SECOND EDITION

PREGNANCY, BIRTH, AND THE EARLY MONTHS

A Complete Guide

Richard I. Feinbloom, M.D.

A MERLOYD LAWRENCE BOOK

PERSEUS BOOKS
Reading, Massachusetts

Many of the designations used by manufacturers and sellers to distinguish their products are claimed as trademarks. Where those designations appear in this book and Perseus Books was aware of a trademark claim, the designations have been printed in initial capital letters (e.g., Milk of Magnesia or Robitussin).

Special thanks are extended to Newton-Wellesley Hospital and Lowell General Hospital for photographic assistance.

Library of Congress Cataloging-in-Publication Data

Feinbloom, Richard I., 1935–
    Pregnancy, birth, and the early months : a complete guide /
Richard I. Feinbloom. — 2nd ed.
      p.   cm.
    "A Merloyd Lawrence Book."
    Includes index.
    ISBN 0-201-58149-3
    1. Pregnancy. 2. Childbirth. 3. Infants—Care. 4. Infants–
    Health and hygiene. 5. Postnatal care. I. Title.
    RG525.F44   1993
    618.2—dc20

92-27998
CIP

Perseus Books is a member of the Perseus Books Group

Cover design by Richard Rossiter
Cover photograph and photographs on pages 28 and 226 by Dag Sundberg/The
    Image Bank
Text design by Anna George
Illustrations by Kathleen Gebhart
Photographs on pages ii, 124, and 234 by Ulrike Welsch
Photographs on pages xx, 184, and 276 by Jim Harrison
Set in 10.5-point Palatino by DEKR Corporation, Woburn, MA

5 6 7 8 9 10–MA–0201009998
Fifth printing, July 1998

Find us on the World Wide Web at
http://www.aw.com/gb/

Contents

CONTENTS

Introduction
to Second Edition

For those fortunate enough to have access to the best care this country offers, having a baby today is safer than ever before. Improved medical care, nutrition, and sanitation have removed most of the risks that accompanied pregnancy and childbirth in earlier centuries. However, our very success in improving safety has spawned an increasing number of issues related to the application of technology to pregnancy and birth as well as raised expectations for the problem-free birth of a perfect child.

On many aspects of maternity care there is reassuring agreement among experts. On other aspects, there is controversy. The controversy extends even to such basic issues as whether it is safe to drink and eat during labor. To dramatize both the controversy and the agreement in prenatal care and birth, I tell at the outset the stories of two contrasting births. These two stories of birth represent the extremes of current practice: one takes place in a *hospital setting*; the other, *in the home*. A third choice, the *family-centered birthing center*—either in a hospital or as a freestanding unit—synthesizes some of the best features of the other two.

The main questions raised in these stories are cross-referenced to complete discussions in Chapter 4 and elsewhere. The rest of the book proceeds chronologically, from care of the mother-to-be during pregnancy (Chapter 2), to care of the baby-to-be (Chapter 3), choices in childbirth itself (Chapter 4), care of the parents in the days immediately after birth (Chapter 5), and then care of the newborn baby (Chapter 6). The more serious complications of both pregnancy and birth are presented in Chapter 7, in alphabetical order for easy reference. Finally, appendices on statistics for home, birthing-center, and hospital birth and on diet organizations, support groups, books on all aspects of pregnancy, birth, and child care and on the policies of the International Childbirth Education Association will enable interested readers to continue the education process that is an integral and never-ending part of becoming a parent.

While much of this book is designed to be referred to selectively, at the appropriate moment, I encourage all parents-to-be to read the sections in Chapter 3 on genetics (pp. 125–139) and on protecting the fetus (pp. 159–182) as early as possible in or even before the pregnancy. We are fortunate in this generation to know so much more about protecting the health and safety of the unborn child.

Since the first edition of this book appeared, a number of the more controversial choices in pregnancy and childbirth have been further clarified. For example, the safety of a vaginal birth after a (previous) cesarean section has been well documented. Other practices on which answers are now more or less "in" include continuous electronic fetal monitoring in labor (no better than listening on a regular schedule with a stethoscope; more likely to lead to intervention in delivery), the value of one-on-one care by a single birth attendant, routine episiotomy (not justifiable), vaginal breech birth (worth considering; cesarean section not needed routinely), and the optimal body position of a woman during delivery (vertical).

In reviewing these issues, I find it striking that many physicians (with important exceptions) have been slow in responding to the research findings. The *New England Journal of Medicine* pointed this out in an editorial July 2, 1992 in which they quoted the *New York Times*, saying "Treatment advances sometimes outpace doctor's willingness to embrace them." For example, the rate of cesarean births climbed from 15.2 percent of all births in 1980 to 23.5 percent in 1990. The rate peaked at 24.7 in 1988 and then fell approximately one percentage point, but the trend is not yet clear. It is worth asking why some in the medical profession and hospitals have been so slow to act upon *new* evidence—for example, the safety of vaginal birth after a previous cesarean section—and why some doctors continue practices that are unsupported by *any* evidence—for example, routine episiotomy.

There are no simple answers to these questions, and space permits only a limited discussion. One answer to the first question is that change of any type is always difficult and has its costs. Take the example of continuous electronic fetal monitoring. This technology has been disproven to be the panacea once expected. It is not better—and in some respects may be worse—than the system it replaced of listening intermittently to the baby's heartbeat during labor. It may contribute to a higher rate of cesarean sections and other interventions. However, most of the hospitals in this country switched over long ago to electronic monitoring (even before it was compared with intermittent listening) and have made a major investment in the high-tech equipment required. Over the past ten to fifteen years their nursing and medical staffs have become habituated to its use. Turning this practice around would require more than simply changing the way the heart rate of the fetus is followed: the overall *approach* to labor and delivery would need redefining. However, inconvenience is not a satisfactory reason for holding on to the status quo.

Another very important factor in the conservatism of doctors has to do with malpractice claims and awards, which have markedly increased in frequency and dollar amounts in recent years. Obstetricians have been particularly affected. In the cases of electronic fetal monitoring, obstetricians see themselves—rightly or wrongly—as more vulnerable to suits if a bad outcome in a baby occurs and a monitor was not used. They believe, with some justification, that in spite what the research evidence shows, a skilled lawyer will be able to produce a witness who will cast doubt on the physician's judgment. Better to use the monitor; why take chances? And similar points can be made with the other examples of conservatism I have cited.

It may well be that in our medical system scientific proof is not paramount (as I believe it should be) in defining how practice is conducted. The history of the use of continuous electronic fetal monitoring (as discussed on pp. 146–147) suggests that the profit motive may have been more important than scientific proof: profit for the inventors, whose good intentions I do not call into question, and profit for the manufacturers, but not necessarily benefit for the public. Also the laws regulating new technologies are not as stringent as those regulating the testing and introduction of new drugs. Some of the dollars spent for expensive but unnecessary services such as continuous electronic fetal monitoring could have been better spent on other aspects of maternity care.

Regarding the second question I raised, of why physicians practice in some instances without proof of the effectiveness of what they do—for example, in the commonly used methods of care for "late-for-dates" pregnant women and babies after the fortieth week of gestation—there are again no simple answers. We are today much more research conscious than we were when many of these practices were put into place. Now that they are in place, it is hard to test them so that we can find out what works and what doesn't. One important reason is that women, quite understandably do not want to take the chance of being part of a study in this, of all experiences in their lives. Insisting on evidence of effectiveness *before* adopting a new practice or technology is even more important for these reasons.

How can maternity care be brought closer into line with the scientific evidence now available? There are now signs of change. One recent approach by some state medical societies, hospital medical staffs, and other groups is to work together in establishing and implementing guidelines for particular practices such as vaginal birth after a cesarean (see pp. 288–291). This self-policing approach has already produced positive results and offers considerable promise for further progress.

Another part of the answer to this complex problem is a more open and full sharing by doctors of the benefits and risks of, and the alternatives to, a particular practice, so that patient and physician can face together, in a spirit of mutual trust, the genuine uncertainty involved in any medical choice (see pp. 29–33). Such collaboration requires time and effort from both parties. The International Childbirth Education Association has adopted a resolution on disclosure of information about obstetrical practices that is consistent with this approach (see Appendix F).

Better public awareness of the issues discussed in this book will also bring about change. In fact, informing the reader was the major reason for my writing this book. To this end I have also listed in appendices C and E the names of other books and of organizations that base their recommendations on the evidence obtained from research studies.

Yet another effort to close the gap between science and practice is public disclosure of practices by care providers. The states of Massachusetts and New York have passed maternity information laws that require hospitals to make available on request their statistics on practices such as cesarean deliveries, vaginal births after cesareans, epidural anesthetics, continuous electronic fetal monitoring, forceps, episiotomies, and use of Pitocin (see pp. 202–205). With such information women will be in a better position to make informed choices about their care.

Reform of malpractice laws will help take some of the pressure off of doctors to practice "defensively," which often translates into more testing and incomplete sharing of the full range of options available. Several states are beginning no-fault insurance programs to compensate families with a poor birth outcome for the considerable financial costs of raising a disabled child—whether or not negligence by a physician or midwife can be proven. (A malpractice settlement, or at least the part of it that gets to the family, may offer the only other major source of funds for this purpose.) Disciplinary action for physicians who have been determined negligent by a panel of their peers and representatives of the law and the public is dealt with separately in this system. In a no-fault program, standards of care based on research evidence probably have a greater chance of a fair hearing than they do in a court of law.

An encouraging development at the time of this writing is the coming together in a national meeting of organizations representing the health professions, government, universities and consumer groups specifically to address the gap between research findings and practice. They seek to answer the question of what steps need to be taken to narrow this gap and accelerate the translation of research into services available to the public. The new federal Agency for Health Care Policy and Research has played a leading role in this meeting and in the implementation of its recommendations. My hope is that among the recommendations will be a call for laws to require that new technologies be proven effective before they are adopted.

A more radical recommendation is that the care of pregnant women be made separate from the current physician-controlled, hospital-based, for-profit medical model of care. For example, midwife Kitty Ernst, the director of the National Association of Childbearing Centers (see Appendix C) has proposed that every pregnant woman be given a tuition credit for enrolling in a birthing-center-based, midwife-run educational and health program that will continue until after the baby is born. Whether or not this direction is the best one to follow, I strongly endorse birthing centers as settings in which the highest scientific standards of maternity care are now being met (see Appendix A). Hospital-based programs still have much to learn from birthing centers and their close relative, at-home births.

I also believe that competing models of care need to be encouraged throughout the country so that women and their families have real choices and can follow their preferences in determining the conduct of pregnancy and birth. Let these models compete not only in the marketplace of consumer choice but also under the consistent scrutiny of scientific evaluation. We are still far from such an ideal.

At the beginning of this Introduction, I stated that having a baby has never been safer "for those who have access to the best care this country offers." The point of this qualification is that the kind of maternity care a woman can receive varies considerably, depending on where she lives and how much money she has. Thirty-seven million Americans (and growing) have no health insurance at all. Our national infant mortality rate, while improving, is still one of the highest in the industrialized world. In some of our inner cities this rate is comparable to that seen in many developing nations. In part, these poor results are preventable through improved care in pregnancy. No discussion of pregnancy, birth, and the early months would be complete without acknowledging this disturbing inequality of services available to women in the United States.

ACKNOWLEDGMENTS

This book is based on the work of many researchers, practitioners, and women (some of whom I attended during labor and delivery) who have advanced our understanding of pregnancy, birth, and the care of infants. Some are mentioned by name; most cannot be. I thank them all.

Since the publication of the first edition of this book, a major advance has occurred in bringing together and evaluating the results of research studies in maternity care. I refer to the establishment of the Oxford University electronic database of perinatal trials in which the world's scientific literature is systematically surveyed on an ongoing basis. From this database Oxford University Press has published a comprehensive 1,500-page, two-volume book entitled *Effective Care in Pregnancy and Childbirth* and, for the general reader and practitioner, the shorter *Guide to Effective Care in Pregnancy and Childbirth*. The authors of these books rate various practices, such as the use of intravenous fluids in labor and the supine (on-the-back) position of a woman during childbirth, according to whether the practice has been *proven* useful or not. The authors recommend stopping some common practices, such as routine cesarean section after a previous cesarean section, and call for more study of practices that look promising but as yet lack sufficient supporting evidence.

The editors of these books, in varying order of authorship for each, are doctors Murray Enkin, Marc J. N. C. Keirse, and Iain Chalmers. I have found the *Guide* to be invaluable in sorting through the evidence and providing a check on other sources of information. It made my work a lot easier.

I also express special thanks to Beth Shearer, Elizabeth Noble, Diony Young, Kitty Ernst, Archie Brodsky, and, for technical assistance, Lucy Wargo, librarian at the Buffalo Children's Hospital, and Paul Karsky and Greg Martin of the data-processing center of the Arnot Ogden Memorial Hospital in Elmira, New

York. For broadening my understanding of how to evaluate maternity care practices and my appreciation of the importance of asking women what they think, I express my gratitude to the editors of *Birth* magazine.

I could not have committed the time to revising this work without the loving forbearance of my wife, Erika Feinbloom. Finally, I acknowledge my editor, Merloyd Lawrence, for (in addition to everything else) convincing me for a second time that yet another book for the general reader on pregnancy would be useful.

PREGNANCY,
BIRTH,
AND THE
EARLY MONTHS

1

Two Births

Birth in the Hospital

On a warm spring night in a suburb thirty minutes from Sun City, Georgia, Joan and Sam Williams were sitting in their living room timing the contractions of Joan's first labor. They planned to have the baby in the local hospital.

The labor pains had begun irregularly in the early afternoon and had settled into a pattern by evening. When the contractions began to come at five-minute intervals, Joan knew it was time to start moving. A good friend, Melissa, had come over about an hour earlier to stay with Karen, Sam's three-year-old daughter by his first marriage. Karen was awakened and hugged by Joan and Sam. They told her that they were finally off to the hospital to get her a new brother or sister.

Joan and Sam lived in a ranch house in the moderately well-to-do suburb. It was not a place where you could easily get from one place to another by walking, and so the couple depended on their two cars for transportation. Although some people continued to go into Sun City for medical care, most used the local hospital.

The community hospital, affiliated with a large university center in downtown Sun City, provided rotations for its resident physicians. It was well run and had a standard maternity floor. Although there were plans to build a birthing center in the hospital, none was functioning at the time of our story. Home births, midwives, and out-of-hospital birthing centers were neither available nor very much discussed in this commmunity. While Joan and Sam's options were limited, their experience was similar in many respects to that of most American parents-to-be.

Joan and Sam were both college graduates. Joan was a real estate broker and Sam ran a retail clothing store well known in the area. Like most of their neighbors, they were politically conservative and socially conventional. They had been referred by friends to Dr. Philip Johnson, who enjoyed a fine reputation in the community. He had recently become the chief of obstetrics at the hospital.

Dr. Johnson was aware of the changes in maternity practice and supported building the proposed birthing center, but his attitude grew more out of a desire to satisfy changing consumer tastes than out of any deep conviction that such a center would make a difference in the quality of the birth experience. He was unalterably opposed to birth at home and could not even imagine himself involved with such a "primitive" practice.

The late-night drive to the hospital over nearly deserted roads took twenty minutes. Joan waited in the lobby next to the emergency room while Sam parked the car. An orderly took Joan up to the labor and delivery area, where she and Sam were ushered into a labor room in which one other woman was already in labor. The room was not entirely strange to them, because they had toured the facility with other members of their hospital-sponsored prenatal class. Wilma, Joan's primary nurse during the rest of the eight-hour shift that had just begun, introduced herself to the couple at the door. She asked Joan about the progress of the labor so far—when she had last eaten or drunk, whether she had any allergies to medications—and recorded the answers on a medical record. She then asked Joan to undress and handed her a pale blue hospital gown. (See p. 219, on sterile precautions.) Once Joan's street clothes were put away, Wilma took her temperature, measured her pulse and blood pressure, and listened to the baby's

2

heart with an ultrasound recorder. "All's well," said said. "Dr. Cooper will be here in a few minutes to check you."

Dr. Ellen Cooper, a house physician in training, entered the room about ten minutes later and introduced herself. She too reviewed the history of the pregnancy and labor, then checked the copy of the prenatal record that Dr. Johnson had sent to the hospital. She examined Joan's mouth, head, chest, breasts, heart, and abdomen. She then asked Joan to lie on her back with knees bent and legs apart to allow her to perform a vaginal examination. This part of the checkup was a bit uncomfortable. "It'll take just a second. Well, you're four to five centimeters dilated and 100 percent effaced." (See "Labor," pp. 186–201). She then pushed a little harder and Joan pulled back. "The head is well engaged, and I think that the occiput, the point of the head, is directed toward your front and left. No doubt about your being in labor. You're off to a good start."

Wilma reappeared shortly after Dr. Cooper left and said, "Looks like you're staying. Mr. Williams, you can go down now to the admitting office to take care of the necessary forms. Then come right on back up." Meanwhile, Dr. Cooper awakened Dr. Johnson by phone to report on Joan's status. They agreed to draw the routine blood studies and to start an intravenous infusion. Dr. Johnson would come in when transition (p. 194) began; for the time being, Dr. Cooper agreed to keep him informed. Dr. Cooper returned to the couple, informed them of the call, and explained that she would now start the I.V. (intravenous injection), which they had been expecting. She placed a tourniquet around Joan's left forearm. When the veins over the top of Joan's hand popped up, Dr. Cooper washed the skin with an alcohol solution; she then injected a small amount of local anesthetic (Xylocaine) to numb the skin. She inserted a needle cover with a plastic catheter painlessly into the vein. When blood dripped from the needle, she released the tourniquet and withdrew the barrel of the needle, leaving the plastic catheter behind in the vein. Before hooking the I.V. into this catheter, Dr. Cooper withdrew several tubes of blood, which was sent to the blood bank for typing and a cross-match with two units of blood that would be held in case of an emergency. After the I.V. was connected and flowing freely, a few twists of adhesive tape secured the catheter in place at the end of the tubing. With the flexible catheter in her vein, Joan knew that her fluid needs would be supplied intravenously, although she would be able to suck ice chips if she wished to. It was hospital policy to avoid putting anything into the stomach that, in the event of an emergency requiring general anesthesia, could be vomited up and aspirated into the lungs, with potentially disastrous consequences. (See "Fluids and Food," pp. 201–202.)

Officially admitted, and certain that this was "the real thing" and not another of the several false labors that had occurred over the past few days, Joan and Sam were able to relax enough to notice the room. It was a twenty-foot-square room, with a bathroom and a single window that looked out over the hospital driveway and the flat, now dark, countryside beyond. The center of Sun City, with its cluster of modest high-rise buildings, could barely be seen off to the left. Dark green flower-print curtains hung beside the window, and two familiar reproductions hung on the light green walls. The two single hospital beds could be enclosed by curtains mounted on ceiling tracks. Next to each was a fetal monitor the size of a large television set. Joan and Sam could hear the indistinct conversation of the nurses and attendants in the hall, punctuated by the distant ringing of phones and the rumble and squeak of passing beds, service carts, and incubators.

Wilma placed the external fetal monitor over Joan's abdomen and obtained a "strip" of the baby's heartbeat over a period of ten minutes and three contractions. (See "Principles of Fetal Monitoring," pp. 144–146.) "Looks good. We can take this off for now." Joan got up and used the bathroom. She had been given disposable paper slippers to protect her feet from the chill of the tile-covered floor. The contractions had become perceptibly less frequent, and Joan proposed taking a walk down the corridor. Her roommate was in active labor, and Joan found her restlessness distracting.

Joan shuffled along as Sam wheeled the I.V. pole and bottle beside her. After about ten minutes of walking, the contractions picked up, and for the first time in the labor, Joan hurt so much that she was forced to stop in her tracks. She wanted to get back to bed as soon as possible.

"Wow, does this hurt, Sam! I've never felt anything like it before." "Try your breathing now," said Wilma. Under her gentle but firm guidance, coupled with Sam's reassurance and back massage, Joan was able to regain her composure. But was clear that her labor was becoming active. It was time for another vaginal examination.

"Very good," said Dr. Cooper. "You're now six to seven centimeters and definitely moving along. The nausea you described goes along with that, too. I'll call Dr. Johnson. I'm sure he's coming in soon. Meanwhile, it's time to attach the internal fetal monitor; but, before we do, we'll have to rupture your membranes. Also, if you'd like some anesthesia now, that too can be arranged. Let me know when you have your next contraction, and we'll go ahead and rupture the membranes."

To nick the amniotic sac, Dr. Cooper used a foot-long sterile, disposable, yellow plastic stick, which tapered into a hook at one end (an Amni-Hook). Joan lay on her back with knees bent and legs apart. As the contraction built up, Dr. Cooper, who had inserted one gloved hand into the vagina, could feel the sac bulging tensely through the cervix. With the other hand she carefully guided the Amni-Hook to the sac and pricked it. Joan could feel the gush of the warm waters. Dr. Cooper kept her hand in the vagina to check for possible prolapse of the umbilical cord, a complication dangerous to the baby because of the vulnerability of the cord to compression by the head and interference with the baby's blood supply. (See pp. 336–337 for a discussion of prolapse of the umbilical cord.) Fortunately, in Joan's case, there was no evidence of this problem. Wilma checked the baby's heartbeat and reported that it was normal.

Dr. Cooper then prepared the fetal monitor wires for insertion. (See "Continuous Electronic Fetal Monitoring," pp. 146–147). She put the index and middle fingers of her left hand into Joan's vagina and rested her fingertips on the baby's head. With her right hand, she guided a hollow plastic tube containing the tiny wires over her fingers to the baby's scalp and twisted their corkscrew-like ends one full circle, tugging gently to verify that they had engaged with the head. She then pulled the plastic tube out of the vagina, leaving the wires behind. The other ends of the wires were plugged into the monitoring device. Red numbers on a screen on the front of the monitor console flashed the baby's changing heart rate in beats per minute as a speaker sounded each beat: "bum, bum, bum. . . ." The volume was adjusted to the level of a steady, soft background noise—a soft, lulling rhythm. Next, Wilma strapped a belt containing a pressure sensor around Joan's abdomen. Also linked to the monitor, it responded to tension in the uterus. A constantly moving strip of graph paper recorded two shifting lines, the upper one representing the fetal heart rate and the lower, uterine tension. As the paper left the machine, it folded neatly upon itself on a shelf next to the monitor, accompanied by the faint whirring sound of the motor-driven roller.

Dr. Cooper showed Joan and Sam how to read the printout. With each contraction, the bottom line, which reflected uterine tension, inched upward, while the top line, which measured fetal heart rate, moved downward ever so slightly, the two lines coming closer together. As the contraction eased, the uterine tension line returned to its previous level, and the fetal heart rate line simultaneously returned to its base. "That's what we call an early deceleration or slowing of the heartbeat along with the contraction. It is probably a normal effect of squeezing the head. Of course, we'll watch the pattern for any signs of stress in the baby." While Joan found these wires annoying, she and Sam felt secure that their baby's well-being was being monitored. (See pp. 146–147, "Continuous Electronic Fetal Monitoring.")

"I'll tell you," Joan said, "I'm really feeling these contractions now, breathing or no breathing, and Dr. Johnson said that I could have an epidural if I wanted one. I think I'm just about ready." Joan settled down in bed, and the anesthesiologist was called.

As long as Joan was attached to the monitor, it was impossible for her to walk around. The wires could be detached temporarily from the monitor to permit her to go to the bathroom, but walking along the corridors was not allowed. Sam sat on a chair next to the bed and held her hand. Together they listened to the heartbeat and watched the monitor. The contractions grew ever more intense. "I don't think I can stand this much longer. Even the breathing doesn't help now." Sam squeezed her hand, feeling more and more uneasy. Just then the anesthesiologist, Dr. Younis, entered the room. "I hear you'd like an epidural." He reviewed her record, repeating the questions asked earlier about allergies to medication, and about general health, and inquired specifically about any back problems. He then asked Sam to leave the room until the procedure was completed. Under the doctor's guidance Joan lay on her side and moved her back to the edge of the bed. Wilma faced her and arched her body over the bed, looping her arms around Joan's neck and behind her knees to keep her from falling over the edge and to position her for the procedure. Joan curled her legs up, curving her lower spine and tucking her head down toward her chest. Dr. Younis explained each move he would make and the sensation she would experience. Joan felt the cool antiseptic solution swabbed over her lower back and buttocks. Next, she felt the needle prick with the local anesthetic, which numbed the skin. The long epidural needle, its hollow core filled with a precisely fitting wirelike metal stylet, was then inserted. The doctor guided it securely between the bones of the vertebral column and through the tough membrane that encased the epidural space. Joan could feel pressure but no pain. As the stylet was withdrawn from the needle, no spinal fluid returned, indicating that the needle, as intended, had not entered the spinal space. (See the section on "Medical Pain Relief," pp. 208–216, for more on epidural and spinal anesthetics.) A small amount of air was drawn into a syringe, which was then attached to the needle. The barrel of the syringe moved in very slightly, further confirming its correct position. The syringe was removed, and a thin plastic catheter was threaded through the hollow needle. Joan reported a twinge of pain in one leg and was reassured that this was a common reaction to pressure by the catheter on a nerve root. The pain passed quickly, as predicted. With its position now verified, the needle was withdrawn from the catheter, leaving the catheter behind in the epidural space. It was taped securely to Joan's back, and she was then asked to roll over and center herself on her back on the bed. Anesthetic solution was now injected into the catheter, the end of which was capped and taped down.

Joan felt a numbness come progressively over her feet, legs, thighs, buttocks, and lower abdomen. She was still able to move her legs when asked, but not as well as before the anesthetic was administered. Most remarkably, her contractions were now barely perceptible. "What a relief," she said with a faint smile. Meanwhile, her roommate had dilated fully and was wheeled off to the delivery room. Joan herself was able to doze off for about twenty minutes. The room was dark, and the fetal monitor was turned down.

A half hour later, or about one hour from the time of placement of the epidural, Sam and Joan were happy to see that her doctor had arrived. On checking her, Dr. Johnson reported that she was still six to seven centimeters dilated, even during a contraction. He had kept his hand on her abdomen through the contraction and was, he said, impressed with the weakness of the muscle action and the long intervals between contractions that sometimes occur when epidural anesthetics are administered. "What I suggest at this point is that we add a little Pitocin to the I.V. to see if we can't move things along a little quicker. The baby is fine. There is no molding of the head and no swelling of the scalp to show that it is not fitting easily into the birth canal."

The idea of stimulating labor sounded good to Joan and Sam—both were growing impatient. Because Joan was beginning to feel the contractions again, more anesthetic was injected, with predictably good results. The Pitocin was added to a bottle connected to the I.V. The tube from this second bottle was connected to a regulator the size of a cigar box, which carefully controlled the number of drops of Pitocin to be delivered. The Pitocin did its job. Within thirty minutes, during which time gradually increasing doses of the hormone were given, labor picked up again with harder, more frequent contractions (barely perceptible to Joan) and with the opening of the cervix to a good eight centimeters. Within another thirty minutes she was fully dilated, and the perineum (the pelvic floor between pubic bone and rectum) was just beginning to bulge. Everyone concerned was pleased with this progress.

Dr. Johnson had intended that the anesthetic lighten up by the time Joan was fully dilated, so that she would be able to push, adding her force to that of the Pitocin-stimulated uterus, to bring about an earlier delivery. As sometimes happens, the timing was just a little off. The anesthetic effect was still present even though dilation was complete. Joan did not feel the urge to push that usually comes at this time. The baby's head was not moving down, even though the Pitocin was still running. In addition, the scalp tissues were beginning to swell, suggesting that the fit might be tight. Since a full bladder can obstruct the baby's descent, Dr. Johnson suggested that Joan try to void. But when Wilma placed a bedpan beneath her, Joan was able to produce only a small amount of urine.

The news from the monitor was disconcerting. There was some loss in "beat-to-beat variability" (see pp. 145–146). This meant that the baby's heart rate was not changing very much from one moment to the next, a subtle point that gave Dr. Johnson some pause when he considered it along with all the other developments. "Basically, everything is still okay, but I'd feel better if we went into the delivery room now and put forceps on the baby's head to get him delivered. [See p. 218.] In the meantime, we'll turn off the Pitocin to give him a rest and have you lie on your side and shift the position of the uterus." Joan was wheeled in her bed to the delivery room. The monitor wires were temporarily disconnected. Sam was directed to the doctors' dressing room to change into a surgical scrub suit before entering the delivery room.

The delivery suite was a fully equipped, gleaming operating room with a surgical operating table, a large adjustable ceiling light, and anesthesia equipment, which included tanks, instruments, face masks, and many different dials. Off to the side of the room was a long table covered with surgical instruments; in one corner was a small table on which lay an open plastic crib over which was mounted a radiant heater for the new baby. Wilma and Mary, the delivery room nurse, assisted Joan onto the delivery table. The fetal monitor was reconnected as Drs. Cooper and Johnson finished their surgical scrub. Dr. Younis reappeared and chatted amiably with Joan and Sam. The atmosphere was friendly. The door to the delivery room then swung open, and Drs. Johnson and Cooper, with dripping hands and arms immaculately scrubbed in antiseptic solution, backed their way into the room with arms raised to avoid touching anything. They, like everyone else in the room, wore surgical caps, face masks, and scrub suits.

"Won't be long now," Dr. Johnson said reassuringly. "How's the anesthesia now?" "Not so good," replied Joan. "Okay, Dr. Younis, how about a little more of the epidural since we're going to need to do an episiotomy [see pp. 219–223] and pull the baby out anyway." Dr. Younis promptly injected some more anesthetic solution through the epidural catheter. Sam watched as the two obstetricians carefully dried their hands and arms, dropping the wet towels to the floor. They put their arms into the sleeves of their sterile gowns, working them on with Mary's help, and put on their sterile gloves. They were now ready. During this preparation Mary placed Joan's legs into stirrup straps. Thus suspended under the knees, her legs felt like lead weights as the effect of the anesthesia returned and the pain of the contraction eased. Wilma then disconnected the monitor, unscrewed the tiny wires from the baby's scalp, and removed the strap from Joan's abdomen. She then cranked a lever near the middle of the table, and the half under Joan's legs folded down to the floor. "Now I'm going to wash you off," she said, and rubbed a wet gauze pad attached to a plastic handle over Joan's perineum and buttocks. Joan could feel the rubbing but not the wetness or coldness of the solution. Mary announced that she would pass a catheter through Joan's urethra into her bladder to empty it. This was accomplished with a return of clear yellow urine, which dripped into a basin Mary held in her other hand. Dr. Cooper now placed sterile green drapes beneath Joan's buttocks, over each leg, and over her lower abdomen. Mary turned on the overhead light and positioned it to illuminate Joan's perineum. "Now I'm going to do an episiotomy. You shouldn't feel it at all, but if you do, let me know." Dr. Johnson inserted the index and middle fingers of his left hand palm downward into Joan's vagina and tensed the perineum, now quite relaxed from the anesthesia, by pulling it toward him. With his right hand he inserted scissors between the fingers of his left hand, one blade on each side of the perineum, and made a two-inch cut, which Joan did not feel. The blades of the forceps were now inserted one at a time and positioned along the sides of the baby's head. Dr. Johnson brought the forceps' handles together and with the next contraction exerted an ever-increasing gentle traction. Soon, curly black hair appeared, followed by the head itself. Sam gasped with excitement. When the forceps were removed, Dr. Johnson gently pulled downward on the head, disengaging the baby's shoulder from beneath the pubic bone. The rest of the baby slipped out in a gush of amniotic fluid. "It's a boy!" The baby gave a lusty cry and immediately pinked up. The

I.V. Pitocin was speeded up to contract the uterus. Joan lay back in Sam's arms, overcome with relief and joy.

Dr. Johnson held newborn Jonathan on his lap, cut the cord, and handed him to Mary, who received him in a warm cotton blanket. She brought him immediately to the head of the delivery table for Joan and Sam to see. "He's beautiful," they exclaimed, almost in unison. "I'll be right back with him," Mary said as she carried the baby to the warming table, where she dried him off and checked him over briefly. Next, she put a name-tag bracelet on his wrist and made prints of his feet for the identification records. She wiped off the feet, rewrapped him, and handed him to Sam, who had been waiting eagerly. "We'll put the antibiotic eye ointment in later when he stops at the nursery," she said.

By this time the placenta had already separated and delivered, and Dr. Johnson was sewing up the episiotomy. He had already checked Joan's vagina and cervix for other tears and found none. The sterile drapes were now removed and the lower end of the table cranked back up. Sam had laid Jonathan in Joan's arms, and both were gazing at him in blissful admiration. "You are finally here!" said Joan, as Sam touched the tiny ears and hands, gingerly, with one finger.

Birth at Home

Andrea Clayborn, thirty-three, was in active labor with her second child in the bedroom of her apartment in College Heights, Massachusetts. She and her husband, Bob, had made a thorough study of the subject of birth at home and concluded that they could accept the risks involved, which they saw as slight. They had invited some close friends to join them in their home for the final hours of labor, along with their midwife and doctor. Andrea had wanted her parents to come, but they were so worried about the delivery that they decided to stay home and wait for a phone call. About fifteen people were now crowded into the bedroom for the last few contractions before the baby emerged. Their collective body heat helped warm the room on that cool New England autumn day.

This particular birth was taking place in a community that

offered possibilities not available everywhere. A cosmopolitan center with two universities and over 100,000 people of diverse ethnic backgrounds, it attracted people like the Clayborns, who enjoyed its intellectuality and traditions of independent thought. Both Andrea and Bob were college graduates and had done postgraduate work. Before the birth of her first child, Andrea worked in a day-care center, and Bob was a member of a management consulting firm. Both were politically active in the community. They had joined with eight other couples to purchase a large apartment building, which they converted into a cooperatively owned group of apartments with a shared backyard and basement-level meeting room. The idea for forming this cooperative resulted from a study project on alternatives in housing that they had undertaken through their church. Andrea and Bob were just the kind of activist people who might be attracted to having their baby at home.

They had attended a series of classes given by one of two organizations that prepared couples for birth at home, and they were well informed about the process of labor and delivery. They were convinced that the risk to them and to the unborn child was very small, especially because they had competent, experienced attendants and lived quite close to several hospitals. The compactness of College Heights allowed them to be anywhere within a matter of minutes (traffic permitting), unlike many suburbs, where distances between home and hospital could be great.

In their community, critical reappraisal of medical practices, particularly those concerned with women's health, had taken root in the previous fifteen years. Consumer groups had brought pressure for a number of changes in hospital practice. The city was also a center of medical schools and teaching hospitals that were highly regarded across the country.

Most of the obstetricians in the city were opposed to home birth on grounds of safety and refused to participate in home deliveries. Therefore, most of the home births in the area were attended by lay midwives, although one group of family doctors did offer home-birth services. The Clayborns had chosen Dr. Bill Greenson, a partner in this group, to attend Andrea's birth.

These doctors had begun attending births in the home in response to requests from people like the Clayborns. Dr. Greenson had a long record of involvement with health-related groups, many with headquarters in College Heights, that called for social reform of one kind or another, and was regarded as a social activist. He had been a physician long enough to know that practices that initially appeared radical could quickly come to be accepted, so that younger people simply would be unaware that things had ever been different. Breast-feeding was a good example. When he began to practice in the early 1960s, doctors, hospitals, and relatives offered little support for nursing newborn babies. But, by the time of Andrea's labor, the situation had changed so completely that there was perhaps too much pressure on women to breast-feed and too little tolerance for women who chose not to. In any event, Dr. Greenson's experience told him that it was important to listen to what the public was saying, and that change often came from outside the medical profession, whose prime role, he felt, was to act as a conservative but flexible arbiter that could resist changing fads while respecting real needs of patients.

Another unusual feature of Dr. Greenson's practice was his work with several lay midwives—women who had received their training in the supervised practice of birthing rather than in midwifery school. He would have been happy to work with formally trained and certified nurse midwives, but these were, by state law, permitted to work in hospitals only and forbidden to attend births at home.

Working as he did on the interface between the majority of his colleagues, on the one hand, and some vocal and assertive patients, on the other, Dr. Greenson knew that his opponents in the medical profession would quickly note mistakes and seize on any problem, or even the mere rumor of a problem, to discredit home birth, even though the problem might just as easily have occurred in the hospital. Such a climate added a burden of stress and extra caution to the practice of home birth.

Andrea's labor had begun about eight hours earlier when vaginal leaking of thick, blood-tinged fluid followed loss of the mucous plug. She had called Lara, the midwife, and told her that labor had begun. Contractions followed soon after, occurring first at intervals of fifteen to twenty minutes. Andrea had busied herself with cooking, tidying up the apartment, and contacting friends and relatives to let them know that labor had begun. Her neighbor and close friend, Jean, agreed to be with her until the midwife arrived. Although the contractions now felt like sharp menstrual cramps, painful enough to make her pause, she did not yet feel the need to use any of the breathing and relaxation exercises she and Bob had so carefully rehearsed. She observed how remarkably calm she was this time in contrast to her first labor, when everything had seemed strange and unknown in spite of childbirth classes and extensive reading.

By early afternoon the contractions had become more frequent and regular, occurring every five minutes. Andrea called Lara and told her it was time. Lara arrived at the apartment within twenty minutes. Andrea also called Bob at work, and he made plans to return home immediately. After sitting through several contractions to get the feel of the labor, Lara did a vaginal examination with a sterile glove and reported that the cervix was four to five centimeters dilated, 100 percent effaced, and that the station was zero. (See p. 188.) Although not entirely sure, she felt that the baby's head was oriented so that the back of the head was pointing toward the front left side of Andrea's body. "No doubt that you're in labor and moving now into the second stage." Lara's words seemed to act as a spur to the contractions. The pains soon grew more intense and more frequent. Andrea moaned, "I think I need some help now." "Okay," replied Lara, "let's see what we can do. How about trying your breathing—light chest breathing with the next contraction." With the next pain, Andrea locked her eyes with Lara and the two of them breathed lightly together, Lara directing the action by shaping the depth and speed of Andrea's gentle panting. They continued for the next thirty minutes or so during contractions until it was clear to both that Andrea was pulling herself together again. As she did, the contractions seemed to space out somewhat, but they were no less uncomfortable.

"It looks like things are slowing down a bit. How about getting up and walking around for a while?" asked Lara. For the next forty-five minutes Andrea returned to working in the kitchen, but now she had to lean against the wall during the contractions. "They're getting stronger again. Maybe you should check me now." Two hours had passed since Lara had first checked Andrea, and she was surprised to find that there had been little change in the cervix. It had dilated barely half a centimeter more, if at all.

All that work and so little apparent progress . . . A look of disappointment came over Andrea's face. "I'm disappointed, and a little tired." "Now," suggested Lara, "is the time for a nice, warm tub bath. That'll perk you up!"

What appeared to be happening to Andrea was not uncommon, for labor oftens gets "hung up" in the latent period of the first stage. Andrea's labor might be regarded as "pokey" (see pp. 197, 199).

The warm bathwater felt soothing and made the contractions much more bearable. Andrea stayed in the tub for half an hour until the pains became more frequent and intense. She reported, for the first time, that she felt slightly nauseated. She had been nibbling food and drinking fluids avidly throughout the labor, but at this point the thought of something to eat or drink made her feel sick to her stomach.

"Let's check you again. Dry off and come back onto the bed." Lara reported "seven to eight centimeters dilation" and phoned Dr. Greenson. "Andrea's in transition and I think you should come now. She's seven to eight centimeters." When Lara put down the receiver, Andrea said, "Let's not call everyone in the house until I'm fully dilated. That'll still give them plenty of time to get up here." Jean, who had been designated "information officer" for the rest of the building, had a different idea. "Why don't I just let everyone know that you're getting near the end so they can put their spouses on alert?"

By the time Dr. Greenson, whom everyone called "Bill," arrived, about thirty minutes after being called, Andrea was fully dilated and reported feeling an urge to push. "Fine," said Bill. "You can begin pushing now." He waited until her contraction was over and then reviewed with her the philosophy of pushing that they had discussed before. "Remember, pushing is not anything you *have* to do. Do it only if it feels good to you. Your baby will be born regardless, and you don't have to rush the birth. Everything is okay and there is no hurry. Just follow your instincts. Let me suggest that you go to the bathroom so that you can sit on the toilet. The john is a great place to be at this point. Also, see if you can urinate. That will make things easier for both you and the baby."

From here on, Lara and the doctor checked the fetal heart rate after each contraction. This was difficult to do, because Andrea was sitting on the toilet and Lara had to get down on the floor to reach the lower part of Andrea's abdomen (under her "overhang") with the fetoscope and check her labia for the bulging that signals the further descent of the baby. As Andrea straddled the toilet with her legs spread wide apart, Lara inserted two fingers into the perineum and pushed down to expose the lower vagina to view with each contraction. Pushing felt so good to Andrea that she groaned her way through each contraction, unmistakable evidence of the imminence of the birth.

When Lara saw the first tuft of new, black hair appear just above her fingers pressing down on Andrea's vagina, she knew it was time to move Andrea back to bed. Soon Andrea was sitting naked on her bed, cradled from behind in Bob's arms. A plastic sheet covered the mattress to protect it from leaking amniotic fluid or blood, and disposable paper pads were tucked under Andrea's buttocks. Midwife and doctor circled the bed, checking the baby's heart rate and descent. They wore street clothes but had removed their shoes. They did not wear masks. Emergency instruments for infant resuscitation were unobtrusively spread out on top of a nearby chest of drawers. Andrea's medical record and a labor chart on which essential information was periodically entered were also there. A ready-to-use tank of oxygen was tucked away behind the door, and a large black doctor's bag, partially open and off in a far corner of the room, bulged with emergency drugs, intravenous fluids, syringes, needles, tape, and similar supplies. Since Jean had called everyone to come up after Andrea had begun to push, a small crowd had assembled in the bedroom.

With each contraction Andrea moved her gaze about the room, pausing briefly to make contact with the others present. She had chosen to pant her way through each pain. The panting started slowly, increased in intensity and volume as the pain intensified, and then slowed down to culminate in a deep sigh. Her friends picked up the rhythm of her breathing and panted along with her. She seemed to draw strength from the collective energy in the room.

During the next contraction the baby's head parted the labia, and a clump of black hair peeked through. Some stool also squeezed out of Andrea's rectum, and Lara wiped it away. "Reach down and touch your baby, Andrea." Andrea put her hand to her vagina and touched the head just before it slipped back in with the end of the contraction. She smiled happily.

"Let's get a mirror down there," said Bill. "There's one in the closet," replied Bob. Dave, a neighbor, got the mirror and placed it at the foot of the bed so that Andrea and Bob could watch the perineum bulge with each contraction. This visual feedback, and Lara's and Bill's guidance, helped Andrea sense how hard to push to allow for the gradual stretching of her perineum.

"You'll see a lot better if you can get some light down there," said Lara. "Right," replied Bob. "There's a flashlight in the first drawer on the left in the cabinet in the entranceway. I just put new batteries in it." The flashlight markedly increased the visibility of the unfolding events.

Andrea had no choice but to push; she was driven by an irresistible urge. When her attendants judged it important to slow down the force of the labor, in order to allow a more gradual stretching of the perineum, they asked her to pant hard in order to stop herself from pushing. This was the only way she could overcome the urge. When she was panting, the only forces moving the baby along were those of the uterus itself and gravity, which came into play because Andrea was in a half-sitting position. All the while, Lara kept one gloved hand over a gauze pad applied to the perineum to guard against an unexpected forceful contraction. During a contraction she would release pressure only periodically in order to inspect the perineum for any sign of tearing. If the skin became white, it would mean a loss of circulation with the likelihood of a tear, and an episiotomy would be considered (see pp. 219–223).

Just then, Bill lost the sounds of the fetal heart with the fetoscope. The most likely explanation was that the heart was simply out of range; but, without hearing it, there was no way to tell if its beating was normal. He put the fetoscope down and positioned the plastic sensor, attached by a cord to the hand-sized ultrasound monitor, over Andrea's lower abdomen, moving it about until the hoofbeat-like "bup, bup, bup . . ." was broadcast for all to hear. Smiles broke out throughout the room. Lara began applying hot, wet, well-wrung washcloths to Andrea's perineum. Jane and Tom, another couple from the cooperative, saw that hot water was always available to heat the cloths. Another neighbor, John, the official photographer, was clicking away. A video camera captured the sights and sounds of the birth for posterity. Between contractions, Lara inserted the tips of her gloved index fingers between the perineum and the baby's head. She poured a little vitamin E oil into the opening created and massaged it into the rim of the bulging vagina, gradually stretching the tissue as she did so (see pp. 42–44, 102–104).

Several contractions later the baby's head crowned; that is, it remained visible at the perineum and did not recede with the end of a contraction. A look of ecstasy came over Andrea's face, and her breathing deepened—she later reported that at this moment she experienced a feeling akin to orgasm.

Lara asked Andrea to slide to the edge of the bed and hang her legs over. As she did, Andrea commented on the burning she felt in her vagina. Two of her neighbors, directed by Lara, sat on the floor next to Andrea and supported her legs. Bob and the pillows were still behind her so that she could comfortably maintain her sitting position at a forty-five-degree angle. When the baby's head crowned, Jean, by previous arrangement, went to wake up four-year-old Joseph, who was asleep in another bedroom. Andrea noticed her leaving and smiled approvingly. Joseph, rubbing the sleep from his eyes as he was ushered into the crowded room, looked with amazement at the scene before him.

Two contractions later, the baby's head emerged completely as the labia folded back after it. "Here's your baby," exclaimed Lara. "Put your hands down to catch your baby."

Although the baby's eyes remained closed, its eyebrows twitched and its lips made continuous sucking movements. "Now hold on to the head and give a little push between contractions," said Lara, whose hand supported Andrea's perineum all the while. Andrea grunted, and the slippery baby slid out. "A girl. Oh, I'm so happy!" Lara and Andrea together firmly held the baby, who quickly let out a lusty, gurgling cry as they lifted her to Andrea's breasts and covered her with a cotton receiving blanket. The tension in the room suddenly yielded to cheering and applause.

Andrea asked Joseph to climb into bed with them. He gently touched the newcomer's head. "Gently—that's right. Here's your new sister, Joseph," said Andrea as she gave him a hug and kiss. She reassured him that the blood he was staring at on the bed didn't mean that anything was wrong with her but was simply part of having a baby. (See pp. 115–119 for more on preparing children for birth.) She then offered little Beth her first meal.

When the umbilical cord stopped pulsing, Lara put a clamp on it about two inches from the baby's umbilicus. She then tied a sterilized white shoelace between the clamp and navel. Bob took sterile scissors and cut the cord between the lace and the metal clamp. Beth's sucking immediately stimulated Andrea's uterus to contract. Within minutes, heralded by a small gush of blood, the placenta was delivered. Both doctor and midwife breathed an inner sigh of relief at this point, because bleeding associated with a retained placenta was one of their biggest worries, particularly with a home birth (see p. 224).

Dr. Greenson asked Andrea once again to move to the edge of the bed so that he could inspect her vagina for tears. After blotting up the blood in the vagina with a sterile gauze pad, he spread the labia apart. With the field illuminated by the flashlight Lara held, he was able to identify two small, superficial tears near the urethra and one tear one and a half inches long, and one-fourth inch deep right in the midline at the site of the episiotomy Andrea had had during her first delivery. In Dr. Greenson's view, sewing up the latter was optional, for healing would occur on its own. No one really knew whether the stitches usually taken would speed it up. Remembering the pain she had felt after the episiotomy and its repair, Andrea was delighted to leave well enough alone.

By now Beth had settled down, and Lara encouraged Andrea to take a shower to freshen up and to allow her bedding to be changed. Before she got out of bed, Bill checked the baby over. "Except for being wet behind the ears, she's perfect!" Bill then applied some erythromycin ointment to Beth's eyes (see pp. 270–271) and emptied the contents of two small glass vials of vitamin K solution into her mouth (see pp. 263–264). Champagne corks began to pop, and the food, which had been arriving steadily throughout the day, was brought out. Lara waited just outside the shower in case Andrea became dizzy. Soon the party began.

Lara and Bill stayed for another hour or so, joining in the

warmth of the occasion. They finished the necessary paperwork, put away their equipment, and waited to observe Andrea for any delayed bleeding or other problems. Lara would also check in on the first and third days following the birth, and both she and the doctor would be available for consultation by telephone. Both congratulated Andrea and Bob on what they said was a "truly superb job." After warm hugs, they took their leave.

Two Births Contrasted

The stories of Andrea and Bob and Joan and Sam represent contrasting approaches toward birth. It would be impossible to capture, even in 100 stories, the wide variety of birth experiences. Between the two are all gradations of experience. For instance, many hospital births now take place in birthing rooms that are as close to one's own bedroom in appearance and feeling as possible. Not every home birth has a festive atmosphere, and not every hospital birth involves anesthesia and forceps. We deliberately chose our exemplary tales to highlight the most extreme differences in tone and approach.

Childbirth in America is in ferment. Pronounced shifts have occurred in the last twenty years. On the one hand, the technology available to deal with pregnancy, birth, and the newborn has expanded significantly. On the other hand, a major movement on the part of a vocal and critical public, spearheaded by organizations like the International Childbirth Education Association, seeks to reclaim family control over childbearing, a natural process that they perceive as having been almost completely ceded to physicians and hospitals since the beginning of this century.

The current scene is the product of the interwoven effects of these two currents. Birthing rooms that make possible homelike hospital births have proliferated throughout the country. This concept is backed by hospitals out of economic necessity as well as ideological commitment. To compete in the childbirth marketplace, hospitals must adapt to patients' special wants and needs.

In most hospitals the birthing rooms are located in the main maternity wing. In others they are in separate facilities on hospital grounds in order to emphasize and develop their own identity. Separate birthing centers, not connected with hospitals, are located in many cities. (The best known of these is the Maternity Center Association in New York City, situated in a town house on the Upper East Side.) Finally, there are home births, which account for a very small but growing percentage of all births in the United States.

The experience of Joan and Sam is typical of many hospital births in this country and probably represents at least 90 percent of all births in the industrialized world. It is the mainstream birth experience. The options of the birthing room, the birthing center, and home birth reflect only a minority experience, but one that appears to be influencing more and more hospitals, as well as the expectations of couples.

As we have seen, the two couples in our stories approached their births differently. Andrea and Bob were concerned with being in charge of their baby's birth. They wanted Dr. Greenson and Lara for support, guidance, and help with possible complications, but not for "delivering" their baby, not for making decisions they regarded as their own. Convinced that having a baby was a normal physiological process, Andrea came to view her body with trust—it was capable of conceiving, carrying, and bearing a child. Problems could arise, but she considered herself a healthy woman built to have babies, the daughter of a long line of women who had borne many children. She and Bob believed that they would, and could, carry out the birth with a minimum of medical intervention. However, they wanted the professional support of a doctor, in view of the possibility that a medical issue could arise.

People like the Clayborns are concerned that the medical profession has a financial stake in intervention: they are not paid as well to "do nothing" as they are to "do something." Patients with insurance don't protest. The Clayborns' is a cynical point of view, but one that others share. It is the concern of women like Andrea that provides so much of the energy underlying the reforms that are occurring in childbirth practices, such as the development of relatively noninterventive settings like birthing rooms and birthing centers.

The Clayborns also objected to many hospital rules, such as

those about eating and drinking. Husbands might be able to come into the delivery room, but their participation would be limited. Being able to have an older child present is not guaranteed, either. Patients must usually stay in the recovery room for one hour. Bob and Andrea were wary of the attempt to control pain with drugs, because they regarded it as a "path of no return," the first step in an unending series of interventions. First, the epidural, next the fetal monitor, then physical immobilization, then Pitocin, then episiotomy, the forceps, the suturing of the episiotomy . . . In their opinion, it all would result in a managed delivery totally out of their control. Medication can slow down contractions, which then must be speeded up for the baby's sake. Complications can arise as the result of previous interventions. In their view, birth should be allowed to proceed as a natural process. The doctor and midwife should be present, always alert, ever on guard, but should not do anything *unless* events dictate. However, for people used to taking the active role, it can be hard just to sit back, watch, and wait—not hurry things along, but simply suggest ways to ease the mother's progress. Andrea and Bob believed that the greatest gift of all is empowering another person to manage for himself or herself, and this was exactly what they wanted from Bill and Lara.

Andrea and Bob saw their relationship with the doctor and midwife as a negotiated partnership, shared decision making based on trust. They realized that every decision they made, from having their baby at home to refusing analgesia, was a gamble in the face of uncertainty.

Throughout the pregnancy both Lara and Bill had informed the couple, as best they could, of the risks they were taking. A bad outcome, even death, can be related to delivery at home, although the odds are low—maybe 1 or a fraction of 1 in 1,000. Birth itself has irreducible risks, even under the best of circumstances and in the finest medical centers. There are special risks associated with the hospital, and risks associated with the home. The order of magnitude of the risks in either site is comparable, although not identical. (See Appendix A.) If something *did* go wrong at home, and the couple had chosen to be there, they would have to live with the fact that they had picked the site. As Dr. Greenson had pointed out, although a chance of failure may be 1 in 1,000, if you happen to be the one, your risk is 100 percent.

While it is easy for a doctor and midwife to talk in these terms, just how well a young couple, whose only experience is one previous birth, can grasp the risk is another question. They had had little enough direct experience with normal birth, let alone its possible complications. Dr. Greenson, having been in practice some twenty years, often thought to himself that if people really knew what they could be getting themselves into, they would likely never attempt anything.

Andrea and Bob wanted to be the stars of their delivery in a special way. For them it was a once-in-a-lifetime opportunity. Bill and Lara knew from previous experience that the power one could experience in oneself by rising to such an occasion could carry over into other aspects of life, setting into motion a cycle of growing self-confidence. They had seen this happen time and time again. Women gained increased self-esteem and a finer sense of their own capacities. Childbirth became, for many, a turning point toward power in a life marked by too little validation. For others, the birth was yet another building block in an already maturing sense of self.

The Clayborns also wanted to feel closeness as a family immediately after the birth. Although they knew that hospital nurses and doctors are certainly caring and responsible, they saw them as strangers. Children and friends are usually excluded from a hospital birth, or involved only as a rare exception. Andrea and Bob reasoned that since relaxation is so important to dealing with pain, the relaxing feeling of being in one's own familiar surroundings could only help in a delivery. Being in an unfamiliar place with unfamiliar people, far away from those closest and dearest to you, was in itself a source of tension that could exaggerate the perception of pain and make it harder to deal with by nontechnical means. Their twenty-minute tour of the hospital, helpful as it was, couldn't compare with the years they had spent together in their cozy apartment.

If a home birth is to work, a couple cannot be rigidly locked into a "natural childbirth," believing that hospitals are to be avoided at all cost. Such ideological attachment is dangerous, because it can cloud life-and-death decisions that must be made in haste. Dr. Greenson and Lara tried hard to undermine such rigidly held positions and refused to work with couples not willing to show flexibility.

The role of the midwife was important to Andrea. Lara had seen Andrea in the office and once at home and had formed a very close relationship with her even before labor and delivery. They were in frequent telephone contact during and after the pregnancy. Lara, a mother of two, had been attending births at home for the past three years. She believed that, as a woman who had experienced pregnancy herself, she brought a special sensitivity. She could offer an intuitive understanding of birth in a way that a man could not. Lara had become a midwife largely because she believed that women should reclaim charge of their bodies and because she wanted to assist families in bringing new babies into the world. Breast-feeding was an area of special interest to her (see pp. 251–262). She was amazed at how often new mothers had difficulty with breast-feeding and how much a little support from an experienced woman could help. Like childbirth itself, breast-feeding had once been part of the traditional lore of women. But people had become distanced from the major events of life—birth, nursing, and death—and had turned to professionals for guidance.

Closely related to the issue of women attending women is the concern for rebuilding a sense of community. The loss of connection with normal life processes in a modern technological society parallels the breakup of the extended family, where such connections were once established. Andrea attended classes organized by a local home-birth group. These classes fostered a sense of community among the participants, who tended to form friendships that endured long after the births of their children.

During such prenatal gatherings (given also in hospital classes for childbirth education) the fear of failure, the ignorance of normal labor and birth, and the feelings of alienation from one's own body are discussed. Gradually the participants come to see their pregnancies as healthy processes for which their bodies are specifically designed. Their fears do not dissipate entirely but recede into the background of their concerns to be viewed as simply part of the process of confronting pregnancy and birth as important life events. While such groups do not romanticize the past with its high infant and maternal mortality rates, they try to draw from the best qualities of the pretechnological and technological years, neither treating every woman as if she were high risk, nor ignoring the potentially lifesaving advantages that modern obstetrics can offer.

Joan and Sam Williams chose Dr. Johnson and the local hospital because they offered the security of experience and modern medical practice. The fact that the doctor and the hospital held the safety of their baby as the paramount concern was comforting to them. From Dr. Johnson's point of view, people like the Clayborns were misguided. He pointed out to his patients that never before had having a baby been so safe, and this safety came directly from the great strides obstetrics had made during the past fifty years: antisepsis, anesthesia, bloodbanks, improved surgical techniques, ultrasound, fetal monitoring, and so on. Advocates of home birth, he felt, took a grave risk in assuming that nothing could go wrong in a delivery.

In his career Dr. Johnson had seen too many things go wrong at the last moment, often suddenly and always unexpectedly, after all had seemed so perfect. He had sweated through these moments, and each had added a few gray hairs to his head. Emergency cesarean sections and other quick action could save mothers and babies if trouble arose. Dr. Johnson questioned whether any woman could be considered truly low risk, so quickly could her condition change. What doctor in his right mind would want to be in someone's house when such a complication arose? He was particularly upset on the several occasions at the hospital when he was asked to deal with a home-birth patient brought in as an emergency after a complication. He had laid eyes on neither the patient nor her spouse nor the lay midwife until that critical moment, and he suddenly had to repair the situation.

Dr. Johnson could understand that some women wanted a "natural" childbirth and were willing to endure the pain involved. If so, they should use birthing rooms like the one his hospital had on the drawing board. In birthing rooms they could have the baby in bed and not even go to the delivery room. He and his colleagues would be right next door to all of the equipment and other resources they might need.

Dr. Johnson felt that couples should ask themselves how they would feel if something *did* go wrong. The issue was not simply having a baby. It was having a baby "well"—having a baby in as good condition as possible, one who would not only be born well but who would grow up free of neurological and other problems. Especially now, when women seemed to be having fewer babies and at later ages, there were real risks to consider (see pp. 315–316). What if someone had a "great birth experience," but a damaged baby?

If having babies were a perfect process, doctors would not be needed at all. The medical profession had moved in to fill the holes left by imperfect evolution and had done so with extraordinarily good results. Take a protracted labor, for instance. It hurts and can hurt badly. A safe, reliable method for dealing with the pain, like an epidural, has been a boon to countless women. True, all such measures have their problems. If the Williams' birth had proceeded without anesthesia, Pitocin or forceps might not have been necessary. But the result was still a more comfortable birth and a healthy baby.

Regarding the question of who should attend birth, Dr. Johnson felt that a midwife or family practitioner might be okay, but that he or she should work only under the supervision of a certified obstetrician. A family doctor could continue with the care of the baby after birth; but, once again, a pediatrician was likely to be even better qualified and trained.

When physicians like Dr. Johnson first began to practice, little was known about natural childbirth. The emphasis in medical school training and residency—indeed, the thrill and challenge—was on complications. Residents did not tally the number of normal births they had attended, but if you asked how many cesarean sections they had done, the number would be right on the tip of their tongue. Also, obstetricians did not concern themselves very much with the "doctor–patient relationship." Many women twenty or thirty years ago neither knew nor cared about the details of labor and delivery. They wanted to have their babies as quickly and as painlessly as possible. Few took classes or read books on the subject. But private practice was different from practice in a clinic, and nowadays, Dr. Johnson recognized, the women are increasingly better educated, expect more attention, and are able to form a personal relationship with their doctor. An obstetrician like Dr. Johnson knew that the success of his practice could be largely attributed to a firm yet gentle bedside manner. Experience had given him a reassuring authority. In four years of medical school, one year of internship, three years of obstetrical residency, and fifteen years of practice delivering hundreds of babies, he had gained this expertise. Joan and Sam Williams saw their doctor as more of an authority than themselves, even though they had taken a course in childbirth education and had read a few books. They felt he was certainly willing to hear their preferences, but they had no intention of crossing his hard-won professional opinion if the unexpected came up in labor. To Dr. Johnson and Joan and Sam, the hospital-birthing system that had developed in this country, while not perfect, was unquestionably the best.

In this chapter we have shown two reasonable and yet opposing points of view on the way a delivery should be handled. Couples planning ahead should be aware of these alternatives and the reasoning behind them. They should also explore birthing centers in their area that might offer the best of both worlds.

While expectant parents must make their own decisions, and while the advocates of out-of-hospital birth and hospital birth feel strongly about their respective views, I should state my own position, which will be evident in later sections of this book. In surveying all the available research on birth practices, I have come to the conclusion that in certain freestanding birthing centers and in well-planned home births conducted by trained professionals, the conduct of normal birth is on the cutting edge of the best current scientific evidence. The basis for this conclusion is contained in the various detailed discussions later in this book of particular practices, such as birth position, eating and drinking in labor, and the continuous presence of a birth attendant. These "alternative" birth settings conform more closely to the research findings than do many hospital settings and are leading the way. The reader is also referred to the discussions of this question in the Introduction and in Appendix A.

2

Making Wise Decisions during Pregnancy

Becoming Informed

The first principle of good decision making is to be informed. Know what your choices are, their pros and cons. If you can, do your homework before discussing issues with your doctor. Be at least as informed about your health care as you would be about buying a new car. This book, many other books on pregnancy and birth, and the presentations in childbirth education classes are good sources of information. (See Appendix E for further reading.)

Whenever possible, attach numbers to the odds of success or failure of a particular choice. This will give you a more concrete idea of your chances and will help you choose more wisely. For example, consider the odds of having a cesarean section with or without an epidural anesthetic. As discussed on page 214, for women having their first labor the best available data reveal that with an epidural, 10.3 percent will need a cesarean section, compared with 3.8 percent without an epidural. Then ask yourself if less pain in labor is worth the increased chance of an operation. Figures are useful in weighing alternatives in medicine, just as they are in weather forecasts. If the chance of rain is 10 percent, you might plan an outdoor picnic, but if the odds are as high as 33 percent (or one in three), you might shift indoors. Good data are not always available on a given question, however. Sometimes the best you can do is make an educated guess.

In addition to obtaining general statistical information, ask your doctor or midwife about his or her own track record. For example, what percentage of patients required a cesarean section? How does this percentage compare with the national norm? and why? What complications has he or she personally encountered? Answers to questions like these will allow you to judge your doctor's philosophy of practice. If a diagnostic procedure such as amniocentesis (pp. 139–141) is proposed, you should, in addition to learning about the risks of this procedure in general, find out the complications rate of the person who will do the procedure on you and how this rate compares with usual standards. What are the chances that the test will have to be repeated? What are the chances that an error will be made, leading to a mistaken diagnosis? If a drug is proposed during pregnancy or lactation, be sure to find out whether or not it has any potential for harmful effects on you or your baby. Except in emergencies, don't agree to any action unless you know what you are getting into, and don't be afraid to ask questions. (See Introduction, p. xv, regarding public disclosure laws in New York and Massachusetts for hospitals with respect to outcomes and practices in maternity care.)

In this book I often refer to randomized control trials (RCT) as the best way to learn about the effects of a particular test, treatment, or policy. In an RCT everything about the group of patients receiving the test, treatment, or other intervention (the experimental group) and the group that is not (the control group) is supposed to match *except* for the variable being studied—for example, routine ultrasound, continuous electronic fetal monitoring, or episiotomy. Then and only then can differences in outcomes— for example, fewer fetal deaths or fewer deep vaginal tears—be attributed to the particular action taken. If the groups are different from the start—for example, one group has more women with a first pregnancy than the other—this fact, rather than the intervention under study, may influence the outcome, thus invalidating the results. Minor differences in the population of women from which the groups are formed, such as age, educational level, and weight, do not *usually* enter into statistical consideration because, if the groups are large enough, random assignment of the women should produce groups that are comparable in terms of these characteristics.

One reason RCTs in pregnancy are difficult to conduct is that as noted in the Introduction, woman may, understandably, refuse to be randomly assigned to a group, such as a hospital-delivery group or a birthing-center one. Physicians, however, are open to criticism for not insisting more often on RCTs *before* they adopt a new practice like continuous electronic fetal monitoring in labor (see p. 149). Once a practice is already in place, it becomes increasingly difficult to conduct an RCT becasue women are reluctant to take the chance of being in the control group. As is often mentioned in this book, data from RCTs are not always available. Then we must make do with the best data we have, recognizing the limitations.

Participating in Decisions

Ideally, your doctor should urge you to participate actively in making decisions. But you may have to assert yourself to get the explanations you need, and asserting yourself in the face of authority may be difficult. (See Appendix F.) To help yourself, make a list of your questions and areas of concern ahead of time. Bring your partner or a friend with you if you need support. Some of the topics you will be discussing are complicated, and having someone else with you as a second listener and questioner can be a real asset. Since remembering exactly what was said can be a problem, you may want to bring a note pad and take notes as your doctor talks. If you run into resistance to your inquiries, or think that you are not being given enough time, share your reaction with your doctor. If you still make no headway, you may need to change doctors. Doctors should have as great a stake in your active participation as you do. After all, they cannot be expected to know in all situations what is best for you. That is too much responsibility for anyone to have to assume.

Be aware that there is not always a single "right" answer that works for everyone. For example, for one woman the very likely risk of pain in labor may outweigh the very small risk of a complication from an anesthetic, but this may not be so for another woman. Decisions involve not only *probabilities* but *values* as well. So making a wise choice involves both knowing the odds and knowing how strongly you feel about each possible outcome. Clarifying your values is a serious, time-consuming process that can be aided in many cases by discussion with others whom you trust—your doctor, partner, family, and friends. Your doctor may be an authority on probabilities, but only you can be the expert on yourself.

Many decisions can be reconsidered as circumstances change. For example, you may choose to keep an open mind about pain medication until you are actually in labor. Of course, this is not always possible, for there are emergency situations when there simply is no time for a full discussion of pros and cons. In circumstances like these, trusting your doctor or midwife is essential.

Sometimes it may seem that pregnancy has become as involved as a course in college, requiring dedication and study to keep up. But the reward, a good childbirth experience, is priceless.

A few words about uncertainty: Keep in mind that there is no absolute certainty, since certainty itself is an illusion. An element of chance is always present, even in the best of hands. Recognizing this uncertainty is the starting point, not only for gaining a degree of control over it but also for maintaining peace of mind.

As a physician, I live constantly with the knowledge of uncertainty. When, for example, I say to a patient, "It looks like you have a viral infection. The odds favor it. I may be wrong, but I'd say that there is a 95 percent chance this is what it is. But if any of the following develop [here I list serious symptoms like higher fever, headaches, and so on], I need to be able to count on you to call me back, even at 2:00 A.M." I mean it just the way I said it. I need the active participation of the patient in order to do my job in the face of unavoidable uncertainty.

The challenging approach of informed choice that we propose is also one possible remedy of the malpractice problem so much in the news. When both doctor and patient are committed to facing the risks and benefits of a particular action before the fact, they are less likely to end up facing each other in court. A greater understanding of the blend of chance and skill, which always operates in medical outcomes, can lead to more realistic expectations. In an atmosphere of trust, of active participation on the part of the informed parents, and of openness on the part of the physician, childbirth can be a triumphant and heartwarming experience for all concerned.

Obstetricians, Family Physicians, and Midwives

One of the first and most important decisions is the choice of a professional who will attend the birth. This can be a family doctor, an obstetrician, or a midwife.

Sources of information include friends who have had babies, doctors who can refer colleagues, local affiliates of the International Childbirth Education Association (ICEA) or La Leche League (while ICEA or La Leche League will not as organizations refer you directly to a doctor or midwife, their members will be willing to speak with you as individuals), the National Association of Parents and Professionals for Safe Alternatives in Childbirth (NAPSAC), hospital departments of obstetrics (the chief of obstetrics may be able to match you to an appropriate doctor or midwife), and nurses who work on maternity services. Most hospitals provide tours of their labor and delivery areas; while there, ask the guide about the styles of the doctors and, if the hospital has them, midwives. The American College of Nurse Midwives (ACNM) will send you a listing of midwifery services in your area, and a listing of freestanding birthing centers is available from the National Association of Childbearing Centers (NACC). The Midwives Alliance of North America, a new organization of lay and nurse midwives that promotes midwifery and provides referrals, will also send you information. (See Appendix C for addresses and other resources.)

At the first appointment with the doctor or midwife, state your own preferences to find out if he or she can satisfy them and if you would be comfortable working with each other. Use the visit as an opportunity to learn, as well, taking advantage of the professional's experience and knowledge. Be open to having your point of view challenged. Having your partner or a friend join you on this first visit is a good idea, to support you, second your reactions, and help by asking additional important questions that might not occur to you immediately.

Make a detailed list of issues of concern to you. These may include policy on intravenous fluids, anesthesia, episiotomy, labor position, and so on. Find out at what point in labor you can count on the doctor or midwife being with you, and clarify coverage arrangements—what happens if he or she is away? In some large group practices the concept of "my doctor" is not even valid. While a woman may see the same person more or less regularly at each prenatal visit, she will be attended during labor and delivery by whoever is on call. This may or may not matter to you.

Obstetricians and *family practitioners* are the two types of physicians who attend births. Both are board-certified specialists. Obstetricians are certified by the American College of Obstetrics and Gynecology (ACOG); family practitioners are certified by the American Board of Family Practice. (Some communities still have general practitioners—general physicians who have not been certified by the American Board of Family Practice.)

One advantage of an obstetrician is that he or she can deal with most complications of labor and delivery. For example, while obstetricians perform cesarean sections, family doctors in general do not, nor do they usually handle complicated births. Under these circumstances, family doctors usually have to call in an obstetrician to assist them. On the other hand, a family physician can continue to care for the family after the baby is born—a major advantage. The family doctor's relationship with the family is not limited to the pregnancy; it includes many other aspects of a family's medical needs. Thus, a family physician offers a family the opportunity for a more extensive and continuous doctor–patient relationship.

Fewer and fewer family doctors provide prenatal care or attend births. Depending on where you live, you may have to search for one who does. The American Academy of Family Physicians is a source of information on family doctors in your area.

When you interview an obstetrician, find out what percentage of his or her deliveries are cesarean sections. Any figure over 10 percent is high, *unless* the physician deals with a high-risk population. Otherwise, a high figure may suggest that his or her criteria for performing cesarean sections are too liberal and that he or she is "too quick to cut." (See pp. 284–291 on cesarean sections.)

If you are planning an out-of-hospital birth, the issues to clarify are discussed in the first section of Chapter 4 (pp. 185–186). If you find physicians willing to attend a home or birthing-center childbirth, ask about the most serious problems they have encountered relating to the site of birth, how they dealt with these problems, and whether they would deal with them differently today. A doctor's openness about his or her practice and willingness to acknowledge errors are qualities generally associated with the best practitioners.

Midwives form the third category of certified attendants. *Nurse midwives* are individuals who have both a nursing degree and midwifery training and who are licensed as such by the state. Midwives attend births in hospitals and birthing centers, but their legal right to attend births at home is more restricted. In some states, midwives can open their own offices for independent private practice. The majority are women, and most belong to the American College of Nurse Midwives. (See Appendix C for information on midwives' associations and the section on "Birth at Home" in Chapter 1 for a description of a midwife's activities and relationship with an expectant couple.)

As a group, midwives are specifically trained to deal with low-risk pregnancies, and they are primarily prepared to deal with normal childbirth and apply nontechnological approaches to helping women with labor and delivery. Unlike many physicians, who are trained in the "disease model" of medicine, midwives do not view pregnancy as an illness or disease. By reputation, tradition, and long experience they are highly attuned to the needs of laboring women. They are "women attending women," a concept central to the thinking of many critics of contemporary hospital childbirth practices. *Midwife* means "with woman."

Nurse midwifery is coming into its own, with the current demand far exceeding the supply. In contrast to the narrow job market they faced ten years ago, nurse midwives are now being

actively recruited by hospitals, private obstetricians, health maintenance organizations (HMOs), and birthing centers. An increasing number are going into private practice. Their styles of practice
are influenced by the settings in which they function.

Midwifery is also practiced by lay (or direct-entry) midwives.
Lay midwives are educated in several ways: some learn on the
job, often at home births, as apprentices to experienced lay midwives; others, in some states, go to school. In the 1970s many lay
midwives worked and studied with family physicians, including
me. Some states certify lay midwives; most do not. In most states
lay midwives operate in a legal gray area. Some prefer it this way
and philosophically reject the notion that pregnancy is a medical
problem and therefore subject to the state regulations that pertain
to medical or nursing practice. My personal experience with lay
midwives has been very positive.

The relationship between nurse midwifery and lay midwifery
is in flux. The two groups of midwives are talking with each
other. Whether they will join ranks or continue their separate
ways remains to be seen.

Other Kinds of Support

Support in labor can take many forms: the *doula* (a Greek word
meaning "a caregiving woman"), the maternity nursing aide of
Holland (who participates in home births and stays on for a week
after the baby is born (see pp. 343–344), and labor coaches and
companions. Studies by Drs. John Kennell and Marshall Klaus of
doulas caring for laboring women in Latin America, Ireland, and
the United States have shown that their participation in labor and
delivery has beneficial effects: significant reduction in the length
of labor, less use of Pitocin for labor stimulation, and fewer cesarean sections when compared with women who lacked continuous labor support. Doula services are becoming more available
in many parts of this country (see Appendix C). My discussion
of the comparably low rates of cesarean deliveries, despite very
different approaches to labor, of American free-standing birth
centers and the Dublin Royal Maternity Hospital (see pp. 199–

200), points up the potential importance of a common feature in both systems of care: one-on-one attendance by midwives. The importance of continuous support by an experienced woman was also found in the research by Drs. Klaus and Kennell and may, I believe, be more significant than any other factor in the excellent outcomes achieved.

Childbirth education classes are offered by most hospitals, by local affiliates of ICEA, and by various home-birth organizations. Hospital classes generally support hospital policies and have an "in-house" quality about them appropriate for preparing families to have a baby in a particular institution. ICEA and home-birth classes take a somewhat more independent stance in their discussion of childbirth practice. Your reading and consultation with childbirth instructors and women who have attended different kinds of classes should help you choose an approach congenial to your personality and needs.

La Leche League provides support for breast-feeding and childcare in general. Its members are available for individual consultation by phone or in person (often in your own home) about problems with nursing. Participation in this group can begin before the baby is born.

All these groups provide opportunities for expectant couples and single parents to meet other couples—one of the most useful functions they serve. For many of today's isolated families, the creation of "community" is an essential step in building confidence for birth and childcare. See Appendix C for the names and addresses of other support groups.

Your History

During your first prenatal visit to your doctor or midwife, a detailed history will be taken. The information you provide will be extremely important in deciding how both you and they will deal with your pregnancy and how risks can be reduced and health promoted.

Your general medical background will include a review of any drugs (prescribed or over-the-counter) you regularly take (see pp. 160–161 on "Drugs during Pregnancy"); any chronic problems that might affect and be affected by the pregnancy, such as recurrent herpes infection (see pp. 171–172), heart disease, phenylketonuria (see pp. 271–272), hepatitis (see pp. 63–64), or diabetes (see pp. 174–175); and past surgical procedures, such as appendectomy, which would be important to know about in evaluating symptoms that may arise, such as abdominal pain (see pp. 76–77).

Your health practices with regard to diet (see pp. 86–93), exposure to cats (see pp. 173–174), exercise (see pp. 94–106), dental care (see p. 72), alcohol (see pp. 176–178), tobacco (see pp. 175–176), medicines (see pp. 160–161), and seat-belt use (see pp. 181–182) will all have a bearing on the pregnancy and should be reviewed.

Your menstrual history, including menarche (age of first period), the interval between periods, and the date of your last period or of ovulation, if known, will be important in dating the pregnancy (see pp. 49–50).

Your past pregnancies, including the date of delivery, complications, the type of delivery, the use of episiotomy (see pp. 219–223) and Pitocin (see pp. 202–204), the weight and condition of your baby at birth and at present, abortions (see pp. 316–322) (both spontaneous and induced), problems in conceiving, and your perceptions of the quality of the birthing experience will all help to highlight aspects of the current pregnancy that require appropriate attention.

It will be useful for your doctor or midwife to know whether you and your partner planned to have a baby at this time and what impact the timing of this pregnancy has on your lives. Do you need professional assistance in resolving ambivalence about the pregnancy or in making the decision to continue or terminate it? Do the answers to these questions relate to the quality of your relationship in any way? Would you benefit from marital counseling or further discussion with your spouse or partner?

Your family history takes on even greater significance in this era of rapidly improving quality of prenatal diagnosis and treatment. (See pp. 125–139 on "Genetics" and pp. 157–159 on "Treating the Fetus,") as we discuss in the section on genetics, clues to increased risk for a genetic disease in the fetus include your age, your racial and ethnic background, a history of having produced a genetically abnormal or retarded individual yourself (or a history of one in your or your spouse's family), recurrent abortions, and birth of a child with a major malformation or chronic illness.

It's a good idea to construct a family tree for each partner, beginning at the bottom of the tree with your own and your siblings' offspring, if any, and tracing back through your generation, your parents' generation, your grandparents', and so forth. List under each person any chronic illnesses, including retardation, and any deaths, and their causes. You will probably have to consult your parents for information and even make a few phone calls to relatives to fill in the details.

Because of the many issues to consider, some experts now advocate that couples make contact with a doctor or midwife even before the woman becomes pregnant. While the effectiveness of this recommendation for "preconception care" has not been proven, there are an increasing number of elements of pregnancy care for which action before conception is or may be useful.* Examples include immunization against rubella (German measles) (see p. 60), testing for AIDS (see pp. 61–63), determination of risk for genetic disorders, and use of folic acid supplements to prevent neural tube defects (see pp. 64–66, 89).

Pregnancy Tests

A hormone indicating pregnancy can be detected in the blood of the pregnant woman as early as three days following fertilization, and in the urine within one week after the first missed menstrual period. This hormone, known as human chorionic gonadotropin (HCG), is produced by the placenta (or, more precisely, by the trophoblast, its earlier form). Currently available tests of HCG done in medical laboratories or physicians' offices are over 98 percent accurate. Over-the-counter urine pregnancy test kits are

---

*See, for example, Brian Jack and Larry Culpepper, "Preconception Care," *Journal of the American Medical Association* (5 Sept. 1990).

somewhat less accurate, giving correct readings 85 to 95 percent of the time.

These highly accurate and useful laboratory tests have taken much of the guesswork out of diagnosing pregnancy in its early stages. They are particularly helpful in confirming pregnancy when a woman has been waiting for a long time to conceive or does not want the pregnancy. They are also useful in identifying possible causes for incompletely explained symptoms, such as those of an ectopic pregnancy (pp. 304–309) or other conditions.

Pregnancy tests are not always necessary. Many women, particularly those who have been pregnant before, "know" when they are pregnant. They notice having missed a menstrual period, experience nipple tingling and breast firmness, and may be aware of an altered body state that is difficult to describe. Pregnancy for these women can be confirmed without testing by noting the physical changes in the uterus detectable on examination (p. 49) and the obvious signs of pregnancy present after several months.

The level of HCG rises rapidly during early pregnancy, doubling every two days. The level peaks at ten weeks of pregnancy, then gradually declines to about one-half of peak levels, where it tends to remain for the rest of the pregnancy. After an abortion, or miscarriage, the level falls off over the course of one week. But occasionally, if trophoblastic tissue has been left behind in the uterus, the hormone may be detectable for as long as several weeks.

Very early in a pregnancy in which a miscarriage is suspected and ultrasound cannot yet provide an answer about the presence or viability of the embryo, measurement of HCG can be helpful, because pregnancies that are failing do not demonstrate the predicted rise in hormone level; it may plateau or actually decline.

Physical Examination

A CHANCE TO LEARN

The physical examination in pregnancy allows the doctor, nurse, or midwife to assess a woman's body for its readiness to carry a

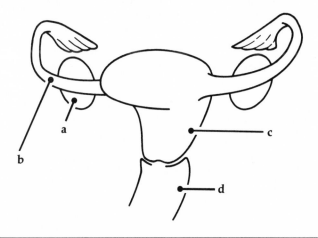

Figure 1. Female reproductive organs: (a) ovaries (b) fallopian tubes (c) uterus (d) vagina

pregnancy and bear a child. It is also an opportunity for you to learn a great deal about the human body in general and the female body in particular. (See Figure 1.) If a woman chooses to include her partner, they both can learn about her body. The exam is also an opportunity for a woman and her doctor or midwife to build up trust between one another. The examination is clearly more than a simple checkup. You can add to the value of this experience in the following ways:

1. Read something about the female body and reproductive organs beforehand. Ask the doctor for any charts or other materials he or she can offer.

2. Ask questions whenever there is something you do not understand. Good, open communication is essential throughout the childbirth experience. Speak up if you feel pain.

3. Try to relax and participate in the examination. For the doctor or other attendant to feel the uterus and ovaries properly, the woman must relax. The examining hands, one in the vagina and the other on the lower abdomen, must move toward each other to feel the structures in between. If a woman's muscles are tense, she actually prevents herself from being examined. Thus,

she has a stake in actively participating in the examination. A maneuver that helps relax the abdominal and vaginal muscles is breathing in and out twice deeply, "bearing down" as though to push out a baby, then "letting go" of the buildup of muscle tension. Often these movements help women relax and allow themselves to be examined.

4. Ask for a mirror to see the cervix and other intravaginal structures. Many women have never seen their cervix, and this is an opportunity to understand its structure.

5. Bring you husband, partner, or a female friend who will be of support later. If you plan to have your husband or a friend present at the delivery, this is a chance to involve them from the start. Make clear to the doctor, nurse, or midwife that these are important members of the labor and delivery "team."

Learning to trust each other, to cooperate and communicate well during the prenatal physical examination, has implications that extend to labor and delivery when it will be vital to work together as a team. In the story of Andrea and Bob in Chapter 1, recall how effectively Andrea and the doctor and midwife communicated with each other as the baby's head was born. Such excellent teamwork during the "big show" grows out of numerous rehearsals in communication (both verbal and nonverbal) during prenatal visits.

THE PERINEAL MUSCLES

One part of the examination that requires collaboration between the examiner and the pregnant woman is the assessment of the perineal muscles. The perineum is the portion of the female body between the lower junction of the labia and the anus. (See Figure 2.) These muscles are used in childbirth, during intercourse, and in the stopping of urination. Since many women are out of touch with these muscles, and relatively few exercise them regularly, their tone is apt to be weak. The examiner can assess them by placing the fingers of the gloved hand onto the perineum just inside the entrance of the vagina and pressing down. The woman is then asked to tighten the muscles. The experienced examiner

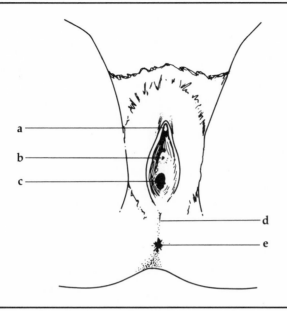

Figure 2. External female genitals: (a) clitoris (b) urethra (c) vagina
(d) perineum (e) rectum

can determine whether tone is nonexistent, weak, average, or
good. If your doctor or midwife does not check these muscles,
you can do it yourself, using two fingers and pressing toward the
spine. If your perineal tone is nonexistent, weak, or average, you
should exercise these muscles. (Our suggestion is to tighten and
relax in units of five contractions, each lasting ten seconds, and
to repeat the unit ten times a day whether or not you are pregnant.)

Toning these muscles can help prevent tearing during birth and
minimizes the need for an episiotomy. Good perineal tone can
also enhance the sexual satisfaction of both partners in intercourse: women can increase their chances for and control over
orgasm, and many men appreciate the gripping sensation they
experience when the perineal muscles are tensed. Strong perineal
muscles also prevent "bladder sagging" as women age (particularly if they have had children), and stress incontinence, the involuntary passage of urine during sneezing, coughing, laughing,

or lifting. These perineal exercises, also known as *Kegel exercises* (after Dr. Arnold Kegel, the physician who first described them), have traditionally been a part of female hygiene in many preindustrial societies, passed on from mother to daughter as part of folk knowledge. (See also pp. 102–104 on prenatal exercise.)

THE PELVIC EXAM

While the initial examination during pregnancy should be complete "from head to toe," its focus is, of course, on the reproductive system. The pelvic examination includes inspecting the labia, determining perineal muscle tone (as we have discussed), inspecting the vagina and the cervix (see pp. 68–69 on physical changes during pregnancy), taking a culture of the cervix for gonorrhea (see p. 61) and possibly chlamydia (see p. 66), doing a Pap (Papanicolaou) test of the cervix (see p. 61), feeling the uterus, ovaries, and rectum, and assessing the size of the pelvis.

The size of the uterus reflects the *gestational age* (the length of time the embryo or fetus is carried in the womb) and is recorded during early pregnancy in terms of weeks; for example, "six to eight weeks' size" (the uterus can first be felt to be enlarged at about six weeks' gestation). Later in pregnancy the size of the uterus is measured with a tape (see p. 84).

The measurements used to determine how easily a baby could pass through the pelvis (as shown in Figure 3) include the following:

1. Estimation of the distance between the lower border of the *symphysis pubis* (where the pubic bones meet in front) and the *sacrum* (forward bend in the spinal column). This distance is judged by using the measured distance between the tip of the examiner's extended middle finger and the thumbward side of the first knuckle of the index finger. In making this measurement, the examiner pushes deep into the vagina, reaching for the curve in the spine, a maneuver that may be slightly uncomfortable for the woman being examined. A distance of greater than 12.5 centimeters (just under 5.0 inches) is considered adequate for the head of an average baby. Often the curve in the sacrum cannot

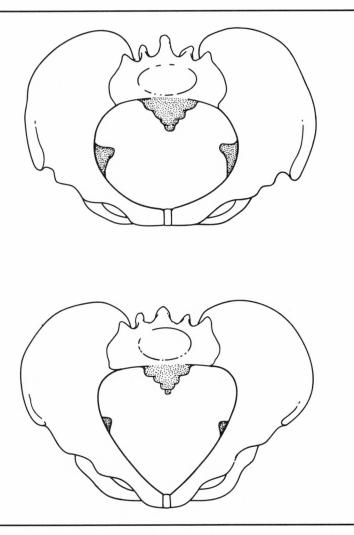

Figure 3.   Pelvis seen from above, showing sacrum and ischial spines.
Female (top) Male (bottom)

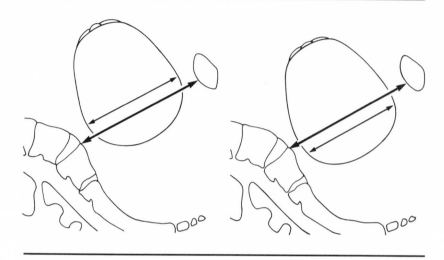

Figure 4. Descent of baby's head into the birth canal, known as engagement. Bold line shows distance between sacrum and pubic bone.

be reached by the examiner, indicating that the distance is at least as long as the examiner's hand. The measured distance between pubis and sacrum is known as the *diagonal conjugate*. (See Figure 4.) Because of the angle of the pubis, the actual shortest distance between it and the sacrum (also known as the *obstetrical conjugate*) is about 2.0 centimeters less than the diagonal conjugate and measures, on the average, 10.6 centimeters (4.1 inches). These two measurements represent the smallest diameters of the inlet of the pelvis, which the baby's head must navigate to enter the birth canal.

2. Determination of the orientation of the sidewalls of the pelvis—whether straight (parallel), convergent (funneling toward the examiner), or divergent (funneling away from the examiner toward the woman's head). Either a parallel or a divergent orientation is considered favorable to passage of the baby; convergent orientation is less favorable.

3. Estimation of the *plane of least dimensions*. This plane is bounded by the lower edge of the pubis, two bony points (spines)

of the ischial bones of the pelvis, and the junction of the fourth and fifth vertebrae of the sacrum (the last two just above the coccyx). The front-to-back diameter of this plane extends from the lower border of the pubis to the juncture of the fourth and fifth sacral vertebrae and measures on the average 12.0 centimeters.

Although a woman herself cannot see or feel her ischial spines, she can become aware of them if the examiner tells her when they are being touched. The spines can also be identified on a drawing or on a model of the pelvis. They are important landmarks of the birth canal and are used as a reference point to stage the descent of the baby. (See Figures 3 and 4.)

The examiner checks to see whether the ischial spines are flat or protruding into the birth canal. The distance between the spines is estimated. It should measure, at least, 10.5 centimeters. Another important measuremment extends from the midpoint between these two spines to the junction of the fourth and fifth sacral vertebrae. This should measure 4.5 to 5.0 centimeters and is a measurement of the depth of the pelvis.

4. The relative convexity or concavity of the sacrum from front to back and vice versa. The more concave, the more room for the baby.

5. Estimation of the angle of the pubic bones, by following these bones downward from the pubis with the second and third fingers of the examining hand. The fingers should separate (pull apart) as downward movement progresses. The angle between the bones should be ninety degrees of greater.

6. Estimation of the size of the outlet to the pelvis is made by measuring the distance between the inner sides of the bones known as the ischial tuberosities, the bones in the middle of the buttocks that one "sits" on. This distance should be at least 11.0 centimeters (4.3 inches). A fist of average size should be able to fit comfortably between the inner borders of the tuberosities. This distance is also known as the transverse diameter of the outlet.

7. Determination of the position and the flexibility of the tip of the spine (coccyx) by pressing on it through the rectum. Ideally, the coccyx should be flat; it should not protrude into the birth canal where it could obstruct labor. It should be movable and thus able to yield to pressure from the baby without cracking.

The "adequacy" of a pelvis for a particular baby is ultimately determined during labor itself, not by measurements made beforehand (see pp. 303–304 on "Disproportion"). However, knowledge of the architecture of the pelvis can be useful in making predictions about the probability of a successful vaginal delivery when labor progress is impaired. It is one of many factors taken into consideration in deciding how to proceed.

BLOOD PRESSURE

Blood pressure is measured at each visit. An inflatable cuff is secured over the upper arm just above the elbow. A stethoscope is placed on the artery that passes under the crease at the elbow. The cuff is inflated to stop the pulse below the cuff, and then it is gradually deflated. The upper reading of the blood pressure, which is called the *systolic pressure* (*systole* refers to the contraction of the heart when blood is ejected with maximum force into the blood vessels), is determined by noticing the reading on the gauge when the pulse sounds first become audible. The lower reading, or *diastolic pressure* (*diastole* refers to the filling, noncontracted phase of the heart cycle), is determined by noting the gauge reading when the pulse is no longer audible. The gauges are calibrated in millimeters of mercury. Thus, a pressure of 120 means that the pressure will balance or support a column of mercury 120 millimeters (about five inches) high in a thin tube. The systolic and diastolic readings are expressed as a fraction: the numerator is the systolic pressure, and the denominator is the diastolic pressure. A reading of 140/90 is regarded as the upper limit of normal. If either figure is higher, blood pressure is too high (hypertension).

Blood pressure varies in a predictable way during pregnancy. There is a normal dip of about five millimeters in the systolic and diastolic pressures during the first and second trimesters.

Blood pressure determination is one of the most important serial measurements made in pregnancy. A blood pressure reading over 140/90 occurring with protein in the urine after the twentieth week defines *preeclampsia*, a relatively common disorder with important implications for pregnancy (pp. 327–329).

Dating the Pregnancy

Many decisions about the growth of the fetus (see pp. 312–315 on "Intrauterine Growth Disturbance") and the timing of delivery of a baby depend on accurate dating of the pregnancy (see pp. 326–327, "Postdate Pregnancies"). Every effort must be made to determine gestational age by twenty weeks, beyond which dating becomes progressively less accurate.

The *date of the last menstrual* period is the primary way of estimating when conception occurred (at roughly fourteen days before the next anticipated menstrual period). Even better is the last *date of ovulation*, as determined by basal body temperature. Another milestone, but not a very accurate one, is the *quickening*, the moment when a mother first feels her baby move, sometime between sixteen and twenty weeks. A mother's recognition of this sensation will vary, depending in part on whether she has had other pregnancies and is familiar with the sensation. Measurement of the size and the height of the uterus is an excellent dating method, particularly in the first trimester. (See Figure 5.) Between eighteen and thirty weeks of gestation, the height of the uterus, measured in centimeters, correlates fairly well with the number of weeks of gestation, especially in first pregnancies. The baby's heart can first be heard with a stethoscope between sixteen and nineteen weeks after conception, and by *doppler ultrasound* by twelve weeks (see pp. 151–154).

With ultrasound, fetal heart movements can be visualized by six to seven weeks. The gestational sac is visible as early as five to six weeks. Between eight and twelve weeks, the distance between the head and buttocks of the fetus, the "crown–rump" distance, dates the gestational age very precisely. Between sixteen and twenty-six weeks, measurement of the diameter of the baby's head can date the pregnancy to within one and a half weeks of the gestational age with 95 percent confidence. Ultrasound re-

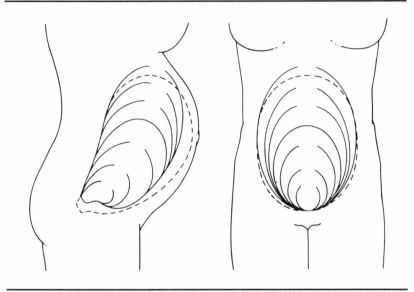

Figure 5. Growth of the uterus. Unbroken curve in middle is size of uterus at twenty-four weeks. Dotted line shows position of uterus after baby's head engages in the pelvis.

searchers have also found that the length of the femur (thigh bone) of the fetus, measured during the second trimester, is 95 percent accurate to within six days of the fetal age. Other physical measurements are being studied for their correlation with gestational age.

Growth of the Fetus

THE FIRST WEEK:
CELL DIVISION AND IMPLANTATION

Egg and sperm cells meet during fertilization to form one cell with

"Growth of the Fetus" is adapted from Boston Children's Medical Center, *Pregnancy, Birth and the Newborn Baby* (New York: Dell, 1972). Reprinted by permission.

forty-six chromosomes. From this one cell, through cell growth, division, and differentiation, the baby and placenta will develop.

After fertilization, rapid cell division produces a hollow sphere, the *blastocyst*. After passing through the fallopian tube and reaching the womb, the blastocyst continues to enlarge. In another three or four days it attaches itself to the surface of the womb's lining. This is called *nidation*.

After seven days, the blastocyst, now composed of several hundred cells, invades the now-prepared lining of the womb, known as the *decidua*, and gains a firm attachment to the mother. In the process, the sphere collapses, like a cooling popover. The cells from the inside of the sphere form the germinal disc from which the entire baby will develop. The rest of the cells compose the invading *trophoblast*, or primitive placenta. The trophoblast is unique, because it is the only human tissue, outside of malignant tissue, that invades another and is not rejected.

THE SECOND WEEK

Once the blastocyst is implanted, its trophoblast grows at an astounding rate, sending out fingerlike projections into the surrounding decidua. These projections become honeycombed with walls and spaces. When the embryo is about two weeks old, maternal tissues are eroded to such an extent that the maternal blood vessels allow the mother's blood to rush into these trophoblastic spaces. Placental circulation is thus established, and the mother's blood begins to nourish the developing embryo.

The trophoblast also produces HCG (see pp. 39–40), without which the entire lining of the womb, including the developing blastocyst, would be cast off. HCG in the mother's blood and urine is the hormone measured in tests used to detect pregnancy.

The embryonic disc, at this point, is a double-layered plate, resembling an empty sandwich. The upper outer layer is called the *ectoderm*; from it the skin, hair, and nails and the entire nervous system will develop. The lower layer is the *endoderm*, which gives rise to the digestive tract, the respiratory system, and many of their accessory glands.

Between these two layers a third layer, the *mesoderm*, soon develops. The muscles and tissues lining the abdominal and pleural cavities derive from it. Scattered between these three germinal layers are loose cells called the *mesenchyme*, which belongs to no single layer but acts as a sort of loose packing tissue between layers. The mesenchyme gives rise to the heart, blood vessels, bones, and cartilage.

THE THIRD WEEK

During the third week the oval germinal disc becomes pearshaped and then takes on the form of the body of a violin. It also bends in the middle, losing its flat shape. Down the center of the ectodermal surface, which will become the baby's back, a couple of parallel ridges form. A groove or trench between them, known as the *neural groove*, will form the central nervous system. The heart and blood vessels also begin to develop during the third week of embryonic life.

THE FOURTH WEEK

Very rapid changes are taking place within the body of the embryo. Shortly after the laying of foundations for the nervous and circulatory systems, the *gut*, or early digestive system, begins to form. By a process similar to the formation of the neural groove, the endoderm gives rise to the foregut in front and the hindgut in the tail region. A blind pouch in front pushes gradually forward, soon breaking through upon the undersurface of the head to form the mouth.

At four weeks and one-quarter-inch long, the embryo does not yet look like a baby. It has a head and a tail, which can be distinguished readily. The neural groove has sealed over completely, and formation of the brain is progressing rapidly. In the head, the beginnings of the eye and ear can be seen. A growing area called the mandibular process is beginning to form the face. The heart is now a large bulge on the underside of the embryo, already beating rhythmically.

TWO MONTHS

By two months the fetus, over an inch long, has assumed a definite human form. It has eyes, ears, and a nose. The hands have fingers and the feet have toes. The head still looks too big for the body, which is potbellied because the liver is too large for the abdominal cavity. The sexual organs have begun to form. From now on the embryo will be called a fetus.

THREE MONTHS

In the third month of embryonic development many different organs of the body become more specialized. In the mouth, a series of ten tooth buds appear in both the upper and lower jaws.

The most dramatic changes of the third month are seen in the sexual organs, especially those of males. Differentiation is more rapid in males than in females, and by the end of the third month, close inspection of the fetus will reveal whether it is a boy or a girl.

FOUR AND FIVE MONTHS

The changes occurring during the rest of pregnancy are much more subtle. Development is largely a matter of simple enlargement and maturation of the various organs. The four-month-old fetus, though tiny, looks like a baby in every respect, although the head is still relatively large and the legs relatively short. The skin is thin, red, and wrinkled.

FROM SIX MONTHS TO BIRTH

By six months of age specialized structures in the baby's skin are formed. On the head and sometimes over the back and shoulders there is a fine growth of hair, whose color has little resemblance to the color of the hair the child eventually will have. Fingernails and toenails appear and grow slowly. At the time of birth they will project slightly at the tips of the fingers, and they will have to be trimmed in the first few days of life to keep the infant from scratching itself. Oil glands appear in the skin and manufacture a greasy, sticky substance known as the *vernix caseosa*, which is like a salve or ointment coating the skin.

By the end of the sixth month the fetus is fully developed. From now until term it needs only to grow in length, weight, and strength in order to face the demands of the world outside the womb.

THE PLACENTA

The *placenta*, or afterbirth, plays a central role in pregnancy. It is a flat, circular structure about seven to eight inches in diameter and an inch in thickness and weighs roughly one pound. It is composed of millions of fingerlike projections, called *chorionic villi*, which are part of the fetal blood vessel system and connect with the rest of the baby's blood vessels via the large umbilical veins and artery in the umbilical cord. In the body of the placenta, the villi are suspended in maternal blood. While there is no actual mixing of circulation between the mother and the fetus, only a thin layer of cells covering the villi separates them. All the nutrients and oxygen pass into the baby's circulation across this layer. The baby also has an active metabolism of its own; the waste products from fetal metabolism, including carbon dioxide, pass into the mother's circulation.

Around the rim of the pie-shaped placenta, membranes are attached. They are a thin, semitransparent sheet of tissue that forms a baglike, round dome. Tethered at the end of the umbilical cord, the baby is suspended throughout pregnancy in the amniotic fluid within this rounded dome. Because of this fluid, it is practically impossible for the fetus to sustain injury from the outside.

The production of hormones is another important function of the placenta. Pregnancy places unique demands on the entire maternal organism; its special requirements must be met by adaptations that involve almost every organ system in the body. The size of the uterus and breasts, and the volume of blood in the body must increase tremendously. To some extent, the pelvic joints loosen. These and many other adaptations are largely brought about by the action of the placental hormones on the mother's body. The placental hormones are also thought to be important in maintaining pregnancy and, finally, in initiating labor. The entire process of growth from conception to birth, as described above, can be visualized in the photographs of the Swedish photographer, Lennart Nilsson (see Appendix E).

Laboratory Tests

Several laboratory tests are routinely performed as part of the initial pregnancy assessment. Since most pregnant women will have contact with these tests, it is good that they have an idea of how the tests are taken and what their results are intended to reveal.

BLOOD TESTS

The *hematocrit* is a reading of the percentage of a thin column of centrifuged blood occupied by the red blood cells. The *hemoglobin* is a reading of the concentration in the blood of the oxygen-carrying pigment hemoglobin contained within the red blood cells. Each test can show whether or not anemia is present. One or both of these tests is usually repeated at thirty-six weeks' gestation.

URINE TEST

A test for protein and sugar (glucose) in the urine is done initially and at each subsequent visit. The presence of glucose in the urine is one way to identify women with diabetes (see pp. 174–175). Urinary glucose in and of itself does not indicate diabetes, which must be confirmed with blood glucose tests. Although as many as 70 percent of women will have glucose in their urine at some time in pregnancy, only 1 percent will also have an abnormal blood glucose pattern. The symptoms of diabetes include increased thirst and urination, increased appetite, and weight loss.

A common practice in prenatal care is measuring the blood glucose in all pregnant women after a glucose test meal in a search for chemical (or "gestational") diabetes. However, for women who show no symptoms of diabetes, a high glucose measurement has not proven valuable in predicting risks for the mother or the fetus. The practice of routine blood sugar testing should therefore be put on hold until researchers prove that it has predictive value and that treatment of asymptomatic women with high blood glucose improves pregnancy outcomes.

It is not uncommon for protein to be present in the urine during pregnancy, and within certain limits, *proteinuria* (protein in the urine) is regarded as normal. The amount of protein is graded from "zero" (none) to "four plus," as determined by a color change in the "dipstick" used for this measurement. During pregnancy a reading of "zero," "trace," or "one plus" is considered to be normal, while "two plus" or greater is considered abnormal, indicating kidney malfunction or preeclampsia (pp. 327–329). An increase in the amount of protein by two gradations (from "zero" to "one plus," "trace" to "two plus," "one plus" to "three plus," or "two plus" to "four plus") is also considered to be significant in defining preeclampsia.

An elevated urine protein may be related to body position and does not necessarily indicate kidney malfunction. In the upright position, the pregnant uterus presses on the veins that drain blood from the kidneys, and protein can leak into the urine from the back pressure. This effect is reversed when a woman lies on her side, thereby rolling the uterus off of these veins. Thus, it is essential to collect urine for protein testing with the woman lying on her side to see whether the cause of the proteinuria was simply postural.

SYPHILIS TEST

The serological test for syphilis, or STS, identifies women with this disease so that they can be treated, thereby protecting their fetuses as well (see p. 173). Women who harbor syphilis often do not have symptoms. However, the micoorganism that causes this disease can cross the placenta to infect the fetus. Treatment can prevent this dread complication. A false positive test for syphilis (in which the test is positive when syphilis is not present) warrants an investigation for the antiphospholipid syndrome, (see pp. 317–318) a cause of recurrent miscarriage and other problems.

BLOOD TYPE, RH(D) FACTOR, AND TESTS FOR ANTIBODIES AGAINST RED BLOOD CELLS

A variety of tests are used to identify women at risk for producing antibodies against the red cells of their own fetus. Such maternal antibodies can cross the placenta to attach to the fetus's cells, causing them to be destroyed and removed from the circulation. The effects on the infant include various degrees of jaundice (pp. 273–274), anemia, and heart failure.

This destruction of the red cells is most common in the case of an Rh(D) negative mother with an Rh(D) positive fetus (RH is now called D). Usually an Rh(D) negative mother beginning her first pregnancy is free of antibodies to Rh(D) positive cells. But during that last trimester of the pregnancy, and especially at the time of birth, small numbers of fetal red blood cells can cross the placenta and enter the mother's circulation. The mother's body recognizes the Rh(D) positive cells as foreign and makes antibodies to eliminate them. These antibodies cross the placenta in the other direction to enter the fetal circulation, destroying the fetal Rh(D) positive cells within the baby. During the first pregnancy with an Rh(D) positive fetus the quantity of anti-Rh(D) antibody produced by the mother is too little and/or too late to destroy enough of the fetus's red cells to cause harm. But should the mother carry another Rh(D) positive fetus during a subsequent pregnancy, the additional exposure to Rh(D) positive cells will restimulate the mother's now-sensitized immune system to turn on antibody production to the Rh(D) factor. The antibody produced can place the fetus in jeopardy. This is why the Rh(D) problem in a previously unsensitized woman is a problem for the second or later pregnancies, not for the first one.

This once-dreaded problem is now almost entirely preventable through the use of a special gamma globulin called RhoGAM, which is rich in anti-RH antibodies. RhoGAM (Rh[D] immuno-globulin) is given to the Rh(D) negative woman in time to attach to and eliminate RH(D) positive fetal cells in the maternal circulation before they are able to sensitize the mother. A first dose is usually given at twenty-eight weeks' gestation, and a second, larger dose is given within seventy-two hours of birth. This one–two punch prevents virtually all Rh(D) negative women from becoming sensitized and has almost completely solved the Rh problem.

The sequence of events described above requires that the blood type of the fetus be Rh(D) positive. The fetus of an Rh(D) negative woman can be Rh(D) positive *only* if the father is Rh(D) positive. (The gene for Rh[D] positive is dominant.) If the father is Rh(D) negative, the situation necessary for Rh(D) sensitization cannot exist. If the father is Rh(D) positive, the baby will have a 50 or 100 percent chance of being Rh(D) positive, depending on whether the father is heterozygous or homozygous (p. 126), that is, whether he carries one or two genes for Rh(D) positivity. At present, there is no way of knowing, short of amniocentesis and fetal blood sampling, whether the fetus is Rh(D) positive or negative until birth, when the baby's blood (from the umbilical cord) can be tested directly. Therefore, RhoGAM is given at twenty-eight weeks when the father is Rh positive (even though the baby might be Rh(D) negative) and again at birth to mothers whose infants are proven to be Rh(D) positive. For the same reasons, RhoGAM is given at the time of amniocentesis and abortion, or if the father's identity is uncertain.

If a woman already has antibodies to Rh(D) positive cells, RhoGAM will not reverse the process and is of no preventive value. Such women will already have antibodies from sensitization due to inadvertent transfusions of Rh(D) positive blood, or from previous pregnancies with Rh(D) positive fetuses in which RhoGAM was not used. (These pregnancies may have involved not only Rh(D) positive babies born at term, but also spontaneous or induced abortions [p. 316] of Rh[D] positive fetuses, or amni-ocentesis [pp. 139–141] involving an Rh[D] positive fetus. In amniocentesis, the fetal blood vessels in the umbilical cord may be torn, resulting in a leakage of fetal blood into the amniotic fluid and thence into the mother's circulation. The fetus itself is usually not harmed during such accidents.) In all of these situations the potential exists for passage of fetal cells into the mother's circulation, with resulting sensitization.

The presence and the quantity of antibodies to fetal red cells can be determined. A rise in antibody titer indicates ongoing sensitization and identifies the fetus that is likely to be significantly affected. Based on this information, additional steps are called for to monitor the baby's well-being and to intervene when appropriate. (See "Treating the Fetus," pp. 157–159.) Antibody levels are routinely checked at twenty-eight and thirty-six weeks and more often, as indicated.

Individuals whose blood type is O have naturally occurring antibodies against blood types A and B. (These antibodies do not arise in pregnancy from sensitization of the mother through fetal–maternal transfusion, as is true for an Rh[D] negative mother with an Rh[D] positive fetus.) Nonetheless, anti-A, and, to a lesser degree, anti-B antibodies can also cross the placenta, leading to destruction of fetal red blood cells, which shows up after birth as jaundice and/or anemia. Since the anti-A and anti-B antibodies already existed in the mother prior to pregnancy, there is no way to prevent their formation during pregnancy. The resulting jaundice and/or anemia in the newborn, known as ABO disease, is dealt with as necessary (see pp. 273–274). If ABO disease has occurred in one infant, there is an almost 90 percent chance of recurrence in siblings with the same blood type.

Some women have rare blood types that can be the basis of antibody production against the incompatible cells of their fetuses. Gamma globulin comparable to RhoGAM is not available to prevent such sensitization. In this circumstance the best one can do is monitor the antibodies and intervene as indicated (similar to the procedure in the case of an already sensitized Rh[D] negative mother). The antibody screening done routinely at the initial prenatal visit identifies women with so-called atypical antibodies that reflect the rarer blood types.

CYTOMEGALOVIRUS

Not yet in general use, the test for cytomegalovirus (CMV) antibodies is likely to become routine in the years ahead (see pp. 167–168).

RUBELLA

The rubella antibody titer identifies the adequacy of the mother's immunity to rubella (German measles), a virus that can cross the placenta to infect the fetus with varying degrees of harm, including deafness, cataracts, mental retardation, and heart defects. (See pp. 172–173 for a discussion of congenital rubella syndrome.) Because of this threat, public health policy in this country promotes immunization of all girls prior to their childbearing years. The suspected exposure of a nonimmune woman to someone with probable rubella during pregnancy calls for monitoring the mother's antibody level to see if it rises. A rising level indicates infection in the mother and possibly in the fetus. Infection in the mother raises the question of aborting the pregnancy, since there is at present no treatment for rubella in either the mother or the fetus.

Women who are not immune to rubella are encouraged to receive rubella vaccine following the pregnancy to avoid this problem in future pregnancies. They should receive the vaccine only when using effective birth control, in order to prevent the vaccine virus from infecting the fetus of an unsuspected pregnancy, although the risk to the fetus of vaccine virus is small.

URINE CULTURE

A significant number of pregnant women harbor bacteria in their urinary tracts without having any symptoms, so-called asymptomatic bacteriuria. These women are at increased risk for developing a symptomatic urinary tract infection (see pp. 75–76). Treating these women with antibiotics can prevent clinical infection from developing. Women with asymptomatic infection can be identified with a urine culture. Accordingly, a urine culture is a recommended routine test during pregnancy.

PAP TEST

The Papanicolaou test (Pap test) of the cervix is used to screen for cancer of the cervix. Pregnant women are not more vulnerable to this disorder; testing in pregnancy simply takes advantage of the fact that a pelvic examination is being performed as part of the initial prenatal evaluation. The Pap test is done again during the postpartum examination.

GONORRHEA CULTURE

The gonorrhea culture of the cervix is performed along with the Pap test. Women who harbor this germ, which can infect the baby at birth, should be treated with antibiotics (see also pp. 169–170).

AIDS TEST

AIDS (acquired immune deficiency disorder), as everyone knows, has become a major and dreaded international public health problem. AIDS is among the five leading causes of death in women of childbearing age in the United States and in children up until age five. The problem is much more severe—alarmingly so—in many developing nations.

Infection with the AIDS (HIV) virus precedes the development of the clinical symptoms of AIDS by months to years. Thus, a mother may be infected but have no symptoms and nevertheless be capable of infecting others, including her baby. The risk of transmission of the virus to babies from infected mothers without clinical symptoms, as reported in a recent collaborative European study (1990), was just over 12 percent. Other studies have reported higher rates of transmission, from 25 to 40 percent. Transmission is higher in women in more advanced stages of infection (whose immune systems are more suppressed), whether or not they have symptoms. Transmission may also occur early in a mother's infection as the virus spreads throughout her body before she has produced antibodies to it. Not all of the studies of transmission rates have characterized the stages of infection of the mothers who were tested.

With the exception of the complications of AIDS itself, such as recurrent pneumonia and other "opportunistic" infections and, at the extreme, death itself, women infected with the AIDS virus do not have more problems with their pregnancies than noninfected women. Nor does pregnancy appear to intensify the effects of AIDS. To date there is no known cure for AIDS, which has been uniformly fatal, although currently available therapy can slow its progress in men and nonpregnant women. The effectiveness of this treatment for pregnant women and their babies is under study.

How the AIDS virus passes from mother to baby is not well proven. There is now evidence that transmission can occur anytime during pregnancy. Following the pattern of similar viral infections, such as hepatitis (see pp. 63–64), a probable route for transmission is directly across the placenta. Breaks in the skin of the fetus are suspected as another means of entry. For this reason, use of scalp electrodes, which are screwed into the skin of a baby's head (see pp. 146–147) for electronic monitoring of the fetal heart rate during labor, is not recommended. The baby can also be infected through swallowing infected maternal blood at the time of delivery and from breast milk containing the HIV virus. Accordingly, breast-feeding is not recommended.

Infected individuals, including pregnant women and babies, produce several types of antibodies to the AIDS virus. Infected pregnant women pass one type of these antibodies to the fetus across the placenta, just as they transmit similar antibodies of this type to viruses such as measles, chicken pox, German measles (rubella), polio, and mumps. What is unique and puzzling about the maternally passed AIDS antibodies is that, unlike the others mentioned, they offer *no* protection to either mother or baby; they do not behave like the usual antibodies, which help the body fight an infection. The detection of a mother's AIDS antibodies in a baby does not necessarily signify that he or she is infected. If antibody, but not virus, has been transmitted, the baby's maternally transmitted antibody level will fall off and disappear over the course of the first year, and the baby will not develop AIDS. If both transmission of maternal antibodies and infection of the baby have occurred, the baby will eventually make antibodies similar to those of the mother and, even earlier, between one and three months of age, antibodies of a type that are not passed from his or her mother. This latter antibody is an early tip-off that infection has occurred. A recent test that detects parts of the AIDS virus offers the possibility of even earlier recognition. An infected infant will go on to develop the symptoms of AIDS, usually by six months.

Because of the spread of AIDS, many public health authorities now recommend that *all* pregnant women, not just those at high risk, be tested, after being counseled about the risks and consequences of AIDS transmission to the baby. (At present most state laws require the mother's permission before AIDS tests are done.) Whether or not testing becomes mandatory, I believe that as a minimum, all pregnant women should be informed about the risks of AIDS and offered the opportunity to be tested and counseled. How mothers will respond to such an offer will vary widely. Some who are concerned about infecting their babies or having their babies grow up motherless will elect to be tested and, if positive, terminate the pregnancy. Others will respond differently.

HEPATITIS B

Babies of mothers who are infected with the hepatitis B virus (most of whom have no symptoms of infection and are called asymptomatic carriers) are at risk for contracting the infection themselves. A minority become infected before birth as a result of passage of the virus across the placenta; the majority become infected during birth as a consequence of exposure to the virus present in the birth canal. Administering to the baby at birth of antihepatitis gamma globulin (antibodies) by a single injection followed by vaccine (several injections over time) is highly successful in preventing infection after exposure to the virus. However, this treatment will not arrest the progression of infection in babies already infected before birth. Pregnant women are now routinely checked for hepatitis B.

Without treatment, a significant percentage of babies who are exposed to the virus during birth will become infected and develop liver disease: inflammation (hepatitis), scarring (cirrhosis), and cancer. Many will die. Because the vast majority of all exposed babies can be successfully treated before the virus has had the chance to infect them, it is now recommended that *all* pregnant women—not, as in the past, just those at high risk for infection—be tested for hepatitis B infection. The babies of women testing positive should be treated at birth as described (see p. 170 regarding new policy to immunize all babies against hepatitis B).

AFP TEST

The alpha-fetoprotein (AFP) test is now being offered to more and more women during the second trimester as a way of detecting open neural tube defects and other severe problems. If it is not offered at your hospital, ask where it is done near you. These abnormalities of the baby's brain and spinal cord include *anencephaly*, failure of formation of the brain, and *meningomyelocele*, a defect of the spinal cord and vertebral column (spina bifida). These anomalies can occur in as many as 1 in 500 pregnancies. Alpha fetoprotein is normally made by the fetus in amounts that increase with gestational age. It is normally secreted into the amniotic fluid and crosses the placenta into the mother's circulation. Fetuses with open neural tube defects secrete increased amounts of AFP into the amniotic fluid. The amount absorbed into the maternal blood also tends to be greater. An elevated level of AFP in the mother's blood can lead to the identification of 90 percent of those fetuses that have open neural tube defects. Ten percent of the affected fetuses are not detected by this test, because the AFP levels in their mothers fall within the normal range and further studies are therefore not done. There is mounting evidence that folic acid supplements begun at or before conception may protect against neural tube defects (p. 89). Also, there is now some evidence that exposure of mothers to hot tubs and saunas during the first trimester increases the risk of neural tube defects (see p. 181).

The AFP test is performed on a sample of the mother's blood

drawn at between fifteen and eighteen weeks' gestation. If levels of AFP are high relative to gestational age, further tests are done.

First, the blood test is repeated after two weeks. If AFP is not elevated this time (as commonly happens), the fetus is considered normal. If the second test is also elevated, an ultrasound (pp. 151–154) examination is performed to date the pregnancy more accurately, to determine the number of fetuses present, to inspect the fetal spine and head for defect, and to determine the normalcy of the placenta. If an error in dating the pregnancy is found (this would account for the increased maternal AFP level on the basis of advanced gestational age), if twins are present (twins produce more AFP than does a single fetus), or if cystic areas are found in the placenta (these could account for direct transfer of AFP), usually no further studies are done, because the elevated maternal AFP can be explained.

If ultrasound testing reveals no explanation for an elevated maternal AFP level (or if a spinal defect is suspected), an amniocentesis is performed to measure the level of AFP in the amniotic fluid. By the standards for AFP measurement now in use, about 98 percent of fetuses with open neural tube defects will be detected through high amniotic fluid AFP level. Chromosomal analysis (see p. 135) is also performed, since high maternal AFP levels are also associated with chromosomal abnormalities of the fetus.

A refinement in testing the amniotic fluid of fetuses suspected of neural tube defects is the measurement of *acetylcholinesterase*, an enzyme normally produced in nerve tissue. It appears to be more specific than AFP for discriminating between fetuses with neural tube defects and normal fetuses. Thus, using this test almost precludes mistaking a normal baby for one with a defect, and vice versa.

A normal amniotic fluid AFP in the presence of an elevated maternal blood AFP can mean that the fetus is normal, or that it falls into a "mixed" group of fetuses that do not have neural tube defects but that, on follow-up, demonstrate other problems that bear close watching. These include various congenital abnormalities, intrauterine growth disturbance (pp. 312–315), likelihood of premature birth (pp. 329–336), miscarriage (pp. 316–322), and an increased risk of fetal death even late in pregnancy. Thus, the yield of the AFP test goes beyond the important goal of identifying the fetus with an open neural tube defect.

To summarize, a consistently elevated AFP level in the blood of a pregnant woman does not necessarily mean an affected fetus, but it does identify those who are *at increased risk* for neural tube and other defects. A normal maternal AFP, it should also be stressed, is no guarantee against having a neural tube defect, since 10 percent of affected fetuses are missed. In this respect, the AFP screening test, valuable as it is, is imperfect. Amniocentesis is much more accurate, but, of course, more risky and costly as well. There is now strong evidence that a low maternal serum AFP level can predict chromosomal abnormalities such as those seen in Down syndrome (see pp. 134–136).

OTHER TESTS

Other nonroutine tests are done in pregnancy when particular risks are suspected. As examples, all discussed elsewhere in this book, we mention the testing of couples of Ashkenazic Jewish background for Tay-Sachs disease (pp. 128–129), the culturing of women for chlamydia, and the testing for serum antibodies (immunity) to cytomegalovirus (see pp. 166–168) and toxoplasmosis (see pp. 173–174). We can look forward to new developments in the years ahead as laboratory science increasingly identifies actual or potential problems in pregnancy. (See "Protecting the Fetus," pp. 159–182.)

Physical Changes

WEIGHT GAIN AND GROWTH OF THE UTERUS

The most dramatic and obvious physical changes in pregnancy are those related to the woman's weight and shape. A woman with an "average" pregnancy, who is carrying one baby, has an overall pregnancy-related weight gain of 25 to 30 pounds. The fetus accounts for 7.5 pounds; the placenta and membranes, 1.4

pounds; the amniotic fluid, 1.8 pounds; increase in size of the uterus, 2.1 pounds; increase in maternal blood, 2.8 pounds; breast size, 0.9 pounds; fluid in the skin and other tissues, 3.7 pounds; and maternal reserves, 7.4 pounds. (See pp. 86–89 for discussion of optimum weight gain.)

During pregnancy the capacity of the uterus increases 500- to 1,000-fold. (See Figure 5, p. 50.) Its existing muscle cells stretch and thicken, and the elastic and fibrous tissues increase markedly, adding to the strength of the uterine wall. Its blood supply also increases.

For the first few weeks of pregnancy, the normal pear shape of the uterus is maintained. As the embryo grows, the uterus becomes more globelike and, by the third month, spherical. Then it elongates more than it widens to assume an ovoid shape. After the third month the uterus is too large to be confined in the pelvis, so it rises into the abdomen. As it grows further, it comes in contact with the front wall of the abdomen, pushing the intestines to the side, and eventually reaches almost to the level of the liver.

Weight gain in pregnancy begins slowly, only to pick up steadily later on. It is obviously correlated with the size of the uterus. About 2 pounds are gained during the first third of a pregnancy; the other 25 or so pounds are gained during the second and third trimesters, with some leveling off during the last few weeks.

The growth in size of the uterus can be represented on a graph in the form of a straight line that is directly proportional to the gestational age. This relationship is true primarily in first pregnancies and less so in later ones. Between the eighteenth and thirtieth weeks of gestation this relationship is particularly good, especially in first pregnancies. A commonly used rule of thumb is that the number of weeks is the same as the number of centimeters of uterine height. The measurement of uterine size is a good indicator of fetal growth.

Any abnormalities in the growth of the uterus need to be explained. As determined over several months, smaller-than-predicted uterine growth suggests *intrauterine growth disturbance* (pp. 312–315) and/or *oligohydramnios* (pp. 311–312), the relatively uncommon condition of insufficient amniotic fluid, and should prompt further evaluation. Excessive uterine growth also requires an explanation. Its causes include errors in dates (that is, believing the fetus to be younger than it actually is); *hydramnios* (p. 311), the condition of too much amniotic fluid; multiple pregnancies (twins or more); *hydatidiform mole* (pp. 310–311); or simply the presence of a large baby, whether or not this reflects maternal diabetes.

From the beginning of the second trimester the uterus contracts irregularly. Toward the end of pregnancy, women are able to perceive these contractions and report that they feel like menstrual cramps. During the last two weeks of pregnancy Braxton Hicks contractions (named for the physician who first described them) can occur as often as every ten to twenty minutes. They may be quite uncomfortable and account for "false labor," or uterine contractions that are not accompanied by progressive dilation of the cervix.

At times a distinct bulge can be seen and felt in the midline of the abdomen between the two rectus muscles that run from the lower rib cage to the pubic bone. This bulge results from a spreading apart of these muscles, which deprives the midabdominal wall of one of its major supports. The gap between the muscles is now bridged primarily by skin and *fascia*, which stretch relatively easily in response to the enlarging uterus. Treatment of this separation of the recti (also called a *diastasis recti*) is discussed in the section on prenatal exercise (pp. 97–99).

CERVIX AND VAGINA

During pregnancy the cervix softens, enlarges, and turns a purplish red. Its mucous glands, along with those of the vagina, markedly increase in number and in the production of secretions. These glandular secretions account for the thick white vaginal discharge so commonly seen. Soon after conception the cervical canal is filled with a clump of thick mucus—the *mucous plug*—which is expelled either during or shortly before labor.

The vaginal wall characteristically becomes duskier, softer, thicker, moister, and more elastic, all in preparation for the stretching it will undergo during delivery. The labia enlarge and turn a dusky blue.

ABDOMEN AND SKIN

In about 50 percent of women, reddish, slightly depressed skin markings, called *striae gravidarum* (the "lines of pregnancy"), are present by the third trimester on the skin of the abdomen and sometimes on the breasts and thighs. Their cause is unknown. After delivery these markings gradually change to silvery colored lines that shrink as the contracting abdominal and breast skin firms up. They are permanent "scars" or *stretch marks* of pregnancy. There is no way to either prevent or eliminate them, and creams and ointments sold for this purpose simply do not work.

In many women (primarily those with dark hair and complexion), the skin of the midline of the abdomen becomes pigmented from the pubic bone to close to the tip of the breast bone. The dark line curves around the umbilicus. Neither the cause nor the significance of this line is known, and it rapidly disappears after delivery.

It is quite common in pregnancy for brown patches to appear on the face and neck. They are known as *chloasma*, or the "mask of pregnancy." They usually disappear after giving birth.

In Caucasians in particular, tiny red spots commonly appear on the face, the neck, the upper chest, and arms. On inspection with a hand magnifying lens, each red dot is seen to consist of several tiny blood vessels branching from a central feeder. If pressure is gently applied to the center with, for example, the point of a pencil, the entire network is deprived of its blood supply and blanches. These *spider hemangiomas*, as they are sometimes called, are believed to be related to increased estrogen levels during pregnancy. Why some women have these spots and others do not is not understood, and their significance is not known. They disappear after giving birth. Another transient skin change is *redness of the palms*. Like the "spiders," this redness is believed to be related to estrogen levels. Its significance is unknown, and the phenomenon disappears after delivery.

BREASTS AND PREPARATION FOR BREAST-FEEDING

Women commonly experience tenderness and tingling of the breasts as one of the earliest signs of pregnancy. The breasts increase in size, often dramatically, and become lumpier as the milk-producing glands enlarge. Delicate blue veins appear beneath the skin and reflect the increased blood flow. The nipples enlarge and darken and are more erectile. Scattered through the *areola* (the dark circle around the nipple) are small bumps, which are enlarged sebaceous (oil) glands (also known as the glands of Montgomery). After the first few months, if the nipple is squeezed, *colostrum*, the thick yellow fluid that comes in before the milk, will come out.

A woman who plans to breast-feed should buy a nursing brassiere large enough to support her breasts both during the last few months of pregnancy and during nursing. The brassiere can be worn day and night if the breasts are heavy, or if she feels uncomfortable.

An inverted nipple can be identified by pressing the areola between the thumb and the forefinger. A normal nipple, or one that is simply flat, will protrude, while an inverted nipple will retract. Inverted nipples are uncommon, since most nipples that appear to be inverted are merely flat and will pose no difficulty for breast-feeding. Inverted nipples are best treated with breast shells (milk cups) during the days after birth. The cups can be worn under the bra between feedings, and a breast pump can be used to draw out the nipple before nursing. Breast shells must fit so that the nipples fit completely into the holes and the base of the cups does not irritate the skin. With the exception of treating inverted nipples, there is no evidence to support measures to toughen nipples by massage or application of creams.

CIRCULATORY SYSTEM

In pregnancy, blood volume increases about 45 percent. The contribution to this increase is not the same for the two major components of the blood—the red cells and the plasma. The red cells increase about 25 percent, while the plasma expands by 40 percent. The result of this disproportionate increase is that the *hematocrit* (the percentage of the blood made up of red blood cells) actually falls, since there are fewer red cells per unit volume of blood during pregnancy than when a woman is not pregnant. Thus, the standards for defining anemia based on the hematocrit are different in pregnancy from those in the nonpregnant woman. The predictable fall of the hematocrit begins between the sixth and eighth weeks of gestation.

During pregnancy the resting pulse rate increases an average of ten to fifteen beats per minute. The volume of blood pumped by the heart increases significantly during the first trimester and even slightly more during the second and third trimesters. *Heart murmurs*, which reflect increased blood flow within the heart, are common in pregnancy. These "flow" murmurs must be distinguished from those related to heart valve disorders, for which antibiotics against infection of the valves may be indicated during labor.

RESPIRATORY SYSTEM

Most pregnant women are aware of an increased desire to breathe during pregnancy. This breathlessness results in part from a decrease in the space available for the lungs as the growing uterus presses up on the chest cavity from below. Women report breathing late in pregnancy to be easier when and if the baby sinks into the birth canal before the onset of labor (see discussion on "Lightening," pp. 80–81).

URINARY SYSTEM

During pregnancy more blood flows through the kidneys. Normally, a small amount of protein is passed from the blood to the urine and can be detected in the urine. As the amount of blood filtered increases, the amount of protein passed in the urine also increases, accounting for the common occurrence of measurable protein in the urine of the pregnant woman (see pp. 55–56).

The urine-collecting system undergoes dilation during pregnancy. The ureters, the muscular tubes that transport urine from the kidneys to the bladder, are relatively lax and dilated, in part a result of hormonal influences and in part a result of partial blockage of the lower ends of the ureters by pressure from the expanding uterus. The right ureter is subjected to further compression by the enlarging veins from the right ovary (which lie directly over the lower end of the right ureter) and by the weight of the uterus, which is usually rotated to the right. The dilation of the ureters and relative stagnation of urine flow through them is believed to be a factor in the increased susceptibility of pregnant women to urinary tract infection (see pp. 75–76).

GUMS AND TEETH

Gums soften and thicken during pregnancy, probably in response to increased blood flow. Even with the mild irritation of toothbrushing, they may bleed very easily. A lump of thickened gum tissue (called a *pregnancy epulis*) may bleed vigorously when touched. Both the normal swelling of the gums and the pregnancy epulis disappear after delivery.

The increase in the size of the gums predisposes pregnant women to *gingivitis*, a gum inflammation that can weaken the supports of the teeth. For this reason, daily brushing, flossing, and regular dental cleanings and checkups are more important in pregnancy than ever before. Contrary to folk traditions you may have heard, pregnancy creates no more long-term dental problems than those encountered in nonpregnant women, assuming, of course, that you pay careful attention to diet and dental hygiene.

Psychological Issues

Drs. T. Berry Brazelton and Bertrand G. Cramer in their book *The Earliest Relationship* beautifully describe the emotional ups and downs, the mixed feelings, and the opportunities for growth provided by pregnancy. They describe the work of pregnancy as divided into three separate tasks, each associated with a stage in the development of the fetus. In the first stage,

> parents adjust to the 'news' of pregnancy, which is accompanied by changes in the mother's body, but not yet by evidence of the actual existence of the fetus. In the second stage, the parents begin to recognize the fetus as a being who will eventually be separate from the mother. This recognition is confirmed at the moment of 'quickening,' when the fetus first announces its physical presence. Finally, in the third and final stage, the parents begin to experience the coming child as an individual and the fetus contributes to its own *individuation* by distinctive motions, rhythms, and levels of activity.

For some couples the change in body size and shape raises certain anxieties. For one, it is a public announcement of their sexual relationship, the only one our society has for an essentially private act. Indeed, some couples may feel embarrassed about "publicizing" what they have been "up to."

The major issue, however, has to do with a woman's self-image as it is affected by society's standards of beauty. Our mass media decry obesity and overvalue extreme slimness as the only real kind of beauty. Being pregnant is often confused in the popular mind, and in the minds of the pregnant woman and her partner, with being fat or unattractive. Because of the intense concern of women in our culture with their weight and figure, growing abdominal girth touches a sensitive nerve. A woman may be concerned that she is no longer attractive to her partner, while a man may worry about whether he can still see his partner as beautiful.

Weight gain and increase in size are not the only issues in the sense of decreased attractiveness. Other body changes, such as large, sagging breasts, puffiness of the skin, stretch marks, swelling of the vulva, increased vaginal secretions (pp. 68–69), and tan spots on the face (p. 69) may also contribute to the sense of loss of physical appeal.

Birth itself involves "distortions" of the female anatomy (bulging of the vulva, bleeding, stretching of tissues, and so on), which can be seen as inconsistent with views of woman as a sexually attractive being. "How would a man ever want to sleep with a woman he's seen giving birth?"—a question frequently asked by men and women alike—reflects this concern. Couples can use such fears and reservations about pregnancy as opportunities to acknowledge their concerns to each other, drawing closer through considering them together.

For all of us, reconsideration of our arbitrary standards of beauty and generally fearful views of pregnancy is in order. To be pregnant is to be beautiful, powerful, and creative, to make a direct contribution to the continuance of human life. While we modern urban people may have lost our direct connection with the beauty of pregnancy and birth, we have access to the ritual, poetry, and art of our own and other cultures to guide us. (See Appendix E for some suggested readings that can help reendow childbirth with awe and respect.) In addition, many of the suggestions given in the section "Children and Birth" (pp. 115–123) can help hesitant or fearful grown-ups welcome pregnancy and birth with the joyful acceptance they deserve.

Common Problems

MORNING SICKNESS

The queasiness very commonly experienced by women during early pregnancy may extend beyond the morning hours. The cause of this loss of appetite, nausea, and sometimes vomiting during the first trimester is not fully understood. Hormonal influences are believed to play a major role, although proof for this hypothesis is lacking. There is no evidence to indicate that the decreased food intake associated with morning sickness is harmful to the fetus, a fact that should be reassuring. Measures that have been proven helpful in relieving the symptom—more by experience than by research—are eating small, frequent meals, such as six per day; separating the taking of liquids and solids by one-half hour; and eating a dry, unsalted cracker or biscuit before

"Common Problems" is adapted from Stanley E. Sagov, Richard I. Feinbloom, Peggy Spindel, and Archie Brodsky. *Home Birth: A Practitioner's Guide to Birth Outside the Hospital.* (Rockville, Md.: Aspen Systems Corporation, 1984).

getting out of bed in the morning. The drug Bendectin, although proven effective and despite FDA approval and lack of conclusive evidence about it as a cause of birth defects, was voluntarily withdrawn by the manufacturer because of controversy (including litigation) over fetal damage. Simple antihistamines appear to be effective and safe, but check with your doctor or midwife.

Severe nausea and vomiting in early pregnancy suggest a hydatidiform mole (see pp. 310–311). Causes unrelated to pregnancy also need to be considered. After eliminating known causes of severe vomiting, the diagnosis of *hyperemesis gravidarum* can be entertained. This serious, but fortunately uncommon, disorder usually requires hospital care to prevent sometimes life-threatening maternal illness. The cause is unknown, although psychological factors have been suggested, and hypnosis as a treatment has been effective in some cases. A 1991 controlled study involving fifty-nine women with severe nausea and vomiting, reported in the journal *Obstetrics and Gynecology*, showed that vitamin B_6 taken by mouth effectively reduced and shortened symptoms.

FREQUENCY OF URINATION

Among several causes of increased urination in pregnancy, the most important is decreased bladder capacity resulting from compression of the bladder by the growing uterus. Another factor that contributes to increased output of urine is the consumption of extra fluids, whether they are intended to relieve constipation or assist in treating urinary tract infections. Frequency of urination may in itself reflect a urinary tract infection and should be watched. When in doubt, a urine culture should be obtained (see p. 60).

URINARY TRACT INFECTION

Urinary tract infection can be frequent and bothersome during pregnancy. The relative slowing of urine flow from the kidneys to the bladder during pregnancy is a factor that both predisposes a woman to urinary infection and interferes with its treatment.

Infection can involve the lower urinary tract (bladder and ure-thra), the upper tract (ureters and kidneys), or both. Upper tract involvement is suggested by symptoms like fever, chills, nausea, vomiting, and abdominal or flank pain. The signs of lower tract infection (*cystitis*) are urgency and frequency of urination along with pain or burning (*dysuria*).

Symptoms and signs of upper urinary tract infection present a more serious problem. Since treatment with antibiotics by mouth customarily recommended for those with lower tract infection may not be adequate, the woman may need intravenous treat-ment, at least initially.

The evaluation of urinary complaints also requires a urinalysis and urine culture. The presence of the typical symptoms described above and the presence of white blood cells along with bacteria in the urine argue for the diagnosis of urinary tract infection and the initiation of treatment.

The cornerstone of treatment for urinary tract infection is an-tibiotics. Several-day, short-course antibiotic therapy for lower tract urinary infections is effective for nonpregnant women and in asymptomatic infections during pregnancy. It has not been sufficiently studied with symptomatic bladder infections in preg-nancy to be recommended yet.

PAIN IN THE LOWER ABDOMEN AND THIGHS

Pain in the lower corners of the abdomen, especially on the right is common in pregnancy and is believed to result from stretching of the uterine supports, especially the round ligaments. This pain, sometimes known as round ligament syndrome, usually occurs at about twenty weeks and must be distinguished from pain arising from appendicitis, cholecystitis (inflammation of the gall-bladder), kidney stones, urinary tract infection, hernia, and other disorders. Pain that arises in the supporting structures of the uterus is related to position. It usually improves when a woman lies down, especially when she is turned to the painful side. It is not normally associated with fever, loss of appetite, nausea, vom-iting, diarrhea, or urinary symptoms. On physical examination, there are no signs of tenderness from pressure over the painful area, a response that is more common in the other conditions mentioned. Most women are able to accept stretching pain as long as they know it does not represent a threat to themselves or their babies.

Numbness or pain in the upper front thigh is believed to result from pressure of the uterus on the nerve that loops toward the thigh over the brim of the pelvic bone. The resulting discomfort is similar to that experienced in the arm as a "funny bone" (also related to pressure on a nerve, in this case the ulnar nerve, which can be subjected to pressure as it crosses the inner part of the elbow). Numbness in the thigh can often be relieved by lying on the back or side, especially on the numb or painful side. This symptom does not usually persist after delivery.

Recognizing *appendicitis in pregnancy* can be tricky. First, loss of appetite, nausea, and vomiting are common in pregnancy, as they are in appendicitis. Second, the enlarging uterus displaces the appendix upward out of its usual position in the right lower part of the abdomen, confusing diagnosis. Third, some degree of white blood cell elevation is common in pregnancy, as it is in appendicitis. A physician who suspects appendicitis must act decisively to make a diagnosis before the appendix ruptures. The safest approach is to err on the side of early operation if appendicitis is suspected. (See also pp. 309–310, "Gallstones.")

Pain in the pelvic girdle late in pregnancy and the feeling of "coming apart" are related to the softening of the ligaments which hold the bones together, which allows the pelvis to "give" during birth. It is a counterpart to the molding of the baby's head, made possible by its open cranial sutures (see pp. 190–193). There is no specific treatment other than avoiding activities that can intensify the strain. Very rarely, the pubic bones actually do separate and require strapping for support.

PAIN IN THE UPPER ABDOMEN

Pain in the upper abdomen deserves a call to the doctor. There are several causes that need to be sorted out, including gallstones (see pp. 309–310), heartburn (see p. 81), and preeclampsia (see pp. 327–329).

FIBROIDS

Fibroids are benign (noncancerous) tumors of the uterus that become more common as a woman gets older. If present, fibroids commonly increase in size during pregnancy. Although they usually cause no symptoms, they can occasionally be mildly annoying or become sources of confusion. For example, a fibroid may suddenly increase in size and cause pain, usually because of bleeding inside the tumor. This difficulty resolves with time alone.

Fibroids may give the false impression that the uterus is larger than it is, thereby leading to a mistake in estimating gestational age. A fibroid that impinges on the cavity of the uterus may be a factor in causing miscarriage. Fibroids that are strategically situated in the lower portion of the uterus may obstruct labor, but this is very rare. Generally, fibroids shrink markedly after delivery. During pregnancy they can be visualized with ultrasound (see pp. 151–154) and differentiated from other masses in the pelvis.

HAIR LOSS

Hair loss, which results from premature cessation of growth in the hair follicles, is one of the more distressing developments of pregnancy and the postpartum period. Fortunately, even though it may persist up to one year, it is temporary. This conversion of the follicles from the growing (anagen) to the resting (telogen) state resembles normal hair follicle behavior at the end of a normal growth cycle. Giving birth is one of the causes of a widespread premature conversion of hair follicles from the growing to the resting state. Diffuse hair shedding during combing may occur for three months after delivery. Should there be any question of this diagnosis, the shedding phenomenon can be duplicated by stroking the hair with a gentle tugging action. The hairs removed can be examined under a microscope, and, in the usual case, all of the follicles will be seen to be in a resting stage.

CONSTIPATION

Less frequent, harder stools that are difficult to pass are common in pregnancy. Hemorrhoids may intensify and in turn be intensified by constipation. Constipation may be corrected through increased fluid intake, increased fiber intake (raw fruit and vegetables, bran, psyllium seeds, and so on), and exercise. Stool softeners like *dioctyl sodium sulfosuccinate* are also useful. Mineral oil and saline cathartics (milk of magnesia, for example) should not be used. So-called irritant laxatives such as senna or bisacodyl can be used on a short-term basis when all else fails.

VARICOSE VEINS AND HEMORRHOIDS

Varicose veins of the legs, rectum (hemorrhoids), and vulva are common in pregnancy, particularly in women whose relatives also have or had them, suggesting a familial susceptibility. The pressure of the pregnant uterus on the large vein (vena cava), which drains blood back from the pelvis and legs, is a major factor in varicose veins in pregnancy.

Although some women complain of aching, the significance of *varicosities of the legs* is primarily cosmetic. They can be relieved by elevating the legs (getting off one's feet and keeping the legs outstretched in a horizontal position) and using elastic ("support") stockings.

Hemorrhoids can bleed and form painful fissures. They are aided by measures to prevent constipation (see previous discussion), sitz baths in warm water, lubricating creams, suppositories (witch hazel, Anusol), and avoidance of straining to eliminate (having what the English call an "unhurried motion"). Thrombosis (clotting) of an external hemorrhoid can be very painful. The clot can be removed under local anesthesia. If bleeding persists, or if the hemorrhoids cannot be pushed back into the rectum or become infected, hemorrhoidectomy (removal of the hemorrhoid) may be required, although this is very unusual in pregnancy. Tying off the hemorrhoids or injecting them with fluids that dissolve them are measures that are preferred over surgery.

Varicosities of the vulva may be contained and relieved with counterpressure by a foam rubber pad held in place by a belt.

While women can look forward to relief from varicosities of all kinds following delivery, hemorrhoids may be more pronounced in labor and the immediate postpartum period. Because of the improvement normally expected after delivery, surgical correction of varicosities should be delayed if at all possible until the necessity for it becomes clear.

DIZZINESS ("LIGHT-HEADEDNESS")

Light-headedness, especially when one quickly stands up after lying down for a while, is common during pregnancy. It is in part related to delay in the return of blood to the heart because of the pressure the uterus exerts on the veins of the abdomen. When insufficient blood is pumped through and out of the heart, dizziness results. Getting up slowly will prevent it.

LEG CRAMPS

Painful spasms of the calf muscles, particularly at night, affect about half of pregnant women. Their cause is not known. Physical measures to relieve a cramp include massage and stretching maneuvers to bend the foot upward at the ankle. When lying in bed, avoid pointing toes straight down or under. Dietary change or calcium supplements have not been proven effective.

LIGHTENING

Lightening is the sensation women experience as the baby drops during the latter weeks of pregnancy. It is not the same as engagement, which refers to the passage of the head (or buttocks in a breech) to the level of the ischial spines (see Figure 3, p. 45). Lightening is accompanied by less shortness of breath, decreased pressure in the stomach, the feeling that the baby has "dropped," increased pressure in the pelvis, increased backache, more fre-

quent urination and constipation, the initial appearance or aggravation of hemorrhoids and varicose veins of the legs, swelling of
the legs and feet, and possibly more difficulty in walking. Nothing
much can be done about lightening except to recognize what it
represents and to bear with its associated discomforts.

HEARTBURN

Heartburn is a common problem in pregnancy and represents
the backing up (reflux) of the acid contents of the stomach into
the esophagus (food tube). Factors that contribute to heartburn
are compression of the abdominal organs, including the stomach,
by the enlarging uterus; the elevation of the stomach above the
uterus; alterations in the action of the "valve" between the esophagus and the stomach; and loss of muscle tone in the esophagus
and stomach.

Heartburn can be largely prevented by eating smaller quantities
at a time and by avoiding lying down immediately after eating
and, if these measures fail, by using antacids at the end of each
meal. If antacids are not effective, there is now evidence that
dilute hydrochloric acid (0.1 milliliters in 10 milliliters of flavored
syrup) may be helpful. If the symptoms come on when a woman
lies down, the head of the bed can be raised six to eight inches
by blocks beneath the bedposts to allow gravity to work against
reflux.

EDEMA

Edema, or fluid accumulation in the tissues, is indicated by visible
swelling and is normal in pregnancy. Edema of the feet and legs
is very common in the third trimester and is related to increased
venous pressure in the lower extremities due to pressure of the
uterus on the large collecting vein in the abdomen (vena cava).
In this respect, it is similar to the swelling of the forearm and
hand that occurs when a tourniquet is tightly wound around the
upper arm. When the uterus acts, in effect, as a tourniquet on
the large veins that drain blood from the legs, backup of blood

and the passage of protein-rich fluid from the vessels into the skin result. When one sits or stands in an upright position, the force of gravity also contributes to this phenomenon. Many women report that late in the day their rings are tight and their faces are puffy, showing fluid retention in the upper part of the body. Neither edema nor weight gain alone during the third trimester is predictive of increased fetal problems.

If edema is annoying, raising the legs will help. The best treatment is to lie down for one hour, one to two times per day, on the left (to tip the uterus off the vena cava). Elastic hose will help reduce the swelling, but some women find these stockings too uncomfortable to be worth the bother. Edema is commonly associated with preeclampsia (see pp. 327–329). In this condition, protein is present in the urine, and the blood pressure is elevated.

VAGINITIS

Vaginal infection is common in pregnancy, and *Candida albicans* (a yeast) is the major culprit. It causes an infection called *Monilialis* or *Monililia* for short. Symptoms of infection are itching, burning, and a vaginal discharge. When the vagina is examined with a speculum, the yeast infection resembles white cottage cheese. Microscopic study of a sample reveals the characteristic branching structure of the budding yeast. Several effective antifungal drugs are used for local treatment.

Candida in the vagina can be picked up by the baby during birth and infect its mouth, producing the condition known as *thrush* (pp. 172). One reason given for performing a vaginal examination late in pregnancy is to detect a monilia infection that may not have bothered the woman enough for her to seek help.

Two other causes of vaginitis in pregnant (as well as nonpregnant) women are *Trichomonas*, a one-celled amoeba-like organism, and infections by certain bacteria. These anaerobic (not requiring oxygen) bacterial infections are commonly referred to as bacterial vaginosis. These infections are diagnosed by microscope examination and culture. Both are treated with *metronidazole* (common trade name, Flagyl), which is considered safe for the fetus after the first trimester.

FATIGUE

Even in the most physically fit women, fatigue is a very common feature in pregnancy. While psychological factors may play a role, it is likely that weariness has a still-unexplained physical basis. Pregnant women tire easily and need to rest and sleep. There is no "treatment" for this problem other than rest, especially rest that is not associated with guilt over being tired or shirking responsibilities. For most women, fatigue is more common during some periods of the pregnancy than others. While some women are tired throughout the pregnancy, others actually report having more energy than ever and experience no fatigue at all.

EMOTIONAL SENSITIVITY

In pregnancy, many women report wide mood swings and unusual sensitivity to the surrounding emotional climate. For no apparent reason, or with only the slightest provocation, an otherwise well-composed woman will burst into tears. This heightened reactivity is no reason to avoid stress or to ask to be treated "with kid gloves." Knowing that emotionality is a normal feature of pregnancy should promote understanding by the woman and those around her that outbursts and withdrawals are normal and need not be taken too seriously.

Later Prenatal Visits

Later in pregnancy the prenatal visits build on the important earlier steps of taking the initial history and performing the first physical examination and laboratory tests. These later visits offer expectant couples an opportunity to take a more active role. Women can weigh themselves, for example, and can check their own urine for protein and glucose. Couples can learn to listen to the fetal heart with the fetoscope and feel the various parts of the baby through the abdominal wall. They can keep their own records, plotting the growth of the uterus and the increase in weight over the course of the pregnancy. A woman can pay particular attention to the first feeling of fetal movement, recording the time and date (p. 144), and she can note changes, especially decreases, in kicking, allowing for sleep periods toward the end of pregnancy. Decreases should be reported promptly to the nurse or doctor. Couples can come to the prenatal visits together and can even include their children (see pp. 118–119 on preparing children for childbirth). They can share their observations, fears, and pleasures with the doctor or midwife. And they can insist on fully understanding what is happening and what choices they have throughout the pregnancy.

It is just as possible for couples to lay claim to their own prenatal care as to labor and delivery. The doctor or midwife then becomes a ready resource and a support, not a director of the birth. Obviously, you need to decide if you want this kind of relationship and will accept the responsibilities it implies. Indeed, many people elect a less active role for themselves.

In uncomplicated pregnancies, visits after the initial examination are traditionally scheduled every four weeks until the thirty-second week, then at thirty-four and thirty-six weeks, and weekly thereafter until birth, thirteen in all. A recent U.S. Public Health Service expert panel has, in the name of efficiency, recommended reducing this number in healthy women to nine for first pregnancies, seven for later ones.

The content of the visits depends on the stage of the pregnancy. Weighing in (pp. 86–87), checking the urine for protein and glucose (pp. 55–56), and measuring blood pressure (pp. 48–49) are standard procedures. Maneuvers having to do with the uterus and baby obviously depend on the size of the uterus, which by the second trimester (twelfth week) has risen out of the pelvis into the abdomen. The height of the uterus is determined by stretching the measuring tape from the pubic bone up and over the uterus to its top (see Figure 5, p. 50).

By sixteen to twenty weeks it is possible to hear the baby's heartbeat with a stethoscope. Since the fetal heart sound transmits best through the baby's back, the location of the loudest sounds suggests the position of the back. In normal head-down (vertex) presentations, the heart tones are generally heard below the mother's umbilicus, while in breech presentations they are heard best above it. Hearing the tones best in front of the abdomen suggests that the back is pointing forward. When the baby's back is pointed toward the mother's back (also called posterior position), the heart tones are apt to be loudest in the mother's flanks.

It is possible for a woman's partner (or another interested observer) to hear the heartbeat by placing an ear directly on the abdomen. An extra-long tubing attached to the stethoscope will allow the woman herself to listen. An inexpensive conical wooden listening device, shaped like a megaphone, may also be used. With an ear against its tip, the examiner places its base directly on the abdomen. These devices are available through the International Childbirth Education Association and its affiliates (see Appendix D) and often from doctors or midwives themselves.

By normal adult standards, the normal heartbeat of the fetus is very fast, ranging from 120 to 150 beats per minute. It is sometimes faint and hard to hear, but this does not mean there is anything wrong. Since the sounds have to travel a variable distance through amniotic fluid, the wall of the uterus, and the fat, muscle, and skin of the mother's abdominal wall, it is easy for them to be muted.

With Doppler ultrasound (pp. 151–154), the fetal heartbeat can be detected as early as the twelfth week. The sounds heard through the ultrasound monitor are not those of the heartbeat itself but are machine-made sounds triggered by the movements of the heart, as sensed by the monitor from echoes of sound waves pulsed to the heart. The visual detection of fetal heart movement by ultrasound imaging can occur as early as the sixth or seventh week of fetal life.

During the last trimester an examiner can feel the baby itself through the abdominal and uterine walls. The firm pressure required to outline the baby will not harm it. The woman can assist the examiner by letting her abdominal muscles relax completely; blowing air out and holding that position helps relax the abdomen. By feeling the location of the baby's head and buttocks, the examiner can tell whether the fetus is head-down (vertex), breech, or transverse (lying horizontally) (see pp. 189–190). Each of these positions has implications for subsequent care in pregnancy. Palpation is also a reasonably good guide to the number of fetuses present, whether one or more (see pp. 338–341 on twins). The baby's size can be estimated as average, large, or small, a judgment useful in predicting the fit of the baby to the birth canal.

It is also possible to tell whether or not the head has descended into the pelvis. The examiner does this by feeling whether his or her fingers can get around the bottom of the head and come toward each other. If the fingers surround the head, it is still high in the abdomen; if not, it has descended into the pelvis. By differentiating between the lumpy hands and feet and the smooth back, and by the location of the heartbeat, the examiner can conclude whether the back is facing left, right, front, or back. Good abdominal relaxation makes this examination easier. Here, too, the pregnant woman can contribute to a successful examination.

Although it need not be done routinely, there are several reasons for repeating the vaginal speculum examination during the last two to three weeks of pregnancy. These reasons include rechecking the measurements of the pelvis (pp. 44–48), determining the "ripeness" of the cervix (its position, dilation, and effacement) (pp. 186–188), and detecting monilial or other vaginal infection (pp. 166–167, 172).

Nutrition and Weight Gain

A good diet is a cornerstone of a healthy pregnancy, necessary to create a healthy baby and to sustain the mother through pregnancy, delivery, and nursing. Nutritional needs of women increase during pregnancy and nursing because the woman is really "eating for two." The best available advice on diet can be summarized as follows:

1. Follow the guidelines in Tables 1 and 2, as well as the recommendations based on the "new" food groups, as described later in this chapter.
2. Gain a minimum of twenty-five pounds, unless you are overweight to start; but do not allow yourself to become overweight.
3. Gain weight gradually and steadily.

Table 1.   Checklist of Recommended Foods*

Foods	Daily Amount
Milk**	1 qt.
Eggs	1–2
Meat	2 servings (liver often)
Cheese**	1–2 servings, additional snacks
Grains (whole, enriched)**	4–5 slices or servings
Legumes, nuts	1–2 servings a week
Green and yellow fruits, vegetables	1–2 servings
Citrus fruit	2
Additional vitamin C foods	Frequently, as desired
Other vegetables and fruits	1–2 servings
Butter, fortified margarine	2 tbsp. (or as needed)
Other foods: grains, fruits, vegetables, other proteins	As needed for energy and added vitamins and minerals

* See discussion of animal-based vs. plant-based diets in text.

** During lactation, add 1 additional serving daily of dairy products and 1 additional serving of grains.

Source: Adapted from Sue Rodwell Williams, *Handbook of Maternal and Infant Nutrition* (Berkeley, Calif.: SRW Productions, Inc., 1976.)

4. Do not attempt to lose weight during pregnancy. Even obese women should gain weight.
5. Do not restrict your intake of salt (sodium); use iodized salt.

The Institute of Medicine currently recommends a weight gain of 28 to 40 pounds for underweight women, 25 to 35 pounds for normal-weight women, and 25 pounds for overweight women. Weight gain that exceeds these guidelines raises the following concerns: larger babies potentially more difficult to deliver vaginally (see p. 337), shoulder dystocia, increased need for a cesarean section, and obesity that persists after childbirth. However, a recent study showed that most women by far will have successful pregnancy outcomes even if their weight gains fall outside these recommended ranges.

Since pregnant women need more nutrients in their diet, increasing servings from each of the food groups will be necessary. Women will weigh, on the average, six pounds more after the postpartum period than they did when they first became preg-

Table 2. Standard Diet for Pregnancy

Food Group	Recommended Serving(s)	Food Source
Calcium	4	2%, skim, whole, and buttermilk. Yogurt, cheese, tofu. Sardines, salmon. Beets, turnips, mustard greens, broccoli, dried beans. Carnation Instant Breakfast drink, custards, puddings, pasteurized eggnog, milk shakes, ice cream.
Protein	2–4	*Animal*: lean meat (beef, veal, lamb, pork), fish, poultry, organ meats (liver, kidney), eggs. *Vegetable*: dried beans & peas (lentils, kidney and navy beans, split peas), peanut butter, nuts, tofu.
Enriched Bread & Cereal	4	Bread, rolls, dumplings, muffins, biscuits, crackers, cereals, cornbread, grits, rice, macaroni, noodles, spaghetti, tortillas, wheat germ.
Vegetable & Fruit (Vitamin C)	2	Oranges & juice, grapefruit & juice, cantaloupe, guava, mango, strawberries, pineapple. Green or chili peppers, tomatoes or juice, broccoli, brussel sprouts, raw cabbage, collards, kale, spinach, greens.
Vegetable & Fruit (Vitamin A)	1	Asparagus, broccoli, chard, brussel sprouts; collards, cress, kale, spinach, turnip greens, or other dark green leaves; pumpkin, carrots, winter squash, yams, apricots, sweet potatoes, cantaloupe.
Other Vegetables & Fruits	2	Potatoes, plums, prunes, dates, peaches, pears, persimmon, berries, apple, bananas, grapes, raisins, lettuce, cucumbers, radishes, bean sprouts, tangerines, watermelon, green beans, peas, corn.
Liquids	6–8	Water, milk, juice, soup, broth, decaffeinated tea or coffee.

SALT should be used in moderation. Use iodized salt.

Source: This chart and sample menu on page 90 draw on information supplied by the Erie County Department of Health, Erie, Pennsylvania.

nant. Many women find that they do not return to their prepregnancy weight. For them pregnancy may be the first step toward a pattern of weight gain, which increases with subsequent pregnancies. Be aware of this risk and watch your weight, diet, and exercise during pregnancy. Extra pounds gained are hard to lose. Notice during prenatal visits where your weight plots out from month to month on the graph of weight gain that is a part of many prenatal charts. If your pattern of weight gain starts to move up and off the normal curve, stop and ask why. After your baby is born, eat carefully and exercise so that you return within weeks to your prepregnancy weight.

The nutrition guidelines in Tables 1 and 2 are for the average, well-nourished woman who has completed her own physical growth. Adaptations of these guidelines are required for adolescents or for women with special nutritional needs. If you find it difficult to include all the recommended food groups, discuss this with your physician. Also, see the books on nutrition listed in Appendix E.

Prenatal vitamins (especially folic acid and iron) are usually prescribed during pregnancy. Until recently there has been little evidence that this practice is necessary for a woman who eats according to the guidelines presented here. Studies done in the past several years have produced conflicting results as to whether women who take a folic acid supplement from the time of conception on are less likely to have a fetus with a neural tube defect (see pp. 64–66). A 1991 randomized control study from England, reported in the *Lancet*, has demonstrated this protective effect of folic acid when begun from the time of conception (usually weeks to months before the average woman begins prenatal vitamins) in women who have had previous babies with a neural tube defect. Whether this finding will be confirmed in women in other countries (where the risk for neural tube defect is usually lower than in England) and how it will be applied remain to be seen.

Taking quantities of vitamins greater than the daily requirements for pregnancy and lactation serves no purpose and should not be done. Megadoses (much more than the recommended daily amount) of some vitamins have been reported to damage the fetus. On the other hand, there is no evidence that a vitamin

Sample Menu for Pregnancy, Standard Diet

Breakfast:

orange juice—½ cup or 1 orange
cream of wheat or grits—1 bowl
soft cooked egg—1
whole grain or enriched toast—1
   slice
butter or fortified margarine—1
   pat
milk—½ cup

MidMorning:

bran muffin—1 medium
milk—½ cup or
apple juice—½ cup

Lunch:

split pea soup—1 bowl
meat or cheese or peanut butter
   sandwich—½ on whole grain
   or enriched bread
mayonnaise—1 tbsp.
lettuce & tomato salad
½ grapefruit
milk—1 cup

MidAfternoon:

milk—1 cup
cheese and crackers

Dinner:

baked chicken—1–2 pieces or 4 ozs.
potato (cooked in skin)—1 small, or
   beans and rice
butter or fortified margarine—1 pat
crisp celery or carrot sticks
green beans or collard greens—½
   cup
custard or ½ cup milk

Bedtime:

hot or cold milk—1 cup
peanut butter or oatmeal cookie—1
   or 2 small

Be Sure to Include These Foods in Your Diet
Foods Rich in Iron:

Poultry	Fish
Eggs	Red meat, liver
Green lima beans	Dried peas and beans
Prunes, dried apricots, raisins	Peanut butter
Molasses	Broccoli

Greens: mustard, turnip, beet, dandelion greens,
   collards, spinach, kale, chard

Your body makes the best use of iron when your diet contains extra vitamin C. Try to use a double portion of citrus fruit or tomato if you are on a
high-iron diet.

supplement designed for pregnancy, along with a normal diet, is harmful to the fetus.

Whether iron supplements are necessary in pregnancy is unclear (see Table 2 for iron-rich foods). The question has not been evaluated with a randomized control study. There is some evidence that taking more iron than required may actually be harmful to the fetus because of a resulting increase in the volume of the mother's circulating red blood cells, which raises blood viscosity (thickness). This increased viscosity of the blood could interfere with blood flow to the placenta. The normal drop in a mother's blood count (hematocrit and hemoglobin—see pp. 55, 70–71) during pregnancy (resulting from an increase in blood volume) should not be confused with anemia and requires no corrective action (see pp. 70–71). How important these concerns about iron supplements are is not clear. Despite the lack of evidence in favor of iron supplements, the common practice is to include iron in the prenatal vitamins recommended in pregnancy.

REVISING THE FOUR FOOD GROUPS

Pregnancy is an excellent time to consider in a fresh and thoughtful way what you eat. I would like to use this book as an opportunity to urge a fundamental change in our eating habits. There is mounting evidence that a grain-based diet, with less (or no) animal (meat, fish, dairy, eggs, and poultry) protein and fat will help prevent heart and blood vessel disease, high blood pressure, kidney disease, osteoporosis, obesity, and even some cancers. While recognizing that the federal government has issued diet recommendations based on this new evidence, many experts on nutrition do not believe that these go far enough. I agree with this concern. Reducing the fat in hamburgers in our kitchens and in fast-food restaurants—a definite step in the right direction—still doesn't get at the heart of the problem, namely, the hamburger itself. I believe that more basic changes in our diets are called for and am convinced that sooner or later these will come to pass.

Apart from the considerable direct health benefits for individuals, a mass public shift toward a diet lower in meat will have highly beneficial ecological and economic effects. For example, a meat-based diet requires the continual creation of new farmland, the raising of more cattle, the clearing of forests, a very costly and inefficient use of crops and of water, and the use of more fossil fuels in food production and processing. Environmental effects range from increased soil erosion to increased levels of greenhouse gases in the atmosphere. Therefore, the shift to a plant-based diet would have crucial health and environmental benefits. The Physicians Committee for Responsible Medicine (PCRM), a national, nonprofit organization of physicians and consumers, has emphasized these problems and has promoted diet reforms. (For more information on the problems associated with animal-based diets and for the PCRM address, see Appendices B and C.)

PREGNANCY AND A PLANT-BASED DIET

The "four food groups" were developed thirty-five years ago to help people plan nourishing meals. However, the concept of an optimal diet has changed since that time. The typical Western diet based on the four food groups is high in animal fat and protein and lacking fiber, and is therefore associated with an increased risk of cancer, heart disease, obesity, diabetes, and osteoporosis. We need new guidelines for meals that will both lower the risk for chronic disease and provide basic nourishment. The PCRM has developed specific recommendations to encourage the shift to plant-based diets and has identified the "new four food groups."

The new four food groups are (1) whole grains, (2) legumes, (3) fruits, and (4) vegetables. A healthy diet includes a variety of foods from each of these groups. Other foods, including nuts, sweets, dairy products, meats, and oils, are options: it isn't necessary to include them in the diet. If you do consume them,

---

This information on new food groups was adapted from information supplied by the Physicians Committee for Responsible Medicine, a national, nonprofit organization of physicians and consumers. PCRM promotes an optimal diet for prevention of disease.

include small amounts only, since these foods can contribute excess fat and do not have fiber.

Current scientific evidence shows that people who eat a diet centered on plant foods have the lowest risk of heart disease, stroke, hypertension, obesity, colon cancer, and osteoporosis. A number of government reports released over the past decade support the need for this dietary shift. These include the surgeon general's *Report on Nutrition and Health*, the National Research Council's *Report on Diet and Health*, and the Department of Agriculture's revised *Dietary Guidelines*.

Many people who are considering a plant-based diet worry about getting enough protein. Protein needs are easily met on a plant-based diet as long as you consume enough calories and eat a variety of plant foods. The average American consumes about twice the recommended amount of protein. Excess protein, especially animal protein, may cause loss of calcium from the body. Animal foods may also raise blood cholesterol levels and may increase the risk for cancer. Therefore, it is a good idea to keep protein intake moderate and to get most protein from plants.

Calcium needs are also easily met on a plant-centered diet. Since a diet high in animal protein causes a loss of calcium from the body, people who consume mostly plant protein probably may need less calcium. Populations who use no dairy products and who consume moderate amounts of calcium frequently have less osteoporosis than Americans do. A few examples of calcium-rich nondairy foods are dark green leafy vegetables, broccoli, cooked dried beans, bok choy, tofu, corn tortillas, and figs.

Many plant foods are rich in iron. Iron-rich foods include cooked dried beans, dried fruit, potatoes, and whole and enriched grains. Vitamin C at each meal helps the body absorb iron more efficiently. Good sources of vitamin C are citrus fruits and juices, strawberries, green peppers, melons, potatoes, and broccoli.

Another concern about vegetarian diets is vitamin B_{12}, which is sometimes present in root vegetables but generally is absent from plant foods. On a diet consisting exclusively of plant foods, the B_{12} requirement can easily be met by eating cereals or other foods that are fortified with this vitamin. People who don't use such products should take a vitamin B_{12} supplement several times a week. The need for this vitamin is very small and is easily met.

Exercise and Relaxation

The purpose of prenatal exercise is to improve muscle strength and stretch tight muscles, since muscles are frequently tensed and shortened, as well as weak. Many common discomforts of pregnancy—backache, varicose veins, cramps, constipation, breathlessness, heartburn, postural discomfort—may be prevented or alleviated through a balanced program of exercise and relaxation. Also, a woman in good physical condition can withstand the rigors of a long or hard labor, as well as the exertion needed to care for the new baby, better than a woman who is "out of shape." But conditioning takes time to develop, and the sooner a pregnant woman begins exercising, the better.

Prenatal exercise has, in addition to strengthening and stretching muscles, several benefits that may enhance the birth experience. Women who exercise regularly throughout pregnancy claim heightened body awareness, confidence in their physiological functions, and knowledge of how these functions are affected by the changes brought on by pregnancy. A woman who learns to trust her body can better trust her uterus and can "let go" during labor and bond with her baby. After delivery the physical fitness skills learned during pregnancy should be continued as an integral part of a healthy lifestyle. The exercises described here can be done in an exercise class or on one's own. Don't feel guilty if, for whatever reason, you can't participate in an exercise program. Look on exercise as an enhancement, but not a crucial aspect of the care you give yourself.

CHOOSING AN EXERCISE CLASS

Although the obstetrics and gynecology section of the American Physical Therapy Association has an increasing number of regis-

---

"Exercise and Relaxation" was written with the help of Elizabeth Noble, P.T., founder of the Maternal and Child Health Center, Cambridge, Mass. and the ob-gyn section of the American Physical Therapy Association. It is adapted from Stanley E. Sagov, Richard I. Feinbloom, Peggy Spindel, and Archie Brodsky, *Home Birth: A Practitioner's Guide to Birth Outside the Hospital.* (Rockville, Md.: Aspen Systems Corporation, 1984).

tered physical therapists who are trained to support women in achieving good musculoskeletal care during the childbearing years, in many communities there are none. Often there are no exercise classes available, either. While health spas, fitness centers, yoga classes, and dance schools may offer prenatal or postpartum exercises, they vary greatly in quality. Unfortunately, many of these programs neglect the muscles of the pelvic floor and reflect little understanding of physiological changes in pregnancy. However, as long as a woman "listens" to her body and does nothing that causes strain or pain, she can usually reap the benefits and avoid the hazards of any reasonably good exercise program. With increasing consumer demand, more quality exercise classes should become available, so women should make their preferences known. If no classes are available, the exercises that follow should be of help.

Exercise classes for pregnant women and their partners may be held separately or as part of general childbirth education classes. In either case, they provide contact with other childbearing couples. In addition to gaining group support, couples in these classes can learn about other resources early in their pregnancies, when they may still be open to making choices and changes in their birth arrangements.

The ideal exercise class has a small number of participants who can be individually evaluated and supervised, rather than trained as a group to "follow the leader." The instructor explains the rationale for each position and movement, along with the role of the muscles in pregnancy, birth, and afterward. The best classes present the exercises in a broad context, coordinated with breathing, relaxation, and psychological preparation for birth.

GENERAL PRINCIPLES

A suggested exercise session lasts for one and one-half hours and consists of roughly equal proportions of calisthenics, stretching, and relaxation. Aerobic exercises can be done for recreation. Good examples are walking, swimming, dancing, and cycling. The exercises need be done only a few times each to be beneficial, but they must be performed slowly and properly. Jerking and straining should be avoided. The goal is increased body awareness and comfort, not training for the Olympics. Quivering muscles or sudden jerky movements designed to bypass a weak muscle group indicate that the exercise is too difficult and should be modified. Once an exercise is mastered and is no longer taxing, it is preferable to make it more challenging, to change the position of the body or the leverage of the limbs, instead of merely doing it more times.

Breathing must be coordinated at all times with exercise movement. A good rule of thumb is "exhale during exertion." Straining while holding the breath in the throat has an undesirable effect on the circulation, especially in pregnant women. It prevents blood from returning to the heart; hence, less blood is pumped from the heart to the lungs to receive oxygen and then into the body. Since less oxygenated blood can reach the mother's tissues, including the placenta, less oxygen is available to the fetus. Exhaling during exertion not only prevents such negative cardiovascular effects but also avoids strain on the pelvic floor and abdominal muscles. In fact, exhaling during exertion actually improves the return of blood to the heart, as positive pressure is maintained in the abdomen relative to that in the chest. This principle is even more important during the pushing stage of labor.

A woman should become conscious of the natural expansion of the chest and abdomen during inspiration and their contraction during exhalation. Strange as it may seem, not everyone breathes in the most physiological way. Some people contract their diaphragms during expiration, rather than the reverse, and need this pointed out to them. Tightening the abdominal muscles on exhalation is a good preliminary exercise that demonstrates the role of these muscles in forced exhalation. Indeed, the abdominals can be strengthened only during exhalation.

While exercise programs can be expanded beyond the basic principles and movements discussed here, it is important that the muscles most stressed in childbearing—the abdominals and the pelvic floor—are emphasized. In the average woman, both are weak. While more visible, the abdominal muscles are rarely exercised in our society, and most of us sit or stand and rarely squat. During pregnancy, these muscles must meet the demands of increased weight gain, changes in the center of gravity, support for the enlarging uterus, and the challenge of the expulsive phase of labor.

ABDOMINAL AND BACK MUSCLE EXERCISE

The abdominal wall muscles provide much of the support for the spine and thus play an important role in the health of the back. Together with the *gluteus maximus* muscles—the major muscles of the buttocks—the abdominals control the angle of the pelvis in relation to the spine, an angle that affects stability and stress of the lower back. The common view is that backache is due to weakness of the back muscles, but, if anything, back muscles are usually too tight rather than too weak. Thus, it is the abdominals that need emphasis in back-care programs.

The abdominal muscles run from the lower edge of the ribs in front and on the sides to the rim of the pelvis. You can feel them if you lie on your back, knees bent, and raise your head and shoulders. Move your hand around over your abdomen from your ribs to your pelvis and feel the firmness over the entire area. The abdominals actually consist of several sets of muscles:

- The *recti*, which run straight down the center of the abdomen and consist of two bundles about three inches in width, one on each side of the midline, separated about an inch and a half of tough fibrous tissue.
- The *obliques*, two layers of muscles that run diagonally, one on each side of the body, from the ribs to the pelvis, crisscrossing in opposite directions.
- The *transversus*, which is wrapped around horizontally.

During pregnancy the growing uterus stretches the abdominals from a straight line between the pelvis and ribs to an expanding curve between upper and lower attachments. Therefore, it makes sense to begin abdominal strengthening exercises as early as possible.

The *curl-up* is the basic exercise for the abdominal muscles. A curl-up is a modified sit-up done to a maximum of forty-five degrees off the surface, with knees bent and the back of the waist flat on the surface used. To exercise all of the abdominal muscles adequately, curl-ups should be done in both straight and diagonal directions.

For a diagonal curl-up, twist one shoulder toward the opposite knee, alternating shoulders on successive curl-ups. Then lie flat after each curl-up. Repeat the exercise up to fifty times, but stop if it starts to hurt.

The work of the abdominals can be progressively increased by changing the position of the arms, as follows:

1. In the initial position, the arms reach toward the knees, assisting the movement (60 percent abdominal muscle effort).
2. The next progression involves a neutral position with arms folded across the chest (80 percent effort).
3. Finally, the arms are clasped behind the head to increase the leverage (100 percent effort).

Each woman begins at the appropriate level and progresses at her own pace. The physical changes that occur in later pregnancy make the more advanced curl-ups (nos. 2 and 3) too difficult.

It is important to check continuously throughout pregnancy for any "separation" of the recti muscles from the stretching of the fibrous band that unites them like a central seam. Such a separation is called a *diastasis recti*. This condition is usually observed after the fifth month but may be seen earlier in women who have it left over from a previous pregnancy. Many women notice the bulging in the midline of the abdominal wall as they get up off the floor after exercising or as they get out of bed or bath. Although diastasis recti is quite painless, it may lead to postural backache because of abdominal wall weakness.

To check for diastasis, lie on your back with knees bent. Raise your head (which activates the recti muscles), allowing your hands to reach toward your knees. You or your exercise coach can then check the width of the soft area between the tense rectus muscle bundles. If three or more fingers can be placed between the contracted recti muscles, diastasis recti is present. With this degree of separation, the bulging can usually be seen as well as felt.

A woman with a diastasis should avoid strenuous work with the abdominal muscles, as in double leg-raising exercises on the back (described later) and heavy lifting or straining. She should also be careful, when arising from the floor or bed, first to roll on one side and then push herself into a sitting position with her arms. It is usually not possible to "close the gap" of a diastasis during pregnancy because of the progressive and continuous stretching of the abdominal wall by the enlarging uterus. However, couples can be reassured that it is possible to bring these muscles together again with exercises after birth. The presence of a diastasis recti requires that a woman's exercise program be modified only with regard to curl-ups; the other essential exercises are still suitable. If the recti muscles cannot stay parallel when the head only is raised, it makes no sense to increase the load by bringing the shoulderss off the floor as well. Furthermore, the oblique abdominal muscles contract when the shoulders curl forward. Because they attach to the sheath covering the recti muscles, their action will lead to further strain and muscle imbalance, which can increase the diastasis.

To perform the modified curl-up, the woman with a diastasis recti lies on her back with knees bent, hands crossed at the area of the gap to support the muscles. She performs head raises only, taking care that the abdominal wall is pulled *in* as the breath is exhaled, in order not to increase the bulging. She should do the exercises frequently for a short time, following the same program postpartum. After a few days postpartum, the woman can evaluate the gap while performing a modified curl-up without hand support. If the diastasis persists, she should continue the modified curl-ups. If the muscles are parallel at the midline, she can slowly increase the curling up by bringing the shoulders off the floor, but only little by little. Too rapid progression can lead to reseparation.

Note the difference between curl-ups and the kind of sit-ups that unfortunately remain popular in many fitness classes. These involve lying flat on the floor with legs extended and straight and literally sitting up. With curl-ups, the knees are bent to stabilize the lower back (lumbar spine). The movement is limited to the abdominals and is never more than about forty-five degrees forward flexion off the surface. A sit-up, which involves a ninety-degree movement, is performed primarily by the hip flexor muscles, which run from the front of the upper thighbones to the lower spine and pelvis. When these muscles contract, they pull the spine and the thighs closer together and hollow the spine—just the effect one wants to avoid. The abdominal muscles, on the other hand, roll the body forward as the ribs approach the pelvis without straining the lower spine. The abdominals do most of the work in the early part of a sit-up. The second half of a sit-up hardly exercises the abdominals at all and may actually conceal weak abdominal muscles, as is typically seen in a person who jerks quickly through the first phase of the movement. Keeping the legs straight and, as is sometimes done in sit-ups, fixing the feet with external force (as, for example, by tucking them under a horizontal bar) further encourages use of the hip flexor muscles and thus increases lumbar strain. *Avoid these sit-ups at all times.* Conversely, bending the knees minimizes use of the hip flexors and brings the abdominals into full play. Please note that the College of Obstetricians and Gynecologists guidelines (see Table 3) recommend against the supine (on-the-back) position for resting or sleeping after the fourth month. Not all experts agree.

PELVIC TILTING AND BRIDGING

Pelvic-tilting movements focus on the lower part of the abdominal wall and can be done in many positions. The action is to decrease the curve of the lower spine (the small of the back) by squeezing the buttocks tightly together and pulling in the abdominal muscles, thus rotating the pelvis to the back (posteriorly). Like curl-ups, pelvic-tilting exercises can be done progressively in three different positions while lying on the back:

1. The knees are bent, the feet flat on the floor.
2. With heels sliding along the floor, the legs are extended as far as possible while the pelvic tilt is maintained. With practice

and increasing muscle strength and control, the tilt will be possible with the legs fully extended.

3. Finally, with the tilt maintained, the legs and thighs are bent and brought over the waist. Then the thighs and legs are simultaneously and gradually lowered and extended to the point where the pelvic tilt is maximally stressed yet maintained. Usually this point occurs before the thighs are lowered forty-five degrees. Many women will be able to lower the legs as far as forty-five degrees only after considerable practice. In late pregnancy this maneuver is difficult for many women. Do not perform this exercise if diastasis recti is present.

There is a difference between leg lowering as described and double leg raising, with which it is often confused. In double leg raising, the woman lies on her back with her legs outstretched and perfectly straight. She then lifts the stiffened legs together from the surface upward. The problem with double leg raising is that, during the most difficult initial part of the movement the pelvic tilt is out of control because the hip flexors, not the abdominals, do the work. As with a seesaw, the short lever of the pelvis rises before the longer lever of the outstretched legs. This exercise has caused much discomfort and aggravation of back pain. The point is not simply to raise or lower the legs. You must be able to maintain the pelvic tilt and protect the lumbar spine while the muscles that do so are challenged and thereby strengthened. *Double leg raising should be eliminated from any exercise program, especially one designed for pregnant women.*

Basic pelvic tilting can also be done in sitting, standing, kneeling, side-lying, and hands-and-knees positions. In the hands-and-knees position, the work of maintaining the pelvic tilt can be increased by extending first one arm, then one leg, then opposite arms and legs together. In this exercise, the abdominal and gluteal muscles hold the pelvis in line with the spine against gravity and the leverage of the different arm and leg positions. This is also a good position for the woman with a diastasis who cannot do curl-ups. The hands-and-knees position also relieves backache and pressure from the uterus, and the progressive exercises mentioned improve balance and strengthen the arms and shoulders.

Bridging is the act of raising the buttocks off the floor. It helps improve the pelvic tilt by strengthening the gluteal muscles, which pull the pelvis down in conjunction with the upward movement of the abdominals. Bridging is done lying on the back, preferably with the legs straight at the knees and heels resting on a low table or footstool. The buttocks are lifted from the floor to form a bridge with the body. If this exercise is done with the knees bent, the woman must be taught to feel the difference between gluteal contractions and the leverage exerted by the hamstrings, which run from below the knee to the "sitting bones" of the pelvis. The closer the heels are to the buttocks, the more substitution occurs with the hamstrings, which can extend the hips when the knees are bent. The value of the exercise is thus reduced. Bridging should be done with the pelvis tilted back and buttocks held as firm as possible. A further progression is to straighten alternate knees while in the bridge and next move the extended leg from side to side, keeping the thighs parallel throughout.

PELVIC FLOOR EXERCISES

The importance of the muscular and fascial layers that comprise the pelvic floor cannot be overemphasized. The pubococcygeus muscle, which connects the coccyx ("tail bone" or tip of the spine) and the pubic bone at its center, is of particular importance. In our culture, the muscles of the pelvic floor are typically not exercised, and many women are actually unaware of them. The three main functions of the pelvic floor are

1. To support the pelvic abdominal organs and the increasing weight of the uterus in pregnancy
2. To provide sphincter control of the anus and urethra
3. To enhance sexual response, since healthy muscles grip and massage the penis during intercourse, and vigorously contract during orgasm to provide increased satisfaction to the woman and her partner.

Structural changes in the pelvic floor—such as laxity and various degrees of sagging of the uterus, bladder, or rectum—are common in Western society, particularly in women who have borne children. Functional changes, such as urinary stress incontinence (the leakage of urine with coughing, sneezing, or straining), lack of sexual satisfaction for either partner, and incomplete emptying of bowels or bladder are also very common. Most women believe that stress incontinence and "falling-out feelings" are normal side effects of pregnancy, since many of their friends suffer the same symptoms. Smoking, obesity, and chronic chest conditions, which all cause increases in intra-abdominal pressure, all aggravate pelvic floor dysfunction. Although softening of tissues related to hormonal and blood supply changes and some descent of the pelvic floor are normal during pregnancy, adequate urinary control can and should be maintained throughout.

Healthy pelvic floor muscles can help facilitate the safe progress of the baby during the second stage of labor. Well-exercised muscles with enhanced blood supply can better withstand stretching before their fibers become underoxygenated or stretched to the point of tearing. Dr. Arnold Kegel, a pioneer in studying the pelvic floor, has shown that during the crowning of the baby's head, a strong pubococcygeus muscle remains protected by the pubic bones, while a thin, fibrous, unexercised muscle is dragged down with the fetal head and is more likely to be injured.

There are problems in learning to contract the pubococcygeus, because the action is internal and out of sight, and no bones are involved in the movement. Without some sort of feedback, women may not be able to judge their efforts and may become discouraged. Many are unaware of the pubococcygeus and cannot contract it in isolation from other muscle groups. Typically, they contract other muscles, such as the buttocks or inner thighs, when asked to tighten this muscle. Since vaginal examinations are not performed during exercise or childbirth classes, it is essential for the woman, perhaps with the aid of illustrations, to locate this muscle herself.

A woman can become aware of this muscle while urinating. Simply stop in midstream several times, paying attention to the muscles you use to accomplish this action. If you cannot do this, you will need to reeducate this muscle. The muscle can also be identified and evaluated during the initial prenatal physical examination (see pp. 42–44). Inserting one or more fingers into the vagina, while at the same time trying to squeeze, is another way for a woman to identify this muscle.

Once a woman has identified the correct muscle, she tightens the anal and vaginal sphincters, thereby also raising the perineum (the region between the lower end of the vagina and the anus). Useful analogies to this action are the rising of an elevator and the drawing up of a hammock. The muscular contractions must be done slowly enough to recruit as many muscle fibers as possible. Contract/relax exercises (also known as Kegeling) can be done at any time. In particular, the pelvic floor should be braced during such exertions as sneezing, coughing, or lifting.

Research has shown that the pelvic floor readily fatigues with exercise and that the average woman cannot make more than a few contractions of consistent strength. Similarly, holding a contraction for more than ten seconds is beyond the ability of most unconditioned women. The exercise should be done "little and often"—just three or four contractions in a series followed by a rest interval. A total of about fifty should be done daily before, during, and after pregnancy. Sexual intercourse is another opportunity for the practice and improvement of pelvic floor control and has the advantage of feedback from one's partner. Pelvic floor exercises can be done anywhere, anytime. They should become as routine as brushing the teeth. In societies where squatting is common, the pelvic floor is always strong, because it must support all the internal organs in this position. Squatting also strengthens the thigh muscles and promotes good lifting habits (instead of bending from the waist).

STRETCHING EXERCISES

For health and well-being, flexibility is as important as strength. The muscle groups that are tight are typically the hamstrings, calf muscles, inner thighs, hip flexors (muscles that bend the thigh toward the abdomen), and back extensors (muscles that straighten out the back as in a position of "attention"). Yoga exercises are particularly suited to enhance flexibility. (See Appendix E.)

The hamstrings can be stretched by standing with one leg

elevated on a chair or table, by "long sitting" (knees straight, legs outstretched), and by lying on the back and lifting *one* straight leg at a time. (Avoid double leg raising, as described previously.) In pregnancy these positions are preferable to bending forward, which usually involves rounding of the back and excessive pressure on the spinal discs (the structures that act as shock absorbers between the individual vertebrae). In stretching the hamstrings it is important to bend at the hips rather than bend the spine.

Calf stretching can be done kneeling on one knee ("runner's stretch") with the foot of the forward leg firmly applied to the floor as weight is shifted progressively forward, or by standing with one foot in front of the other; the knee of the rear leg is kept straight with its foot planted squarely on the floor as the forward knee is bent. The hip flexors can also be stretched in the half-kneeling position, one foot in front of the other, with the weight transferred onto the forward foot until a pull is felt in the opposite groin. The back can be stretched in a "tailor-sitting" position (knees bent, ankles crossed, and legs allowed to fall apart). The trunk is then bent forward to bring the head toward the floor. A modified back stretch can also be done in a "half-tailor-sitting" position (one leg outstretched and one leg bent) with trunk bent to either side. Sitting with the legs extended ("long sit") and holding the back at a ninety-degree angle (without leaning on the arms) is an excellent stretch and postural exercise. The back can also be buttressed against a wall and the exercise made more difficult by raising the arms while keeping contact with the wall. Squatting with the heels flat is another recommended sitting position. It is ideal for the second stage of labor, even essential with a large baby, breech presentations, or CPD (cephalopelvic disproportion) (see pp. 303–304).

The adductor muscles (which pull the thighs inward toward each other, and contract to hold an object between the knees) can be stretched in a sitting position with the soles of the feet together, allowing the force of gravity to let the thighs fall apart. The "pelvic clock" exercise, arching the pelvis around like the hands of a clock, of Moshe Feldenkrais can also be done in this position and increases pelvic awareness. This maneuver involves sitting on the floor with the soles of the feet together and rotating the pelvis, first clockwise, then counterclockwise.

AEROBIC EXERCISE

Aerobic exercise refers to activities that increase the pumping of blood by the heart and the movement of air in and out of the lungs. They include any combination of walking, skipping, jumping, jogging, and dancing, using backward, forward, and sideways directions for variety. Other aerobic activities include running, cross-country skiing, brisk walking, and non-weight-bearing activities, such as swimming and cycling. "Warming up" and "cooling down," including stretching before and after the aerobic exercise, are particularly important to prevent injury and too often overlooked. Women should continue with their favorite sports, listening to their bodies for signs about what to do and how much, as the pregnancy progresses and after delivery. Table 3 contains guidelines for planning appropriate aerobic activities.

RELAXATION

An ability to relax is a great asset during birth when a couple learns that actively "being" is as important as "doing." For one thing, relaxation during labor allows the mother to conserve energy. Giving birth involves using the forces that push the baby down the birth canal as well as reducing the forces that oppose this descent. "Tightening up" increases resistance; "opening up" decreases it. In a sense, a pregnant woman "allows" her baby to be born simply by yielding to the forces pushing the baby out. As in sexual intercourse, a woman must allow birth, like orgasm, to happen. "Letting go" through increased body awareness is a skill that can be learned and practiced.

Sheila Kitzinger, noted British childbirth educator, has described the "puppet-string" approach to relaxation. In a comfortable lying position, with plenty of pillows, one imagines various parts of the body attached to strings operated by a puppeteer who can pull the strings straight up or at various angles. The strings can be pulled in any combination: for example, the right shoulder and the right index finger can move together, or the right shoulder can move with the left knee, and so forth. A woman can "activate" the strings herself. Or she can ask her

Table 3. Exercise Guidelines

Pregnancy and Postpartum

1. Regular exercise (at least three times per week) is preferable to intermittent activity. Competitive activities should be discouraged.
2. Vigorous exercise should not be performed in hot, humid weather or during a period of febrile illness.
3. Ballistic movements (jerky, bouncy motions) should be avoided. Exercise should be done on a wooden floor or a tightly carpeted surface to reduce shock and provide a sure footing.
4. Deep flexion or extension of joints should be avoided because of connective tissue laxity. Activities that require jumping, jarring motions or rapid changes in direction should be avoided because of joint instability.
5. Vigorous exercise should be preceded by a 5-minute period of muscle warm-up. This can be accomplished by slow walking or stationary cycling with low resistance.
6. Vigorous exercise should be followed by a period of gradually declining activity that includes gentle stationary stretching. Because connective tissue laxity increases the risk of joint injury, stretches should not be taken to the point of maximum resistance.
7. Heart rate should be measured at times of peak activity. Target heart rates and limits established in consultation with the physician should not be exceeded (see table below for recommended postpartum heart rate limits).
8. Care should be taken to gradually rise from the floor to avoid orthostatic hypotension. Some form of activity involving the legs should be continued for a brief period.
9. Liquids should be taken liberally before and after exercise to prevent dehydration. If necesssary, activity should be interrupted to replenish fluids.
10. Women who have led sedentary lifestyles should begin with physical activity of very low intensity and advance activity levels very gradually.
11. Activity should be stopped and the physician consulted if any unusual symptoms appear.

Pregnancy Only

1. Maternal heart rate should not exceed 140 beats per minute.
2. Strenuous activities should not exceed 15 minutes in duration.
3. No exercise should be performed in the supine position after the fourth month of gestation is completed.
4. Exercises that employ the Valsalva maneuver should be avoided.
5. Caloric intake should be adequate to meet not only the extra energy needs of pregnancy, but also of the exercise performed.
6. Maternal core temperature should not exceed 38°C.

Heart Rate Guidelines for Postpartum Exercise

	Beats per Minute	
Age	*Limit**	*Maximum*
20	150	200
25	146	195
30	142	190
35	138	185
40	135	180
45	131	175

*Each figure represents 75% of the maximum heart rate that would be predicted for the corresponding age group. Under proper medical supervision, more strenuous activity and higher heart rates may be appropriate.

From "Exercise During Pregnancy and the Postnatal Period," American College of Obstetrics and Gynecology Home Exercise Programs. Washington, D.C. Copyright 1985.

partner to do so and to let her know which ones are being "pulled." After a string has been pulled, so to speak, she can allow the muscle to relax and the body part involved to sink back into a resting state.

The method of relaxation based on Stanislavsky acting techniques uses imagined activities. In a relaxed sitting or lying position, with eyes closed, get in touch with various parts of your body by imagining them engaged in activities such as chewing sticky taffy, walking barefoot on sharp pebbles at the beach, kneading dough, following an airplane overhead to the distant horizon, tasting a sour lemon, and so forth. Do not actually make these movements. Do them only in your mind.

In point of fact, relaxation cannot be taught. People learn how to relax *indirectly*. Although childbirth classes often include training for "conscious release," this is not physiologically possible because the receptors that control muscle tension do not reach a conscious level in the brain. Thus, the most effective "body work" approach to relaxing a muscle is to tighten the muscle that has the opposite action. Examples of this approach include "dragging down" the shoulders for tense and elevated shoulder muscles, "fingers long" to extend overactive finger flexors, and "dragging down" the jaw for tension in the face. As you do these exercises, note which muscles are tense and which are relaxed. In actively dropping your jaw you can become aware of relaxation in the muscles of your cheeks. Further details of this approach, which works key areas of tension in the body, can be found listed in Appendix E under "Exercise and Comfort."

Mental relaxation must be encouraged along with physical release. These skills form the basis of yoga and meditation programs. Focusing on the natural rhythms of breathing will quiet the mind and facilitate general body relaxation. Controlling the breath, on the other hand, requires effort, diminishes body awareness, and impairs relaxation. Couples can experience these phenomena for themselves by alternating control of the breath with simple observation of it. (See next section.)

The passive state of mental relaxation can also be obtained by repeating the number "one" or any other word silently to oneself, or by using a mantra, as in meditation. The procedure, adapted from Herbert Benson's *Relaxation Response*, is as follows:

1. In a quiet environment, on an empty stomach, select a comfortable chair, sit in a relaxed position, and close your eyes. Place your feet comfortably on the floor, and rest your head against the wall or back of the chair.

2. Deeply relax all of your muscles, from your feet to your face—toes, ankles, calves, thighs, lower torso, chest, shoulders, neck, head. If this is hard, try tensing each part and then relaxing it. Squeeze your fists and arm muscles. Then let them relax and hang loosely at your side on the arms of the chair or in your lap. Repeat with your feet and legs, squeezing them first and then letting them loose.

3. Breathe normally through your nose. Pay attention to your breathing and to the air moving through your nose. Do not overbreathe. As you breathe out, say "one" or another word silently to yourself. Rather than focusing on breathing, some people find it easier to imagine a pleasant scene.

4. When other thoughts and feelings float into your mind, just let them be. Do not push them away, but do not pay attention to them either. Be indifferent; adopt an "oh, well" attitude. If a reminder (to do something, for example) comes into your mind,

open your eyes, get up, write it down, sit back down, and start again from the beginning.

5. Continue for ten to twenty minutes. Open your eyes to check the time, but do not use an alarm. If you have done the exercise for too short a time, close your eyes and go back to it. Then sit quietly for several minutes, at first with your eyes closed and then with them open.

6. Do the exercises daily. Do not expect immediate results, and do not expect any results unless you do it on a regular basis. Some people prefer doing the relaxation exercises at the beginning of the day, others at the end of the day. Some do it both at the beginning and the end of each day. Once you have practiced the exercise and feel comfortable with it, you can also use it at times of particular stress.

The relaxation exercises just described do not work well after a heavy meal.

Breathing in Labor

As part of a changing emphasis in childbirth education, many practitioners are reevaluating traditional psychoprophylactic breathing techniques, such as the Lamaze and Bradley methods. This rethinking recognizes that each woman's labor is different and that women, left to themselves and encouraged to experiment, are capable of finding the laboring position and breathing patterns that work best for them.

Increasingly, controlled patterns of breathing are coming to be considered excessively rigid. This view in no way minimizes their historical importance as a reaction to the totally anesthetized childbirth advocated in the earlier part of this century, nor does it deny the continuing appeal of these methods to women who would consciously "control" pain in childbirth. All too often, however, there is a preoccupation with fixed patterns of breathing that do not respond to the needs of the body. Breathing normally, and in response to internal cues, may be more beneficial. The purposeful alteration of breathing, with the goal of pain control through distraction, consumes energy and limits feeling and awareness. Women who have had a normal childbirth often report that it is lack of energy, rather than unbearable pain, that is their most common difficulty during labor. This lack of energy may result from anxiety and tension and may be exacerbated, rather than helped, by the distraction techniques and breathing interventions taught by childbirth educators and in books.

On the one hand, shallow chest breathing does not permit sufficient fresh air to enter or sufficient stale air to leave the lungs for adequate gas exchange to occur in the tiny air sacs. On the other, if this type of breathing becomes rapid, dizziness and light-headedness (symptoms of hyperventilation) may occur as the woman accelerates her breathing to "stay on top" of her intensifying contractions. Hyperventilation also leads to chemical changes in the blood that decrease it oxygen-carrying capacity and change its acidity. Both effects are transmitted to the fetus, impairing its well-being.

Although women are commonly taught to achieve an inverse relationship between the speed and depth of respiration (the slower, the deeper; the faster, the more shallow), research has shown that, as the breathing rate increases, women in labor do not naturally decrease the amount of air they breathe in and out with each breath. The rate of breathing is the only practical guide for couples. It should not exceed twenty breaths per minute, and ideally—to stay within optimum limits—should be much less.

Traditionally, women have been told after full cervical dilatation to "breathe in, hold your breath, and push!"—an effort that results in a forced expulsive effort against a closed glottis. This approach is now being reconsidered. The closed pressure system formed after even five seconds of forced breath retention leads to increased pressure inside the chest, reduced return of blood to the heart and lungs, and a reduction of the amount of blood pumped by the heart to the body, including the placenta. Thus, blood flow to the fetus can be impaired. This breath holding also results in reflex tensing of the pelvic floor, which increases resistance to the baby's descent—just the opposite of what is desired.

A more beneficial approach, according to our recent thinking, is to push with lips pursed to let air out gently during bearing down—in effect, "breathing the baby out." Furthermore, women

111

need bear down only to the extent that such pushing brings a feeling of relief. They should follow their internal body cues.

The birthing center at Pithiviers, France, directed by world-famous obstetrician Dr. Michel Odent, works on the assumption that women know how to give birth if left alone. No formal prenatal instruction is given. Instead, women come to the center about a week before their due date and learn what they need from other women who have just given birth. They spend much time singing around the piano, and, when they go into labor, they are free to assume any comfortable position, sometimes even laboring in a warm pool. The reported results are excellent.

My personal opinion is that childbirth education, including breathing techniques, should be kept simple, with emphasis on natural events and normal physiology. If childbirth can be seen as an involuntary process, one that need only be allowed to unfold rather than be controlled, the laboring woman will be better able to direct her energy within instead of dissipating it by attempting to put her mind outside her body. Each woman should strive to find her own way, fully realizing that women already know how to have babies if left to themselves.

Sex during Pregnancy

Sexual feelings fluctuate widely during pregnancy and may at times disappear altogether. For example, in early pregnancy a woman with morning sickness is likely to be little interested in intercourse with her partner. Several studies indicate a drop-off in desire in the third trimester as well. At other times, some women report a strongly increased desire for sex.

The dramatic changes in a woman's body that are part of a normal pregnancy run counter to some of our society's most cherished ideals of beauty. This may affect a woman's own attitude and her partner's. In our culture, which tends not to acknowledge and respect the sexuality of the pregnant woman, these changes are thought of as anything but sexual turn-ons. Couples would do well to concentrate on their own positive feelings toward each other, deemphasizing any stereotyped negative feelings toward sexuality, pregnancy, and sex and pregnancy.

Intercourse is perfectly permissible during pregnancy, although adjustments in position and penetration will have to be made to accommodate the woman's expanding abdomen. The man-on-top ("missionary") position is too uncomfortable for late pregnancy; a side-by-side or sitting position is preferable. After the baby has "dropped," rear-entry positions are particularly comfortable , with the woman kneeling, crouching, or lying. Lots of pillows can be used for support, to keep weight off the abdomen. Pillows and more pillows are to intercourse during pregnancy what a rocking chair is to breast-feeding.

Sheila Kitzinger has pointed out that, in advanced pregnancy, it may be better for the man to ejaculate just before a woman comes to orgasm. An erect penis in a heavily pregnant woman may prevent her from making the kind of pelvic movements that will bring on orgasm. In pregnancy, as at other times, the man should be aware that the clitoris can be overstimulated. A good general rule is that, once the clitoris has become swollen, the man should ask the woman when she wants penetration.

During pregnancy, many couples prefer forms other than intercourse to express sexual feeling: cuddling, showering together, massage, or caresses that lead to orgasm. The sensitivity of a woman's breasts and nipples often markedly increases in pregnancy. They can become the focus of erotic arousal but need to be handled gently.

Pregnancy offers couples the opportunity to explore what for them may be new forms of expression, which can be continued after the birth. The topic of lovemaking during pregnancy has inspired much recent interest and a number of books (see Appendix E).

Labor and delivery can be a profoundly sexual experience. Pioneering childbirth researcher Niles Newton has identified eleven points of comparison between undisturbed childbirth and sexual excitement:

1. Change in breathing
2. Tendency to make vocal noises
3. Facial expression reminiscent of an athlete under great strain

4. Rhythmic contraction of the upper segment of the uterus
5. Loosening of the mucous plug from the opening of the cervix
6. Periodic abdominal muscle contraction
7. Use of a position in which the woman's legs are drawn up and spread apart
8. A tendency to become uninhibited
9. Unusual muscular strength
10. A tendency to be unaware of the world, and a sudden return to alert awareness after climax (orgasm) or birth
11. A feeling of joy and well-being following the orgasm or birth

Obviously, the degree to which a couple can experience labor and delivery in such sexual terms will depend on the setting in which birth takes place and how it is conducted. Relaxation and a sense of security are important factors.

Common fears regarding intercourse and orgasm during pregnancy relate to precipitation of an abortion (miscarriage), initiation of premature labor, and harm to the baby in some way. In point of fact, there is no evidence that intercourse causes miscarriages, although it may be the last straw in a pregnancy that was going to abort anyway (see p. 319). While there is some evidence that intercourse and orgasm may trigger the onset of labor, research findings are divided on this question. The general consensus is that intercourse is not considered to be a factor in premature labor, and there is no evidence that intercourse harms babies.

In a few situations intercourse during late pregnancy is best avoided. These include the following:

1. After the breaking of the amniotic sac, which allows communication between the uterus and vagina, increasing the chances of infection of both the uterus and the fetus (see pp. 332–333 on "Premature Rupture of the Membranes")
2. Premature labor controlled with drugs (see pp. 330–331)
3. Placenta praevia (pp. 323–324)
4. Impaired well-being of the fetus, as, for example, in the infant suspected of having intrauterine growth disturbance (see pp. 312–315)

It is possible for all expectant couples to achieve better sexual response. Many women who were unable to or could only occasionally reach orgasm before pregnancy report becoming orgasmic thereafter or for the first time achieving multiple orgasms. Such women also report that they feel more pride in their bodies, have more confidence in themselves as sexual beings, and are more sensual and sensitive, that sex is more relaxed, less pressured, more playful; and that trust and intimacy with their partners have increased.

Pregnancy presents a couple with the opportunity for close, honest communication about sex and other issues. Every "problem" mentioned is also an opportunity for enhanced growth and understanding in the magnificent context of creating a new life.

Children and Birth

As more people now strive to make birth a family-centered experience—whether in the hospital, the birthing room, or the home—they are becoming more concerned with preparing an older child for the birth and arrival of the new sibling. Since many couples find this complex and difficult, I have gathered some specific advice from parents who have successfully done so. Some of them chose to include an older child during labor and delivery; many did not. In any case, thoughtful preparation of the child is always important.

Most parents I consulted emphasized three points:

1. The key to success in preparation is the attitude of the parents—if the child is to be unafraid, enthusiastic, and excited about the birth, the parents must be that way, too.
2. The bonding that takes place after birth should occur not only between the parents and the newborn but between the older child and the new sibling as well.
3. Children participate to the degree that they are comfortable. They should not be forced or pressured to do more than they

"Children and Birth" is adapted from *Children at Birth*, a non-published essay used for prenatal classes, with the kind permission of Jenifer M. Fleming.

want to do; and they should be permitted as much, or as little, involvement as they can deal with comfortably.

CONVEYING THE UNFOLDING OF PREGNANCY AND THE TIME OF BIRTH

Tell your child about the expected baby as soon as you are sure you are pregnant. Many parents say their child needed the nine months as much as they did. Even though time is a difficult concept for small children, they seem able to grasp it if it is linked to their own experiences. Some parents used the signs of the seasons to convey the passage of time. If, for example, the baby is due in June, a parent may say something like this: "First there will be fall when the leaves turn pretty colors, then winter when the trees are bare and it is cold and snow is on the ground, then Christmas when we have a tree and presents and Santa Claus comes, then spring when the crocuses peep above the ground and the willows turn yellow. Then the forsythia, then the lilacs, . . . and then 'our baby' will be born when the roses bloom." Of course, when you try to convey time this way, the age of the child will be a factor; but several parents found this pattern understandable to children who, some as young as two and one-half years, quickly memorized the sequence.

One mother said she used pictures showing the month-by-month changes in the uterus and fetus to make up a "time line" for the wall of her daughter's room. Many physicians and midwives give out illustrated booklets that lend themselves to this use; you can buy special sets of posters, or copy the illustrations in available picture books on pregnancy (see Appendix E). Each month the child adds the appropriate picture to the time line. This way the child gets a clear sense of the progression of the pregnancy, not only from the pictures but from her mother's increasing girth as well. Another idea for a time line is a series of photographs of the mother, taken throughout the pregnancy, showing her changing body configuration. These can be taken by the child.

Inspired by Advent calendars used at Christmastime, several parents successfully used this idea to prepare their children for the birth of a sibling, particularly children from two to eight years old. (We suggest making the calendar run at least two weeks beyond the due date in case the baby arrives late.) Simply make a calendar of those days around the due date with little movable doors or windows for each day. Behind each window put a surprise, preferably one related to new life—a baby animal toy, a robin's egg, or seeds.

FAMILY CELEBRATIONS AND ACTIVITIES

Family celebrations—holidays, birthdays, festivals—can be used to convey passage of time before the birth of the baby. For some families, Christmas, with its focus on baby Jesus, is the time to celebrate babies in general, first anticipating their coming, then marveling at their birth, and finally rejoicing in their arrival. Repeating Christmas traditions that center around the birth of a baby (like the calendar just described, candles around the house, or familiar music) helps young children get into the spirit of the event and makes it real for them. The same can be achieved with birthday customs already followed in the home—cake and candles, presents, singing, and retelling family members' memories of past birthdays. Children of all ages, and adults too, love to hear the story of their birth. Retelling and rehearing their own beginnings helps them prepare for another birth in the family.

Many parents found that focusing attention on a pet helps a child understand that another being needs care and space of its own, that it has a will of its own, and that its needs must be respected. Try to visit younger animals in pet shops or in children's zoos or in the homes of friends to provide children experience with new lives. With pets children can learn, over a period of time, that care is an ongoing, never-ending circle of love and attention. Of course, contact with human babies is even more to the point.

The idea of a nickname may come from the child when he or she refers to the baby during the pregnancy. If not, parents can suggest one, realizing it may not catch on. One eighteen-month-old had a beloved doll she called "Wolly." When she saw her mother's belly growing, she transferred the name to the baby inside. She would talk to "Wolly" and would pat her mother's stomach. The nickname, thank goodness, did not persist after little sister Katy's birth, but it did help the toddler relate to her new sibling during the pregnancy.

Often it helps to talk about the baby as a special gift to the whole family, to be cared for by everyone, just as the older child was a special gift to the parents. The older child may then more easily appreciate the idea of preparing gifts for the baby when it is born (receiving blankets, quilts, decorated T-shirts, mobiles, special songs). Children can participate in making these gifts. Families who enjoy music together can make up or choose a particular song to welcome the new baby. They can rehearse it together before the baby comes so that it becomes a kind of theme song in the home for many days, or even years, after the birth.

PREPARING THE CHILD FOR THE PHYSICAL ASPECTS OF PREGNANCY, LABOR, AND BIRTH

Include older children in visits to the midwife or doctor. Explain that these people will be at the birth to help you have the baby. As the pregnancy advances, children usually enjoy listening to the heartbeat and feeling the baby kick and move around. Whether or not you have your child present at examinations and any other special procedures depends on your inclination, the preferences of the caregiver, and the age and developmental level of the child. If at all possible, include the child in visits to the hospital to meet the doctor or look through the nursery window. If you plan a home birth, explain to an older child that you might have to go to the hospital for help.

You may wish to bring your child to certain birth classes. Classes that use slides and pictures of births are particularly useful, depending on the interests and age of the child. Birth movies can give a child who will be attending a home birth a real sense of the sights and sounds of birth. Let children meet the midwife, nurse, or labor coach. Ask class leaders and check libraries and bookstores for well-illustrated, informative books on birth and the arrival of a new baby (see Appendix E).

Visit friends who have new babies, especially those whose

pregnancies you and the child may have followed. Contact with babies gives children a better idea of what newborns are like—how tiny and helpless they are, and how gentle and loving one must be with them. Children often enjoy watching and imitating the exercises a woman does in preparation for birth, including relaxation and breathing techniques.

Depending on the age and temperament of the child, you may want to discuss any fears he or she has about the birth, for example, what happens if the baby does not breathe right away. Be alert to the child's questions and observations and aware of the deeper meanings they convey. You will be amazed at the distorted ideas children at any age can have, and you will have a good chance to correct them then.

INCLUDING THE CHILD
AT THE ACTUAL BIRTH

If you plan to have children present at the actual birth, you need to do extra preparation. Talk about the hard work of pushing the baby out, and the concentration and patience it takes to have a baby. Show them the different positions you might assume, and let them hear the kinds of sounds you might make. One family played a tape of their first labor to their older child, to accustom him to the sounds. These were, of course, the sounds of his own birth.

Don't forget to talk about blood—the "good blood"—and its purpose and value when the baby is born. Talk about how a baby looks when it first comes out of the mother and about the importance of the placenta to the baby.

Give the child a task. Four- and five-year-olds can be a great help giving you ice chips and orange juice, for example. Older children can help time contractions, wipe your face with a washcloth, hold your hand, breathe along with you, hold a flashlight, and so forth. Although most children want to feel useful at a birth, expect that they may also need to be out of the room for a while. Make them as aware as possible before the birth that they can choose to be there or not, and that whatever they choose is all right with you.

Identify a caretaker for the child. Unless children are well into their teens, most will need someone at the birth who is there solely for them. Explain to the child that while Mommy is having the baby, she won't be able to give him or her the same kind of attention and care that she normally does. For this reason, this other familiar and loved person will be there. The person you choose for the caretaker role should be comfortable with birth in the setting you have chosen. Consider having this person join you at several childbirth classes, and show him or her the books about pregnancy and birth that you particularly like. Also, this "birth-sitter" should understand that if the child does not want to be present at the birth, that is fine, and his or her job is to stay with the child.

Define the father's role at the birth. Will he be the caretaker for the child and leave others to support the mother, or does he want to be primarily involved with her? The child should know in advance what role the father will play.

A surprise bag of goodies, suitable to the age of the child, will keep most children interested and peaceful during what might be a long labor. For young children, these small treats are often the most exciting part. Their interest will alternate between the items in the bag and aspects of the labor and delivery.

Parents who have included their older children in a birth say that it does not eliminate sibling rivalry. But, as one parent reported, "there seems to be a deep reservoir of trust and love from the older to the younger," because, as her three-year-old said to the baby, "I saw you born."

If given the chance, children have a wonderful capacity to respond to an experience in ways that adults find difficult to imagine. One four-year-old was overheard describing to a friend of the same age the recent birth at which she was present: "Mommy cried, the baby cried, and there was blood, but it was good blood."

AFTER THE BIRTH

After the birth when you first see your older child, at the hospital or at home, reassure him or her that you are fine—physically tired, perhaps, but in no way hurt or unrecognizable. You are still the same person, still the child's mother. Birth is such a dramatic happening that a young child may feel that the world has turned upside down. The child, especially one under six, should see you behave "normally" again—walking, talking, and laughing. This is especially important if the child has been present at birth and has seen you assuming strange positions and making extraordinary, possibly frightening, noises.

Make time during the days following birth for some quiet cuddling and attention to the child alone, perhaps when the father or a friend is with the baby. Depending on age and temperament, your child may ask for a lot of this kind of physical reassurance immediately, or the child may act reserved and appear to reject you. Sometimes this diffidence comes from a feeling of awe toward you and the new baby, and sometimes from feelings of anger and the fear of rejection. Don't be alarmed; such withdrawal is a common reaction, particularly in children aged five to eight.

Children need time to integrate the experience of birth, just as you do. If you continue to show that you love and care for them as well as for the new baby, they can begin to share affection and positive feelings toward you and the baby at their own pace. Older children, as well as parents, need time to bond with the newborn. Give them as much freedom as you can, within the limits of safety for the infant, to explore, touch, kiss, and handle the new sibling. With a younger child, you may have to make it very clear from the beginning that you are not going to allow the baby to be hurt or even pressed too firmly. Demonstrate touch to your child by encouraging him or her to gently hug the baby; touch the baby's hair, hands, and feet; and even hold the baby. Each day set aside special play time for the newborn and the sibling.

A festive birthday party for the newborn can be a long-remembered highlight for the sibling. Include children in the preparations, such as making and decorating the cake. The party is the time for the special song or version of "Happy Birthday." If you are celebrating with champagne, offer children their own small glass with juice or soda, so they can join in the toasts. Children love to receive and give gifts, and gift giving can express love within the family. Gifts to the older child from the parents, the new baby, and others, and gifts from the older child to the new brother or sister are all appropriate. For preschool children, well-chosen books are particularly fitting. If a child likes dolls, nothing makes a more appropriate gift. Consider setting up an area some-where especially for the older child, where he or she can care for the doll with replicas of the equipment you use for caring for the real baby—changing table, diapers, and bottles. Over the suc-ceeding days additions can be made to keep up interest.

To head off difficulties with the older child during nursing times, keep a big jar filled with packets of nutritious snacks (rais-ins, nuts, sesame sticks) especially for the older sibling. (This is an old La Leche League suggestion.) The child can then have a snack at nursing time and sit with mother and baby. The child might enjoy decorating the jar and putting his or her name on it. Select a jar the child can open, and keep it within reach.

Bath time can be a delightful time to include the older child. Newborns love water, and it seems to have a soothing and plea-surable effect on children of all ages, whether they need to be scrubbed or not. With adult supervision, the older child can sup-port the baby in the water and feel very useful and trusted. Time spent touching and caressing during the bath and immediately after can teach lessons in gentleness and care. After the bath, a little warm oil can be massaged into the skin.

Make a picture sign to teach a small child about the importance of not disturbing a sleeping infant. Such a sign can depict each member of the family engaged in quiet activity while the baby is sleeping. At times when the baby needs to sleep, have the older child hang the sign on the baby's door. The child will quickly learn about a baby's need to be on his or her own and to sleep without being disturbed.

Older children will probably experience jealously toward the baby and long for "the good old days" when they had their mother all to themselves. It is important that children understand and eventually accept that the baby is here to stay, but it is equally important that both parents take time to do things individually or together with older children. If you have more than one older child, make sure that whoever had been "the baby" does not get dropped by the older siblings in favor of the new arrival. You may need to talk about this with the older children before the birth. Even if the father is the primary caretaker for the older child during the few weeks following birth, it is important that the mother spend time with him or her as well. After those first few weeks, even if a woman is busy nursing the baby full-time, there will always be some brief periods when the sleeping baby can be left with the father or a friend while the mother takes the older child on one of those favorite trips to the library, park, or ice cream parlor. There should be special time each day at home for the older child to read, talk, cuddle, and play with the mother while the baby sleeps.

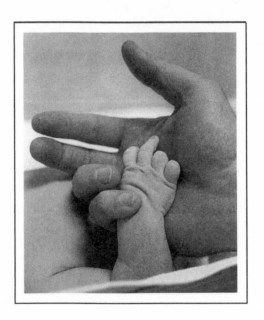

3

Caring for the Baby-to-Be

Genetics

NEW OPTIONS FROM GENETIC SCIENCE

There are many exciting aspects of the rapidly developing field of genetics that offer the possibility of actually correcting gene abnormalities. This discussion, however, focuses on only those advances in genetics that already have applications in family planning. To understand these advances, you need to know the meaning of several technical words and understand one or two elementary concepts. You should find the small effort amply rewarding, for genetics is a subject that will affect us more and more in the years ahead.

Gregor Mendel, the founder of modern genetic science, showed that the first generation of a crossing of two distinct varieties of any organism (yellow- and green-seeded peas in the case of Mendel's famous experiments) received a *dominant* hereditary unit from one parent and a *recessive* unit from the other. We now call these hereditary units *genes* and know that they occur in pairs, each parent contributing one gene. Genes are found in the nucleus of each cell, carried on rodlike structures called *chromosomes*. When the offspring has obtained a combination of a dominant gene from one side and a recessive gene from the other, the dominant gene always prevails. Individuals with this combination of a dominant and a recessive gene are said to be *heterozygous*, having two unlike genes for a particular characteristic. If they receive the same type of gene from both parents, they are said to be *homozygous*, whether the gene is dominant or recessive. For a recessive gene to be physically expressed, the offspring must be homozygous, having received that one recessive gene from each parent. Recently, scientists have discovered that the "same" gene may function differently in an offspring, depending upon whether it came from the father or the mother. This important new understanding does not change the discussion in this chapter.

Mendel's theories are usually expressed in symbols. Dominant genes are shown in capital letters (XX). Recessive genes are designated by the corresponding lowercase letters (xx). A pure dominant strain of yellow-seeded peas, for instance, is symbolized as YY. This genetic formula is known as the *genotype*. A pure recessive strain (for instance, of peas with green seeds) is shown by the genotype yy. When these two strains are crossed (YY by yy), all progeny will have the same genotype Yy. You will see how this works if you think of the four possible combinations: the first Y combining with the first y to produce one Yy, and then with the second y to produce a second Yy; then the second Y combines with the first y to produce the third Yy, and with the second y for the fourth Yy. These are known as *heterozygous hybrids*, and they all have the same demonstrable characteristic known as the *phenotype*, which in this case is yellow seeds, since yellow (Y) is dominant over green (y). (Note that the letter Y is used here as an abbreviation for the phenotype "yellow." Later in the discussion Y will be used in a traditional way to refer to the male sex chromosome.)

GENES THAT CAUSE DISEASE

All of us carry both dominant and recessive genes. These genes control our individual characteristics, both those that are obvious, like hair color, and those out of sight at the level of chemical molecules. A gene may cause a characteristic harmful to its bearer—in other words, a disease. The disease-causing gene may be either dominant or recessive, and it may be located on the sex chromosome or on an autosomal (nonsex) chromosome. An example of a dominant gene is the one that determines *retinoblastoma*, a cancer of the retina of the eye. Dominant conditions carried on the autosomal chromosomes (those not linked to sex) are the most frequent types of inherited disorders. Well over a thousand have been identified. The usual criteria are that (1) the trait appears in each generation; (2) the trait is transmitted by an affected individual to approximately half of his or her children, regardless of sex; (3) unaffected individuals do not transmit the trait to their children; (4) males and females are equally likely to have the trait and to transmit it. (A discussion of the related topic of dominant genes linked to sex chromosomes follows.)

When a disease-determining gene is recessive, one recessive gene from each parent is required to produce the disease in question. The most common recessive genes are located on autosomes, but recessive genes can also be carried on the sex chromosomes. Many recessive genes are lethal; when one is matched with another, they produce a fertilized ovum so defective that it cannot survive. Such defective conceptions account for a significant percentage of spontaneous abortions (miscarriages) (see pp. 316–317).

A person who carries the recessive, disease-causing gene, along with a different, dominant gene, is said to be a *carrier* of the gene. While most recessive, disease-determining genes do not cause difficulties in the carrier (heterozygote), this is not always the case. For example, in one inherited disorder of blood fats, the person with two genes for the disease (homozygote) is at increased risk for having a heart attack before the age of twenty. Yet the more mildly affected carrier does not develop problems until a later age—in the forties or fifties. The carrier for sickle-cell anemia usually has no problems. However, in unusual circumstances of low oxygen, such as are found at high altitudes (in nonpressurized airplanes, for example), the carrier's blood cells can also undergo sickling (collapsing into the shape of a sickle) and cause symptoms. It is crucial to understand the difference between being a carrier of a disease and actually having the disease. The carrier usually (but not always, as just described) has no symptoms, while a person with the disease is symptomatic in some way.

A very important point in understanding the role of recessive genes in reproduction is that the outcome in the offspring is determined *by chance*. Consider the marriage of two people, each a carrier of the gene for sickle-cell anemia. Each child would have a one-in-four chance of being homozygous and having the disease. The fact that the first child was or was not affected does not alter the chances for the next child. Some families could have four affected children and some, none. But overall, in the population at large, one out of every four children born to all carrier couples would have the disease.

In summary, the characteristics of autosomal recessive genes are as follows:

1. The condition determined by the gene appears only in siblings and not in their parents, offspring, or other relatives.
2. On the average, one-quarter of the siblings will be affected, which is the same as saying that the recurrence risk is one-quarter for each pregnancy.
3. Males and females are equally likely to affected.
4. With especially rare disorders, the likelihood is that parents are blood relatives, a factor in the occurrence of certain diseases in isolated and inbred groups.

The frequency of recessive genes in a given human population varies according to the disease in question and the population. Some recessive genes are very common in certain groups, such as the gene for *sickle-cell anemia* in blacks. It has a frequency of 10 percent; that is, 1 out of 10 blacks carries the recessive gene for sickle-cell anemia. A random marriage between any two blacks, thus, has a 1-in-100 (or one-tenth of one-tenth) chance of bringing two carriers together. Each child of such a marriage of carriers has a 1-in-4 chance of being homozygous and having the disease of sickle-cell anemia.

In the case of *Tay-Sachs disease*, 1 in every 30 Ashkenazic Jews (Jews of Eastern European descent) is a carrier. A random marriage of any two individuals from this ethnic group has a 1-in-900 chance of uniting two carriers. Each child born of such a marriage has a 25 percent chance of being homozygous and having the disorder.

In *cystic fibrosis*, a disease involving abnormal production of mucus in the lungs, intestines, and other parts of the body, somewhere between 1 in 30 and 1 in 60 individuals is a carrier. Thus, 1 in 900 to 3,600 random marriages is likely to bring two carriers together, with a 1-in-4 chance of each child being affected.

The gene for *thalassemia* (or Cooley's anemia) occurs in about 1 in 30 to 1 in 12 people whose origins are in the Mediterranean basin (primarily Greeks and Italians), Africa, and Asia. This means that random pairings have a 1 in 900 to 1 in 144 chance of bringing together two carriers. Again, the chance for each one of the offspring to be affected is 1 in 4.

A recessively transmitted disease for which newborns are routinely checked is *phenylketonuria* (or PKU). It occurs once in every 10,000 births and is amenable to treatment with a special diet (see pp. 271–272). *Galactosemia*, another rare, recessively inherited disease, occurs perhaps only once in 100,000 births. This condition, which involves the lack of an enzyme that normally orders the conversion of galactose, a common milk sugar, into glucose, causes brain damage, liver disease, and cataracts. The treatment is a diet free of galactose.

Another relatively common disorder recessively inherited is an abnormality deficiency of the liver-produced plasma protein *alpha antitrypsin*, which leads to chronic lung disease (emphysema) and liver disease (cirrhosis). About 1 in 2,000 to 4,000 whites have this disorder, and 10 to 20 percent of these demonstrate symptomatic liver disease.

It is now possible to identify genes in cells both from adults and from fetuses (obtained by amniocentesis [see pp. 139–141] or chorionic villous sampling [see pp. 141–142]). By testing parents, the risk for their fetus having the gene in question can be known. Then the fetus-at-risk can be checked for that gene (or genes). At present, treatment of affected fetuses is still experimental (see, for example, "Treating the Fetus," pp. 157–159) and, for practical purposes, not available. Cure of affected babies after birth is also still experimental. In the absence of an available treatment, many parents choose to abort fetuses destined to have serious diseases for which there is no cure. But developments in gene therapy are moving rapidly, and breakthroughs are expected in the near future. Also just around the corner in this fast-moving field of genetics is the testing of genes of infants and young children for susceptibility to certain diseases and the institution of preventive measures. For example, children found to have genes that place them at risk for arteriosclerosis could be started on a special diet early in life.

Gene testing is currently offered to parents at risk for various common recessive disorders, such as Tay-Sachs disease, thalassemia, and sickle-cell anemia, by virtue of their membership in ethnic groups with a high frequency of the disease, or, with other disorders, because of the presence of a disease in a member of the parents' families, including themselves. For some common diseases, such as cystic fibrosis, multiple variations of the causative gene have made screening programs for all parents too complicated to be practical at this time, but they do not stand in the way of testing particular families at high risk.

POLYGENIC INHERITANCE

Many important characteristics (such as height, intelligence, and special aptitudes) appear to be transmitted by several genes rather than only one. These characteristics are said to be *polygenic* in origin. In predicting the outcome of mating when multiple genes are involved, we follow the Mendelian laws. But we find that the problem rapidly becomes very complex as the number of possible combinations soars.

Most congenital abnormalities are polygenic. They include congenital heart disease, club foot, congenital dislocations of the hip, cleft lip and palate, and open neural tube defects. The last group includes *meningocele* (failure of closure of the back of the spine, with a saclike protrusion of the membrane that covers the spinal cord), *meningomyelocele* (a meningocele containing the spinal cord and nerve roots), and *anencephaly* (failure of formation of the brain). When the spinal cord or nerves are involved in a meningomyelocele, there is usually an associated neurological defect, like paralysis of the legs or bladder.

Couples at risk for these disorders are usually identified through a review of their family histories. Genetic counseling in these situations must be highly individualized. Although the prevention or cure of most polygenic disorders prenatally is not yet possible (see pp. 157–159, "Treating the Fetus"), prenatal diagnosis of serious congenital abnormalities (like meningomyelocele and hydrocephalus) can provide couples with information on which to base the decision about continuing a pregnancy. For example, prenatal diagnosis of open neural tube defects is already available with considerable accuracy, beginning with the measuring of *alpha-fetoprotein* (AFP) levels in the blood of pregnant women. (See pp. 64–66, "Laboratory Tests," and pp. 139–141, "Amniocentesis.")

MUTATIONS

Occasionally, genetic information changes when it passes from parent to child. Consequently, the offspring has characteristics different from those of either parent and his or her ancestors. *Mutations* are changes in genes that produce permanent, transmissible characteristics in the offspring. Should the right mutation occur, it would be possible, at least in theory, for a couple of redheads (from families in which no one but redheads had ever been born) to produce a child with black hair. The children of this child would receive the gene for black hair also.

Mutations account for the spontaneous appearance of some diseases, known to be hereditary, for which no previous family history can be found. For example, a significant percentage of children with retinoblastoma (see p. 127) will be the first ones in their families to manifest this usually inherited disorder.

Two types of genes appear to be more unstable than others and vulnerable to mutation: oncogenes (tumor genes) and the p53 tumor-suppression gene. Mutated oncogenes signal cells to grow without restraint, that is, to become cancerous. The p53 tumor-suppression gene, which resides on the number 17 chromosome, produces a protein that controls cell growth by regulating other genes. It is a kind of master gene. In many cancers this gene is mutated, unleashing the cell to grow wildly, a characteristic of malignancies. Scientists speculate that this gene mutates in response to environmental exposures such as certain toxins in food. Viruses may be another stimulus for mutation. Further research offers possibilities for better understanding of triggering factors for gene mutation, for identifying people at risk for future cancer (i.e., carriers of the gene), and for early identification of potentially treatable existing cancer. (The shedding in the stool of mutated oncogenes by cancerous intestinal cells also offers possibilities for early detection.) Recent studies have shown that a mutated p53 tumor-suppression gene may also be inherited, thereby placing children of parents with the mutated gene at risk.

CHROMOSOMAL ABNORMALITIES

As previously mentioned, genes are strung together on chromosomes. In ordinary cell division, each chromosome makes a copy of itself (*mitosis*), with one copy going to each of the two daughter cells produced by the division. Each daughter cell thus receives exactly the same number and kind of chromosomes the parent cell had. In the formation of egg and sperm cells, however, a different and unique type of division occurs, called *meiosis*. In meiosis, each daughter cell receives only half the number of chromosomes, one from each of the paired parental chromosomes. Human egg and sperm cells have twenty-three chromosomes each. When they combine, the new individual formed by their union has forty-six, the characteristic number for the human species. (If the chromosomes were not halved before fertilization, they would double with each succeeding generation.)

On occasion in meiosis there is an uneven apportioning of chromosomes to the daughter cells, causing them to form with an extra or missing chromosome. This is called *nondisjunction*. Another accident that may happen in mitosis is *translocation*, in which a segment of one chromosome shifts to another chromosome. Egg and sperm cells that have experienced either nondisjunction or translocation may be incapable of fertilization. Or, if such a germ cell participates in fertilization, the combination may give rise to a defective fetus that is spontaneously aborted (see pp. 316–322), to an abnormal individual such as one with Down syndrome, or to an individual who is normal in appearance (phenotype) but who carries the rearranged chromosomal material in a *balanced translocation*. The fetuses produced by such an individual are at risk for abortion, for Down syndrome and other chromosomal syndromes, and for carrying balanced translocations themselves. The couple with frequent (three or more) spontaneous abortions (miscarriages) or with one spontaneous abortion and a malformed stillbirth or live birth is at increased risk for having a translocation and should be studied for it (see pp. 316–317).

The study of chromosomal conditions is called *cytogenetics*. In recent years knowledge in this field has grown enormously. Newer chemical methods of separating and staining enable geneticists to work from photographic prints of the chromosomes enlarged 3,000 to 4,000 times. The pairs of chromosomes are assigned numbers (from 1 through 22) according to the length and position of the *centromere*, the sharply constricted region that joins the halves of each pair. Pairs 1 through 22 are the *autosomes*, or nonsex chromosomes. In addition, there are 2 chromosomes that determine the sex of the individual, making the total of 46 chromosomes per person.

The sex chromosomes are of two types, X and Y. The female has two X chromosomes; the male, an X and a Y. In meiosis, one of the mother's X chromosomes goes to each daughter cell (egg). The father's sperm cells are equally divided between those carrying an X and those carrying a Y chromosome. The union of a Y-bearing sperm with the X of the mother produces a male. The union of an X-bearing sperm with the X-bearing egg produces a female. Thus, it is the father who determines the sex of the baby.

The X chromosome is longer than the Y and contains more genes. In males, the genes on the X come from the mother only. If a recessive gene on that part of the X chromosome that is unopposed by the shorter Y chromosome is abnormal, there is no dominant gene to oppose it, and the male will be affected with the disease. In the female, the action of the sex chromosomes is more complex. One of the two X chromosomes that exist in every cell in her body (except the egg) will become inactivated early in fetal development. This happens on a chance basis. In other words, about half of her cells will have an active X chromosome inherited from the mother; the other half, an active X chromosome inherited from her father. Therefore, in an *X-linked chromosomal disorder*, the female will be only partly afflicted. She will, however, be a *carrier* of the abnormal gene, capable of passing it on to her children. Therefore, the characteristics of an X-linked recessive gene are as follows:

1. The incidence of disease is much higher in males than females. If affected, females are rarely affected as seriously.
2. The trait is never directly transmitted from fathers to sons.
3. The trait is passed from an affected male through all of his daughters, and from her to half of her sons.
4. The trait may be passed "silently" through a series of carrier females before manifesting itself in affected males.

Many of the *hemophilias* follow this X-linked recessive inheritance, with females as carriers who do not show symptoms and males who have the disease. On an average, one-half of the male offspring of a mother who carries the defective gene will have hemophilia. The other half, having received a maternal X chromosome that does not contain the abnormal gene, will be normal. On an average, one-half of the female offspring of such a mother will be carriers like the mother and the other half, normal noncarriers. *X-linked dominant conditions* also occur but are rare.

All the genetic diseases now known to be associated with chromosomal abnormalities appear to stem from either too much or too little genetic material. The most common of these is *Down syndrome*, known earlier as *mongolism*, in which chromosome pair 21 is involved. Individuals with Down syndrome have physical characteristics that make early recognition possible—they are invariably retarded, and many have associated heart anomalies. It appears that this abnormality arises during meiosis. Instead of half the chromosomes going to each daughter cell in the normal manner, an ovum or sperm is formed that has two number 21 chromosomes. When this abnormal germ cell subsequently joins with its counterpart to receive another number 21 chromosome, the result is a cell with three number 21 chromosomes instead of the normal pair. In this most common form of Down syndrome, known as the *nondisjunction type*, the mother and father are cytogenetically normal by our present measurements.

Although we know how Down syndrome comes about, we still do not know exactly why it happens. In the nondisjunction type the abnormality in the ovum is more common with increase in the age of the mother, particularly over thirty-five, but abnormal sperm appear to be less related to a father's age. While either parent can contribute the extra chromosome at any age, the older a couple is, the more likely the contribution is made by the mother.

The risk for Down syndrome varies according to maternal age as follows:

	Age			
	20–24	25–29	30	33
Live births	one per 1,352	1/1,133	1/885	1/592
	35	37	40	42
Live births	1/365	1/225	1/109	1/67

The age of thirty-five has been chosen as the usual cutoff point on a cost–benefit analysis for routine fetal chromosome testing based on maternal age alone. This analysis takes into account the costs, to society as a whole, of screening and therapeutic abortion of affected fetuses (as well as the risks of the procedure itself; see pp. 321–322) as balanced against the costs of lifetime care for affected individuals. Markers for increased risk of Down syndrome for women under thirty-five include low maternal serum levels of alpha-fetoprotein (AFP) (see p. 66), unconjugated estriol, and human chorionic gonadotropin. The AFP test is the most widely available. Use of these markers combined with chromosomal studies leads to identification of most affected fetuses. However, many affected fetuses will still be missed.

At present the only way to come close to 100 percent detection would be through chromosomal analysis of all fetuses through amniocentesis (see pp. 139–141) or chorionic villous sampling (CVS) (see pp. 141–142). (Analysis of trophoblasts from the placenta circulating in the mother's blood [see p. 143] is still experimental.) Such a program of detection would be very costly and would result in many unintended miscarriages of normal fetuses because of the risks of the procedures themselves (see pp. 142–

143). On the other hand, even though the frequency of affected fetuses increases with maternal age, most babies with Down syndrome are born to younger women simply because younger women have most of the babies who are born. Hence, our current practice of testing only those younger women considered to be at increased risk based on the markers currently used leaves something to be desired if the goal is the detection of all fetuses with Down syndrome. Parents who are concerned about this question may want to explore it further.

In about one Down syndrome child in fifty, a different type of chromosomal abnormality has occurred, indicating that one of the child's parents is a carrier of a *balanced translocation* (see p. 132). In this particular type of translocation, part of one of the number 21 chromosome pair has split off to join another chromosome.

When a Down syndrome child is born, cytogenetic analysis of the child is required to determine if the nondisjunction type or the translocation type is involved. If the translocation type of chromosomal abnormality is found, the parents and their close relatives should also be checked to see if they, too, have the translocation. In either situation, the parents need genetic education and counseling to understand their child's condition and to plan for future pregnancies.

There are several other well-recognized chromosomal abnormalities. In the disorder known as *Klinefelter's syndrome*, males have an extra X chromosome. Instead of being XY, they are XXY. The disorder becomes manifest usually in adolescence, when the testes fail to develop and growth of the breasts occurs. Puberty may be delayed. The abnormal testes produce neither sperm nor testosterone, the male sex hormone. About 8 to 10 percent of these boys are mentally retarded (usually mildly). Treatment consists of psychological counseling and the administration of sufficient male sex hormones to promote sexual development. Klinefelter's syndrome occurs in about 2 males per 1,000 in the population and is more common in the pregnancies of women over forty.

In *Turner's syndrome*, which affects females, an X chromosome is missing; such girls have only one X instead of two. The disorder occurs in about 1 in 2,500 live-born females and in about 5 percent of aborted fetuses. Individuals with Turner's syndrome fail to mature sexually at puberty because their ovaries do not develop.

A disorder that is the leading cause of inherited mental retardation is known as the fragile X syndrome, so named because one or both tips of the X chromosome are partly or completely detached from the body of the chromosome. Identifying the disorder through chromosome analysis has been problematic because the fragile site has not been easily demonstrable. The difficulty in its demonstration has varied according to the age of the person being studied and has often required elaborate techniques. A recent major breakthrough, by researchers at Emory University, is the isolation of the specific abnormal gene. This discovery will lead to a much more thorough understanding not only of the distribution of the gene in human populations but also of the relationship between the gene and symptoms of disease and between the gene and the fragile X chromosome. (Some individuals with a fragile X chromosome, for reasons not yet understood, apparently have no symptoms at all.) It will greatly improve prenatal diagnosis.

Based on chromosome studies, fragile X affects 1 in 1,000 males and 1 in 2,500 females, which means that it is *very* common. (Because it is an X chromosome–linked disorder, more males would be expected to be affected and more seriously affected). When genes rather than chromosomes are studied, even more people will probably be found to have the abnormal gene than has been thought to be the case.

At puberty some males with a fragile X chromosome have, in addition to retardation, large testicles (three to four times the average size), prominent chins, large ears, and often an enlarged head size. In additional to mental retardation and learning problems, fragile X may account for a certain percentage of other serious mental disorders such as autism and schizophrenia. The apparent commonness of the gene, coupled with its seriousness, will probably fuel the argument for genetic testing of all pregnant women and their partners.

GENETIC COUNSELING

Genetic counseling involves knowledge of both the principles discussed in this chapter and the principles of making decisions under conditions in which outcomes are uncertain. This kind of decision making involves knowing the probabilities of outcomes and how they mesh with one's values (see pp. 29–31).

Questions involving genetics arise in families in several ways. When a baby with a congenital abnormality is born, or when there is a stillbirth, parents understandably seek to find out the cause of the defect and the chances of recurrence. Recurrent miscarriages also raise the question of a genetic cause. Those who should seek counseling include the following:

1. Couples who already have a child with some serious defect, such as Down syndrome, spina bifida, congenital heart disease, a malformed limb, or mental retardation
2. Couples with a family history of a genetic disease or mental retardation
3. Couples who are blood relatives (first or second cousins)
4. Blacks, Ashkenazic Jews, Italians, Greeks, and other high-risk ethnic groups
5. Women who have had a serious infection early in pregnancy (rubella or toxoplasmosis) or who have been infected with the AIDS virus (pp. 166–174)
6. Women who have inadvertently taken some potentially harmful medication early in pregnancy, or who habitually take certain drugs (pp. 160–161), including alcohol (see pp. 176–178)
7. Women who have had multiple X rays taken early in pregnancy
8. Women who have had two or more of the following in any combination: stillbirths, deaths of newborn babies, miscarriages
9. Any woman thirty-five years or older (see p. 135 for full discussion)
10. Women who have had a screening test that is positive for a genetic disease, for example, a consistently elevated blood alpha-fetoprotein level (see pp. 64–66)

Ideally, a careful genetic history should be part of every premarital health checkup before children are planned. It should be done, at the latest, early in the first pregnancy. Certainly, the birth of a baby with a congenital problem should occasion a careful family history. The study of any stillborn baby for genetic defects is also important. We can improve the quality of our genetic histories by preparing and keeping up-to-date family trees and family medical histories. The better the data, the better the genetic counseling and prediction that can be offered. (See pp. 37–39, "Your History.")

Genetic counseling may be obtained at most large medical centers and, without exception, at university teaching hospitals. Family physicians, pediatricians, and obstetricians are all good sources of information on genetic disorders and possible courses of action. A registry of counseling centers is maintained by the March of Dimes (see Appendix C).

The discussion of specific genetic disorders given in this chapter is far from exhaustive; only the more commonly encountered problems have been considered. (See Appendix C for further reading.)

Tests

AMNIOCENTESIS

Amniocentesis is the procedure of passing a needle through the abdominal wall into the uterus and amniotic cavity of a pregnant woman to obtain amniotic fluid for study. By means of amniocentesis it is possible to identify a fetus afflicted with certain inherited disorders (pp. 125–139); to assess the maturity of the fetal lungs when preterm delivery is under consideration (pp. 329–336); and, in some cases, to provide medical treatment before birth (see pp. 157–159).

Amniocentesis for inherited disorders is generally performed between fourteen and sixteen weeks, but increasingly it is being offered earlier, between eleven and fourteen weeks, thereby making it, in this respect, more competitive with chorionic villous sampling (see pp. 141–142). When amniocentesis is performed to test for amniotic alpha-fetoprotein (see pp. 64–66), it is usually done between sixteen and eighteen weeks because of increased validity of the chemical tests after the sixteenth week.

Before an amniocentesis, the uterus and fetus are examined

with ultrasound to find the site of the placenta (to avoid puncturing it), to check for the presence of twins (each of whose sacs may need to be entered), and to verify the gestational age of the fetus. The woman's abdomen is washed with antiseptic solution and draped with sterile towels. The skin is numbed with a local anesthetic. Under ultrasonic guidance, to avoid injuring the fetus or the placenta, a hollow needle three to six inches long is passed into the uterus. Amniotic fluid is withdrawn through a syringe attached to the needle. Occasionally, no fluid is obtained after the first pass with the needle, and another attempt is made. If the second pass also fails, the usual policy is to stop and wait a week before trying again.

When amniocentesis is performed for chromosomal and gene analysis, the amniotic fluid obtained is separated in a centrifuge into cell-rich and cell-free layers. The cell-free layer is subjected to biochemical tests and may be cultured for microorganisms. The cell-rich part, containing about 10 to 100 living cells, can be studied directly to determine the sex of the fetus and the presence of certain enzymes. More often the cells are cultured; in a few weeks the harvested cells can be studied biochemically and genetically. Two million cells are required for certain biochemical tests, while 100,000 are enough for chromosomal analysis.

In about 10 percent of women more than one amniocentesis must be done, either because of failure to obtain fluid on the first attempt or technical failure of the laboratory to process the sample. If the fluid contains blood, it may be unsuitable for certain analyses, and a new sample will have to be obtained.

Minor complications occur in about 1 out of 100 procedures: uterine cramping, vaginal bleeding (from the uterus), and leaking of amniotic fluid through the vagina. In the rare event that the fetus is pricked, the result can be a permanent skin dimple.

More serious complications can occur. Even in the most experienced hands, amniocentesis appears to carry the risk of about one-half of 1 percent for miscarriage, maternal bleeding at birth, or injury to the fetus. In any case, for women over thirty-five, the risk of the fetus's carrying a chromosomal abnormality is between two to five times the highest estimated risk of pregnancy loss as a result of amniocentesis.

The inadvertent puncturing of the placenta may lead to transfer of fetal red blood cells into the mother's circulation. If the mother is Rh(D) negative and the fetus Rh(D) positive, the mother can be stimulated to produce antibodies to the transferred fetal cells (pp. 57–59), which can destroy the baby's red blood cells. Because of this potential complication, all Rh(D) negative mothers of Rh(D) positive fetuses are considered candidates for RhoGAM, the anti-Rh(D) antibody that binds to Rh(D) positive fetal cells in the mother's circulation, causing their removal before maternal sensitization.

Several problems in chromosomal analysis may lead to either no answer or an uncertain result after amniocentesis. For one, the cell culture may fail altogether. Few good laboratories have failure rates exceeding 5 percent. If cells from the mother have been shed into the amniotic fluid, these may grow out in the culture and be mistaken for those of the fetus. This problem occurs in about 1 to 2 per 1,000 studies. If male cells are grown from the fluid, they must of necessity be from the fetus; but if female cells grow, there is a possibility that they are those of the mother rather than those of the fetus. Accordingly, a separate chromosomal analysis of the mother's blood cells is recommended for comparison with the chromosomes of the cells grown from the amniotic fluid. (Another way of identifying a male fetus is to measure testosterone levels in the amniotic fluid.)

Laboratory errors are not completely avoidable, even in the best of hands, and can result in aborting a normal fetus or allowing an abnormal one to continue to term. The error rate for prenatal diagnosis, however, is remarkably low, ranging from 0.2 percent to 0.6 percent. For many couples, the waiting period—one and one-half to two weeks—is a time of increased anxiety. For most, however, their risks and anxiety are well balanced by their peace of mind when certain very serious abnormalities of the developing fetus have been ruled out.

CHORIONIC VILLOUS SAMPLING

Chorionic villous sampling (CVS) is a painless procedure that can be performed in the hospital or a doctor's office as early as the fifth week of pregnancy. In the most common approach, a thin, hollow tube (catheter) is inserted into the uterus through the vagina, or through the abdominal wall, and guided by ultrasound or by hysteroscope (a fiberoptic viewing tube) into a position between the uterine lining and the *chorion*, a tissue layer that surrounds the embryo for the first two months of its development and then develops into the placenta. A syringe attached to the tube sucks up several of the *chorionic villi*, projections of tissue that transfer oxygen, food, and waste between the mother's circulation and that of the embryo and are genetically identical with the embryo. Analysis of the cells of the villi thus reveals the genetic endowment of the fetus. Certain kinds of cell analysis can be done on the same day, thereby enabling couples at times to avoid the anxiety of the long wait for the results of amniocentesis.

AMNIOCENTESIS AND CHORIONIC VILLOUS SAMPLING COMPARED

Until recently there have been no randomized control studies that compare CVS with amniocentesis. Caution has therefore been needed in interpreting the results of existing nonrandomized control studies. One of the largest studies to date (reported in the 9 March 1989 issue of the *New England Journal of Medicine*) compared 2,278 first-trimester CVS's with 671 amniocenteses performed at sixteen weeks of gestation. Successful cytogenetic diagnoses resulted for 97.8 percent of the CVS's and 99.4 percent of the amniocenteses; 0.8 percent of the women who had had a CVS later needed an amniocentesis to clarify an uncertain initial result. The rate of combined fetal losses due to spontaneous abortions, termination of abnormal pregnancies, stillbirths, and neonatal deaths was 7.2 percent with CVS and 5.7 percent with amniocentesis. The combined pregnancy loss with CVS exceeded that with amniocentesis by 0.8 percent, possibly representing complications of the procedure itself. However, the difference was so small that it probably is not significant. Other nonrandomized studies, not discussed here, have yielded similar findings, but there are differences in outcomes from one institution to another.

The first (and, at the time of this writing, only) randomized control study was reported in June 1991 in the *Lancet*. It involved

3,248 European women cared for in medical centers in several countries. The most significant finding was that women who had an amniocentesis had 4.6 percent more babies who survived than women who had a CVS; 91 percent of the women who had an amniocentesis delivered a live baby, in comparison with 86 percent of those who had a CVS. This study suggests that CVS, as an effect (complication) of the procedure itself, is slightly more likely to result in a fetal death sometime during the pregnancy than is amniocentesis. (In the CVS group there were more spontaneous fetal deaths before twenty-eight weeks' gestation [2.9 percent], more terminations of pregnancy for chromosomal abnormalities [1.0 percent], and more neonatal [at the time of birth] deaths [0.3 percent].) These are important findings because of the design and quality of the study, and they will allow parents to make more discriminating decisions about the two procedures. As found in other studies, about 1 percent of the CVS's had to be followed by amniocenteses to clarify uncertain chromosomal analyses. However, a recent (1992) multicenter study organized by Jefferson Medical College in Philadelphia (designed to look at a different question—the comparative safety of transcervical and transabdominal CVS) showed *no* differences in miscarriages after CVS compared with the best results following amniocentesis, underlining the importance of checking the statistics of the physician who will actually be doing the procedure.

As previously mentioned, CVS makes chromosome analyses possible on the same day, while results after amniocentesis require up to two weeks. On the other hand, an amniocentesis may have to be done anyway after a CVS (about 1 percent of the time) because of uncertain results. Performing amniocenteses in the first trimester (yet to be critically evaluated) narrows some of the difference between the procedures with respect to the earliest gestational age at which a diagnosis can be made.

Amniocentesis is easier for doctors to learn and is therefore more generally available than CVS, which is performed at only a few specialized maternity hospitals. When it comes to your own care, as with all procedures related to pregnancy, I encourage you to ask about the individual outcome statistics of the particular physician or clinical service you are considering.

A still-experimental but promising diagnostic procedure in

chromosomal analysis is the study of trophoblasts (see p. 51) normally found circulating in a pregnant mother's blood, readily obtained by venipuncture (drawing of blood from a vein, usually in the arm). Because trophoblasts have the same chromosomes and genes as the fetus, studying them (assuming that the technical details can be worked out) could provide the same genetic information as CVS or amniocentesis at far less risk, cost, and inconvenience.

WHAT A WOMAN CAN TELL

During recent years there has been some interest is seeing whether women on their own can assist in identifying fetuses in difficulty by counting the number of fetal movements that occur in a set time period. To date, studies have provided mixed results, and such self-monitoring has not become an established part of prenatal care.

We suggest that any woman who notices a *significant decrease in fetal activity,* even if she cannot precisely describe it, report this promptly to her doctor or birth attendant. An increase in activity, on the other hand, is probably a good sign and has not been shown to predict fetal problems.

PRINCIPLES OF FETAL MONITORING

Because there is some controversy surrounding fetal monitoring, it is good to know a few basic facts about its methods and purpose. Heart rate and oxygen supply are the main concerns:

1. The fetal heart rate reflects fetal oxygen supply, which depends on the delivery of oxygen to the placenta from the mother's circulation and the function of the placenta itself.
2. Contraction of the uterus temporarily cuts off the blood supply to the placenta, enabling the fetus to draw only on oxygen already present in the placenta at the time of onset of the contraction.
3. The fetus whose oxygen supply is already borderline when the

uterus is not contracting will be tipped into a state of oxygen deprivation during a contraction. This lack of oxygen will be reflected in a prolonged slowing of the fetal heart rate with slow recovery.

During a uterine contraction the fetal heart rate normally slows in response to pressure on the fetal head and returns to its baseline as the contraction ends. In electronic fetal monitoring terms, this is called an *early deceleration.* However, given an inadequately functioning placenta and a marginal oxygen supply to the fetus to begin with, a contraction will tip the fetus into a state of oxygen deprivation, and the heart rate will drop. It will not recover until well after the contraction is over. In the language of monitoring, this is called a *late deceleration.* A third kind of deceleration, called *variable deceleration,* bears no consistent relationship to uterine contractions. It is believed that this pattern is caused by compression of the umbilical cord due to pressure by the baby or twisting. The precise mechanism of these three most important monitor patterns is not entirely clear.

Normally, the fetal heart beats at a baseline rate of between 110 and 150 to 160 beats per minute. A rate of 100 to 110 is termed *mild bradycardia* (literally, "slow heart"), and a rate less than 100 is called *marked bradycardia. Tachycardia* (literally, "fast heart") is termed "mild" if the heart rate ranges from 160 to 180 and "marked" if it is greater than 180.

Tachycardia alone is not an indication of fetal distress, since it may be due to maternal fever, drugs given to the mother, or intrinsic abnormalities in the rhythm of the fetus's heart. Similarly, mild bradycardia without other changes is not necessarily a sign of fetal distress. Severe bradycardia has several causes, among them congenital heart defects in the fetus, sudden lowering of the blood pressure in a pregnant woman with hypertension, or decreased oxygen supply to the fetus.

Another term used in connection with electronic fetal monitoring is *variability,* which refers to the variation in heart rate from beat to beat. When a fetus is awake and healthy, its heart rate speeds up and slows from second to second. Although these changes are probably too subtle to detect simply by listening to the heart with a stethoscope, the internal fetal monitor, which produces a printout of the fetus's electrocardiogram (see the next section), graphically displays variability. Decreased variability is observed in a fetus that is asleep, in an otherwise-normal premature infant, in babies whose mothers are medicated with drugs such as Demerol, morphine, and Nisentil, and in those who are experiencing distress.

INTERMITTENT MONITORING

The traditional way to monitor the fetal heart rate is to listen with a stethoscope or, more recently, with a hand-held ultrasound device called a Doppler (after its inventor). With practice, skilled attendants can use a stethoscope in much the same way they can an electronic monitor. They can follow heart-rate patterns through a contraction and thereby identify the normality or abnormality of the pattern. Monitoring with a stethoscope can also be used in the nonstress test (see pp. 149–150).

CONTINUOUS ELECTRONIC FETAL MONITORING

Continuous electronic fetal monitoring (EFM) records uterine contractions and the fetal heart rate over time. The uterine contractions are measured by a pressure gauge strapped to the mother's abdomen. The changing shape of the uterus during a contraction is sensed and transmitted as electrical signals, activating a needle that imprints a lumpy line (blip) on a rolling strip of graph paper. The fetal heart rate can be picked up either by an *external* ultrasound monitor placed on the abdomen over the uterus or *internally* by a wire—leading through the vagina and attached to the fetal scalp—that produces an electrocardiogram tracing. (The electrical impulse associated with heart contraction spreads throughout the fetus's body. A sensor placed on any part of its body—in this case, the scalp—detects the impulses generated by the heart and provides accurate information about heart rate.) In measuring the variability of the heart rate, the internal (EKG) monitor has a decided advantage over the external (ultrasound) monitor.

The electrode commonly used for internal monitoring is attached to the fetus by twisting the corkscrew-shaped wires at its tip into the scalp. It is likely that the baby feels this jab, although we know, from observations made on newborns receiving injections or having blood drawn, that the pain is probably experienced for only a short time.

Complications of internal fetal monitoring are rare, but not insignificant. They include infection of the scalp of the fetus at the site of attachment of the electrode; damage to fetal blood vessels, with resulting hemorrhage in the case of a low-lying placenta (see pp. 323–324 on placenta praevia); and an increased risk of infection within the amniotic cavity.

An important practical issue connected with internal fetal monitoring is that the woman must lie in bed for as long as the wires are attached. Telemetry systems, in which the fetal heart rate is broadcast to the monitor without maintaining connections by wire, have been developed, but such attractive systems are not widely available.

COMPARISON OF INTERMITTENT AND CONTINUOUS ELECTRONIC FETAL MONITORING

To date, there have been nine randomized control studies involving over 17,000 labors (including labors at term and preterm) that compared a group of women whose fetuses were intermittently monitored (listened to every fifteen minutes during the first stage and every five minutes during the second stage of labor) with a group whose fetuses received continuous electronic fetal monitoring. Fetal pH scalp sampling (see pp. 154–155) was available in all of these labors as needed.

These studies did not demonstrate any differences between the groups in the initial newborn assessment at the time of birth, in the number of deaths of babies around the time of birth, or in the number of infants requiring care in the intensive care units of the hospitals. In the largest study reported, one difference, whose significance is unclear, was that, for reasons unknown, more intermittently monitored babies, especially those whose mothers received Pitocin (the trade name for oxytocin, a hormone) to stimulate their labor, had a convulsion during the newborn period. However, there was no difference between the groups in the proportion of babies with seizures who survived. Nor was there any difference between the groups in the frequency of cerebral palsy or in the mental or neurological development of the babies as of their fourth birthdays. Nonetheless, some authorities are still concerned about the increased incidence of seizures and conclude that a case can be made for continuous monitoring when a labor can be characterized as unusual in some way, for example, in requiring Pitocin stimulation. Interestingly, for reasons not well understood, continuously electronically monitored fetuses were more likely by about a third to be delivered by cesarean section or by forceps. In summary, either method of monitoring appears acceptable, with intermittent monitoring appearing to have a significant edge in preventing operative delivery and continuous monitoring *possibly* more advantageous in complicated labors.

None of the studies to date have included women who had had a previous cesarean section and were attempting a vaginal birth. However, there is no reason to believe that the outcomes would be different. The American College of Obstetrics and Gynecology approves of both ways of monitoring and has even more liberal requirements for frequency of intermittent listening during the first stage—every thirty minutes. More studies are needed to define the optimal frequency of intermittent monitoring as well as special circumstances when one or the other approach is superior.

There are no studies that compare the time it takes to monitor by the two approaches. A common view is that continuous electronic monitoring requires less staff time: one nurse (in this era of shortages of nurses) can watch several patients. I find it hard to believe that there is any significant difference in the time required to listen and the time required to review a tracing, assuming that the tracing is being reviewed in a timely manner. (If it is not, what good is it?) With respect to dividing a nurse's attention among several patients, it is worth noting that the best outcome statistics among babies and mothers are achieved in settings where there is one-on-one continuous attention by a birth attendant who monitors intermittently (see pp. 199–201).

Many obstetricians have operated under the belief that a fetal monitor tracing would protect them in a malpractice suit brought for a sick baby. It is unclear whether this view is valid or whether, to the contrary, the tracing becomes a "smoking gun" that incriminates them.

One limitation of continuous electronic fetal monitoring is lack of agreement even among authorities about the significance of certain heart-rate patterns. This uncertainty probably has contributed to overdiagnosing of fetal distress and may be a factor in the higher incidence of operative deliveries seen in electronically monitored babies.

Several aspects of the history of continuous electronic fetal monitoring are worthy of comment. First, this technology, which is quite expensive, was introduced and was widely adopted in hospitals (but *not* in birth centers or home births) *before* comparison studies were done. Advocates of the technology claimed and persuaded others that it was superior to intermittent listening. Even after the first research results showed no differences in the well-being of babies, along with a higher operative delivery rate, the technology continued to spread. And the "no difference" findings of the studies to date have still not resulted in a significant return to the less expensive intermittent monitoring. Thus, until very recently, the history of the use of this technology has been characterized by practitioners not insisting on scientific proof in the first place and then disregarding such evidence when available. I sincerely hope that in the future the medical profession and the federal government will *insist* on a standard of proven effectiveness *before* a new technology is adopted, thus preventing such gaps between research findings and actual practice.

NONSTRESS TESTING AND FETAL BIOPHYSICAL PROFILE

The basic principle of nonstress testing (NST) is that a healthy fetus's heart rate will increase in response to movement of the body. In the standard method of performing the test, an external fetal monitor detects the fetus's heart rate by ultrasound while a continuous recording of the heartbeat over twelve minutes is printed out on a moving strip of paper. When the mother feels a kick, she depresses a switch, which identifies the movement on the paper with a mark that can be related to the fetal heart rate at the time. The most widely accepted standard of normality (there is lack of agreement on this point) is two accelerations of fifteen beats per minute lasting fifteen seconds per ten minutes. A normal test is known as "negative," or "reactive." An abnormal test is also known as "positive" or "nonreactive."

Another version of this test involves simply clocking the fetal heart rate with a stethoscope over five minutes. The fetus is considered to be reactive when a single acceleration of fifteen beats per minute lasting ten seconds is observed. This form of the nonstress test is less expensive than ultrasound monitoring and more readily available. It may also have advantages over the use of ultrasound in women with obesity or hydramnios (p. 311), in whom the ultrasound waves are dampened by the intervening fat and/or fluid.

The nonstress test is a reasonably good screening test for fetuses at high risk for distress. In a low-risk fetus the high false positive rate will result in an unacceptably high rate of unnecessary intervention. In fetuses at high risk, it is usually combined with ultrasound assessment of amniotic fluid volume along with fetal body tone and limb and breathing movements into what is called the fetal biophysical profile. This study is thought to predict fetal well-being as accurately as the contraction stress test (discussed in the next section) and is much easier to administer.

CONTRACTION STRESS TESTING

Contraction stress testing involves monitoring the fetal heart rate with an external monitor while the uterus contracts spontaneously or is stimulated to contract with intravenously administered oxytocin. (Remember that internal fetal monitoring is used only with women in labor because of the need to rupture the amniotic membranes.) The contraction stress test is done in the labor and delivery sections of hospitals and is usually performed on women and fetuses who have failed the nonstress test. It takes from one to two hours. For fifteen to thirty minutes, "baseline" uterine activity and the fetal heart rate are recorded along with fetal movements. If spontaneous uterine contractions lasting forty to sixty seconds occur approximately three times in ten minutes, the test can be done without oxytocin stimulation. In the absence of demonstrable uterine activity, oxytocin is infused to produce such contractions.

The correlation between a negative contraction stress test and a favorable outcome is good. Positive contraction stress tests are divided into nonreactive and reactive groups. Both exhibit a significant increase in the incidence of intrauterine growth retardation, low five-minute Apgar scores (see pp. 235–236), and fetal distress during labor in comparison with fetuses whose contraction stress tests are negative.

If the test is positive, labor can still be normal and, on the average, will be so about 25 percent of the time, depending on the study reviewed. About 7 percent of tests do not yield clearcut results and must be repeated the next day.

Despite the widespread use of nonstress and contraction stress tests and the biophysical profile, there is no evidence that they have had an impact on the well-being of babies. They must be regarded as still experimental. Two other still-experimental, but promising, tests of fetal well-being during labor measure the response of the fetal heart rate to a loud sound transmitted through the abdominal wall or, after the amniotic sac is broken, to pinching of the fetal scalp with a padded surgical clamp. A response is considered normal when there is an increase in the heart rate.

ULTRASOUND

Ultrasound (sonography), a constantly improving diagnostic technology, is having a major impact on maternity care and medical practice in general. Its origins date to World War II, when high-frequency sound waves were first used to detect enemy submarines. The echoes of sound waves beamed into the water were reflected back from any object encountered, to be "heard" by electronic sensors.

The use of sound waves in medicine follows the same principle. Intermittent high-frequency (inaudible to the human ear) sound waves are generated by applying an alternating current to a device known as a transducer. A transmitting solution like mineral oil is placed on the skin, and the transducer is applied. In its use in pregnancy, the transducer sends pulsations of sound through the mother's abdomen to the interior of the uterus.

As the sound waves penetrate tissues of different composition (fetal skull and brain or amniotic fluid and fetal skull, for example), some of the sound energy is reflected (echoed) back to the transducer. The transducer alternates rapidly between emitting (sending) and receiving (listening) states. In the listening state, the echoes received generate a small electrical voltage, which is amplified and displayed on a black-and-white television screen. Thus, the ultrasound technique identifies the location of anatomic structures by measuring how long it takes for ultrasound waves to reach them, be reflected at the interface between them and other structures, and return to the sensor. The echoes can also be converted into audible sounds, making it possible to "hear" the beating of the fetal heart.

Ultrasound can be used in several ways. It can measure the size of a structure such as the fetal head, which is useful in dating a pregnancy, and it can follow the growth of the fetus. It can produce a cross-sectional picture or "slice" of the fetal body. A "slice" through the fetal abdomen can show the size and location of the organs inside. A "slice" through the brain can identify the ventricles (fluid-filled cavities), providing information about their normality or enlargement (*hydrocephalus*). Ultrasound can be used to observe actual movements of fetal structures such as the beating of the heart, emptying of the bladder, movements of the chest, and sucking of the thumb. (See "Fetal Biophysical Profile," pp. 149–150.)

The clinical applications of ultrasound include the following:

1. Identifying an embryo in order to diagnose pregnancy
2. Monitoring the growth of the fetus
3. Determining whether a fetus has or has not been aborted (pp. 320–322)
4. Determining a tubal (ectopic) pregnancy (pp. 304–309)
5. Identifying multiple pregnancies (pp. 338–341) and fetal position (see pp. 277–283, "Breech Presentation")
6. Identifying fetal abnormalities such as meningomyelocele, hydrocephalus, or limb defects (pp. 130–131)
7. Locating the placenta and determining placental abnormalities (pp. 323–324 on placenta praevia)

8. Measuring the amniotic fluid (see pp. 311–312 on hydramnios and oligohydramnios)
9. Guiding needle insertion in amniocentesis (pp. 139–140)
10. Measuring the fetal heart rate during prenatal visits (p. 49), stress and nonstress tests (pp. 149–151), and labor
11. Treating the fetus before birth (pp. 157–159)
12. Identifying the umbilical blood vessels to obtain fetal blood samples (see p. 156)

A still experimental use of ultrasound is measuring the pulsations of the mother's arteries, which deliver blood to uterus and placenta, and of the fetal arteries in the umbilical cord, which deliver blood from the fetus to the placenta. Measurement of what is called the velocity wave force of these arteries holds the promise of being one of the best ways to identify fetuses at risk for illness in utero.

The question of the safety of ultrasound is of concern. All that can be said to date is that there is no evidence of fetal abnormalities related to its use. Nor have changes been observed in living cells in tissue culture after exposure to the doses used in humans. However, ultrasound has been in use in pregnancy in a major way only for the last fifteen years or so, a relatively short period for follow-up studies. Concern has been expressed about possible harm not only to the developing fetus but also to the ovaries of the mother and the ovaries of the female fetus as well. These important concerns are at present hypothetical and not based on any evidence.

Despite the fact that ultrasound examination is increasingly being used in all pregnancies, whether or not a specific indication exists, studies to date of performing a single routine ultrasound test or two tests, one early and one late in pregnancy, have not indicated that outcomes for babies are improved. The studies do show that such routine testing leads to earlier identification of twins, revision of the expected date of delivery, and earlier detection of fetuses with congenital malformations. In the case of severe malformation early detection allows for early abortion as an option. How often routine ultrasound detects a malformation that is surgically correctable in utero (see pp. 158–159) is not yet known. Because ultrasound is an expensive technology in an era of runaway medical costs, determining its effectiveness and weighing that against its cost during routine prenatal care are important steps—ones that should have been done *before* its widespread adoption.

How much can be learned from ultrasound depends on the resolution power of the equipment and the skills of the tester. Most of the tests done in obstetricians' offices are useful for determining fetal age, the number of fetuses, and the presence of gross malformations. Detailed studies of fetal anatomy (including more subtle malformations) and function (such as breathing and swallowing) require more complex machines and more specialized observers. Each level of testing has its own place and goals.

The experience by parents-to-be of seeing ultrasound images of their babies has introduced a new graphic dimension into the fetal–parental relationship. New family albums often open with a streaky ultrasound portrait.

FETAL SCALP BLOOD PH TESTING

One measure of the well-being of the fetus is the amount of oxygen in its blood, supplied by the placenta. Since the fetal heart rate reflects oxygen supply to the heart, it is a good, although indirect, measure of blood oxygen. More precise monitoring would measure oxygen level itself. While work is under way to use the internal fetal monitor to obtain such data, at present the closest measure of fetal oxygen is the closely related acidity of the blood, measured by what is called the pH.

In order to perform this test, an endoscope (illuminated tube) is inserted through the cervix and pressed against the baby's head. The skin is then wiped clean with a cotton swab, sprayed with ethyl chloride to stimulate increased blood flow, and coated with a silicon gel to cause the blood to coalesce as easily collected globules. Immediately after a uterine contraction, one or two tiny cuts are made through the skin to a predetermined depth. The blood is collected immediately in a long, pointed glass tube and analyzed.

In general, a pH reading of 7.25 or greater (i.e., more alkaline, as opposed to acidic) is considered to be normal, 7.20 to 7.24 borderline, and less than 7.20 abnormal and indicative of too little oxygen in the blood. In general, the baby should then be delivered promptly. However, the test is not always reliable. Rarely, pH results with "high" readings can be associated with hypoxia, and some "low" ones can be associated with normal oxygen values. A deceptively low reading, which indicates danger when there is none, can occur when the baby's scalp is swollen and the blood is not circulating well, when the blood of the mother is too acid, or when the blood sample is inadvertently taken from the mother rather than the fetus.

The pH can be deceptively normal under the influence of pain medications and anesthetics given to the mother, as well as when infection is present, when the blood of the mother is alkaline, when the baby has certain congenital anomalies, and when the blood sample is obtained at times other than immediately after a contraction.

Overall, if a fetus's scalp blood pH is normal, there is an 80 percent chance of a good Apgar score (see pp. 235–236) after delivery and a 20 percent chance of a low Apgar score. On the other hand, if the pH is too low, there is a 60 percent chance that the Apgar score will be low. Thus, while the scalp blood pH test is very useful, it is a far-from-perfect means of identifying babies who are stressed.

At present, pH testing is used to check babies with abnormal fetal monitor traces and as a result, improves the ability to detect the fetus at risk. Fetal scalp sampling should not be done when a fetus is suspect for hemophilia or when the mother has an infection that could be transmitted to the fetus at the electrode site: herpes (pp. 171–172), HIV (pp. 61–63), hepatitis (pp. 63–64), gonorrhea (pp. 169–170), or group B streptococcus (p. 170).

THE L/S RATIO

Late in normal pregnancy certain cells in the fetal lung produce fat-rich chemicals that coat the inner walls of the air sacs, which are, of course, collapsed prior to birth. This coating prevents the sacs from sticking together after respiration begins following birth. A major problem for premature babies, particularly those of less than thirty-two weeks' gestation, is that these surface chemicals have not yet been produced. Without treatment such babies develop *respiratory distress syndrome.*

Some of the surface chemicals produced by the fetal lung are washed up through the airways to the mouth and out into the amniotic fluid, which can be examined by amniocentesis (see pp. 139–141). Two of the chemicals secreted are lecithin (L) and sphingomyelin (S). The ratio between these two (the L/S ratio) is a good predictor of maturity of the lungs.

An L/S ratio of greater than 2.0 indicates that the risk of respiratory distress is slight, unless the mother is diabetic, the fetus has an illness caused by incompatibility between its blood type and that of its mother (see pp. 57–59), or the fetus is very sick for any reason at the time of testing. In newborns, for whom the L/S ratio is 1.5 to 2.0, respiratory distress will occur 40 percent of the time; if it is below 1.5, distress occurs 73 percent of the time.

Thus, the L/S ratio is a useful, although imperfect, measure of fetal lung maturity. Whenever preterm delivery is considered, as, for example, in suspected intrauterine growth disturbance (see pp. 312–315), the risk of continued intrauterine life must be weighed against the dangers of prematurity, particularly the respiratory distress syndrome. The L/S ratio helps in this decision. Babies who are candidates for early delivery, but whose lungs are immature, can be treated with steroids to hasten maturation of the lungs (see p. 158).

FETAL BLOOD SAMPLING

Blood from the fetus for diagnostic purposes can now be obtained under ultrasound guidance by passing a needle (attached to a syringe) through the mother's abdominal wall and the wall of the uterus into the fetus's umbilical vessels. The fetal blood can be analyzed for various characteristics, including such diseases of the blood cells as sickle-cell anemia (see p. 128) and thalassemia (see p. 129), chromosomal abnormalities, blood protein deficits as in hemophilia, platelet deficiencies (see pp. 132–137, 325–326), and antibodies to infectious agents such as toxoplasmosis (see pp. 173–174) and cytomegalovirus (see pp. 167–168).

With the information obtained from the fetus's blood, physicians can make decisions regarding therapy. In some instances treatment may be administered using the ultrasound-and-needle technique, for example, in transfusing blood cells into the umbilical cord of a very anemic fetus (see below). Before doing the procedure, the physician should talk with the mother about the risks of fetal blood sampling for her and for the fetus.

Treating the Fetus

Of all recent developments in prenatal care, one of the most exciting is that of actually treating an ill fetus. As noted in the preceding section, our capacity to judge how well the fetus is developing and to take action, or to leave things alone, based on the information obtained, has grown enormously in recent years. The field of *fetal medicine* has come into its own. In the following discussion I will touch on the highlights of this developing field, focusing on the active treatment of the unborn.

One of the oldest treatments involves the fetus whose survival is threatened by anemia and heart failure, most commonly caused by incompatibility of the blood types of mother and fetus (pp. 57–59). Such a fetus can be saved by blood transfusions performed in utero. Blood cells are injected into the fetus's abdominal cavity or into an umbilical blood vessel through a needle that has been passed, under ultrasonic guidance, through the mother's skin, abdomen, uterus, and amniotic fluid. Several such transfusions may be needed to assure the survival of the fetus.

Treatment of the fetus can involve medication. For example, antibiotics are used to treat a mother and fetus with syphilis (p. 173). Fetuses with heart failure (also detectable by ultrasound) caused by rapid heart action (*tachycardia*) have been treated successfully by giving digitalis, which slows heart rate, to their mothers. The digitalis crosses the placenta to the fetus. Fetuses with underfunctioning thyroid glands (*hypothyroidism*) and goiter (enlargement of the thyroid) have been successfully treated by injecting thyroid hormone directly into the amniotic fluid. In swallowing the amniotic fluid, the fetus also swallows the hormone, which is absorbed into the body. Similarly, overfunctioning of the fetal thyroid gland (*hyperthyroidism*) has been prevented by administering to the mother (and thereby to the fetus) a drug to decrease thyroid activity. If accomplishing premature birth is necessary, usually because of a need to end a pregnancy to protect mother or baby or both, the lungs of a premature fetus can be matured to a more functional level by giving the mother hydrocortisone-like hormones. (See pp. 155–156 on L/S ratio.)

The fetus in severe distress during labor (as detected by fetal monitoring and scalp pH sampling) can be resuscitated prior to an emergency cesarean section with oxygen given to the mother (and hence to the fetus) or terbutaline (see p. 163) to stop uterine contractions. Also, the mother can be positioned to roll the uterus off her major abdominal blood vessels, thereby increasing blood flow and oxygen supply to the placenta and baby.

Prenatal surgical treatment for problems that would damage the fetus if left uncorrected is in its infancy. A pioneer in fetal surgery is Dr. Michael Harrison of the University of California Medical Center in San Francisco, where an international registry of fetal surgery is maintained. As an example, with ultrasound it is possible to detect obstructions of the male urinary tract, which, if uncorrected, can lead to stretching and progressive destruction of the kidneys. Obstructions of this type are located at the juncture of the bladder and urethra, so-called posterior urethral valves. At several medical centers, operations have been performed to relieve such obstructions by passing a plastic catheter (small thin tube) through the fetus's abdomen into the bladder to drain off excess urine continuously into the amniotic fluid. An alternative approach, with some advantage for younger fetuses in whom the tubes tend to block off with time, is to open the uterus under anesthesia and operate directly on the fetus. In the case of bladder obstruction, an incision is made into the fetal bladder that allows the urine to drain into the amniotic fluid. After birth, another operation is performed in which the valves are removed and the incision closed.

Operations have also been performed on fetuses to correct a diaphragmatic hernia. In this condition one of the diaphragms (the muscles that separate the lungs from the abdomen and that play an important role in breathing) is missing. The result is that the abdominal contents, for example, stomach and intestines, move (herniate) into the space for the lung above it. The lung collapses and after birth may not expand and function even if a technically difficult operation is successful in correcting the hernia. Operating before birth has the advantage of protecting the lung. Results of this still-experimental procedure are awaited.

The potential for surgical correction of other kinds of malformations before birth is unclear. After an initial rush of enthusiasm for fetal surgery, much more attention is now being given to selection out of cases in which other problems of the fetus might be incompatible with normal survival even if surgery for a correctable defect is technically successful. Fetal surgery has led to several exciting discoveries even more significant than correction of anatomical malformations. One discovery is that an incision into the skin of a fetus, up until a certain gestational age, heals without scarring—a phenomenon with far-reaching implications for clinical practice.

Another profoundly significant discovery is that, up until a certain gestational age, a fetus, unlike a child or an adult, will not reject certain cells injected into its body. The injected cells will survive and reproduce, coexisting with the fetus's own cells. If the DNA in a fetus's own genes is defective, resulting in a disease, the transplanted normal cells can make up for the deficit. Thus, some inherited diseases can potentially be cured by cell transplant. Additionally, after birth the baby is more likely to accept an organ donation from the donor of the cells transplanted before birth. Cell transplantation in utero thus may pave the way for easier and more successful organ transplantation. The kinds of cells currently being transfused and studied are called stem cells, the undifferentiated parent cells of circulating blood cells.

A recent issue that has arisen in hospitals and in court is the treatment of a fetus when the pregnant woman dies or becomes mentally incompetent. For ways women can make their wishes known in this regard, see the address for "Choice in Dying" in Appendix C.

Protecting the Fetus

Every day, it seems, the list of things known to harm the growing fetus increases. In this section I present what is really known about drugs in pregnancy, vaccines, infections in the mother, addictive substances, and environmental hazards.

In general, I advise a conservative approach to drugs, vaccines, and other outside influences that may be harmful to the fetus. If a medication or vaccine does not directly benefit the fetus, I advise you to avoid it if at all possible. If you cannot, try to minimize exposure. Confine drug treatment to drugs that have not been shown to harm the fetus.

The climate of suspicion that surrounds drugs makes it difficult to study their effects during pregnancy. Since effects may not be apparent until many years after the drugs are taken, causal connections between a problem and prior drug exposure are often hard to draw. A prime example is the hormone diethylstilbestrol (DES), taken by many women a generation ago to prevent miscarriage. Years later a small percentage of their offspring in their teens and twenties were discovered to have abnormalities of the genitalia.

While reading this chapter parents-to-be would do well to remember that most babies are born healthy, as they have been for thousands of years. Worrying over imagined or exaggerated hazards will help neither mother nor baby. After following sensible precautions, such as those outlined here, parents should try to relax and put their confidence in the age-old natural process of childbearing. (See also discussion of exercise, pp. 94–106).

DRUGS DURING PREGNANCY

In Table 4 most drugs are identified by their generic names, which are usually not the way they are known to the public. For example, the well-known drug Tylenol will be listed as acetaminophen. To use the table, you will need to ask the pharmacist or physician for the generic name or check it yourself on the label or package insert. (Space does not permit a listing of all of the many trade names by which these drugs are marketed, hence, the use of generic names.) Please read (at the bottom of the table) the explanations for any superscripts (the little letters just above and to the right of the end of the name of the drug). (See p. 260 on drugs to avoid while nursing.) Please note that commonly used but illegal drugs, such as marijuana, are also listed. Their listing in no way signifies my approval of their use at any time. Please also note the caution called for in using any vitamin in doses above those recommended for pregnancy. (See pp. 89, 91 regarding the question of need for vitamin supplementation in pregnancy.) For those readers wanting more details, I refer you to the sources. Again, I want to emphasize the importance of talking with your physician or midwife about any drug you might use during pregnancy and lactation.

VACCINES

Vaccines are of two types: those containing dead and those containing live microorganisms, usually viruses. *Live-virus vaccines* are generally avoided in pregnancy for fear of infecting the fetus. The most commonly used live-virus vaccines are those against measles, rubella (German measles), mumps, and polio (the widely used Sabin vaccine).

Of these vaccines, the *polio vaccine only* can be given with relative safety during pregnancy. Even so, its use is recommended only during polio epidemics in which the risk of contracting paralytic polio clearly outweighs the risk of any complication associated with taking the vaccine, however small.

The *rubella vaccine* currently used can infect the fetus in a minority of exposures, but to date no cases of congenital rubella syndrome (see pp. 172–173) have been reported after its use. The risk of vaccination within three months of conception appears to be so small as to be almost negligible. Thus, the rubella vaccination of a pregnant woman should not in itself be a reason for therapeutic abortion, even though the final decision is, of course, an individual matter. Despite this reassuring information, we recommend a conservative course of action. Pregnant women should avoid the rubella vaccine, and nonpregnant women should not become pregnant for three months following vaccination. Women whose blood antibody levels show that they are not immune to rubella should receive the vaccine prior to pregnancy or, if pregnant, after delivery.

In contrast to live vaccines, *killed vaccines*, which contain no

Table 4. Drugs in Pregnancy

Type of Drug	Safe to Use[a]	Relatively Safe, or Limited Information[b]	Some Risk Associated[c]	Contraindicated[d]
Analgesics/drugs for arthritis	Acetaminophen Codeine[e] Meperidine[e] Morphine[e]	Isoniazid Percodan[e1] Percocet[e2]	Aspirin[g] Ibuprofen[g] Indomethacin[g] Naproxen[g] Propoxyphene Sulindac[g]	
Antibiotics	Ampicillin Erythromycin Penicillin	Amoxicillin Cephalosporins Clotrimazole Isoniazid Lindane Miconazole Nitrofurantoin[g] Oxacillin, dicloxacillin	Acyclovir Bacitracin Chloroquine Ciproflaxin Metronidazole[f] Sulfonamides[g]	Tetracycline
Anticoagulants	Heparin			Warfarin
Antiemetics	Trimethobenzamide	Meclizine	Hydroxyzine Prochlorperazine	
Antihypertensives	Hydralazine	Alphamethyldopa Atenolol Metroprolol Nadolol Propanolol	Benzapril Captopril Enalapril Lisinopril Quinapril Ramipril	

Category			
Bronchodilators	Albuterol Beclomethasone Cromolyn sodium Terbutaline	Aminophylline Metaproterenol Theophylline	
Cardiac drugs		Atropine Digoxin	
Cough medicines	Terpin hydrate	Potassium iodide[c] Robitussin-DM[4] Robitussin-CF[5]	
Decongestants/ antihistamines	Nose drops and sprays	All over-the-counter cold preparations Astemizole Brompheniramine Diphenhydramine Phenylephrine Phenylpropanolamine Promethazine Pseudoephedrine Terfenidine	
Laxatives and antidiarrheals	Milk of magnesia Kaopectate[6]	Docusate Loperamide Paregoric[e] Psyllium	
Sedatives			Alprazolam Chlordiazepoxide Diazepam Flurazepam Triazolam

Table 4. Drugs in Pregnancy *continued*

Type of Drug	Safe to Use[a]	Relatively Safe, or Limited Information[b]	Some Risk Associated[c]	Contraindicated[d]
Thyroid preparations	L-Thyroxine		Propylthiouracil	
Other drugs	Ferrous sulfate Vaccines[f] (hepatitis B, polio [killed], rabies) diphtheria-tetanus toxoid, influenza Vitamins in usual doses (see pp. 89, 91)	Allopurinol Antacids Caffeine (in usual amounts) Cimetidine Corticosteroids Probenecid Ranitidine	Carbamazepine Fluoxetine Iodide Methadone Nicotine skin patches Phenytoin Primidone Sertraline Tricyclic antidepressants Trimethadione Vaccines (polio—live) Valproic acid	Amphetamines, LSD, ethanol Antineoplastic drugs Bromocriptine Cocaine[e] Disulfiram Estrogens, DES Heroin Isoretinoin Lithium Marijuana Vaccines (measles, mumps, rubella, smallpox)

[1]Trade name for oxycodone and aspirin.

[2]Trade name for oxycodone and acetaminophen.

[3]Trade names for iodinated glycerol.

[4]Trade name for quaifenesin with dextromethorphan.

[5]Trade name for quaifenesin with dextromethorphan and propanolamine.

[6]Trade name for kaolin with pectin.

[a]Although no drug can be used with certainty that there will be no adverse effects, drugs listed in this column are used at Barnes Hospital in St. Louis, Missouri.

[b]Many drugs in this column are relatively new, but no consistent adverse effect has been attributed to their use. Data on these drugs are limited.

[c]These drugs have some associated risk when used in pregnancy. The potential benefit derived from these drugs should be weighed against possible adverse effects.

[d]These drugs have been well documented to produce adverse fetal effects and should not be used in pregnancy.

[e]Possible neonatal addiction and withdrawal symptoms may occur after long-term use; possible neonatal depression may occur with intrapartum use.

[f]Avoid in first trimester. Discontinue breast-feeding while taking until 24 hours after last dose.

[g]Avoid use in third trimester or near delivery.

Sources: Adapted by the author from the following sources: Gerald G. Briggs, Roger K. Freeman, and Sumner Y. Yaffee, *Drugs in Pregnancy and Lactation* (Baltimore, Md.: Williams and Wilkins, 1990); Department of Medicine, Washington University, *Manual of Medical Therapeutics* (Boston, Mass.: Little, Brown, 1989); and *Physician's Desk Reference*, 45th ed. (Montvale, N.J.: Medical Economics Data, 1991).

living microorganisms, can be used safely after the first trimester. (Consult Table 4 for specifics.) The most commonly used killed vaccine is directed against tetanus and diphtheria and is recommended to be administered to adults every ten years up to the age of sixty-five. The "flu shots," made available to protect against the three strains of influenza expected to be common in any one winter season, are also killed vaccines, as is the Salk vaccine for polio and the vaccine against hepatitis B (see p. 170).

INFECTIONS

The fetus is generally well protected from infection that the mother contracts before or during pregnancy. Common colds, flu, stomach viruses, strep throat, sinusitis, and even pneumonia will not harm the fetus. There are, however, important exceptions to this general rule, and these are presented here.

AIDS. (See the discussion of "AIDS Test," pp. 61–63.)

Chlamydia. Chlamydia, a bacterium little known to the public, causes more infections to the newborn than any other infectious agent. Like gonorrhea, Chlamydia inhabits the mother's cervix and is picked up by the baby as it passes through the birth canal. Depending on the population surveyed, between 2 and 40 percent of women harbor the bacteria, and between 18 and 50 percent of the babies of these women will pick it up, although not all will show symptoms. About one-third of exposed babies will develop conjunctivitis if preventive treatment is not undertaken. Although Chlamydia conjunctivitis is not well prevented by the silver nitrate eyedrops traditionally used, it is both prevented and treated with erythromycin eye ointment now widely used.

Chlamydia can also cause pneumonia in infants less than three months old (with peak occurrence between four and twelve weeks). Erythromycin taken by mouth is the antibiotic proven most effective to date in treating conjunctivitis and, probably, pneumonia.

Whether all women should be tested for the presence of chlamydia during pregnancy is not clear. There has been no randomized control study regarding the benefit of treatment for the mother or the baby at birth. An argument can be made for taking cervical cultures of women at high risk for infection and treating those who are positive with a course of antibiotics. Erythromycin is the favored drug.

Cytomegalovirus. Cytomegalovirus (CMV) is a virus most people know little or nothing about. Recently revealed as the leading congenital infection in humans, it infects 1 percent of all babies. Thus, of the approximately three million births annually in the United States, 30,000 newborns are infected. About 3,000 of these are obviously sick at birth, and about 600 actually die of the illness. The remaining 2,400 who recover are likely to suffer nerve damage, deafness, eye impairment, mental retardation, and stunted growth. Of the 27,000 infected infants who appear well at birth, between 2,700 and 7,600 will eventually develop hearing impairment, inflammation of the eyes and perhaps impaired vision, tooth infections that cause loss of baby teeth, and intellectual handicapping.

Fetuses who are at greatest risk are those whose mothers become infected with the virus for the first time during the pregnancy. Mothers who have antibodies to the virus from a previous infection—and thereby a degree of immunity—are less likely to transmit the virus to their fetuses. There is a growing consensus that pregnant women should be routinely tested for antibodies so that those who are not immune can take precautions against infection, as will be described.

Infected newborns can harbor and excrete CMV for months, perhaps years, and so are a major reservoir for the spread of the disease throughout the community. Day-care centers in particular are notorious in this process. Since the infected babies who play an important role in the cycle of CMV infection do not usually appear ill, pregnant women, women who could become pregnant, and those who work in these centers are at risk.

To prevent the infection of nonimmune, pregnant day-care workers, several steps might be useful. (They have not been put to the test yet.) First, such women can be offered blood testing for antibodies to the virus. Those who are not immune and continue to work should be counseled to wash their hands frequently; to use gloves, especially when handling diapers or respiratory secretions; and to avoid mouth-to-mouth contact or excessive kissing. The family is another common setting for infection of the nonimmune pregnant woman. The best advice is to minimize contact with the urine of toddlers and with their saliva by limiting kissing and the sharing of drinking glasses and utensils.

In the older child or adult, CMV infection can take the form of a subclinical infection that produces no symptoms at all. Or it may cause symptoms similar to those of infectious mononucleosis—sore throat, fever, swollen glands, and an enlarged liver. Fortunately, CMV infection after infancy does not appear to have the risks of handicapping associated with the disease in the newborn.

Like the herpes virus (see the following discussion), CMV can remain in the body indefinitely, perhaps for life. Periodically it becomes active, spreading throughout the body reinfection without necessarily causing symptoms. When a pregnant woman experiences either such a flare-up or, especially, when she is initially infected early in pregnancy, the virus can spread across the placenta to the fetus or from the cervix to the baby during birth. The risk to the fetus of reinfections does not appear to be as great as an initial infection of the mother, insofar as serious illness at birth is concerned. Apparently, the previously infected mother has produced antibodies that protect the fetus (and later the baby) from damage by the virus. Nonetheless, chronic subclinical infection and contagiousness do occur, and the long-range consequences to the child of such reinfections are not yet known.

CMV can also be present in breast milk. In such cases the baby may already be immune, at least temporarily, because antibodies to CMV have been transmitted from the mother across the placenta before birth. Transmission of CMV via breast milk is a strong argument against pooling the milk of several mothers into a milk bank to feed a premature infant who may lack maternally transmitted immunity.

To date, there is no drug to combat CMV. A vaccine now under development offers the most likely long-range solution to this major health problem, but no quick solutions seem likely.

Fifth Disease. Infection of a pregnant woman with the virus (parvovirus B19) that causes fifth disease—so named because it once was the fifth most common rash in children—can be damaging or lethal to the fetus, but the risk is very low. Most women (and men) are already immune to fifth disease (also known as *Erythema infectiosum*) because of previous exposure to the virus, usually in childhood. An antibody test is available to determine previous infection and probable immunity. Women who are exposed to individuals with fifth disease—usually, children—should talk with their midwife or doctor about the desirability of being tested for immunity.

Fifth disease in children and adults typically causes fever and a distinctive rash: affected people have an intensely red facial rash with markings as though someone had slapped their cheeks. The redness characteristically does not affect the skin around the lips. Commonly a lacelike red rash appears first on the arms, then spreads to involve the trunk, buttocks, and thighs. The rash can recur for weeks and sometimes months. The infection can produce arthritis and joint pain in adults or a mild respiratory illness, or there may be no symptoms. Even without symptoms fifth's disease is contagious, primarily through airborne spread. The disease is most contagious before the rash appears, when it is least suspected. No treatment for this viral infection is available yet, and permanent control awaits the development of a vaccine.

Gonorrhea. Since germs that cause gonorrhea are present primarily in the cervix, gonorrhea infection is a problem for the newborn, who can pick up the germs during passage through the birth canal, than for the fetus in utero. Gonorrhea can infect the baby's eyes, causing a virulent conjunctivitis that can sear the corneas and even cause blindness if untreated. Gonorrheal conjunctivitis is prevented by routinely treating the eyes of the newborn with silver nitrate, tetracycline, or erythromycin very soon after birth (see pp. 270–271).

On the expectant mother's first prenatal visit, and later visits if the risk of exposure is high, a culture of the cervix is performed to detect possible gonorrhea infection. If the culture is positive, the woman is treated with antibiotics. But the eradication of gonorrhea at any time in pregnancy does not guarantee that the mother will not become reinfected. For this reason the eyes of the newborn are treated routinely, regardless of the mother's medical history.

Group B Streptococcal Infection. In recent years it has been discovered that group B streptococcus (different from the bacterium that causes the familiar "strep throat") is responsible for between 12,000 and 15,000 infections in newborns per year in the United States, affecting two to three babies per thousand. Without prompt recognition and treatment of the disease, about half the infected newborns will die; and half of those who become ill and develop meningitis will show long-term neurological effects. Despite the commonness of this infection, it has received scant public attention.

The group B streptococcus is carried in the intestines of about 10 percent of women and spreads from the anus to the vagina. As far as is now known, it causes no symptoms in the woman. The baby picks up the bacteria during passage through the birth canal and can also acquire the infection after birth. About 40 percent of infected mothers transmit the bacteria to their babies.

The signs of illness in the newborn are nonspecific. They include irritability, fever, vomiting, lethargy, and labored breathing. Even mild symptoms may signify the potentially lethal spread of the bacteria throughout the baby's body.

The best way to prevent infection of the baby, according to the evidence, is to treat women considered to be at high risk for harboring group B streptococcus with antibiotics during labor. A rapid test that could be used at the first examination in labor would permit a more selective approach to treatment. Such a test is under development.

Hepatitis. As discussed on p. 63–64, hepatitis B transmitted from an infected mother to the fetus or to the baby at birth is an important health risk to the baby. Current policy is to immunize all infants at birth with hepatitis B vaccine and to give gamma globulin as well to infants whose mothers test positive for hepatitis B. (See discussion on p. 63.)

Herpes.   The herpes virus occurs in two varieties, *type 1* and *type 2*. *Type 2* produces the cold sores commonly encountered on the mouth and lips. *Type 1,* which causes blisters on the genitalia of men and women, is a frequently occurring sexually transmitted disease. After the first outbreak of infection, herpes virus can remain in the human host indefinitely, erupting periodically and usually, but not always, causing visible, painful lesions. During such a herpes flare-up or during an initial attack the virus can be transmitted to others. Thus, herpes virus present in a woman's birth canal can be picked up by her infant during labor and delivery. Particularly contagious is a first-time infection of a mother around the time of delivery.

Herpes infection of the newborn can be fatal or disabling, even with the partially effective drug therapy now available. To date, there is no vaccine against herpes, and available drug treatment for the disease has not been tested in pregnant women, out of concern for possible harm to the fetus from the drug itself.

At present, the best way to keep a baby from getting herpes is to prevent its exposure to the virus. When herpes virus is known to be present in the cervix and vagina, the baby is kept away from this infective environment by being delivered through cesarean section. For this preventive approach to work, the amniotic membranes must either be intact or have been broken no more than four to six hours before the operation is performed.

Women considered most at risk for shedding virus that can be transmitted at birth are those with visible herpes sores. These are the women who are considered prime candidates for cesarean delivery. Following this policy will be successful in many, but not all, cases because herpes virus may be present in the birth canal even in the absence of visible sores. All too often women may be shedding virus in their vagina with no symptoms or signs at all. Another preventive approach, still in a research stage, is testing both partners for antibodies to the virus. When a woman, but not her partner, lacks antibodies and is therefore vulnerable to infection, safe sex practices should be initiated to prevent viral transfer.

If the pregnant woman's partner has a documented herpes infection, it is recommended that the couple avoid genital contact in the last several months of pregnancy. If the partner has cold sores of the mouth (caused by type 2 herpes virus), oral-genital contact should be avoided, since herpes type 2 can also infect the genitalia and is transmissible to the infant. After the birth, people with cold sores of the mouth or lips should avoid kissing or nuzzling the infant, cover any exposed lesions, and wash their hands before handling the baby.

Listeria monocytogenes. *Listeria monocytogenes* is a germ that can infect the pregnant woman and the newborn, leading to spontaneous abortion, stillbirth, and serious illness in the neonate. It is not recognized as a common problem. The germ is widespread in streams, sewage, silage, and soil, and infects primarily farm animals. It is passed in their stools, from which it can contaminate vegetables grown with infected manure. It is commonly present in chicken, particularly commercially prepared, and in cows' and goats' milk and soft cheeses made from them. Thorough washing or cooking of vegetables should be preventive. Pasteurization of milk usually destroys this organism. Pregnant women are probably best advised to avoid store-bought cooked chicken salad, which may have been sitting for a while.

Monilia. *Monilia,* a yeast (technically known as *Candida albicans*) commonly present in the vagina, can cause vaginal infections in the mother and a condition known as *thrush* in the newborn, as noted in Chapter 2 (see p. 82). While many women with monilial infections have an itchy vaginal discharge, which leads to early diagnosis and treatment, monilial infections may also be silent (with no obvious symptoms) or go unnoticed. The vaginal speculum examination usually performed late in pregnancy is done in part to detect monilial infections. Treating the infection minimizes the possibility of transmitting the yeast to the baby.

If a baby picks up the yeast in the birth canal, it can infect his or her mouth or tongue, causing the white coating known as thrush. Although troublesome, thrush is easily treatable.

Rubella. *Rubella,* or *German measles,* usually a mild childhood infection, can have severely damaging effects on the growing fetus. In fact, the capacity of some viruses to damage the fetus was first established in connection with rubella. Investigators noted that epidemics of rubella preceded the birth of a significant number of babies with a group of birth defects known as *congenital rubella syndrome* (these include deafness, a small brain, and mental retardation).

The development of an effective vaccine (see p. 161) against this virus was given impetus by the serious problem of infection of the fetus. Now girls and women are routinely immunized against rubella, and the occurrence of rubella-induced birth defects has been virtually eliminated (see also p. 60 on test for rubella immunity).

Syphilis. Syphilis is caused by a corkscrew-shaped microorganism that can reach the fetus of an infected woman by crossing the placenta from the mother's blood to that of the fetus. Infection can cause widespread and progressive damage to any part of the body of the fetus, including the brain, eyes, and bones. Although treatment with antibiotics can arrest infection of the fetus, the damage already done cannot be reversed. Because of the danger of syphilis, women are checked for the presence of the disease with a blood test at their first prenatal visit and, if indicated, at later visits as well. If syphilis is diagnosed, immediate treatment is given (see pp. 56–57).

Toxoplasmosis. Toxoplasmosis is an infectious disease caused by a one-celled organism called *toxoplasma*, which resembles an amoeba. Commonly found in the feces of cats, it is also encountered encysted (in dormant form) in the raw meat of several animals, especially pigs. Up to one-fourth to one-third of all people have contracted this infection at some time in their lives, usually without being aware of it, and have measurable antibodies to *toxoplasma* in their blood. Infected humans harbor the cyst form of this organism in their tissues, apparently without ill effect.

If a woman becomes infected during pregnancy, the fetus can become infected in turn, suffering possible widespread damage, especially to the brain and eyes. The baby may suffer mental retardation, epilepsy, and blindness. The infected woman herself may have no symptoms at all or may show symptoms that resemble those of infectious mononucleosis: sore throat, fever, and enlarged lymph glands in the neck.

The pregnant woman can best avoid exposure to *toxoplasma* by not eating raw meat, especially pork; by washing her hands carefully after handling raw meat; and by avoiding contact with stray cats. If she has a pet cat, she should wear disposable gloves and a face mask (against dust) while changing the litter box or delegate this task to someone else for the duration of the pregnancy. Litter should be changed daily to prevent *toxoplasma* larvae from maturing to the stage of infectivity. The pet cat should be confined to an area where it cannot hunt birds and rodents, kept away from the stool of other cats, and fed canned or cooked food rather than raw meat.

Efforts to detect and treat an infected fetus have been less than satisfactory. While it is possible to detect a fetus at risk for infection by measuring maternal antibodies to toxoplasmosis and then testing the fetus's blood (sampled from the umbilical vessels under ultrasound guidance), it is not known whether the antibiotics available are effective in treating a fetus or by what stage in the fetal infection they must be given.

DIABETES

Although diabetes and pregnancy do not mix well, attentive care can do much to reduce risks to the mother and the developing fetus. Pregnancy intensifies the metabolic derangement in this disorder in women who already have it, and pregnancy can "bring out" diabetes in a woman with an underlying tendency to it, even though she has not previously shown signs or symptoms of the disease. During pregnancy such women may develop such typical symptoms as weakness, weight loss, increased thirst, and increased urination.

The effects of diabetes on pregnancy include the following:

- Increased risk of preeclampsia and eclampsia (see pp. 327–329)
- Increased susceptibility of the pregnant woman to infection
- Increased size of the fetus, which may complicate delivery (see p. 337, "Shoulder Dystocia," and pp. 303–304 on cephalopelvic disproportion)

- Increased incidence of polyhydramnios (see pp. 311–312)
- Increased incidence of congenital abnormalities (birth defects)

Diabetic pregnant women require insulin therapy. With careful control of their blood glucose levels initiated early in pregnancy (the earlier the better), aided by home blood glucose testing, many can achieve pregnancy outcomes not significantly different from those of nondiabetic women. Ideally, plans for diabetic care should be made even before pregnancy occurs. The less tight the control, the more likely are the adverse consequences listed. Interventions during pregnancy such as cesarean sections should be based on indications that apply to any pregnancy, not on diabetes itself. Because of the increased risk of fetal malformations, a detailed ultrasound study of the fetus during the second trimester is appropriate. Diabetic women should have their urine checked for infection more frequently than nondiabetic women.

Women with long-standing diabetes are at increased risk during pregnancy for deterioration of kidney and eye function and may require treatment for these problems. Some women may demonstrate the first signs of kidney and eye problems during pregnancy. Diabetic women should discuss the risks to them of pregnancy *before the fact.* For some, pregnancy is not a good idea at all, for others, continuation of a pregnancy can be dangerous. (See pp. 55–56 on tests for diabetes.)

TOBACCO

There is good evidence that the babies of women who smoke are likely to be smaller and lighter by several hundred grams than those of nonsmokers, and they are likely to be born several days earlier.

Complications in pregnancy are also more common in women who smoke than in nonsmokers. They include spontaneous abortion (see pp. 316–322, placenta praevia and abruptio placenta (pp. 323–324), premature rupture of the membranes (pp. 332–333), and bleeding in labor. Exposure of the pregnant woman to smoke in the air, produced by others, contributes to the smoke levels in her blood, although not to the same degree as would her own smoking. Tobacco products (*thiocyanate,* for example) are found in the cord blood of the baby at birth, even in mothers "passively exposed" to cigarette smoke. There is mounting evidence that even passive smoking harms health.

There is also good evidence that children of smokers show greater susceptibility to respiratory infections (colds, bronchitis, ear infections) during childhood, are more likely to take up the smoking habit themselves in later life, and are more likely to develop lung cancer as adults even if they do not themselves smoke. By stopping during and after pregnancy, parents not only become positive role models for their children but also improve their own health and prevent the many diseases associated with smoking.

ALCOHOL

The babies of women who are heavily drinking alcohol during pregnancy are at risk for widespread defects that are apparent at birth and may impair the child's functioning for life. These babies have a cluster of defects known as the *fetal alcohol syndrome* (FAS). They share four characteristics:

1. Prenatal growth retardation
2. Central nervous system abnormalities, including a small head and brain (microcephaly), a history of delayed development, attention deficit disorder, hyperactivity, learning disabilities and/or seizures
3. Multiple abnormalities of the face, including small eyes, a short distance between the corners of the eyelids, a poorly developed groove in the skin between the upper lip and the bottom of the nose, a thin upper lip, and/or flat cheekbones
4. Other malformations such as heart and genitourinary defects.

Only recently have babies with FAS been followed up in adolescence. Researchers from the University of Washington Medical School (where in 1973 FAS was first described in this country) and the University of Vancouver (Canada) reported in 1991 in the *Journal of the American Medical Association* that the characteristic facial abnormalities of affected children become less pronounced with time, but that they tend to remain short and have small heads. The average IQ was a (low) 68 but there was considerable variation. Average school performance was at a second- to fourth-grade level, with striking deficits in arithmetic skills. Maladaptive behaviors such as "poor judgement, distractibility, and difficulty perceiving social cues were common." FAS is now the major known cause of mental retardation in this country. In Seattle it is estimated that 1 in 700 children is affected. In one Canadian Indian village the prevalence is 1 in 8. The lifetime-care costs for one affected child are estimated at $1.4 million in today's dollars. The consequences of chronic high-dose alcohol exposure in utero are devastating.

The mothers of babies with FAS have been alcoholics drinking over four shots of hard liquor (or the equivalent in beer or wine) per day. Some experienced delirium tremens (DTs) or alcoholic stupor during labor. Fetuses exposed to lower amounts of alcohol, two to four shots per day, have demonstrated lesser degrees of the physical and mental abnormalities of FAS. These are referred to as FAE (fetal alcohol effects). It appears that the severity of FAE and FAS is related to the extent of exposure to alcohol, but the precise dose–response relationship (how much alcohol over what period of time in what stage of fetal development to produce what abnormalities) is not known. Preliminary results from a new study from the National Fetal Alcohol Research Center in Detroit suggest that not until a woman regularly drinks more than three shots of whiskey per day (or its equivalent) do fetal alcohol effects begin to show up.

It is not known and probably never will be known for certain whether there is any safe dose of alcohol during pregnancy. There is no question that the safest policy is simply to abstain. Such a policy underlies the familiar warnings on the labels of bottles of alcoholic beverages and on the signs posted in restaurants and stores. Some authorities believe that this campaign overstates the problem (and also fails to reach the alcoholic women who most need the advice). Average social drinking in pregnancy (an occasional drink) *probably* is of no consequence. A 1991 report in the *British Medical Journal* involving 592 pregnant women is reassuring: During early pregnancy, 43 percent of the women consumed no alcohol, 48 percent consumed one to five drinks weekly, 6 to 10 percent had five to ten drinks weekly, and 3 percent had more than ten drinks weekly. At eighteen months of age in this study the children of drinkers had the same motor and mental development scores on a standardized assessment as the children of nondrinkers. Even heavy drinkers who lowered their intake before the third trimester, according to some reports, have been able to reduce the effects of alcohol on fetal growth. In many communities genetic counselors are the health professionals best able to advise women on the risks to their fetuses resulting from any particular pattern of drinking.

CAFFEINE

Although caffeine in large doses has been shown to cause birth defects in experimental animals, no such effect has been demonstrated in infants born of mothers who consumed caffeine during their pregnancies, in the several studies that have been done. For example, a 1982 report of more than 12,000 births at the Boston Hospital for Women showed no correlation between caffeine consumption during pregnancy and birth defects in newborns.

MARIJUANA

The impact of marijuana smoking on the fetus has been difficult to assess, partly because marijuana smokers also commonly drink alcoholic beverages and smoke tobacco (see previous sections), and they are prone to have inadequate diets. Any defects noted in the babies of marijuana smokers may be the result of the interaction of several factors, making it difficult to isolate the specific contribution of marijuana.

With this cautionary note, the best available evidence is that marijuana is likely to result in smaller babies and ones who have features compatible with the fetal alcohol syndrome (see pp. 176–178). The best recommendation, of course, is to avoid marijuana during pregnancy.

COCAINE

The impact of cocaine exposure on the fetus is not yet well understood. The evidence to date, based on retrospective studies, is that chronic cocaine exposure is associated with low birth weight, intrauterine growth retardation (see pp. 312–315), small head size, brain injury in utero from strokes, abruptio placenta (see p. 324), premature rupture of the membranes (see pp. 332–333), and preterm labor (see pp. 329–332). At birth many exposed babies temporarily demonstrate significant impairment not only of orientation but also of motor and state regulation, as measured by the Neonatal Behavioral Assessment Scale (see pp. 237–238). They often also demonstrate tremor, poor feeding, irritability, and, occasionally, seizures. Later, cocaine-exposed babies are more likely to die unexpectedly as victims of the sudden infant death syndrome. The precise role of cocaine (or crack) in these adverse outcomes is not clear because many of the mothers of these babies also have other behaviors and problems that can harm the fetus, such as cigarette smoking and poor nutrition. A 1991 report from the Boston Children's Hospital indicates that cocaine-exposed babies are ten times more likely to have structural defects of their hearts. Although long-term effects on the growth and development of these infants and children have not yet been isolated, there is clearly cause for great concern, particularly in view of the widespread use of cocaine within segments of our society.

X RAYS

The possibility of harm to the fetus from diagnostic X rays has aroused great concern. Much of the concern over radiation originated in the aftermath of the atomic bombing of Japan, because of the increase in abortion and birth defects observed there. It is important to realize, however, that there is no reported case of a human birth defect caused by a diagnostic X-ray study. Radiation to the fetus during diagnostic X rays, while hard to measure accurately, is without question significantly less than that received by some fetuses in Hiroshima and Nagasaki. Although it is also true that X radiation has been shown to be damaging in experi-mental animals, the doses used were far larger than those used in humans.

The risk of radiation exposure to the fetus from diagnostic X rays appears to be quite low, certainly not high enough to con-traindicate medically needed X-ray studies. Nevertheless, unnec-essary exposure is unwise, especially in the first trimester. If a study can be delayed, so much the better. The following guide-lines are suggested:

1. A sexually active woman in her reproductive years should assume that she is pregnant unless proved otherwise. Evidence of not being pregnant includes the following: onset of menses in the previous ten days, use of oral contraceptives, use of an IUD, no sexual intercourse since the last menstrual period, having had surgical sterilization, or a negative result on a very sensitive preg-nancy test (see p. 40).

2. If a woman known to be in the first trimester of pregnancy needs an X ray, the pelvis should not be included in the X-ray field if at all possible.

3. Women should always wear a shield over the pelvis and abdomen when having X-ray studies (including dental X rays), whether or not they are pregnant. They will offer some, but not complete, protection.

4. If there is medical indication to perform a diagnostic X-ray study in pregnancy, the importance of the information to be ob-tained will generally outweigh the remote risk of harm to the fetus. However, each situation must be evaluated on its individual merits.

5. If a woman receives a relatively large amount of radiation (more than five rads) to the pelvis in the first trimester of preg-nancy, she may have suffered an increased risk for birth defects, the exact percentage of which is not well understood, perhaps 1 to 3 percent. For some couples, such a risk may be enough to justify a therapeutic abortion after careful discussion with a phys-ician.

6. With any X-ray exposure during pregnancy, there may be a small increase in the incidence of leukemia during childhood, although this issue is not yet well understood.

The preceding discussion does not apply to the therapeutic use of X rays, administered in much larger doses, usually to treat cancer. These doses can be sufficient to damage the fetus.

HOT TUB AND SAUNA USE

There is now reasonably good evidence that women should avoid the warming effects of hot tubs and saunas early in pregnancy. As reported in the August 19th 1992 issue of the *Journal of the American Medical Association*, researchers at Boston University found that the fetuses of women exposed to heat sources during the first trimester were at increased risk for neural tube defects, a problem that develops during the first trimester (see pp. 50–53, 130). Use of a hot tub increased the risk 2.8 times; sauna, 1.8; fever, 1.8; and electric blanket, 1.2. There is little information yet about the risks of heat exposure during the last two trimesters.

VIDEO DISPLAY TERMINALS

Concern has been expressed about the effects on the fetus of radiation from computer screens, an issue for many women. Research to date has been reassuring, so far revealing an absence of demonstrable risk.

AUTOMOBILE SAFETY

A woman of childbearing age is more likely to be killed or crippled by an automobile accident than by disease or other threat. Thus, if a woman could take only one preventive measure during pregnancy, she might be well advised to insist on using seat belts herself and demand that others in the car do the same. Both lap belts and shoulder harnesses can be used safely in pregnancy. To the extent possible, the shoulder harness should be used in the usual way, and the lap belt should be fastened over the hips beneath the uterus. For maximum protection of the pregnant woman, all other passengers need to be restrained, too, since a crash can send unrestrained riders flying with unbelievable force (over one ton at a car speed of twenty-five miles per hour) that can seriously harm them and others.

I also encourage expectant parents to plan ahead for their baby's car safety by obtaining a crash-tested infant restraint before the baby's birth, so that even the first ride will be a safe one. These restraints are held in place by the car's own safety belts. It is simply not safe to carry an infant or child on one's lap, even when sitting in the back seat. It is also best not to use the car's safety belts alone until a child weighs about forty pounds. (If the alternative, however, is no restraint at all, the standard belt will do once a child can sit up alone.) More and more states have laws requiring child restraints.

The Boston Children's Hospital, in its book, *The New Child Health Encyclopedia*, offers the following guidelines for selecting an infant restraint:

- Infant seats, which are usually tublike devices, and convertible seats, which are larger than infant seats and shaped more like a small chair, are the only types of car safety seats recommended for use with babies less than 17 pounds.
- The safest place for the infant to ride is in the center of the back seat. Infants ride in a semireclining position facing backwards. In the event of an accident, the baby's back absorbs the force of the crash.
- Infant seats are usually lined with soft padding. Folded blankets should be placed around the baby to help keep the head steady until head control is achieved. A safety harness holds the baby firmly in the chair, and the chair is anchored to the car with the vehicle's regular safety belt.
- Infant seats should be used until the baby's legs become cramped or until the child exceeds the weight limitations set by the seat's manufacturer. When the child outgrows the infant seat, parents should have a toddler seat installed in the car and ready to use.
- Convertible seats are usually economical, because the same seat can be used for infants and toddlers. Infants ride in the semireclining, backward-facing position in the convertible seat. When the child approaches 20 pounds, the seat is turned toward

the front of the car, the harness system is revised according to manufacturing specifications, and the frame of the seat is converted to an upright position.
- Flimsy, lightweight plastic feeding seats or car beds, which may be more convenient for carrying infants into buildings, should be restricted to household use. Infants should be transported only in federally approved car seats, which have been crash-tested under strict government guidelines.

The American Academy of Pediatrics and the American College of Obstetrics and Gynecology, including its nursing association, joined the campaign for the use of car seat restraints in the mid-1980s. The members of these professional groups, working in concert, are in a strategic position to reach pregnant women and the parents of infants and children. They will be happy to inform you on the effective use of infant restraints and seat belts and to recommend effective types.

4

Choices in Childbirth

Where to Give Birth

Choosing where to have the baby is one of the most important decisions a pregnant woman and her partner must make. Their decision must be based on available local options, which, regrettably, are limited in many communities. In Chapter 1, I described two different approaches: a hospital birth and a home birth. As of this writing, less than 1 percent of all births in this country occur at home, and about 15,000 occur annually in freestanding birthing centers. (There are now 135 of these centers, with 50 more under development.)

At this point there are no randomized control studies of out-of-hospital versus in-hospital births, which means that existing comparative data are less than satisfactory. However, there is a growing literature of European and American experiences with different birth sites. In order to help couples who want more information, I have given an overview of this literature in Appendix A.

Apart from medical considerations in hospital delivery, women who choose to have their babies in hospitals do so for many different reasons: a sense of security, access to a range of pain medications and technical backups, the particular hospital affiliation of the obstetrician they chose and trust, or simply the relief from routine pressures and duties that a few days in the hospital would offer. Some husbands who feel more secure with the idea of their wives giving birth in a hospital encourage this choice.

Women who choose an out-of-hospital birth also have different reasons for their decisions: a preference for homelike surroundings, the chance to have children or friends present, a greater opportunity to make their own decisions surrounding the birth, a sense of intimacy, greater involvement of the father, and less cost.

As I discussed in the Introduction, the out-of-hospital settings are the ones in which, in my opinion, scientific standards in maternity care are best being met today. Birth in such settings, assuming well-trained attendants and defined protocols for management (including indications for transfer to a hospital), is at least as safe as it is in the hospital. In other respects it is superior—sometimes far superior. Hospitals have much to learn from the out-of-hospital experience.

For a healthy, low-risk pregnancy, the probability of a complication (like fetal distress or severe postpartum hemorrhage) that would make the loss of time in transit to a hospital a serious disadvantage in managing the labor is very low, although how low is not known. In making this comment, I assume that the out-of-hospital site is staffed by competent attendants, is close to a backup hospital, and has a reliable system of transport.

Labor

By convention, labor is divided into three stages. The *first stage* begins with dilatation of the cervix and lasts until the cervix is completely dilated, marking the onset of the next stage. This first stage is divided into latent and active phases. We discuss these later on. The *second stage* of complete dilatation ends with the birth of the baby, as the *third stage*, the delivery of the placenta, begins.

The progress of the first stage of labor is judged according to the diameter (width) of the cervix. The size of the opening ranges from "zero" (completely closed) to "fully dilated," at an average of ten centimeters (just under four inches) with a full-term baby. (See pp. 188–189.) The smallest discernible dilation usually noted is a "fingertip"; that is, it allows for the introduction of the tip only of the examiner's finger. The cervix may be dilated several centimeters before labor begins, especially in first pregnancies.

The definition of labor encompasses regular uterine contractions and progressive cervical dilatation. For practical purposes, the cervix should open to three or four centimeters before it is concluded that labor has begun, even though the length of labor, once in progress, is timed from the onset of regular contractions. It is both possible and common for a woman with a slightly dilated cervix and the experience of contractions *not* to be in labor, since, during the latter part of pregnancy, uterine contractions that may be quite painful are common. These are known medically as *Braxton Hicks contractions,* as noted in Chapter 2. A run of Braxton Hicks contractions constitutes what is commonly called false labor. These false labor contractions are usually irregular. They do change unpredictably in length, strength, or frequency and often stop with a change in activity. Shifting from standing to lying down (or vice versa) or taking a warm bath will often make them stop.

In contrast, "true labor" contractions increase in regularity, length, strength, and frequency. They do not subside, growing stronger with activity. The onset of labor is often heralded by loss of the *mucous plug,* which fills the crevices in the cervical canal. Bloody mucus leaks from the vagina or is noticed on toilet paper. This "bloody show" may appear just before the onset of labor or may come intermittently over several days. One way or another, it signifies that the time is drawing near.

Labor is announced in about 10 percent of pregnancies by the breaking of the "bag of waters" or *amniotic sac* (see pp. 54–55), experienced by the woman as a slow leak or gush of warm fluid, which she may mistake for urine. Such "premature rupture of the membranes" exposes the uterus and fetus to the bacterial naturally present in the vagina and calls for special care to prevent infection if labor does not proceed quickly.

The essential distinction between true and false labor is dilatation of the cervix. Many a woman has thought she was in labor,

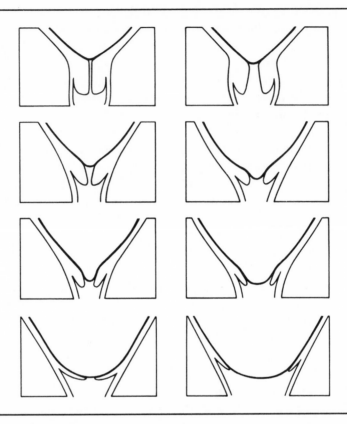

Figure 6. Dilatation and effacement (thinning) of cervix. Left-hand column shows cervix in a first birth; right-hand column shows the cervix after two or more births.

only to find out she was not. False alarms result in futile trips to the hospital and anxiety. Because contractions do not always mean that labor has started, official admission to the hospital is delayed until the width of the cervix has been observed for a while.

During labor, or even sometime before it begins, the cervix not only dilates but "effaces," or thins out. (See Figure 6.) This *efface- ment* is measured as a percentage of its full thickness—25 percent, 80 percent, and so on. At the onset of labor, effacement of the cervix varies from zero to 100 percent. As a rule it is completed, at the latest, when labor enters its *active phase.*

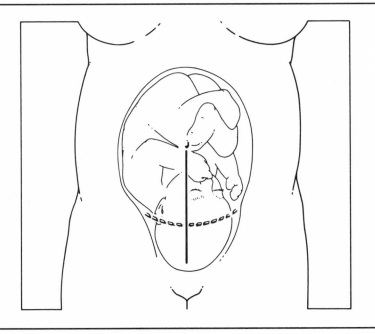

Figure 7. **Axis of birth canal (bold line). Midpelvis (dotted line)**

Thus, before labor begins, the cervix may be said to prepare for the work ahead. This "ripening" of the cervix for labor consists of its dilatation, effacement, softening, and forward rotation as it shifts from a position facing the woman's spine to one facing forward.

Another important consideration in assessing the progress of labor is the location of the baby in relation to the birth canal. (See Figure 7.) The position of the leading edge of the baby, the part that first enters the birth canal (usually the head), in relation to the center of the mother's pelvis is known as the *station*. The midpelvis is called "station zero." When the head reaches station zero, it is said to be "engaged." (See also pp. 44–48 on pelvic measurements.) Above the level of the midpelvis the station is called negative; below the midpelvis, positive. "Plus one," then, means 1 centimeter below or beyond the midpelvis, while "minus two" means 2 centimeters above the midpelvis. Descent of the baby is recorded in sequence as "minus three," "minus two," "minus one," zero (at the midpelvis), "plus one," "plus two," and "plus three" (when the baby's head is visible).

In addition to determining where the baby is located, it is also essential to know what part of the baby will appear first—head, face, hands, buttocks—and how it is oriented in space. This can usually be determined during vaginal examinations. Determining the way the head, for example, is turned requires identification of its "landmarks," or topical characteristics, with reference to an imaginary line or axis passing through the birth canal. For example, *sutures*, or *fontanels*, distinguish the front from the back of the skull. These sutures are the seams between the still-unknit bones of the skull. The fontanels are the triangular spaces at the junctions of the sutures, a large one in front (anterior) and a smaller one in back (posterior). (See Figure 8.) Using these landmarks, it is possible to determine whether the head is facing forward, backward, or crossways. In medical terms, the location of the *occiput* (point of the head) is described as being to the left or right of center, pointing forward (anterior), backward (posterior), or crossways (transverse), ninety degrees to the right or left of the midline. Thus, "LOA" (left occiput anterior, the most common position), means that the occiput (the *O*) is directed left and forward. For a summary of the various positions, see Figures 9 through 12.

In touching the baby's head, the examiner determines whether or not the scalp is swollen. Swelling is called *caput succedaneum*, and a caput signifies that the ring of pressure exerted by the cervix on the scalp has interfered with the return of blood from the skin in the center of the ring. The presence of a caput (see Figure 13) suggests that the cervix is not yielding to pressure from the head and may mean some degree of obstruction to the descent of the baby. At times a caput can be several centimeters thick, suggesting a greater degree of descent than is the case.

Another effect of pressure on the baby's head is known as *molding*, the shaping of the head by the architecture of the birth canal. At birth a baby's head, unlike that of the adult or child, can be squeezed and elongated because the separate bones of the skull have not yet fused. (See Figure 8.) The seams are open and the bones can overlap. This overlapping of the bones can often

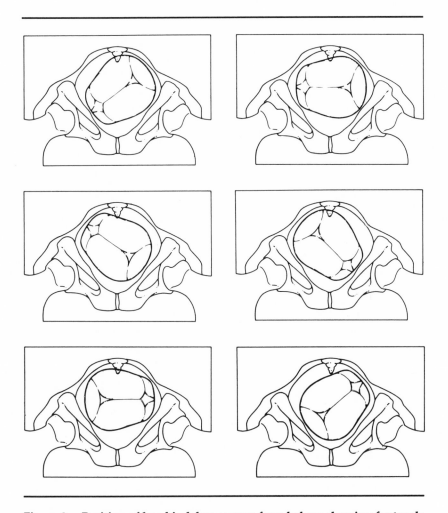

Figure 8. Position of head in labor as seen from below, showing fontanels

be detected in a vaginal examination. Molding is seen at birth in the form of elongation of the head and usually reverses spontaneously within a few days. The capacity of the head to "mold" is an adaptation of our species to the stresses of labor. The "give" of the skull prevents it from cracking and permits a birth that otherwise would have been obstructed. The molding of the baby's head is complemented by the looseness of the joints of the moth-

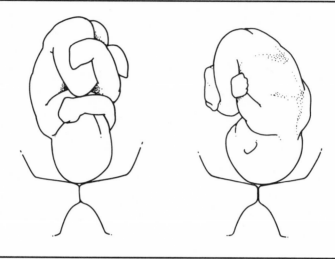

Figure 9.   Head pointing forward   Figure 10.   Head pointing backward

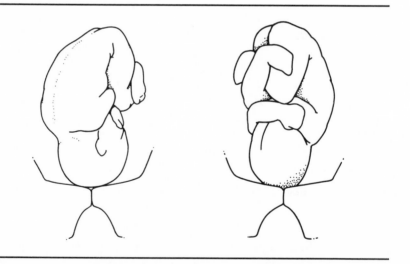

Figure 11.   Head pointing right   Figure 12.   Head pointing left

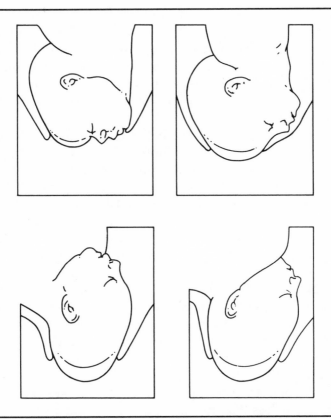

Figure 13. **Caput (swelling of baby's scalp due to pressure from the cervix or vagina)**

er's pelvis, which also allows for some give of the birth canal to accommodate the infant as it passes through.

During a vaginal examination the mother will usually hear the examiner report his or her observations on the following: dilatation of the cervix, its effacement, the station, the presenting part of the baby, and the orientation of the presenting part. For example, "six centimeters, 80 percent, minus one, LOA" means that the cervix is six centimeters dilated and 80 percent effaced, and that the head is one centimeter inside the midpelvis and oriented with the occiput, pointing forward and to the left.

These measurements are usually made during a contraction,

when dilatation and descent are maximal. A variation of this principle is used to assess the roominess of the pelvis early in labor: the examiner pushes the baby down and into the birth canal by pressing the abdomen on the top of the uterus with one hand while feeling the head in the vagina with the other. The ease with which the baby descends reflects the fit between the baby and the birth canal.

Dr. Emanuel Friedman of the Beth Israel Hospital in Boston has studied hundreds of labors, plotting the dilatation of the cervix and the station against the amount of time elapsed. In many maternity centers the *Friedman curve* serves as a useful guide to the normal progress of labor, since the labor curves of individual women are compared against this standard. The first stage of labor, as I mentioned, includes two phases of cervical dilatation, the *latent phase* and the *active phase*. The active phase is further divided into the *acceleration phase* and the *deceleration phase*. The latter part of the acceleration phase and the early part of the deceleration phase are referred to as the *transition*, that part of labor in which the cervix usually opens rapidly, from about seven centimeters to full dilatation. Transition is often the hardest part of labor, and its pain may be unbearable. It is often accompanied by nausea and vomiting.

In first labors the latent phase, according to Friedman's data, normally lasts less than twenty hours; in second and subsequent labors, normally less than fourteen hours. In the active phase in first labors the cervix normally dilates about 1.2 centimeters per hour; in second and subsequent labors, 1.5 centimeters per hour. The latent phase is subject to many influences, such as drugs, and its duration (see following discussion) has little bearing on the subsequent course of labor. A prolonged active phase, on the other hand, may mean a misfit between the baby and the birth canal (see pp. 303–304 on disproportion). It would be interesting to repeat Dr. Friedman's study with women who are not in bed and are encouraged to be up and around during labor, as much as is comfortable.

Each stage and phase of labor has its own characteristics. A sensitive attendant, or the laboring woman herself, particularly if she has given birth before, can often tell the status of labor by the frequency, duration, and intensity of contractions, the presence or absence of pressure sensations in the birth canal, and the presence of associated symptoms such as nausea or vomiting.

Early in the latent phase of the first stage, contractions are five to thirty minutes apart and last from fifteen to forty seconds. They are often described as "mild cramps," "gas," "back pain," or "pressure." During the active phase, the contractions come two to five minutes apart, are forty-five to sixty seconds in duration, and are stronger, more intense. In transition the contractions occur one and one-half to three minutes apart, last for forty-five to ninety seconds, and are the strongest they will be during the whole labor. Often, one follows the other so rapidly that rest may be impossible. Once full dilatation is achieved, the contractions may then space out to three to five or more minutes apart, so that some women are able to doze off between them. As the baby descends to the perineum, many women report a "burning" sensation. The contractions are now less intense, and discomfort shifts from the uterus to the rectum and vagina and includes a sense of pressure and an "urge to push."This urge should be followed to the extent that it feels comfortable to do so. (See pp. 16, 111 on pushing during birth.)

The second stage of labor, when dilatation is completed, usually lasts less than two hours. As long as progress is occurring and both mother and baby are well, no arbitrary limit at which intervention is indicated need be set on the second stage.

Having discussed the characteristics of an average labor, it is important to emphasize how variable labor can actually be. While the average first labor lasts about eight hours, with 95 percent lasting sixteen hours or less, and average subsequent labors last six hours, with 95 percent lasting twelve hours or less, these are averages only. Experienced birth attendants never cease to be amazed at the variability of the normal pattern. In my practice, I have seen first labors go on for two days, but I have also seen more than one first labor in which the cervix dilated from two centimeters to "full" in less than an hour. I vividly remember one woman who had irregular but distressing contractions without progress in dilatation for over forty-eight hours—no doubt, as I thought, a prolonged latent phase. To stimulate her labor, one of the midwives administered castor oil and an enema in the office. Within minutes this woman, who had never experienced labor before, felt the urge to push. My initial reaction was that the enema was working, and I suggested that she try using the toilet. When she was unable to produce a bowel movement, I suggested that she lie down in a chaise longue in our treatment room until the urge ceased. But the urge to push continued. I did a vaginal examination and found, to my utter disbelief, that she was fully dilated. There was no time to get to the hospital. We hastily pulled supplies together, and she had the baby right in the office. Both baby and mother came through in fine condition.

Each woman's labor is truly her own, and its particular course needs to be respected and attended to. Some common patterns, as well described by midwife Peggy Spindel, are as follows:

1. Some women go very slowly through early labor, then take off quickly when active labor is reached. This is the pattern described by Friedman as the norm.

2. Some women involuntarily "tighten up" and resist stronger contractions (especially at dilatation of four to five centimeters) to the point where those present begin to worry about the lack of progress. When these women seemingly can hold back no longer and are able to "let go," they dilate very easily.

3. Some women progress in steps rather than continuously, resting as each new step is reached. It seems as if they successively interpret, integrate, then yield to each new set of sensations.

4. Some women resist when descent, with its strong genital sensations, begins to occur, even though they may have dilated rapidly until then (the late active stage), and pushing may be very slow.

5. Some women do not show their labor very much at all. It is hard to tell when they are having a contraction and how strong it is. Vaginal examinations must be done periodically to assess progress. Often these women dilate quite well.

6. Some women stop their labor entirely at some point, either to deal with a problem or to rest, or seemingly for no apparent reason. This unusual variant of labor, while deviating from the norm, may still be compatible with a trouble-free birth.

The configuration of the birth canal varies along its course. It is not like a curved tube or tunnel with a constant diameter throughout. At the entry to the birth canal the widest measurements are the oblique distances running from the right back to the left front and from the left back to the right front. At the outlet of the canal, the widest dimension is from front to back, from the tip of the spine (coccyx) to the juncture of the pubic bone in the front. As the baby's body descends in the birth canal, it turns and twists to accommodate to these shifts in dimension. The baby apparently plays an active role in moving himself or herself along. In the LOA position, the head approaches the perineum at an angle and then moves to a direct front-to-back orientation just as it is being born, while the shoulders and back, following behind higher in the canal, are still at an angle. When the head fully emerges, it immediately turns back into alignment with the rest of the body. As the shoulders are born, they move into a direct front-to-back position with one shoulder under the pubic bone as the other emerges over the coccyx. As the shoulders turn, the head turns with them, and the baby's face looks directly to the side. (See Figures 14 and 15.)

While the posterior position (occiput pointing to the back) is a normal but minority presentation from which babies are safely born, it is one that is often associated with the prolongation of labor and the experience of back pain. If a baby is posterior and progress in labor is slow, efforts are usually made to help the head (and the baby) to rotate forward, either by having the mother change position or by having the attendant turn the head manually in the vagina.

Prolonged early labor (or *prolonged latent phase*) is the term generally used to describe delays of twenty hours or more in first labors and fourteen or more in subsequent ones. A prolonged early labor can be a major source of distress to a woman, who may become discouraged and physically exhausted. Her condition is compounded by lack of sleep and dehydration.

Two basic approaches to this problem are to stimulate labor or to slow it down. The course to follow depends on how tired the woman is. She may need to rest for a while, or she may have enough reserve to get on with her labor after brief stimulation. If she has the will to move along and still has some energy, there are certain measures that can pick up a labor, particularly, having her walk around and, in the hospital, administering oxytocin (see pp. 203–204). In any case, she needs reassurance that failure to

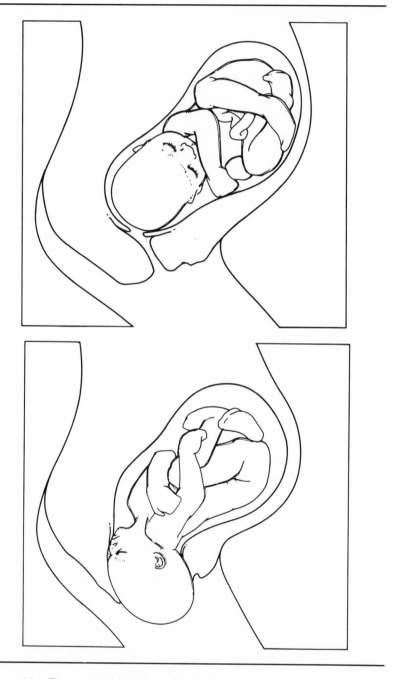

Figure 14.   Descent and rotation of baby in birth canal

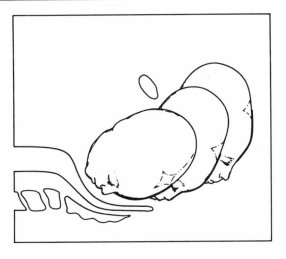

Figure 15.   Rotation of baby's head during birth

progress is not of her own doing, for a woman can do everything "right" and still have this problem. Reassurance from a trusted, familiar attendant that both she and the baby are basically well can bolster her flagging spirits.

An approach that takes a very different view of prolonged early labor (actually eliminating it as a possibility) and is attracting wide interest (possibly because of shortening hospital stays) is called the active management of labor. Popularized by the Royal Maternity Hospital of Dublin, Ireland, active management involves (1) a strict definition of labor onset involving regular and painful uterine contractions at least once in 5 minutes in association with either complete effacement ("taking up"—see pp. 188, 332–333) of the cervix or spontaneous rupture of membranes, (2) rupture of the membranes (see p. 187) of all women in labor in whom such rupture has not occurred spontaneously, (3) use of oxytocin (see pp. 202–204) when the cervix dilates at less than one centimeter per hour, and (4) cesarean section if delivery does not occur within twelve hours.

The primary birth attendant in the Dublin program is a midwife who gives one-on-one care to the laboring woman. In Dublin, active management has resulted in excellent outcomes among the babies, including a cesarean delivery rate of less than 6 percent, which is remarkably low by American standards even when allowance is made for differences in the populations of women served. However, this cesarean rate is no lower than that achieved in American birthing centers (see pp. 345–347) that do not practice active management, suggesting that other factors account for the high rate of vaginal births. One common element in the care provided in both settings is the midwife. As mentioned in Chapter 2, Drs. John Kennell and Marshall Klaus, in their multinational studies of labor support by one female attendant, whom they call the *doula*, (see Appendix E) have brought to our attention just how important continuity of care by a birth attendant can be. I suspect that what may be most significant in the low cesarean rates of the two settings is not so much use or non-use of oxytocin and rupture of the membranes as the attention of a midwife attuned to the needs of the laboring woman.

In a study from Northwestern University, reported in the February 13th 1992 issue of the *New England Journal of Medicine* Dr. Lopez-Zeno and colleagues conducted a controlled trial of active management during first labors and achieved a cesarean section rate of 10.5 percent, compared with 14.1 percent in the control (traditionally managed) group. In this study, not using midwives, the average length of labor was shortened by 1.66 hours, and significantly fewer infections occurred among the mothers who were actively managed. Almost three-fourths of the women at Northwestern received epidural anesthetics. More studies are clearly needed.

(In the Northwestern study, the cesarean section rate in the traditionally managed labors was less than the rate in the same hospital during the six months preceding the study for women with their first labors, dropping from 20.9 percent to 14.1 percent. Apparently the performance of the study, with its avowed goal of a lowered cesarean rate, had an important institution-wide effect. These results exemplify laudable efforts now underway at many hospitals to reduce cesarean rates [See discussion on cesarean births on pp. 284–291]. Nonetheless, birthing centers have achieved, in my opinion, still more impressive results both with respect to cesarean rates and other measures such as non-use of anesthesia and lower rates of episiotomies. This suggests to me that the low-technology, patient-oriented, research-based approach to labor and birth used in the birthing center is pointing the way to reform of maternity care and should be carefully watched by all those setting policy in hospital obstetrical units [see p. 346].)

If the decision is to quiet the labor down and allow the woman to rest, a less common approach than in the past, measures that can help include warm baths and medications. *Hydroxyzine* (also known by the trade name Vistaril) slows contractions and can be given either by mouth or by injection. It is sometimes combined at home births with two shots of whiskey. Morphine sulfate in relatively large amounts is probably the most effective drug for allowing a woman to rest. Administered by injection, two doses fifteen to twenty minutes apart are usually required. It should be given only in the hospital. While most women fall asleep after receiving morphine, many report that they are still aware of their contractions but better able to tolerate them. At the very least, morphine does seem to permit rest and the recuperation of energy. Sometimes labor stops completely, to resume within several days, but more commonly it is only temporarily dampened.

Fluids and Food

The basis for the traditional hospital recommendation that laboring women avoid eating and drinking in labor and rely on intravenous fluids (I.V.s) exclusively is that in an emergency, should a general (gas) anesthetic (see p. 215) be required to deliver the baby (usually by cesarean section), there is a danger that, during the induction of anesthesia, the woman will vomit and breathe the stomach contents into her lungs. This is indeed a serious problem; chemical pneumonia and even death can result.

Critical review of this policy, however, finds it flawed in several ways. First and foremost, proper anesthetic technique (compression of the upper airway by pressing on the neck) can prevent aspiration of vomited stomach contents during anesthesia induction. Second, general anesthesia is little used today, certainly compared to fifty-plus years ago when the policy of no food or fluid by mouth was developed. Third, it is not proven that a stomach empty of fluids and food will prevent the aspiration problem. The acid normally present in the stomach is itself highly irritating to the lungs if aspirated. In light of the evidence, the question becomes Why base a policy affecting millions of women on a theoretical risk that affects only a few?

There is also accumulating evidence that glucose given to the mother intravenously may have negative consequences for the baby. The glucose passes across the placenta into the baby's blood, where it stimulates the baby's pancreas to secrete insulin. At birth when the outside source of glucose stops, the extra insulin drives down the baby's blood sugar, with potentially harmful effects. Despite the lack of evidence to support the policy of no fluids or food in labor, this practice persists in many hospitals (but not in birthing centers or home births; see pp. 15, 347)—another example of the gap between practice and science.

Early in labor, where permitted, easily digested carbohydrate foods—such as bread, fruit, rice, and pasta—and light protein foods—such as cheese and yogurt—can safely be taken as long as a woman wants them. As labor progresses, the emphasis should shift to high-calorie liquids. In general, water, Gatorade, iced tea, and noncitrus fruit juices are well tolerated. Honey or sugar can provide calories for women who want to drink plain water. Women should optimally consume eight ounces of fluid and 200 calories an hour. (As examples of frequently used foods, a tablespoon of honey contains 64 calories; one cup of grape juice, 167 calories.)

Some home-birth attendants have noted that citrus and apple juices and dairy products can cause vomiting in heavy labor. They advise women to freeze cranberry or grape juice in ice trays to use in the event of nausea. Crushed ice from these juices, plain ice chips, or small sips of cool water tend to be kept down if taken in small amounts between each contraction. Dry toast or crackers also often help reduce nausea.

Drugs That Contract the Uterus

Oxytocin (trade names Pitocin and Syntocinon), *ergonovine maleate* (Ergotrate), and *methylergonovine maleate* (Methergine) are drugs that stimulate contraction of the uterus. They play an important role in the care of women during and immediately after labor.

Oxytocin is the synthetic form of a hormone normally secreted by the pituitary gland to contract the muscles of the uterus and the glands of the breasts, leading to the ejection of milk. In the postpartum period, the secretion of this natural hormone accounts for the "afterpains" of uterine contractions familiar to nursing mothers, particularly with their second and subsequent babies. The secretion of natural oxytocin is stimulated by nerve impulses that reach the brain and pituitary from the breasts during nipple stimulation. Thus, stimulation can initiate and augment labor as well as initiate both the letdown of milk and the uterine contractions that help prevent postpartum hemorrhage. Because oxytocin is metabolized readily and lasts but a short time in the blood, it is ideal for artificially inducing uterine contractions in labor.

When used intravenously to enhance labor, an ampule of ten units of oxytocin is thoroughly mixed with one liter of salt-sugar solution to produce a concentration of ten milliunits (one one-thousandth of a unit) per milliliter of solution. Oxytocin is delivered intravenously through a constant infusion pump set to carefully regulate the amount of hormone entering the woman. When using oxytocin, attendants must be on constant guard to prevent the uterus from contracting either violently or for a prolonged period, lest it rupture or the fetus be harmed from poor circulation or head injuries. Oxytocin is immediately discontinued if worrisome heart-rate patterns develop. Intrauterine pressure monitors inserted via a tube through the vagina are sometimes used to measure the intensity of uterine contractions during oxytocin stimulation.

Oxytocin can be used only when there is reasonable evidence that the baby adequately fits the pelvis (see pp. 44–48 on pelvic measurements and pp. 303–304 on disproportion). Because of the risk of uterine rupture, oxytocin is generally avoided in cases of gross uterine overdistension, as in hydramnios (p. 311), with twin pregnancies (pp. 338–341), and in women who have had more than five full-term pregnancies.

Oxytocin is sometimes used to initiate labor. In the past, such "elective" inductions were routinely done for the convenience of the family and/or the obstetrician. Unfortunately, the price paid for this convenience was a prematurity rate of about 3.5 percent, due to errors in estimating gestational age. Elective induction is now frowned on, but medical grounds for inducing labor *do* exist. For example, in intrauterine growth disturbance (pp. 312–315) or preeclampsia (pp. 327–329), induced delivery of the baby may be essential for fetal and maternal well-being. Nipple stimulation is also used as a "natural" alternative to the administration of synthetic oxytocin, leading the mother to produce her own.

Finally, oxytocin can be used to help contract the uterus after the baby is born. There is now good evidence that such use decreases postpartum bleeding (hemorrhage). For this purpose it can be given by injection or added to an intravenous infusion already in place.

Multigravidas (women who have had more than two full-term pregnancies) seem to be more sensitive to oxytocin than women who are pregnant for the first or second time. They experience more cramping and pain from administered oxytocin or from the natural hormone they produce themselves. As just mentioned, their afterpains are characteristically more intense. For these reasons, oxytocin should be given to these women in lower doses.

Oxytocin is not always effective. The earlier in pregnancy, the less likely the uterus will respond or an "unripe" cervix will undergo dilatation. When labor must be induced to deliver an immature fetus that has died in utero, a prostaglandin (see pp. 291–300) is used instead.

There is also a limit to the amount of oxytocin a woman can tolerate before harmful side effects occur. Since the hormone also inhibits the capacity of the kidneys to excrete water, an overdose can put a woman in danger of water intoxication.

Ergonovine is a chemical derived from the ergot fungus found in rye and other grains or produced synthetically in the laboratory. Ergonovine causes uterine contraction. Unlike oxytocin, the effects of ergonovine last for hours, making it unsuitable during labor but useful for maintaining a contracted uterus after delivery of the placenta.

Ergonovine and methylergonovine are administered by injection after the placenta has been delivered and can be given in conjunction with oxytocin. They can also be given by mouth as needed to maintain the uterus in a contracted state. Both can be used to contract the uterus and prevent bleeding after a D and C (pp. 321–322).

Because of undesirable side effects of ergonovine preparations, including nausea and elevated blood pressure, they are less used today.

Prostaglandins are another widely used group of chemicals that cause uterine muscle contraction, and are usually administered as a vaginal gel to induce labor. They have the advantage, over oxytocin, of being effective even when the cervix is unripe. (See also the discussion of the use of prostaglandins in abortion on p. 300.)

Pain in Labor

The pain of labor is different from other kinds of human pain because it signifies a normal physiological process, one of the few kinds of pain (besides teething) that does. Because we usually associate pain with a health problem, our first objective in dealing with labor pain is to break that association. Contractions mean progress; each labor pain means that the baby is one step closer to being born. While labor pain per se cannot be reduced, the fear that exaggerates it can be. Nor does pain in labor contradict the view of the female body as essentially healthy, designed to conceive and bear children. Instead, it may be seen as a prototype of the anguish and difficulty so often associated with the creative acts of all human beings. It is not coincidental that creative persons often liken their work to giving birth. A woman can use the pain of labor as an opportunity to come into touch with her own basic resiliency. Trusting in one's own body and self is the first step toward dealing with pain in labor in a nontechnological way.

Women point out that there are times when it seems impossible to cope with even one more contraction, when it truly seems as if they "can't go on" and would gladly accept "anything" to "end it all." Transition is usually the stage when this sense of impossibility arises. Often when a woman feels worst, she has just about reached the top of the mountain. At this point she needs to mobilize all her resources to make it to the summit. Awareness of this paradoxical mixture of pain and progress can inspire her to continue.

A useful perspective on pain in labor is to consider its duration:

only a few hours out of a lifetime are at stake. Dealing with pain in labor can contribute to a woman's sense of achievement, fulfillment, and satisfaction with her own capacities and can bolster her physical and emotional integrity.

Such an ideal, however, must not be so rigidly adhered to that it inappropriately deprives a woman of needed pain relief. There is a distinction here between heroism and martyrdom. The use of anesthesia or analgesia may represent the best decision and need not be regarded as a sign of inadequacy or failure. Pain in labor, if it overwhelms and terrifies the woman, may inhibit the strength of uterine contractions and decrease the flow of blood to the placenta, stressing the baby. Every birth attendant has seen an injection of epidural anesthesia convert a labor that was becoming a nightmare to an exhausted, frightened woman into a satisfying birth experience. In many situations, analgesia or anesthesia can be a blessing. Even women who are most committed to unmedicated birth find support in knowing that these technological measures are available if needed and that they need not feel abandoned to useless suffering when other "natural" measures have failed.

One of the hardest judgments an attendant must make during childbirth is whether to be firmly encouraging ("Remember how much you wanted to do it on your own. We're going to help you do it. You are doing very well, so let's keep it up!") or to decide to intervene technically. The woman herself may not be the best judge, for there are few women who, while suffering the intense pain of labor, would refuse medication if offered. Yet the experience of many attendants and pregnant women shows time and time again that motivated women *with the right kind of support* can pull themselves together and go on to deliver without medication. Knowing the woman well helps attendants make such distinctions. Midwives often spend hours during the prenatal period getting to know their clients—their strengths, weaknesses, and coping styles. At the same time, of course, the clients are getting to know them. This mutual knowledge proves invaluable when decisions must be made in the intense atmosphere of labor. If it is unlikely that familiar people will attend a woman in birth, compensatory supports can be built in. Her partner may serve as labor coach, as in "husband-coached childbirth," or another relative or friend can perform this service.

The importance of trust and empathy also argues for the greater involvement of women as birth attendants, especially women who have themselves had babies. Women who have experienced childbirth have a built-in advantage over male doctors in terms of their capacity to empathize with the laboring woman. You will notice in both of the stories in Chapter 1 how inventive the midwives and nurses are. They seem to have an endless bag of tricks to draw on in providing physical and emotional comfort and support.

Responding to the complaints of a woman in pain, as labor coaches and other attendants know, is complicated. Responses are almost automatic. We try to reassure ("Everything's okay; don't worry"), to offer what relief we can, to assume responsibility ("If only I could do something for you . . . "), and risk invalidating her experience ("Other women have done it, and you can, too").

Real communication with a woman in pain begins with the recognition that it is *she* who is in pain and who needs, first and foremost, an acknowledgment of her feelings: "It sounds as if you're feeling that you can't make it one step further." This show of understanding validates her experience and lessens some of her fear of the unknown in feeling crazily outside the bounds of human experience. A woman in labor needs to know that regardless of her bewildering feelings and embarrassment at not being able to cope, she can count on the unqualified support of others. Actively "being with" a woman in labor—quite apart from "doing for" her—such as supporting her in breathing through a contraction, is half the job of coaching. No woman should ever labor alone.

On a more practical level, pain can often be reduced through a change in position. A woman in pain can try turning on one side or another; can sit up, stand up, or walk around; or can get down on all fours, experimenting until she finds what works best. Back pain is often relieved by lying on one's side, sitting upright, walking, or getting on hands and knees. Firm pressure with the wrist or the palm of the hand against the most painful spot can help. Sometimes a light stroking motion feels better than pressure. Taking a warm bath or shower also lessens pain, as does massaging, singing, or listening to music.

Relaxation and breathing techniques are now the classical approach to coping with the pain of labor. They have been featured in childbirth education classes for the past forty years. Both are discussed in the section on prenatal exercise, along with the current rethinking of the role of breathing in labor (see pp. 94–110).

Medical Pain Relief

ANALGESICS

Analgesics and anesthetics are medications used for pain relief. Analgesics reduce pain to make it tolerable, while anesthetics are intended to eliminate it completely. Analgesics in everyday use include aspirin and acetaminophen (Tylenol). Among the stronger analgesics are codeine, Percodan, and some newer drugs like Zomax. The strongest analgesics include morphine, meperidine (Demerol), alphaprodine (Nisentil), and nalbuphene (Nubain).

The analgesics most commonly used in labor are meperidine and alphaprodine. They are sometimes combined with the antihistamine promethazine to enhance their effect, producing a dose with more impact and greater effectiveness. These drugs are given by injection. In addition to relieving pain, they produce some drowsiness and euphoria. Many women find that these drugs help them regain their strength during a long, difficult early labor. Analgesics pass through the placenta to the fetus where they can depress those centers in the baby's brain that drive respiration, an effect of clinical importance only if the baby is called on to breathe on its own, not while the work of respiration is being done by the mother. Analgesics can also sedate babies, resulting in drowsiness that can interfere with the baby's responsiveness and feeding during the first few hours after birth, or even longer. Because of their depressant and sedative effects, these drugs should be given long before the expected time of birth, and preferably only during the first stage of labor (see p. 186). Barring an unexpectedly rapid birth, as in an emergency cesarean, their effect on an infant's respiration should be over well before delivery. If the effect is not over, and if the baby's respiration is depressed, assistance can be provided as needed with a breathing bag and oxygen. The drug naloxone hydrochloride (Narcan) can also be administered to the baby as often as needed to reverse the respiratory depression effects of analgesics.

ANESTHETICS

Anesthetics are drugs that can eliminate pain. Two broad classes are used—local nerve-blocking agents (which prevent the nerves from passing messages to the brain), such as those used in dental work or in surgery of the skin, and gases that are inhaled through the lungs to affect the entire body. Lidocaine (Xylocaine) is a popular example of the former, and nitrous oxide, the latter.

Blocking Agents.   In general, the nerve-blocking agents are quite safe as currently used. One known drawback is that even though the drugs are injected into a defined place in the body, they are absorbed into the mother's bloodstream in small amounts and passed through the placenta to the fetus. The issue of persisting drug effects in the baby after birth, especially as they affect the newborn's behavior during early parent–infant interaction, has largely been laid to rest.

Accidental injection of the blocking drug into the mother's blood, which sometimes occurs despite all precautions, may result in high circulating levels in the blood. The mother may experience light-headedness, dizziness, slurred speech, a metallic taste in her mouth, numbness of her tongue and mouth, muscle twitching, loss of consciousness, and, in the extreme, generalized convulsions. Her blood pressure may fall because of the drug itself and because she is lying flat on her back, still a common laboring position for women who have received blocking anesthetics. Fetal distress may occur as a direct effect of the drug or as a result of decreased oxygen due to diminished blood flow to the placenta from the drug complications described in the mother. These rare problems of inadvertent overdose of the mother, which can occur even in the best of hands, are usually treated successfully but obviously are best avoided altogether.

The blocking agents are most commonly given as *spinal* or *epidural anesthetics*. "Spinals" and "epidurals," as they are called for short, have the advantage of allowing the woman to remain awake and aware during labor and delivery. Both can be used for either vaginal or cesarean birth. Epidural anesthesia is used for pain relief during both labor and delivery, while spinal anesthesia is used only for delivery.

In *spinal anesthesia,* a needle inserted between the vertebrae of the lower back introduces the blocking agent into the spinal canal. The drug bathes the spinal nerves in the canal before they exit to pass to lower parts of the body. Both sensory and motor nerves are temporarily blocked so that the mother's pelvic area and legs are numbed and cannot be moved voluntarily. The "level" of anesthesia (that is, how high on the abdomen the anesthesia reaches) is largely determined by how much drug is given and by the position the mother assumes immediately following the injection. For a vaginal delivery, the goal is to anesthetize only the perineum and legs. For a cesarean section, anesthesia should be achieved to the level of the rib cage.

A spinal anesthetic can be given while the woman is either sitting or lying on her side. First the skin is cleaned with an antiseptic solution. Next a sterile drape with a central hole is placed over the lower back. The anesthesiologist numbs the skin with some of the blocking agent, infiltrating the solution down to the spinal column so that the "channel" between skin and spinal column is anesthetized. The woman is then asked to curl forward to open the spaces between the vertebrae. A thin, hollow needle containing a removable stylet is pushed through the now-numbed area until it enters the canal. The stylet is removed, and the location of the needle in the spinal canal is verified by the return of clear spinal fluid. A syringe containing the anesthetic solution is then attached to the needle, and the medication is introduced between uterine contractions. For a vaginal delivery the woman is asked to sit up for forty-five seconds to allow the medication to settle to the bottom of the spinal canal. For a cesarean section, the woman lies first on one side, then on the other, to allow the anesthetic to travel upward in the canal to block the nerves that supply the entire abdomen. The level of anesthesia is controlled to some extent by tilting the operating table either up or down as indicated. The anesthesiologist checks the level by checking the woman's response to the prick of a needle moved up or down the abdomen.

In vaginal delivery, spinal anesthesia causes the mother to lose the ability to bear down. The higher the level of anesthetic, the less voluntary control. In addition, spinal anesthesia decreases the force of uterine contractions. For both reasons, forceps and an episiotomy (see pp. 218, 219–223) are almost inevitably needed. Because of these effects on the course of labor, spinal anesthesia is not given for vaginal deliveries until the cervix is fully dilated, at the onset of the second stage of labor (see p. 186), and delivery is usually accomplished soon after its administration.

Spinal anesthesia carries several risks. The most common is a drop in the mother's blood pressure due to a blockage of the sympathetic nerves that control the tone of muscles in arteries. When the arteries dilate, the same volume of blood is contained in a larger volume of vessel, and thus the pressure of blood falls. This fall in blood pressure is made worse if a woman lies flat on her back to deliver; in this position, the uterus rests on the large vein in the back of the abdomen (inferior vena cava), interfering with the return of blood to the heart and the pumping of blood from the heart. For this reason, the delivery table is tilted to the side. (See pp. 216–218 on position in labor.) Another way to minimize the fall in blood pressure due to spinal anesthesia is to give the woman a liter or more of intravenous sugar-salt solution before beginning the procedure. If a drop in blood pressure occurs despite fluids and avoidance of lying flat, medication to contract the dilated muscles in the arteries is administered. Because of the risk of low blood pressure, spinal anesthesia is not used when a woman's blood volume is already compromised, for example, when blood loss has occurred or when preeclampsia is present (see pp. 327–329).

Another problem with spinal anesthetic, far less common today than it was in the past, is headache, often referred to as "spinal headache," which usually comes on several hours after the procedure. This pain is believed to be due to the slow leakage of spinal fluid through the puncture site, which results in loss of the cushioning of the brain that the spinal fluid provides. As a result, the brain tugs on its attachments, producing pain. Spinal headache is minimized by using a very thin needle, which produces a very small hole. Bed rest and analgesics are helpful, and abdominal support with a girdle is also useful. If all else fails, a "blood patch," or injection of a few cubic centimeters of the woman's own blood into the area just outside the puncture site, has proven effective in sealing off the tear. Occasionally, spinal anesthesia causes temporary loss of control of the bladder, which may necessitate bladder catheterization during the first twenty-four hours after delivery.

A dreaded rare complication of the inadvertent introduction of an excessively large dose of anesthetic into the spinal canal is blockage of all nerves, which produces temporary total body paralysis. In this emergency, hypotension (low blood pressure) is treated by using the measures just discussed and by elevating the legs to allow blood now needed elsewhere to drain back into the heart. The depressed respiration is treated by passing a tube through the mouth and into the airway to move oxygen in and out of the lungs with the use of a hand bag or respirator. Fluids and drugs to constrict blood vessels are also given. Spinal anesthesia is not used in women who have had allergic reactions to local anesthetics, whose skin at the injection site is infected, or who have chronic low back pain, which could be aggravated by the spinal needle.

In the *epidural anesthetic,* the nerves are numbed after their exit from the spinal canal into the space just outside it, which is known as the epidural space. In this space, the sensory nerves that transmit external stimuli are less well insulated and more susceptible to blockade than are the motor nerves that govern movement. Thus, pain and other sensations are eliminated while voluntary movement is preserved, an advantage over spinal anesthesia. But because the woman's sense of position and tension is blocked, her use of these voluntary muscles is less effective. Unlike the spinal anesthetic, which is given only during the second stage of labor, the epidural can be given earlier. Usually, however, it is not given until the active phase of the first stage, because the anesthetic can stop labor altogether if it is administered during the latent phase. The procedure for performing an epidural is similar to that used in the spinal. Once the needle enters the epidural space, a thin plastic catheter is passed through it. Often the woman will experience a twinge of pain in her back or leg as the catheter touches a nerve. When the needle is withdrawn, the catheter is left in place and the anesthetic solution is injected into the space. The catheter is then taped in place on the woman's back until delivery. A major convenience of the epidural block is that additional solution can be introduced as needed. A common approach is to give a "top-off" every ninety minutes. Less drug is used this way than by continuous infusion. Fewer drug-related effects occur as well. This approach has proved superior to allowing mothers to self-administer additional anesthetic through a syringe device.

Several uncommon problems may be encountered about 0.5 to 1 percent of the time. For one, inadvertent entry into the spinal canal, unrecognized before anesthetic injection, can result in a high level of spinal anesthesia, which can cause widespread temporary paralysis and respiratory and blood pressure problems similar to those described as possible consequences of spinal anesthesia. The resulting leak of spinal fluid may also cause a "spinal headache" (as previously described) even if no anesthetic was introduced. Also of major concern is inadvertent injection into the mother's bloodstream through a vein. Proper technique, which includes using small, safe test doses, can reduce these risks and minimize their consequences.

Epidural anesthesia is not always completely effective even in the most experienced hands. In one study, 85 percent of women were free of pain, 12 percent had partial relief, and 3 percent experienced no relief at all. An epidural given to relieve labor pain, with the catheter pointing upward (toward the head) to direct the solution to the nerves supplying the uterus, may not effectively numb the perineum during the second stage.

As with spinals, epidural anesthesia can produce a decrease in blood pressure. Much of this effect, as noted earlier, is due to the once-common practice of lying flat, with the resulting pressure of the uterus on the great blood vessels in the abdomen. It is important that women with epidurals not lie flat on their backs. (See pp. 216–218 on position in labor.) Intravenous fluids are also used to prevent hypotension.

Epidural anesthesia decreases uterine contractions, slows labor, and limits pushing during the second stage. These features may necessitate an episiotomy and the use of vacuum extraction or forceps, and add up to a highly medical type of birth—one managed and controlled by the doctor, not the woman. Local anesthetic is also frequently used to numb the perineum as an episiotomy is performed, as a perineal laceration is sutured, or as an episiotomy incision is repaired. The anesthetic is injected directly into the tissues involved.

In a 1989 article in the *American Journal of Obstetrics and Gynecology*, Drs. James Thorp, Jay McNitt and Phyllis Leppert reported the results of a study of 711 women in their first labor, 447 of whom received epidural anesthesia and 264 of whom did not. Some of the women in the no-epidural group received analgesics. The frequency of cesarean section was significantly greater in the epidural group (10.3 percent) than in the no-epidural group (3.8 percent). A limitation in the study is that the design was retrospective, was not randomized, and lacked controls: characteristics of the women other than the use of an epidural may have accounted for the difference in the cesarean rate, although none were apparent on review of their labor records. Randomized control studies of this question, which are difficult to organize, are needed. Regarding long-term effects of epidurals, not much is yet known. A report in the *British Medical Journal* in 1990 showed that among women who delivered vaginally, long-term backache was almost twice as common for those who had received epidurals than for those who had not, a finding well worth a close look in future studies.

Epidural anesthesia is now being widely promoted by anesthesiologists and obstetricians. It is often featured in articles in popular women's magazines as the best way to have a painless childbirth. Anesthesiologists make themselves readily available on the labor and delivery floor for epidurals, especially for insured patients. An expectation is being created that epidural anesthesia is and should be a routine procedure. I find it regrettable that the full story about epidural anesthesia is not being presented so that women can make a truly informed choice. The consent form that women sign for the procedure presents the risks in far too narrow terms. Neither epidural nor spinal anesthetics are used in birth centers, where the best outcomes in labor and delivery are achieved today.

Intrathecal Injection.   A promising new use of the technique of spinal anesthesia, referred to as intrathecal injection and involving use of morphine and similar drugs rather than anesthetic agents, is now gaining popularity. When injected into the fluid of the spinal canal early in labor, morphine and closely related compounds can reduce pain sensation while interfering minimally with muscle control, for up to eight to ten hours. Thus, a woman in labor can move her legs, walk around, and push as needed. Undesirable side effects are nausea and itching of the nose, face, and upper chest. More studies of this approach are needed to compile cumulative data on effectiveness and side effects.

General Anesthesia.   While less commonly used in obstetrics than blocking agents, gas, or general anesthesia, still occupies an important place in labor and delivery. The great advantages are ease of administration and the rapid onset of effect. Thus, in emergencies in which time is critical, it is the anesthetic of choice. The great disadvantage of general anesthesia is that it passes directly to the fetus, anesthetizing it as well. This is rarely serious unless the fetus is threatened by some other problem. Of course, during labor under general anesthesia the mother is asleep or nearly asleep and misses out on much of the birth. The most serious problem of general anesthesia is the possibility that the laboring woman may vomit and aspirate the stomach contents into her lungs, producing a chemical pneumonia. As I pointed out earlier, this problem is to a large extent preventable through proper anesthetic technique, including external pressure on the airway in the neck to prevent aspiration of any stomach contents vomited during the early stage of anesthesia administration. (This topic is also discussed more fully under "Fluids and Food," pp. 201–202.)

Learning about Anesthesia.   In some hospitals anesthesiologists meet with pregnant women and their partners to answer their questions about anesthesia and the role of the anesthesiologist. Some obstetricians routinely refer patients for these consultations, which may be regarded as part of childbirth education, being equally informative to both those who have definitely decided they want anesthesia and those who would use it only if needed. The topic of anesthesia is also covered in most childbirth education classes. Couples should inform themselves about anesthesia prior to, rather than during, labor itself, when decision making is more pressured. (For further discussion on the topic of pain in labor and of alternatives to the use of drugs, see pp. 205–208.)

Position in Labor and Delivery

In a traditional hospital birth, a woman lies on her back with her legs in stirrups. This supine, or *lithotomy,* position is often associated with episiotomy and the use of anesthesia and forceps. It was designed primarily to allow the physician easier access to the birth canal and perineum for the manipulations that often characterize this type of delivery. In fact, it is the supine position that makes these interventions necessary, and it has come under considerable criticism for several reasons.

First, when a woman lies flat on her back, the uterus presses down on the large artery and vein that run adjacent to the spine, interfering with the return of blood to the woman's heart, the outflow of blood from her heart, and blood circulation to the uterus, placenta, and fetus. Fetal distress (see pp. 144–146) can result; moreover, the uterus, deprived of its normal circulation, is less able to contract, potentially interfering with labor. A second problem is that bearing down during the second stage is much more difficult and less effective when lying on one's back than when upright. Third, as Dr. Michel Odent, obstetrician of the famous birthing center at Pithiviers in France, claims, based on extensive clinical experience, tearing of the perineum may be reduced to a very low level in the upright position, and episiotomies are rarely if ever needed.

Births in preindustrial societies have almost always been conducted with women either standing (by holding or being held up) or squatting, in both cases taking full advantage of the force of gravity to help push the baby out. (A similar effect was achieved by Andrea in our home-birth story, when she sat on the toilet seat, an excellent place for a woman to labor in the home or a hospital.) X rays of the pelvis show that the outlet of the birth canal is increased by 28 percent (almost a third) when a woman squats! An increase of this magnitude can make the difference between a vaginal and an operative delivery.

The upright position (standing, sitting, or squatting), is also an excellent one in which to labor, especially if it relieves pain. This observation is based both on clinical experience and on studies that show a shortening of labor in the vertical position. A small, but controlled, study from the University of Southern California showed that walking was as effective as oxytocin in stimulating labor.

The upright position also appears to be as advantageous in delivering the placenta as it is in delivering the baby. While there are no controlled studies yet, the evidence available suggests an advantage in expelling the placenta while squatting.

The results of a randomized control study of birth in the squatting position were reported in the July 8th 1989 issue of the *Lancet*. With squatting there were fewer forceps deliveries (9 versus 16 percent) and shorter second stages of labor (thirty-one versus forty-five minutes). There were fewer perineal tears, but more labial tears. Eighty-two percent of the women who squatted maintained the upright position for most of the second stage. The women reported great satisfaction with being vertical during the latter part of labor and during delivery.

Another position that is more effective than lying on the back is sitting up, at least at a forty-five-degree angle, drawing the legs up if desired to provide more effective pushing and possibly to enlarge the diameter of the birth canal. (The newer birthing chairs let the woman achieve this position very well.) Since the baby normally first moves downward, once the head is out (that is, toward the mother's back in whatever position she may be), the sitting woman either brings her buttocks to the edge of the bed or elevates her buttocks with a firm object (such as an inverted bedpan covered with a soft pad) in order to provide room for the emerging baby.

Another effective position for labor and delivery, but one not yet subjected to critical evaluation, is lying on the side with the upper leg held up by an assistant and the back and buttocks near the edge of the bed. The attendant stands behind the buttocks with one hand supporting the perineum and the other arched over the uplifted leg to control the baby's head. This position also helps the woman to see her baby emerging.

Forceps and Vacuum Extractor

Forceps are metal instruments like tongs with blades at one end that are designed to grasp the baby's head to pull it from the birth canal. The vacuum extractor is an alternative to forceps that appears to be as effective and less traumatic to mother and baby. The version most commonly used in the United States consists of a plastic suction cup attached to a hollow handle and air pump. The cup is applied to the baby's scalp, and a vacuum is created in the cup by a pump connected to the handle. This vacuum sucks the fetal scalp tightly against the interior of the cup (an effect similar to that produced by a toilet plunger), and it fills the hollow of the cup to form a firm seal. The handle can then be pulled to draw the baby down and out through the birth canal. The cup is usually applied during a contraction and released between contractions.

The major risks of both techniques are to the baby's skull and scalp. Forceps can crack the skull (rarely seriously), and extractors can cause the skin beneath the skull to swell. However, a 1991 *Lancet* report from Israel of 52,282 infants born in Jerusalem between 1964 and 1972 is very reassuring on the safety of forceps and vacuum extraction. There was no evidence of increased medical or mental impairment at age seventeen years among those who had been delivered by either of these methods.

Neither forceps nor the extractor are normally needed. They are useful when progress in delivery is arrested and when emergencies arise. They are more likely to be used when the woman is in the supine position and when epidural anesthesia is used.

Sterile Technique

The two births described in Chapter 1 show two different approaches to the question of how sterile a birth should be. In the traditional hospital birth, surgical sterility is the goal, while in an at-home birth cleanliness is the standard, as is the case for many births in birthing centers. At home, street clothes are worn by all, while in the hospital surgical scrub suits are required. The "prep" performed in the delivery room is completely bypassed at home. In both settings, however, sterile examining gloves are used to avoid introducing germs directly into the birth canal.

There is no evidence to suggest that elimination of sterile technique at home births is associated with any increased risk to either the mother or the baby. From the point of view of the baby's health, it could be argued that the baby at home is born into the environment in which he or she is going to live, and for which he or she has adequate protection.

Common hospital practices that have not been proven to prevent the spread of infection include the requirements for mothers to use hospital gowns (rather than garments brought from home) and for nurses and doctors who care for babies in nurseries to wear gowns, caps, and masks. While gowns protect regular garments from the messes associated with care of babies, no evidence proves that they control the spread of infection. Such dress codes should be eliminated or at least relaxed.

Hospitals also commonly restrict visiting by well children on the grounds that they will spread infection to mothers and babies. There is no evidence to support this policy, and it should be stopped.

Episiotomy

An episiotomy is an incision or surgical cut made with (sterile) scissors or a scalpel in the perineum, the area between the lower junction of the labia and the anus, performed to widen the open-

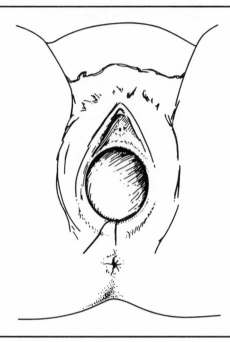

Figure 16.   Episiotomy: midline or angled to the side

ing of the vagina to ease passage of the baby's head. It may be
made in the midline (median) (more frequently done in this country) or angled to the side (mediolateral). (See Figure 16.) Usually
an episiotomy is repaired (sewn up) following delivery of the
placenta. Absorbable sutures that dissolve and so do not require
later removal are used. Of these, polyglycolate sutures (Dexon or
Vicryl) have been shown to be associated with less pain. Unless
a spinal or epidural anesthetic has been administered, making
and repairing an episiotomy are usually done under local anesthesia.

The mainstream medical view of episiotomy, which supported
its almost routine use, was described in a well-known textbook,
Williams Obstetrics, as "the most common operation in obstetrics."
It

> substitutes a straight, neat surgical incision for the ragged laceration
> that otherwise frequently results. It is easier to repair and heals better

than a tear. It spares the fetal head the necessity of serving as a battering ram against perineal obstruction. If prolonged, the pounding of the fetal head against the perineum may cause intracranial injury. Episiotomy shortens the second stage of labor.

Episiotomy is alleged to prevent vaginal and pelvic relaxation following birth and to prevent urinary (stress) incontinence, but there is no evidence to support these claims. It has also been recommended during the birth of premature babies to minimize trauma to the fetal skull, which is more delicate than that of a full-term infant, but here again, evidence is lacking. Episiotomy has its place in removing a barrier to progress of labor when the perineum is the barrier and in relieving distress of the mother or baby, or both.

The topic of episiotomy can arouse strong feelings. Many prominent obstetricians say that they "*always* do an episiotomy." But Sheila Kitzinger, a well-known critic of contemporary childbirth practices, termed the procedure "ritual genital mutilation," in which males exert power over women's bodies and deny women the opportunity to experience birth as a sexual act.

Critics of routine episiotomy point to the pain of the healing episiotomy and its negative effects on lovemaking, urination, and defecation. These discomforts are far worse, they believe, than the pain of a "natural" and "more physiological" tear in the perineum. Indeed, several early studies have shown that women who have episiotomies do report more postpartum pain and are slower to return to full activity, including sexual intercourse. The problem with such reports is that those women who had the procedure and those who didn't may have been different to start with. For example, it could be that only those most likely to tear badly received an episiotomy and would have been in even worse condition without it.

One study, in which women were allocated *at random* to either a restricted "conservative" or a "liberal" use of the procedure, was done by Dr. Adrian Grant of Oxford. The episiotomy rates of the two groups, who were otherwise similar in characteristics and were handled similarly in labor, were 10 percent and 51 percent, respectively. Interestingly, there were *no* differences between the groups with respect to the amount of pain reported after birth, the time it took for the perineum to become pain free, or problems with controlling urination. The one difference in outcomes was that women who were in the restricted group were more likely to have resumed sexual intercourse within a month after delivery (presumably because it was less uncomfortable for them). Despite the differences in episiotomy rates, there was little difference in the frequency with which suturing of the perineum was required. The women who did not receive an episiotomy were more likely to tear on their own, so that not having an episiotomy did not spare women from tearing and being sutured.

In 1992 an important randomized control study from Canada under the direction of Dr. Michael Klein, Professor of Family Medicine at McGill University, convincingly showed that women who had episiotomies had worse outcomes in all respects than those who did not: more pain, poorer perineal tone, and slower return to sexual function. Vaginal tears sustained during delivery healed better than did episiotomies. This study provides persuasive evidence that there is no justification for doing an episiotomy routinely. The only valid reasons for episiotomy are distress in the baby where delivery must be quickly accomplished or an inability of the mother to overcome the resistance of the perineum to delivery, an unusual circumstance.

A number of measures appear to minimize tearing and the need for episiotomy. (Few of these, we hasten to add, have been subjected to controlled clinical studies.) What follows is based on the experience of many colleagues.

1. As long as mother and baby are doing well, birth should be gradual and unhurried, in order to allow the perineum to stretch slowly. Women should "push" only if pushing increases their comfort. (There is little doubt that episiotomies facilitate quicker births, as do forceps, and so one inevitably wonders whether the time factor may not play a role in the popularity of this procedure with some obstetricians and their patients.)

2. In order to prevent undue stretching, the prepared mother can respond selectively to her urge to push, according to the status of her perineum. Attendants can give verbal feedback and show her the effects of her pushing with a mirror. If pushing causes too forceful stretching, the woman can stop pushing and allow

her uterus to do the work alone. A gentle push between contractions can then ease the baby's head out.

3. Maintenance of flexion of the baby's head (chin to chest) results in the smallest part of the head pushing through the vulva. Flexion is supported by downward pressure on the top (vertex) of the head by the attendant's hand during contractions.

4. Supporting the perineum is another way to minimize tearing. This is accomplished by maintaining constant counterpressure with the hand applied to the perineum as it gradually stretches.

5. Position in giving birth is also very important. There is accumulating evidence that the upright position, either standing or squatting, minimizes tearing, another good argument for avoiding lying flat on the back during delivery (see also p. 216).

6. Preparation of the perineum through Kegel exercises, by their "toning" effect on the muscles and fascia, is believed to make them more stretchable and less likely to tear, a point analogous to the minimization of muscle pain in joggers who stretch their muscles before running. (See pp. 94–110 on prenatal exercise and pp. 40–49 on the physical examination.)

Delivery of the Placenta

The third stage of labor begins with the birth of the baby and ends with the birth of the placenta. To facilitate separation and delivery of the placenta and minimize bleeding, an effective active management approach has been developed. This approach includes giving Pitocin (see pp. 202–204), cutting the umbilical cord just after the birth of the baby, and gently pulling on the cord to help the placenta separate. Sometimes the Pitocin is given on the appearance (birth) of the baby's shoulder. Early clamping of the cord is avoided when a mother has an Rh(D) negative blood type in order to minimize the transfusion (across the placenta) of Rh(D) positive fetal cells that could cause her to produce antibodies to the Rh(D) factor (see pp. 57–59). There is some evidence that the squatting position can aid in the expulsion of the placenta. Massage of the uterus also causes it to contract after the birth of the placenta. A mother can massage her uterus to keep it firm and contracted.

If the placenta fails to be delivered within a half hour of birth, or if there is brisk bleeding, it must be removed manually to prevent hemorrhaging. This painful procedure is ideally done under anesthesia. Once removed, the placenta is carefully inspected. In the unlikely event that a large piece is missing, the uterus must be explored manually under anesthesia to identify and permit removal of the fragment left behind.

CHAPTER

5

*After the Birth: Care of the Parents**

Postpartum Care

As more and more parents take their babies home soon after delivery, either in the hospital or in a birthing center, and as more women have their babies at home, they all have to rely more on themselves and less on professionals for dealing with common postpartum issues. Postpartum care includes the procedures outlined here.

Immediately after the birth the mother should be careful to *urinate frequently*, because a full bladder may keep the uterus from contracting as it should. To relieve stinging, a woman can dilute her urine by using a squeeze bottle to spray warm water over the perineum during urination, or she can urinate while under the shower with water running over her body. Signs of possible urinary tract infection—elevated temperature, burning on urination in which the discomfort is "inside" the bladder rather than on the sore perineum—need to be noted and treated (see pp. 75–76).

The postpartum woman may not have a *bowel movement* for the

*This chapter is adapted in part from a non-published essay "Postpartum Care," by Peggy Spindel, R.N.

first several days after giving birth. There is no need to strain, for it is not necessary to defecate immediately, and straining may be harmful. Prune juice, increased fiber, and fluids can soften or stimulate stools. Hemorrhoids, which may have begun during pregnancy, usually improve on their own after delivery.

The *uterus* should be checked every fifteen to thirty minutes for the first few hours and hourly for the rest of the day after delivery. If it is not hard like a softball (or coconut), it needs to be massaged until it firms up. If massaging does not work, the midwife or doctor should be informed. Nursing can be expected to lead to uterine contractions, sometimes called afterpains. The feeding of the infant is naturally linked to the tightening up of the uterus and the prevention of postpartum bleeding. The uterus should be monitored until it is too low in the abdomen to feel, about the tenth day after delivery. The vaginal flow (*lochia*) should not be greater than a heavy menstrual period. It should not be green or have a foul smell. By the tenth day it is usually just a light pink to brown discharge. Sanitary pads, rather than tampons, should be used for the first two weeks, since tampons may introduce germs into the vagina and the uterus.

A woman may *shower* when she feels steady on her feet. Tub baths have traditionally been discouraged for two weeks, in the interest of preventing infection from bacteria washed into the uterus. The validity of this teaching has not been confirmed. Perineal pain may respond to hot sitz baths (one and one-half inches of water) several times a day. A strong brew of the herb comfrey (available in health food stores) added to the water is alleged by many midwives to promote healing, but this is unconfirmed.

Ice applied to the perineum during the first twenty-four hours will help reduce labial swelling at least temporarily. Crushed ice is packed in a rubber glove, which is tied at its wrist, then wrapped in a sterile gauze pad. A sterile cotton ball soaked in refrigerated witch hazel can be placed under a perineal pad over sore regions— rectum, perineum, and labia. Local anesthetics—whether in the form of creams, sprays, or lotions—have been proven to provide pain relief. Foam rubber rings for sitting are popular. There is preliminary evidence that proteolytic enzymes taken by mouth can decrease swelling and pain associated with sitting and walking, but more study is needed. In contrast to these measures, treatment with ultrasound and pulsed electromagnetic energy have proven both ineffective and expensive. Of the analgesic medications available, acetaminophen (Tylenol) and ibuprofen (Motrin, Advil) are probably the safest and most effective. The exercises described in Chapter 2 (pp. 102–104) are all useful, if gradually introduced as the new mother feels stronger.

Emotions

For parents, it takes time to incorporate the birth experience. Mothers and fathers describe three general emotional stages in the postpartum period.

The first may be called the taking-in stage, after an extraordinary, possibly once-in-a-lifetime, experience. During this period mothers think and talk about the delivery a great deal and in detail. While taking stock, they work on resolving any mixed feelings. In this stage a mother can feel very focused on herself and inwardly directed and may even welcome being mothered herself.

The second stage, taking hold, is a time when a mother feels motivated to take charge of herself and her new baby. She feels less dependent on her family and wants to move quickly into asserting the new role she sees for herself. The pitfalls of this stage of rising expectations and mobilized energy are overtiredness and anxiety about one's competence as a mother.

Last, there is a letting-go, or settling-in, phase, in which the transition represented by the birth experience is resolved and put away, when the baby's separateness is realized and enjoyed, and the parental role is incorporated into one's identity.

Women often report *feelings of grieving* after a birth. They discover that the sense of loss they experience is the loss of being pregnant. The special feeling of fullness within, the self-conscious pride, and the attention of others can all be sorely missed once the baby arrives and "steals the show." Mothers sometimes feel like a cross between an anonymous cow that supplies the milk and an ignored maid who cleans up the messes, while it is the baby who is the focus of everyone's loving attention. To prevent this, families should keep up a little extra loving and mothering of the mother for a month or so. The result is likely to be a mother who has plenty of love to give because she is receiving much love and who is strong and more confident because she feels valued. During this time a father is called on to provide a lot of extra attention and do extra work—and he deserves extra love, too.

Mothers often describe a feeling of "fluffiness in the head," as one postpartum mother put it, finding it hard to imagine a life separate from mothering. It is as if they have forgotten how to do anything except care for the baby. Especially troublesome is the inability to find or remember a word or carry on a coherent conversation. This state of mind is probably related to a combination of factors that include hormonal effects, lack of sleep, and the intense emotional involvement with the baby. Among the many reactions it can elicit from others in the family are amusement and annoyance. The "fluffiness," luckily, will soon pass.

Sexuality

During the postpartum period, the sexuality of new parents can take a special, less genitally focused form. Childbearing is so overwhelming a part of a woman's sexual existence that it can entirely overwhelm her libido. Birth and adjustments to the baby during the postpartum and nursing periods can be such powerful sexual experiences that for a time intercourse can feel like an irrelevant intrusion. Men, too, normally have fears and concerns about causing another pregnancy too soon, injuring or causing pain to the new mother, or pushing to have sex before their partner is ready. All of these factors can color sexual relationships and inhibit the expression of sexual feelings. The couple needs to take advantage of the opportunity these changes present for empathic communication. Each can come to understand how the other experienced the birth in terms of his or her own body and psychological makeup.

Genital sex is but one expression of intimacy, and it may be temporarily suspended during late pregnancy and after birth. Other forms of warmth and caring can flow in both directions— massage, mutual masturbation, showering together, for example—to take its place. Even when a couple is ready for genital sex again, they may not return immediately to the prebirth relationship, for physical or psychological reasons.

The timing of the reinitiation of genital sex is best left to the discretion of the couple. Traditionally, doctors have recommended abstention until the six-week checkup. Although on theoretical grounds there would appear to be a heightened vulnerability to infection until the uterus is fully returned to its nonpregnant form, there are no data to support this concern.

If the vagina is dry or has tender spots, a water-soluble lubricant like K-Y jelly will help relieve irritation. Adjustments in positioning can help reduce pressure on a sore area. Many of the positions and other forms of intimacy suggested for late pregnancy are appropriate for the postpartum period, too. Milk ejection may occur spontaneously with arousal and seem bizarre and/ or humorous to both partners.

Many couples report increased sexual enjoyment following birth, especially women after their first child. However, this may take several months to achieve, while the mother's body returns to normal and the baby's schedule evolves.

Although breast-feeding suppresses the mother's ovulation, it is *not* a foolproof form of contraception. Since ovulation occurs *before* the return of menstrual periods, menstruation is not a reliable guide to resumed fertility. The combination of a condom with contraceptive foam or jelly is a very effective contraceptive that can be used indefinitely or until other birth control arrangements are made.

Oral contraceptives containing both estrogen and progesterone (combined pills) are generally not recommended during nursing. In some women they have been shown to decrease both the volume and the protein content of breast milk. There is also concern about possible effects on the baby of the birth control hormones passed into the milk. If combined pills are used, nursing should first be well established. In contrast, progestin-only pills (minipills) do not substantially affect breast milk. The minipill and nursing, with its own contraceptive effect, are a very effective *combination* in preventing pregnancy. Minipills can be started right after the baby's birth.

Family Crises

Combinations of physical and psychological problems can precipitate genuine family crises in the days and weeks following birth. A sluggish baby who won't nurse, combined with a mother who is exhausted and whose breasts are painfully engorged with sore nipples, is one. Another is the combination of a screaming baby with well-meaning, but intrusive and undermining, grandparents plus parents who feel frazzled and incompetent. The "superwoman" with older children, who refuses to stop waiting on everyone else long enough to care for herself, is a prime candidate for exhaustion and problems with the baby.

Such situations, which in the extreme can become nightmarish, call for active involvement by the doctor, midwife, friends, and others in the family's support network. Phone contact with the doctor (or midwife) is helpful, for he or she can assess the family's needs, provide loving support, and offer concrete suggestions. An exhausted mother should be encouraged to get into bed and take her baby with her. Relatives, friends, and members of a couple's prenatal class can be mobilized to bring cooked food, do laundry and shopping, and care for other children while the parents focus on themselves and the baby.

I vividly remember one mother who got into such a state of anxiety that her milk dwindled and her baby became dehydrated, almost to the point of needing hospitalization. A team of nursing mothers, who had used my practice, were quickly recruited to supplement this woman's depleted milk supply and to allow her to rest and successfully recoup her strength and confidence.

For those whose obsessive neatness is a barrier to their relaxation, the postpartum period offers an opportunity for them to learn that people can take priority over things. If a family is besieged by well-wishers, limited, brief visiting hours can be arranged and the phone taken off the hook. Public health and

Visiting Nurse Association nurses, supervised home health aides, and commercial homemakers can also provide support. Ask your physician or the hospital or birthing center about such resources.

Other formal support groups for the postpartum period include independent counseling services and childbirth preparation organizations, such as the local affiliate of ICEA and La Leche League. Help is usually available if one only asks for it. (See Appendix C for a list of resources.)

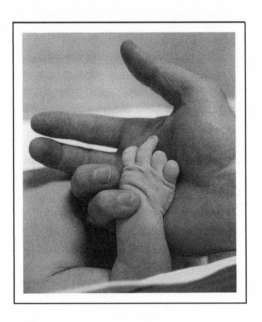

6

After the Birth: Care of the Baby

The Apgar Score

Immediately after the birth the health and well-being of every newborn is judged according to a test named for Dr. Virginia Apgar, an American anesthetist who worked at Columbia Presbyterian Hospital in New York. She identified the critical nature of the several minutes immediately following birth and developed a rating scale to help attendants decide whether resuscitative efforts are necessary.

The Apgar Score rates a newborn baby on each of the following five signs:

- Appearance or color
- Pulse (heart rate)
- Grimace or reflex irritability
- Activity
- Respiration

Sixty seconds after birth, the baby is rated on these measures using a scale of zero to two. In appearance, the newborn is given a score of two (the maximum) if the skin is pink all over; one if the body is pink but the arms and legs blue; and zero if the entire body is blue. A score of two is given when the pulse is greater than 100 beats per minute, one if it is less than 100, and zero if it is not present at all. An infant who cries vigorously when given a slap on the soles of the feet is scored two for reflex responsiveness; a grimace or slight cry counts for one; no response is zero. A newborn who makes active motions is scored two for activity or muscle tone; some movement of the arms or legs is rated one; zero is the score if the baby is motionless and limp. Strong efforts to breathe, along with vigorous crying, count for two; slow, irregular breathing is rated one; no respiration, zero. The five components are totaled to give the one-minute Apgar score (maximum ten, minimum zero).

Most newborns score seven to ten points one minute after birth. Infants with scores of four, five, or six usually require immediate help and oxygen to assist their first attempts at breathing. Mucus in the throat, if present, must be suctioned before they can breathe adequately. A baby with an Apgar score of less than four is unresponsive, pale, limp, usually not breathing, and possibly lacks a heartbeat. The throat of such an infant requires immediate suction to clear the airway, and the lungs require external inflation. Several minutes of attention may be necessary before the baby can take over on its own. Premature infants and others with breathing difficulties may need continuous respiratory assistance in the intensive care nursery.

The Apgar scoring is repeated five minutes after birth, and both scores are recorded. Studies have shown that good scores, especially at the five-minute mark, are strongly predictive of the baby's chances for survival and normal development in early infancy. The one-minute score, on the other hand, alerts the attendants to the immediate, sometimes urgent, need for life support to protect the baby from either imminent death or lifelong neurological problems. Recently, the value of Apgar scoring has come under critical review, and some authorities are challenging its usefulness.

Behavior of the Newborn

In recent years scientific studies have greatly expanded what we know about newborns' extraordinary capacity to interact with their environment. For example, babies at birth can turn their heads repeatedly toward the source of a human voice, their faces assuming an alert expression as they search out the sound. Babies will choose a female voice over any other, and prefer humanlike sounds to pure tones of an equivalent pitch range. Babies' responses to sound can be measured by their sucking patterns. Babies pause briefly after a pure auditory tone, then go on sucking steadily. When babies hear a human sound, however, they stop, then continue sucking in a "burst-pause" pattern, as though expecting something to follow; then they pause in sucking to hear more. Babies will notice and follow the picture of a human face, turning a full ninety degrees, but will not follow the picture of a "scrambled" face, although they will look at it wide-eyed for long periods. Babies prefer the odors of milk to those of water or sugar water, and they can taste the difference between human milk and a cow's milk formula designed to be identical to breast milk.

The remarkable complexity and individuality of the newborn are captured and made vivid by the Neonatal Behavioral Assessment Scale (NBAS) developed by Dr. T. Berry Brazelton. This scale recognizes six states of alertness, twenty-six items of behavior, and twenty neurological reflexes. The twenty-six items of behavior are grouped into six types:

1. *Habituation:* the infant's ability to shut out disturbing environmental stimuli
2. *Interactive* (orientation): the newborn's ability to notice and process both simple and complex events in the environment
3. *Motor:* the ability to maintain muscle tone, control motor actions, and perform integrated motor activities
4. *Range of state:* the intensity and variability of the infant's state of consciousness during the assessment
5. *State regulation:* the newborn's ability to control and modulate states while attending to social and inanimate stimuli
6. *Automatic regulation:* the newborn's vulnerability to such automatic behavior as trembling, startling, and changes in skin color

The pediatrician may perform the NBAS (in whole or in part) and the general physical examination with the baby's parents present. This is a splendid opportunity for them to observe the remarkable capacities of their baby. By understanding his or her individual temperament or personality, parents are better able to care for the baby, to discriminate between themselves and the baby, and to gain some insight into the responses the baby elicits in them (and vice versa). For example, an intense, easily startled, hard-to-quiet newborn can be predicted to be a fussy, even "colicky" infant. Parents of such a child can expect a stressful start with great potential for self-blame and feelings of inadequacy, desperation, and depression. The frazzled parents risk playing into the infant's irritability, setting into motion a cycle of mutually stimulating and reinforcing negative behaviors. But with the insight derived from watching as the pediatrician examines the baby, parents can discover how to help such an excitable infant become calm. The examination or the time the assessment scale is being carried out is an ideal opportunity for building an alliance with the doctor—family practitioner or pediatrician—who will be caring for the baby.

The interactiveness of the newborn grows rapidly in complexity. For example, by the age of three or four weeks, clear differences in the baby's response to mother and father can be demonstrated. As Dr. Brazelton says in his book *Infants and Mothers:*

> With the mother in sight, it is the baby who is likely to set the pace of their interactions. His face will brighten, his hands and legs will "reach out" gently toward the mother moving smoothly back and forth in a rhythmic fashion. If we watch the baby's face and eyes, we see that they alternately brighten with an intensely interested look as his mother, responding, attempts to engage him, and then become dull as the child retreats into himself and his mother desists.
>
> Father and infant synchronize, too, though their rhythmic pattern is different from that between mother and child and it is the father who is more likely to "set the pace." In our studies we have found that fathers are likelier . . . to "jazz up" the baby. Exaggerated gestures or expressions seem to say, "Come! It's playtime!" At first the baby will watch the father's antics as if trying to take them in and adjust to them. His shoulders will hunch, his eyebrows go up, his face show anticipation. Then the interaction will begin. As the baby gets older he will laugh out loud and bounce up and down in his eagerness to continue his games with his father.

Many of the visible and audible signs and responses of the newborn change over the first few days. After enduring the trying experience of birth and the one to two hours of intense alertness that follow, permitting peak interaction with parents (see pp. 248–251 on parent–infant attachment), many babies withdraw into a state of toned-down activity or disorganization for the next twenty-four to forty-eight hours. The baby may not suck long or hard and appears to have little interest in eating. This normal withdrawal following delivery may confuse parents eager for interaction with their newborn. Nursing usually picks up once the milk comes in, on the third and fourth day, as though the baby's changing needs are timed to coincide with milk production. The nursing that occurs earlier, however, is very important for the baby, for he or she receives nutrition and immune factors from the mother's colostrum to help ward off infection. This often low level nursing is also essential for the mother because it stimulates milk production, promotes uterine contraction, and reinforces the closeness between mother and baby that nursing represents. So pokey feeding in the first several days need not be a worry.

REFLEX BEHAVIOR

The newborn is endowed with certain coordinated patterns of behavior known as reflexes, which operate from circuits within the lower centers of the brain and have little to do with the process of rational thought or purposeful action.

Appropriate stimulation in the quiet alert state will automatically elicit these reflex responses. If the cheek of a sufficiently awake and hungry newborn is stroked, she will turn her mouth toward the stroking object, be it a finger or, as nature intended, the nipple of her mother's breast. This reflex is known as the *rooting response*. It is completely automatic and serves to orient the baby toward her source of nutrition before she "knows" where food comes from. Sucking occurs by reflex if something touches the lips, the mucous membranes of the mouth, or the soft palate.

If the newborn is startled by a loud noise or sudden change of position, particularly one with an element of falling, his arms and legs respond in a characteristic way. They move symmetrically first outward, then upward, and then inward. The hands first open, then clench tightly into a fist, as though the infant were echoing remote primate ancestors in trying to grasp a branch of

239

a tree or its mother's body to prevent a fall. The legs go through a similar, although less consistent, sequence of movements. In addition, the baby's head bends down and forward. This reflex, known as the *startle* or *scare response* is named the *Moro reflex*, after the neurologist who first wrote about it.

If pressure is applied by a finger to the palms of the baby's hands or to the balls of her feet, the fingers and toes will curl in to "grasp" the pressing object. The hand grasp is often so strong that the infant can be lifted out of her crib. This automatic response of hands and feet is known as the *grasp reflex*. If the soles of the feet are stroked, the foot will pull up, the toes fan out, and the large toe elevate. This response is known as the *Babinski reflex*, again for the neurologist who first described it.

If you support a baby by holding him under the arms and move him across a tabletop with his feet just touching the surface, his legs will make movements that are very similar to walking. This response to movement and pressure of the feet is reflexive and should not be confused with early walking.

There is a group of hand–mouth reflexes that can be elicited by stroking the cheek or the palm of the hand. The baby roots toward the stroking finger. Her arm flexes and she brings her hand to her mouth. She opens her mouth, puts in the fist, and begins to suck. Stimulating the baby at either end of the line, cheek or hand, leads to the same complex series of movements. (No doubt this reflex is a precursor of thumb sucking. Even in the newborn and fetus, nature has seemingly endowed the infant with a way to handle tension.)

If you place a cloth across the nose of a baby, he will first attempt to mouth it. When this fails, he will twist his head and flail with both hands in an effort to remove it. (This reflex makes it all but impossible for a baby to smother in his bedding.) If one leg is stroked, the other leg will move over by reflex to push the stroking finger away. Babies withdraw by reflex from such painful stimuli as pinches or pinpricks.

If a baby's head is slowly turned to one side while she is lying either prone or supine, the body will predictably assume the attitude of a fencer. The arm on the side toward which the head is turned will be extended, and the other arm will bend at the elbow; the legs will move in exactly the reverse pattern—one bent, the other extended. This response of the extremities to head turning is known as the *tonic neck reflex*. If the baby is suspended in air by her feet (a position not harmful or bothersome to the infant), she will first assume the fetal position, flexing both arms and legs and curling into an upside-down ball. Then she will extend her legs and arms outward and arch her back, like an athlete in a swan dive.

Reflexes are part of the baby's equipment at birth. As the forerunners of voluntary control, they demonstrate that the "circuits" for complex movements such as walking have been laid down long before actual walking begins. The reflexes persist until voluntary control is developed to the point where it dominates behavior. Thus, when a baby begins to reach and grasp objects at the age of about three months or so, the grasp reflex disappears. When the baby becomes aware of his surroundings and visually searches out his bottle or his mother's breast, the rooting reflex vanishes. In the newborn, reflexes give information on the normalcy of a baby's nervous system. Not all of the reflexes just described are routinely elicited in the normal newborn during a physical examination.

Appearance

With physical aspects of the newborn, a great deal can be learned simply by looking. During the first day or two babies may have bluish (*cyanotic*) fingers and toes from a clamping down of circulation to their extremities, perhaps to conserve heat. The rest of the body is pink. This is quite normal. In a few days the fingers and toes will take on the same coloration as the rest of the body. If a bluish or dusky color remains, the doctor will check for heart or lung disorders.

The normal breathing pattern of newborns is variable. They may breathe as rapidly as sixty or seventy times a minute, then slow down to twenty or thirty times per minute, all within the space of two or three minutes. While breathing is noisy, it should not be labored or require hard work. A quality of struggle characterizes the breathing of babies with pulmonary difficulties and makes it different from normal rapid breathing. The vigor and quality of the baby's cry give information about her airway, vocal cords, and general strength. When stirred up, she is apt to move all four of her limbs and thus give an observer an excellent opportunity to detect any impairments of motion. When she cries vigorously, her color usually changes from pale pink to a beet red.

A newborn's skin is usually dry and flaky, as though he were shedding his skin. The soft, lustrous appearance of the skin seen in pictures in baby magazines will take weeks to develop. At birth, the skin is covered with a greasy coating known as *vernix.* Even though most vernix comes off in the first sponge bath given, bits may remain behind the ears and in the folds of the buttocks. Actually, it is unnecessary to remove vernix at all; it may be massaged into the skin. It is thought to have antibacterial properties. The long hairs on a newborn's body are known as *lanugo.* They characteristically fall out over the first few weeks.

A baby's hands and feet will normally feel cool, while his or her body will be warm. There is no need to add clothing unless the baby seems uncomfortable.

Forceps used in a delivery may leave marks on the skin of the baby's face and head, but these fade within several days. The small yellow or white spots present on the noses, cheeks, or chins of many babies represent trapped collections of sebum, the fatty secretion of the sebaceous glands of the skin. These require no attention and disappear in a matter of weeks.

Small, faint red spots or blotches are often seen on the upper eyelids, at the nape of the neck, and in a diamond shape over the bridge of the nose and the forehead. Clusters of tiny blood vessels (or capillaries) present in the immediate newborn period and early infancy account for these markings. Why they occur is not known. In the old days, marks at the bottom of the neck were often called stork bites (since the back of the neck was the part of the anatomy grasped by the beak of the mythical stork who delivered the infant to his new home). Stork bites tend to blush and become darker when the baby cries. They disappear gradually over the first year. The diamond-shaped spot on the forehead fades with time, but in some individuals it may persist for life, barely visible except during emotional upsets, when it may flush.

The common *strawberry patch* is a mole (*nevus*) made up of blood vessels. Usually not present in the newborn, it shows up after the baby is brought home. A small bright red spot on the skin is the first sign of such a mark, which predictably will grow rapidly after the baby leaves the hospital. Such nevi enlarge over the first year and gradually resolve over the next several years. They do not usually require treatment.

The newborn's skin is highly reactive. When a baby is excited by hunger or stimulated by the poking fingers of a nurse or doctor, large red blotches or mottling may appear over the body, sometimes more prominently in one part than another. Why babies are susceptible to this blotching and mottling is not known for sure, but it is thought to be related to immature regulation of the flow of blood to the skin. These irregularities of coloration have no medical significance, and in several months the exaggerated skin responses disappear.

A common rash seen after the first day or two, and for the next several weeks, is *erythema toxicum*. The characteristic of this rash (its exact cause is unknown) is a red blotch with a small, white, raised center. It resembles prickly heat, or heat rash, which is usually finer. The rash is more prominent on the face, neck, and trunk than on the arms and legs. It comes and goes right before one's eyes. Neither the cause nor the treatment is known, for the condition is so transient and harmless that it has not stimulated the interest of researchers.

Prickly heat, or *heat rash,* is caused by trapped sweat that accumulates deep in the skin and sets up an inflammation. It can afflict people of all ages but is more common in babies. Heat rash manifests itself in small, often pinpoint, red blotches with slightly raised whitish centers. The rash characteristically comes and goes rapidly; it may be present in the morning and gone by noon. It is a condition best left alone, since the application of powders and creams on the skin only aggravates the plugging of the sweat ducts and tends, if anything, to make the condition worse. Keeping the baby in a relatively cool environment will reduce heat rash but may not eliminate it. Fortunately, babies seem to be less troubled by it than parents.

The head of the newborn often shows the effects of passage through the birth canal. If *molding* (see pp. 190–193) has occurred, the result may be a transient lopsidedness. The bones of the baby's skull are not as tightly knit as they are in adults and can shift and overlap to a degree. Thus, the head can usually adapt to the squeezing at birth without injury. The normal separations between the bones (*sutures*) can be felt by running the finger over the head. You will have the distinct impression of a small groove separating one bone from the other. In the middle of the head toward the front is the major (anterior) *fontanel,* or soft spot. There is a smaller posterior fontanel at the "point" of the head in back. The coverings of the fontanels are very tough and can be pressed on without fear of damage. As the baby grows, the skull bones fuse, closing the fontanels and suture lines. For most infants, closure of the anterior fontanel occurs between six months and one and one-half years, while the posterior fontanel closes in a few weeks to months. The anterior fontanel in a quiet baby held in a sitting position sinks in and pulsates. When the baby cries, the soft spot tenses. The veins of the baby's head are more prominent than those of adults because they are closer to the surface of the skin. Also, there is less hair to conceal them.

Swelling of the scalp from pressure of the cervix during birth is known as a *caput succedaneum* (see p. 190). It gradually resolves in twenty-four to forty-eight hours and so is of no special significance. Trauma to the head during delivery may result in a linear crack (fracture) in the skull and lead to bleeding between the skull and the scalp. The accumulation of blood can be seen as a swelling over the side of the head and is known as *cephalohematoma.* It requires no treatment and gradually resolves over several weeks.

The eyes of the newborn are fully formed. The whites often have small reddish blotches, which are tiny hemorrhages produced by squeezing of the head in delivery. These specks of blood clear in a week or so and have no significance. The color of the eyes is almost always blue. If there is to be a change of color, it comes on gradually. The eyes are examined by a nurse or doctor with an ophthalmoscope, a special adaptation of a flashlight with a peephole and magnifying lenses, used to check the lenses of the eyes for cataracts and the retina (the sensing part of the eye) for its normal red color. If this red reflex is present, it excludes the possibility of congenital retinal tumors and other abnormalities.

244

Infants see more than was once thought. Infants can fix on a red or pale-yellow object dangled before their eyes and follow it. Shining a bright light causes the lids to shut tightly. If you spin a baby about, her head will turn reflexively in the direction of the spin, and her eyes, in a rhythmical series of alternating fast and slow movements known as *nystagmus*, will try to keep up with the spin. When the baby stops short, the eyes continue quick, rhythmical movements in the direction of spin for several seconds. These reactions depend on the complex position-sensing connections in ear and brain. If you pull a baby up to sitting position by her hands, her eyes will open much as do the weighted eyes on old china dolls. This response is called the *doll's eye reflex*.

The ears are inspected for proper formation and normal location of the canals. Since vernix in the canal often blocks easy inspection of the eardrum, it is not routinely checked in the newborn. As for hearing, fully awake infants usually respond with a startle to any sudden loud noise. Immediate repetition of the noise usually elicits no reaction. The infant seems able to shut out the repeated stimulus as a kind of self-protection. (Might it even be that babies do not hear their own crying after a point?)

The lips and mouth, including the gums and palate, are examined for defects. In rare cases, babies are born with teeth, which usually will be "extras" rather than the standard primary and secondary teeth. The tip of the tongue is joined to the floor of the mouth by a little band known as the *frenulum*, which is sometimes quite short. In the past, short frenula gave rise to the concept of being "tongue-tied," and accordingly, many frenula were clipped. In point of fact, babies with short frenula do not usually have problems with sucking or, later, with speaking.

A fuzzy white coating on the tongue, noticed usually after the third or fourth day, signifies thrush, an infection with the yeast known as *Monilia*. The baby picks up the yeast from the mother's vagina while passing through it before birth (see p. 172).

The neck is inspected and felt for masses. There are several kinds of congenital cysts, some of which may have sinuses, or small openings, in the skin. While they may require surgical removal, this is not usually done in the newborn period. The sternocleidomastoid muscles run from the mastoid bone of the skull just behind the ear down to the inner third of each collarbone and come into play when the head is bent forward or turned to the side. Bruises of this muscle, which possibly occur during or even before birth, may produce a swelling and later a scarring and tightening, the condition known as *torticollis*. When the neck is examined, the position of the windpipe (*trachea*) is checked. Normally in the midline of the neck, it may be tugged to one side in certain abnormalities of the lungs. The thyroid gland at the lower part of the front of the neck is also checked.

The chest should expand and contract symmetrically. Unequal movements of the two sides point to lung problems that require further investigation. Attached to the lowest point of the breastbone just at the top of the abdomen is a distinct little bone known as the *xiphoid*. While it may be particularly prominent and slightly pointed in newborns, it has no special significance. The doctor listens to the chest with a stethoscope to check on the flow of air in and out of the lungs and to detect any fluid within the lungs.

The rhythm and rate of the heartbeat are also checked with the stethoscope. While heart murmurs are common in the newborn, the majority are normal and do not signify heart disease. Most disappear promptly. The explanation for murmurs lies in the radical reorganization of the circulation that occurs at birth. Before birth, blood almost completely bypasses the lungs; with the newborn's first breath, blood begins to circulate through them. This shift in blood flow is accompanied by the opening and closing of various channels within the heart and large blood vessels. The process of reorganization may not be complete for a few days, and blood flowing through partially opened or closed channels generates the noise called a murmur. Later murmurs, too, are in and of themselves not abnormal, for about one-third of normal children have murmurs that do not signify any heart disease.

Feeling the pulses in a baby's groin assures the examiner that there is no significant constriction of the aorta, the major artery leading from the heart to the body. Sometimes these pulses are difficult to feel in a newborn, but they can be detected later.

The stump of the *umbilical cord* is prominent and firmly attached to the *umbilicus* ("belly button"). The stump, shiny and moist for the first day or so, gradually dries, shrivels, and falls off in about seven to fourteen days. More than a small rim of redness of the skin of the umbilicus signifies infection and requires medical attention. In newborns, unlike adults, the size and shape of the abdominal organs—the liver, spleen, and kidneys—can be felt under normal conditions. The examiner searches for abnormal masses, such as a blocked kidney. The bladder of the newborn normally rises up much higher in the abdomen than in the adult and can be felt when full of urine. If stools are being passed normally, no examination of the anus or rectum is called for beyond mere external inspection.

The skin of the *scrotum* reflects the maturity of the baby boy. The normal rough appearance develops only in babies whose gestation was close to term. In premature infants the scrotal skin is likely to be smooth and shiny. The testes should be present in the sac. Hernias and hydroceles (fluid accumulations) can be detected as swellings in the scrotum, and hernias require repair even in the newborn period. The urethra, the thin tube that runs the length of the inside of the penis, should open at its tip. In a noncircumcised infant, the foreskin may conceal the urethral opening (*meatus*). Seeing (or feeling) urine shoot out in males assures that there is no obstruction to the lower urinary tract.

The legs of the newborn are normally bowed from the curled-up position in the womb, and the feet are likely to be turned inward. Both bowing and in-turning of feet persist until the child walks, demonstrating the principle that the shape of the bones depends largely on the forces they sustain. Until the stress of walking is put on them, the legs remain bowed because nothing has stimulated them to change. The legs and feet of babies born by breech (pp. 277–283) may show the effects of their uterine position. The legs turn outward, with the kneecaps touching, and the feet may also turn outward. In time, these effects disappear.

The hips are checked for dislocation, since congenital dislocation of the hip is a progressive condition, and success in treatment depends mainly on early recognition. Careful note of the hips should be taken at all examinations in infancy, for dislocations may make their appearance only after several months and even as late as a year after birth.

Bonding and Attachment

Both of the birth stories in Chapter 1 demonstrated the importance of keeping parents and infants together immediately after birth. This commonsense practice was neglected earlier in this century as birth moved from home to hospital. Although we are again taking it for granted, only recently have hospitals "permitted" fathers to be with their partners at birth, and rooming-in is not a universal practice in hospitals.

Midwife Raven Lang studied a group of mothers having home births in California and identified a seemingly species-specific behavior in mothers who have access to their babies immediately after birth. Even before delivery of the placenta, the mother, in an apparent state of ecstasy, reaches for her infant and moves so that they can lie face to face. After the infant quiets down, she almost always rubs her baby's skin with her fingertips in a gentle stroking motion, beginning with the face. Most of the parents talk to their infants in high-pitched voices, and all other participants are drawn to the infant as well (see pp. 115–123, "Children and Birth"). Breast-feeding begins within minutes as the infant licks the nipple. As noted earlier, this sucking leads to contraction of the uterus, reducing bleeding. At the same time the colostrum delivers nourishment to the baby along with antibodies and antibody-producing cells to help ward off infection.

During the hour or so following birth, the baby is alert to interactions with his parents. This availability must be taken advantage of before the baby becomes sleepy. The richness of the newborn's psychological skills has only recently been described by researchers (see pp. 236–241), even though it is likely that mothers have always known that their babies recognized them. In the parents and other participants, these interactions are accompanied by the welling up of intense, at times overwhelming, feelings of warmth and love for the baby and a desire to nurture him. Thus it is that "babies will make parents of us all."

The effect of medication on the baby's alertness and responsiveness after birth (see pp. 208–209 on analgesics in labor) is of continued interest. In the doses currently used in early labor, they do not interfere with early bonding between infants and parents.

The answer to this question is obviously of great importance, since it will affect decisions about the use of these medicines and parents understand and correct for possible drug effects when responding to their baby's early behavior.

Follow-up studies of the interactions between parents and infants who had early contact with one another, versus ones who did not, suggest some interesting differences. In one study, for example, mothers who played with their nude babies soon after birth spent much more time with them during the first three months than mothers who did not. Mothers who had early contact spent more time with the baby during the first month, stood closer to and soothed the baby more during an office visit to the doctor, and came to the baby's aid more readily in a stress situation (such as vaccinations). Two years after the birth, they spoke to their babies differently, asking more questions, making fewer demands, and using more adjectives and adverbs. A study of premature infants who had contact with their mothers on the first day, as opposed to the twentieth day, showed a significantly greater developmental quotient at four years of age. Not all studies, however, show such effects, and even those that do can be faulted, because they involved small numbers of mothers and infants. Nevertheless, the burden of proof seems to be on those who claim no differences in behavior. The clear human advantages of having infants and parents together seem to override any objections.

Drs. Marshall Klaus and John Kennell, who have done important work on parent–infant bonding, have identified seven principles of attachment:

1. There is a "sensitive period" during the first minutes and hours of life in which the close contact of the mother and father with their newborn, in a private situation, is desirable in order for optimal later parental behavior to develop.

2. There appears to be species-specific behavior in the human mother and father when they are first given their baby.

3. The process of attachment is structured so that the father and mother will become attached to only one infant at a time. With twins, this explains why mothers dress them alike, and it

also argues for keeping twins together and discharging them together from the hospital, even if the larger one must wait.

4. During the process of a mother's attachment to her infant, it is necessary that the infant respond to her with some signal. The mother needs feedback from the baby in order to invest her love and nurturing efforts. Babies, it has been demonstrated, follow and attend to spoken words for short periods even on the first day after birth.

5. People who witness a birth process become strongly attached to the infant.

6. The processes of attachment and detachment are mutually incompatible. Thus, it is difficult to go through a process of attachment to one person while mourning the loss of another person. For example, if a mother loses a baby, she should get over the process of the loss (which might take seven to eight months) before she becomes pregnant again.

7. Early events can have long-lasting effects. Anxiety about the well-being of a baby with a temporary disorder may result in enduring concerns, which may adversely shape development.

Even though bonding is a real and important process, it should not be interpreted too rigidly or literally. I would like to add several strong notes of caution.

First, bonding and attachment take place over a long period of time. They can start slowly and gather strength. There is no evidence that infants and parents whose normal contact is disrupted for some reason (say, for example, the need for a premature infant to be put in an incubator in an intensive care nursery) are unable to recoup and proceed with normal subsequent development. It would be tragic if parents separated from their infant at birth believed that what they had lost could never be regained, and there is certainly no support for such a conclusion.

While early contact is highly desirable and should be encouraged whenever possible, dire consequences are not likely if it cannot occur. There are no rules about human development—except, perhaps, for its extreme plasticity. We must guard against the "tyranny of the normal," which can be as destructive as the practices it seeks to correct.

Most parents would agree that bonding proceeds over many days, if not weeks and months, and is a very individual matter. Not all mothers or fathers experience an instantaneous rush of love for the infant. Some work their way slowly into attaching to the baby—in stages, with occasional steps backward, too. For all parents there will be ups and downs and much room for patience and steady caring. As Dr. T. Berry Brazelton says in his book *On Becoming a Family*, "Falling in love with a baby may well happen at first sight, but staying in love is a learning process—learning to know oneself as well as the baby."

It is important for parents to follow their own feelings and not be too caught up in expectations of what should and shouldn't happen. If there is any "should" in this discussion at all, it is that hospitals should adopt policies that permit parents unlimited and free access to their newborns from the time of birth onward.

Another misconception that can interfere with the pleasures of early parenthood is the notion of "spoiling." This is a concern of many parents. All of us want babies to grow up to be self-reliant, independent individuals who do not need or expect to be coddled. However, such worries are completely irrelevant when it comes to the newborn baby. Lavish all the love and affection you can muster and do it unstintingly. There is no more important contribution to a baby's well-being than giving him or her a sense of self-worth and lovableness and trust in parents and home environment. As long as a baby responds positively, it is hard to see any problem in extensive physical contact. There will be time later in the first year to begin the important job of setting limits.

Breast-Feeding

Breast-feeding is a wonderful way to nourish a baby. It is too bad that more women don't do it. Unfortunately, in the United States there still is a generalized lack of support for nursing although not nearly so much today as even fifteen years ago. Most women don't have the opportunity to learn about breast-feeding by being around nursing women, as is true for girls growing up in breast-feeding societies, many in the developing world. (Movies and videotapes can make up for this deficit only in part.) Negative attitudes toward breast-feeding (more common in families of lower socioeconomic status) include an (ungrounded) fear that the breasts will permanently sag and lose their attractiveness and that breast-feeding is primitive and animal-like. For some couples a commitment to an equal sharing of parenting argues for a father's participation in feeding for which formula is seen as the only solution. (In fact, a mother can express her milk into a bottle for immediate use or freeze it for later use. A father can then feed it to the baby. The real question may be who will get up in the middle of the night.) This attitude of couples and particularly of women has always struck me as a rather odd interpretation of the principles of equal rights for women.

Other barriers to breast-feeding are institutional and societal. In the past—less so today—doctors and nurses discouraged nursing because of their own ignorance and their unwillingness to take the extra time required to deal with breast-feeding problems. Hospital practices of separating babies from mothers, routine feeding of water (or formula), and feeding according to a fixed schedule (rather than on demand, facilitated by rooming-in) have a chilling effect on breast-feeding. Commercial formula manufacturers with a strong financial stake in promoting their products make it all too easy to use formula by providing free starter supplies for distribution by hospitals. (In the developing world, the promotion of formula feeding by manufacturers approaches the level of scandal in terms of negative health and economic consequences. This practice has been strongly condemned by UNICEF, the United Nations International Childrens Emergency Fund, which is working—not too successfully—with various national ministries of health to curb it.) The early separation of working mothers from their babies also discourages breast-feeding. Some enlightened companies now provide on-site day-care services for employees so that mothers can drop in to nurse. This practice is widespread in the People's Republic of China.

Such barriers provide a backdrop that may make breast-feeding problematic even for the woman who chooses it. Her feelings may be mixed. She may approach nursing to "prove" that she can do it. Or she may know that the father is "just going along" in his support but really is negative about nursing. Deep down this woman is ready to give nursing up at the first sign of trouble. Such ambivalence doesn't help matters. Nursing works when women trust in themselves. Women in traditional societies don't even think about this question. Of course it works!

The benefits of breast-feeding are many. From a nutritional point of view it has never been equalled let alone surpassed. The more we learn about breastmilk the more we marvel at it. For example, it contains disease-fighting antibodies and white blood cells. These are particularly important for protecting babies against infection in parts of the world with less than optimal levels of sanitation but are important to all high-risk newborns, such as those born prematurely or with intrauterine growth retardation. When you think about it, we shouldn't be so surprised at all about the wonders of breastmilk. After all, it is an essential link in human evolution and survival over these many thousands of years.

Breast-feeding is supremely convenient and instantly available without preparation. Nursing from the breast, unlike a bottle, contributes to correct positioning of the baby's erupting teeth. Mothers claim that it promotes a unique physical and emotional closeness. Breast-fed babies smell sweeter, and their stools tend to be softer. (See pp. 268–269 for a discussion of babies' bowel patterns.) Breast-feeding is considerably less expensive than formula feeding, at a time when the high cost of living is a national problem. No additional foods are required for a breast-fed baby up to six months. No vitamin or iron supplements are needed, as vitamins and iron from the mother are secreted in abundant quantities into breastmilk. (Fluoride is not, so it needs to be added to the baby's diet. See p. 264.) Breast-feeding has some contraceptive effect (though *not at all foolproof*), particularly during the first year, which plays a role in population control.

Both production and ejection of human milk are regulated by hormones produced in the mother's pituitary gland. The primary stimulus for release of these hormones is the suckling of the baby and the emptying of the breasts. In some women even the sound or thought of the baby will initiate letting down of the milk from the milk glands into the collecting ducts, with leaking or squirting of milk from the nipple. During a feeding the cycle of milk production and ejection can occur several times. As babies grow and require more milk, they nurse more and stimulate increased production. The breast is finely tuned to adjust its production according to the baby's needs as expressed by nursing activity. But the breast can meet a baby's demands only if *all* of the baby's nursing is directed at the breast. If a baby is also feeding from a bottle, the breast will respond to the lessened total nursing by reducing production. The baby, unsatisfied by the breast, will then need even more milk from the bottle. And so on. Eventually, milk production will stop altogether. (This is exactly what happens during weaning.) The basic physiologic point is that to nurse successfully, a baby from the time of birth must have unrestricted access to the breast without supplementation. A hungry baby should be breast-fed as often as necessary. Milk production will increase to catch up with his or her needs.

Babies nurse best when they are hungry. Mothers can learn to identify the earliest signs of hunger and not wait for babies to work themselves into a fit of crying that requires settling down. They should follow the baby's lead, not the clock's. During the first few weeks many babies nurse as often as twelve times in twenty-four hours. Some of the nursings may occur as often as an hour apart. There may be a bunch of nursings during one part of the day, while at other times they may be spaced out.

Milk production, letdown, and ejection are remarkably sensitive to a mother's emotions. A strong emotional shock has been known to stop milk production altogether. By the same token, successful nursing is a good sign of maternal contentment and happiness. When a problem in nursing develops, a mother's worry and upset make it even worse—all the more reason to have identified a knowledgeable and supportive expert in breast-feeding, known as a lactation coach, for quickly getting back on track.

Although not all crying by a baby is caused by hunger (see "Colic," pp. 266–267), crying often becomes the basis for concluding that nursing isn't working and an excuse for stopping. Often this thinking is grounded in mixed feelings about nursing in the first place. As I advise new mothers, be honest with yourself. If you clearly and deeply feel that you want to nurse and your partner supports you fully, you can rest assured that you will be able to deal with the baby's crying and continue nursing. You can do it! It is also true that an inconsolable baby can trigger so much anxiety in a mother that breast-feeding can be adversely affected, compounding the problem of crying. Consult a lactation coach if you're becoming frazzled.

A baby who is getting enough appears content, urinates frequently, and has bowel movements. It is not necessary to weigh babies after a feeding to see whether they have gained weight. Such a practice is bound to make you a nervous wreck and to interfere with milk production. Periodic weighings during well-child checkups will confirm the weight gain that is obviously occurring. There are occasional "good babies" who require special handling if they are to be adequately nourished. They don't cry or even seem hungry.

A baby nurses by drawing areola and nipple (together forming a teat) into his or her mouth. Latch-on is accomplished by the baby's rooting reflex (see p. 239), which leads to turning of the mouth in the direction of any stroking of the cheek or lips (by breast or finger) and then opening of the mouth for the insertion of the teat. The mother needs to cup the breast with four fingers from beneath to support its weight and keep it from pulling away from the baby's mouth and then position the baby to facilitate latch-on (see Figure 17), all the while supporting the baby comfortably so that he or she need only nurse, not hold up or turn the neck or head. Proper positioning will also minimize trauma to the nipple and maximize the effectiveness of nursing.

Properly positioned, the baby's gums will close over the areola behind the nipple, drawing the teat within the mouth. The nipple elongates under tactile stimulation, and the teat dynamically expands to fill much of the mouth. The teat is held in place by the roof of the mouth (hard palate) from above, the tongue from below, and by the lips and gums in front. When correctly positioned, the baby's lips should be everted (rolled out) on the areola (or on the skin of the breast behind the areola) as opposed to pinched or pursed (as in whistling). The body of the breast should be clear of the nose. The teat is "milked" by a wave of muscle contraction (peristalsis) of the tongue that spreads from front to back, while the length of the tongue maintains contact with the

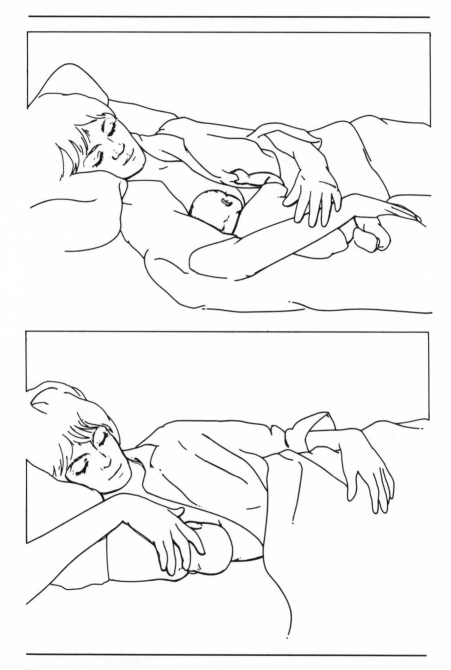

Figure 17. Nursing positions

Figure 17.   Nursing positions, *continued*

teat throughout. (Sucking milk from a bottle with a nipple involves an entirely different set of coordinated mouth and tongue movements. Many babies, particularly younger ones, are unable to switch back and forth from breast to bottle. Breast-feeding usually suffers in the competition, another reason for avoiding bottles.)

There should be no friction or tugging on the nipple itself either

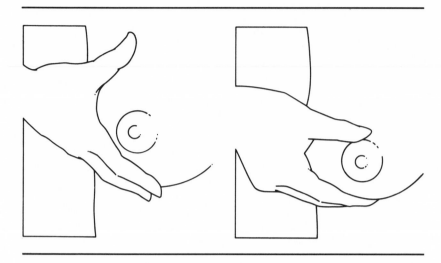

Figure 18.   Expressing milk with the hand

during latch-on or feeding. The nipple is not designed to withstand such trauma and if so subjected will become painful and cracked. With correct positioning of the baby there is no reason to arbitrarily limit the duration of nursing—as was often advocated in the past—in order to protect the nipples. The baby can simply be nursed until you see signs of fullness. As one breast feels emptier, the other can be offered. Breast-feeding should not be painful for the mother (with the possible exception of some very brief pain in the teat after latch-on during the first few days of nursing). On the contrary, most mothers find nursing to be physically and emotionally pleasurable.

To break the hold of the baby on the teat, the mother can insert the tip of a finger between the baby's gums and the areola and then pull the teat away and/or move the baby away. If the breast is too full (extreme fullness is called engorgement) at the beginning of nursing and the areola is firm and noncompliant, latch-on will be difficult and the nipple is vulnerable to being bitten and injured by the baby's gums. In this case, the mother needs to soften the teat by expressing some milk either manually (easiest) (see Figure 18) or with a breast pump. (The technique of hand expression is an important, readily learned skill for breast-feeding and allows a mother to empty her breasts or start the flow of milk as needed, for example, to leave a supply of breast milk when she must be separated from the baby.) Engorgement also suggests that the baby is not being put to breast on demand, so more frequent nursing may be needed.

Most women who are first-time breast-feeders will need support initially from a knowledgeable and experienced coach, who can make the difference between success and failure. Women should be sure before labor that such coaching will be available either from the staff of the institution (hospital or birthing center) or from another privately arranged source, for example, a friend or lactation consultant. (The early behavior of the baby as it affects nursing is discussed on p. 239.)

There is no need for a mother to drink extra fluids while nursing. She need merely follow her thirst and drink according to need, as when not nursing. Guidelines for a healthful diet are provided in Chapter 2 (see pp. 86–93). Following these guidelines will provide both mother and baby with sufficient vitamins so that a supplement is unnecessary. Mothers who are anemic after delivery may need additional iron.

Many drugs taken by a mother pass into the breast milk, and some require temporarily stopping nursing (while continuing to pump the breasts). Combined birth control pills should not be used while nursing, as they interfere with lactation (see pp. 231–232). Alcohol passes undiluted from the mother's blood into the milk. A 1991 study in the *New England Journal of Medicine* showed that the odor and taste of milk containing alcohol is significantly changed and that babies consume less of it. This does not necessarily mean that mothers should abstain entirely while nursing, but they should be aware of possible negative effects. For more information on drugs during nursing, see Table 5.

Nipples are best left to air dry, and creams and ointments should be avoided. Friction from a bra or other clothing should be minimized, particularly early on. True inverted nipples are uncommon (see p. 70) (most will become erect upon stimulation); these can be corrected by a breast pump to draw out the nipple at the beginning of a feeding and between feedings by breast shells (milk cups), which promote the eversion (coming out) of the nipple. Painful nipples, including cracked and bleeding ones,

Table 5 Drug Use during Breast-feeding

Contraindicated	
Chlordiazepoxide (sedative)	
Cocaine	Marijuana
Diazepam (sedative)	Metronidazole (antibiotic)
Flurazepam (sedative)	Primidone (anticonvulsant)
Heroin	Tetracycline (antibiotic)
Iodinated glycerol (expectorant)	Vaccine: polio (withhold
Lithium	breast-feeding)

*Drugs that pose some risk during breast-feeding
or for which no information is available
as to their effects on the baby*

Albuterol (antiasthmatic)	Phenylephrine (decongestant)
Allopurinol (antigout medicine)	Phenylpropanolamine
All over-the-counter cold medicines	(decongestant)
Antidepressants	Probenecid (antigout medicine)
Astemizole (antihistamine)	Prochlorperazine (antinausea
Bacitracin (antibiotic)	medicine)
Beclomethasone (antiasthmatic)	Promethazine (decongestant)
Caffeine	Robitussin-DM and -CF
Clotrimazole (antifungal)	(cough medicines)[a]
Cromolyn sodium (antiasthmatic)	Sertraline (antidepressant)
Fluoxetine (antidepressant)	Terfenadine (antihistamine)
Hydroxyzine (antiemetic)	Theoplylline (antiasthmatic)
Ipratropium (antiasthmatic)	Trimethobenzamide
Loperamide (antidiarrhea medicine)	(antinausea medicine)
Meclizine (antinausea medicine)	Vaccines: diphtheria-tetanus-toxoid
Metaproterenol (antiasthmatic)	(dT), influenza, measles, mumps
Miconazole (antifungal);	
Percodan (analgesic)[a]	

Note: Drugs listed in Table 4 (pp. 162–165) that are not in the above table are probably safe during breast-feeding, but you should check with your doctor before taking *any* drug during breast-feeding.

[a]Trade name.

suggest that the nursing technique is incorrect, and immediate attention should be given to reviewing technique and making required corrections. Breast shields for painful nipples interfere with nursing (those made of silicone less so than others) and are rarely indicated. Whenever a problem with nursing that you cannot figure out occurs, such as nipple pain, an unsatisfiable baby, or lack of weight gain, consult promptly with a knowledgeable coach lest a spiral of lactation failure be initiated from which recovery becomes increasingly difficult. Be particularly wary of any advice to give the baby a bottle of formula. Such advice is all too forthcoming from the most well-meaning people, including grandmothers. It can spell disaster for nursing.

If supplementary feeding becomes necessary under special circumstances, the current recommended approach makes use of feeding devices other than an artificial nipple, which can confuse the baby and make return to the breast difficult. An example is a device known as a *supplementer*, a thin plastic tube taped to the breast and ending at the nipple. A syringe with milk is attached to the upper end of the tube. The baby is put to breast with the nipple end of the tube along with the teat in his or her mouth. Milk is then injected through the tube into the baby's mouth.

A tender lump in the breast signifies a blocked milk duct. The overdistended milk glands behind the blockage may allow substances to leak into and irritate the overlying skin, causing redness and other signs of inflammation, including fever, chills, and generalized achiness. Continued nursing on that breast is crucial to draining the blocked region. Massage may also help. As with sore nipples, a blocked duct also suggests faulty nursing technique, and a review with an experienced coach is in order. Streaks of redness that spread out from the tender area signify infection of the breast with bacteria, for which antibiotics will be needed.

Once breast-feeding is well established—ideally, after two to three months—and the frequency of feedings begins to space out, it is often possible to introduce the baby to bottle feeding for use when a mother needs to be away, for example, at work. She can pump her breasts (at home or at work) and leave her own milk or use a commercial formula. Even if the baby is given a formula, a mother may still need to pump her breasts for maintenance of her milk supply or simply for comfort. The best way to deal with this issue varies a great deal, depending on the age of the baby and the family circumstances. One woman in my practice successfully reduced her nursings of her eight-month-old to once a day and when on vacation built her milk supply up by more frequent nursing. This raises another point: there is no set age when nursing needs to end, and more women are breast-feeding well into the second year and beyond.

If a baby becomes jaundiced (see pp. 273–274), it is important in most cases to continue nursing without interruption and *not* to offer the baby extra water. With respect to nutrition during jaundice, breast milk is effective in helping treat the problem. Other measures may need to be taken as well. Sometimes breast-feeding contributes directly to jaundice through excess quantities of natural substances in the mother's milk that reduce the elimination of bilirubin, the chemical that in excess accounts for jaundice. In these instances temporarily stopping nursing (for several days) will allow the baby to clear the excess bilirubin. The jaundice will not return when nursing is resumed. To maintain her milk production during the break in nursing, a mother should regularly empty her breasts manually or with a breast pump. On the other hand, there is no evidence that breast milk jaundice is harmful. It can be left alone.

Breast-feeding can be accomplished in a number of special situations such as prematurity and cleft lip/palate. Even relactation (starting milk flow when none exists) is possible. No condition of the baby should be automatically written off as permanently incompatible with breast-feeding. A knowledgeable coach and a determined mother are the ingredients for success.

For women with breast discomfort from fullness who choose not to breast-feed, fluid restriction is helpful, as are several medications that inhibit milk production, including bromoergocriptine and stilbesterol.

Finally, a word of acknowledgment. The La Leche League, mentioned earlier, was organized fifty years ago by a small group of mothers in a Chicago suburb. At the time, a middle-class woman who nursed her baby was looked upon as just short of crazy; a support group was essential. From this small but determined circle of women the movement back to breast-feeding was launched. The founding mothers also realized that something was very wrong with the medicalized management of labor and delivery in hospitals. In those days "twilight sleep" was still popular: women were given a mixture of drugs that wiped away their awareness and memory of childbirth. In response, the La Leche mothers had their babies at home! They never talked about home birth publicly lest they be labeled as really off-the-wall.

For references and resources on breast-feeding, please see Appendices C and E.

Bottle Feeding

Even though formula lacks some special features of human milk, such as germ-fighting antibodies and white blood cells, babies do very well on it. In the relatively sanitary conditions in the United States today, such advantages of human milk are less critical than in underdeveloped areas of the world.

Cans of formula base come in the right size for making single batches of formula. If you have some left over, you can store it safely in the refrigerator for forty-eight hours, covered tightly with plastic wrap. The bottled formula also can be kept safely in the refrigerator for forty-eight hours. A bottle can stand at room temperature for an hour without spoiling and, if unopened, go back in the refrigerator. If, however, the baby has taken some formula from the bottle, the remainder should not be kept for more than an hour (half an hour in a hot climate) and should not be returned to the refrigerator.

Hot water and soap should be used in washing bottles and nipples. Sterilization in the presence of a safe water supply is unnecessary.

Vitamins and Minerals

Babies, like people of all other ages, require vitamins. Breast milk contains all the vitamins and iron a baby will need. Iron and vitamins are added to commercial formulas. There is no need to give extra vitamins or iron, despite the common practice of doing so. Nursing mothers must ensure an adequate vitamin intake themselves, which can usually be done by diet alone.

Vitamin K is necessary to the production of blood clotting factors. Without it, there can be bleeding throughout the body. Newborns have only small amounts of this vitamin and require about a week to make enough on their own to facilitate normal clotting. Therefore, vitamin K is routinely administered at birth to boost the level immediately.

Vitamin K is traditionally given by injection right after delivery. It is also possible to give it to the baby by mouth. It may be given prenatally by way of the placenta. The mother takes five to ten milligrams daily, beginning fourteen days before the estimated date of birth and continuing until birth. These methods have the advantage of being painless, but they have not yet been carefully studied. It is very likely true that there is enough vitamin K in commercial formula to meet a baby's requirements, but studies have not yet been performed to look at this question.

Fluoride is of proven benefit in preventing dental cavities. Populations of children exposed to fluoride, either in the water supply or as supplements, show a 50 percent reduction in cavities. Fluoridation of water has proved to be one of the most effective of public health measures. Fluoride is incorporated into growing teeth and can also be applied to the surface of teeth with a fluoridated toothpaste or a special fluoride solution. Since fluoride passes poorly through breast milk and is not added to prepared ready-to-use infant formulas, parents will need to give it directly to the baby. If your town water supply is fluoridated and you are bottle feeding, using the water to prepare formula, you will not need to give fluoride drops. Too much fluoride stains the teeth. As the breast-fed baby grows older and takes more town water, directly or in foods, taper off the supplements. By a year they are probably not needed. Check with your doctor or nurse about obtaining fluoride drops and determining the doses to use.

Feeding, Sleeping, and Crying

FEEDING

Babies regularly swallow air with feedings and usually *burp* it up. Sometimes they seem uncomfortable before burping, as though their stomachs are too full. Since air rises, the upright position is the best one to facilitate burping, traditionally assisted with a gentle pat on the back. Along with burping, many babies bring up ("spit up") some milk, which may exit through their noses as well as their mouths. Spitting up is of no consequence to the baby. It is likely that whenever a baby burps, some milk enters the esophagus (food tube). Since the distance from stomach to mouth in a baby is only a few inches, it does not take too much extra force to bring the milk all the way up and out. If spitting up is bothersome, you can burp the baby midway through a feeding and let up on nursing as soon as the baby slows down, thus not giving more milk than he or she can hold and thereby tending to prevent spitting up.

Babies also *hiccup*. They even have hiccups in utero, which mothers can often distinguish from kicking. Hiccups seem to bother babies little if at all, and most will merrily hiccup their way to sleep. There is no need for concern.

Babies have no need for *solid foods* for at least the first four months, and preferably six. Certainly they need not be given them until they can take them from a spoon. There is no evidence that the earlier introduction of solid foods reduces the number of nighttime awakenings.

SLEEPING

Sleeping patterns vary widely. Your baby will give you plenty of clues about what his or her schedule is. Most babies sleep twenty out of twenty-four hours in the first week or two and slowly taper off to sixteen to eighteen hours by the end of the first month. Some infants have predictable sleep/wake patterns; other babies are much more irregular. Some sleep more at night, while others catnap during the day in a variable pattern. Most infants do not sleep through the night until four or more months, although you can count on hearing about the exception who does so within the first one to two weeks. Many infants seem to mix up nights and days during the first several weeks of life. The introduction of solid foods does not affect the age of "sleeping through."

Light and noise do not usually bother infants, but if your baby startles easily or is a restless sleeper, you may have to arrange some dark and quiet spot. The best recommendation for sleep position of most infants until at least six months is on the back (supine) or side. Recent studies have demonstrated that these positions are less likely to be associated with crib death (also known as sudden infant death syndrome, or SIDS). Exactly how sleep position contributes to SIDS is not yet well understood.

If you are breast-feeding a fussy, wakeful baby and are drinking caffeine-containing beverages (coffee, tea, cola drinks), prudence suggests stopping, since there is evidence that caffeine reaches the baby through breast milk. It could act as a stimulant to keep her awake, active, and irritable.

CRYING

Crying is an infant's major means of communication and expression. It can mean "I'm hungry," "I'm tired," "I'm uncomfortable," "I'm letting off steam," or "I'm bored." Not all crying can be readily explained, and, of course, babies cannot be asked about their inner experiences. Many babies will cry without obvious cause for up to several hours a day, often in the late afternoon and early evening (one hopes not in the middle of the night). Do what you will—feed, change, rock, swaddle, hug, coo—nothing works for long. Interestingly, babies of all cultures and child rearing practices show this common behavior, meaning that the source probably lies within the infant rather than his or her environment. (In other words, it's not your fault.)

An extreme degree of inconsolable crying, when a baby seems truly miserable, is known as *colic*. Colic is believed to be related to intestinal cramps, but no one knows for sure. Cow's milk allergy may be a factor for some babies.

Babies who cry swallow air. It rumbles through their stomachs and intestines and is passed through the rectum. It is possible that the air contributes to intestinal cramps and leads to still more crying, more air swallowing, and so on. It is also possible that babies cry when they hear themselves cry, in a kind of self-imitation or contagion of discomfort.

When all else fails, you may have to let a baby "cry it out." Pick him or her up every fifteen minutes to provide comforting. If this does not help, put the baby back to bed, close the door, and cover your ears. If the crying is driving you up the wall, ask someone else to take over while you go for a walk. A rested person with a fresh point of view may be able to figure out a few tricks that have eluded you—little ways of working around a baby's individual quirks.

There are few forces on earth that can make one feel more

inadequate, or so undermine one's self-confidence, as the crying of a baby who cannot be comforted. Don't be surprised if you feel a little helpless, incompetent, or guilty in dealing with this behavior—you are not alone. And you can reassure yourself that, as far as anyone can tell, colicky crying leads to no permanent physical or emotional scars. Such babies grow up well anyway. Another piece of good news about even the worst colic is that it does not go on forever. By three months, or four at the outside, it is only a memory. (See crying and breast-feeding pp. 254–255 and Appendix E for books on babies in the first year.)

Bathing and Diapering

BATHING

Young babies do not need baths; they are not dirty at birth. *Vernix* (see p. 242), which coats the skin in utero, is healthy for the skin and may protect it against infection. If vernix accumulates in the skin folds, spread it around and rub it in like lotion. Wash the baby's bottom with warm water on a soft cloth.

Traditional practice directs that until the stump of the umbilical cord falls off, the baby should be sponge bathed with warm water and not immersed—presumably to prevent infection of the cord. To our knowledge, however, this has never been critically studied.

The bathing procedure is simple. Wash the eyelids with a clean cloth or cotton ball. While a Q-tip can be used to remove visible ear wax, it should not be used to dig into the ear canal. (Ear wax is normal. It becomes a problem only when it blocks a doctor's or nurse's view of the eardrum, when *otitis media* is suspected.) Use a mild soap to wash the baby from neck to feet, soaping the creases in the neck, under the arms, and in the groin. Wipe a girl's genitals from front to back to minimize the chance of a urinary tract infection. (This practice should be followed by the girl herself later in life when she begins using toilet tissue.) Use mild shampoo or soap for the scalp. Remove head scales ("cradle cap," or *seborrhea*) by rubbing with a cloth. If the scales are particularly resistant, soften them first with some baby oil. You may have to rub hard to get them off.

When using a baby tub, support the infant with one arm. You can also use a shallow bathtub. *Never leave an infant alone or unsupported in the water.* Since babies usually enjoy being bathed, a bath is a nice time for socializing and a useful diversion during fussy periods.

The *umbilical cord* stub should fall off on its own in seven to fourteen days. Do not pull it off. Until the cord falls off, keep the diaper rolled down under the navel. The effectiveness of the common practice of dabbing alcohol on the stump at each diaper change has never been proven. If more than the rim of the skin around the base of the cord becomes red, call the doctor promptly, since this could mean infection. Following the separation of the cord, the umbilicus ("belly button") may be wet and red, and the raw area left behind may bleed when touched. This area will usually heal within a few days. If it does not, the doctor or nurse can treat it by applying dried silver nitrate on the tip of what looks like a long matchstick.

DIAPERING

The baby should urinate and have a *bowel movement* within twenty-four hours. The first stool, called *meconium,* is black and sticky, almost like tar. The appearance changes first to a "seedy" yellow, then finally to a golden yellow with the consistency of scrambled eggs after the mother's milk comes in.

Bowel patterns vary from infant to infant. Some babies will have a bowel movement with every feeding, while others will have but three or four a week. Breast-fed infants are notorious for skipping days, and may even go a week between stools. The stool pattern may change dramatically after the first few weeks, from six stools a day to one every other day. The all-time record holder in my practice went three weeks between stools and was perfectly well!

Babies commonly strain and turn brick red when passing stools, but their discomfort usually lasts no more than a few minutes. None of this straining means that the baby is constipated. *Diarrhea* is characterized by frequent, watery, sometimes foul-smelling, sometimes green, loose stools. The doctor should be called if your baby develops diarrhea. (The green color, incidentally, comes from bile that has not undergone processing because of the rapid passage of the stool through the intestine.)

A baby boy's *foreskin* will not retract completely at birth. Retractability increases with age and is usually not complete for several years. During baths it is not necessary to retract the foreskin over the head of the penis for cleaning. Periodically, gently test the foreskin for retractability; *do not* force it.

A *circumcision* takes about ten days to heal. Wash the area with warm water on a cotton ball at each diaper change.

Regarding the necessity of circumcision, there is no medical or hygienic argument for it, (possibly some reduction in the already low risk for urinary tract infection) and there are risks that should be faced. I advise against routine circumcision. If the procedure must be done, a local anesthetic can be injected at the base of the penis to minimize pain to the baby.

Pinkish urine is common during the first few weeks, particularly in baby boys. The pink stain, lighter in color than blood, is often noticed on the diaper but is no cause for alarm. The color comes from urate crystals and is of no special significance.

A baby girl may have a *pink-tinged vaginal discharge* during the first ten days. This is caused by the withdrawal of stimulation of her uterus by maternal hormones that passed to her body via the placenta. It is a normal response.

Babies of both sexes may temporarily have *swollen breasts* and nipple secretions caused by the transfer of hormones from the mother across the placenta. This swelling disappears in seven to ten days.

An accumulation of *mucus* in the corner of the eye, particularly on awakening, is very common. It probably represents a transient partial blockage of the duct that drains tears from the eye into the nose. Wipe the mucus away with a moist washcloth or cotton ball. Redness of the whites of the eye (except for red spots present at birth, mentioned on p. 244) signifies infection (*conjunctivitis*) and should be reported to your doctor or nurse.

Diaper rash is the almost inevitable result of using diapers, a price we seem willing to pay for the convenience of dry sheets, clothes, and laps. For an infant, wearing wet diapers is analogous to an adult's having a wet bathing suit on most of the day. Since infants vary in their susceptibility to rash, care of their bottoms can be individualized.

The following procedures will prevent rash and help clear up rashes in progress:

1. Change diapers as soon as they are wet, or at least every two to four hours, including a change at night. Gently rinse the skin with clear water, allowing it to air dry as much as possible.
2. Avoid overnight use of plastic pants over a cloth diaper. Instead, use a "triple diaper" made of cloth diapers and a rubber pad to protect the bed.
3. In washing cotton diapers, use an extra rinse with diluted vinegar added.
4. The "super" disposable diapers bind with water and not merely absorb it, thereby providing a drier environment for the skin.
5. There is evidence that disposable diapers are less likely to cause a rash.
6. Use ointments to protect the skin. These are probably better as preventives than as treatments for established rashes. Zinc oxide, A and D, Desitin, and Vaseline Intensive Care all will do. Air exposure will also reduce rash.
7. Check with your doctor or nurse about any rash that resists your efforts to clear it up. Medicated creams or ointments may be required.

Preventing Eye Infection

In the United States, all states mandate by law the treatment of the newborn's eyes to prevent gonococcal infection (see pp. 169–170). Most states follow the standards of the Centers for Disease Control in allowing a choice between silver nitrate and an antibiotic ointment (erythromycin or tetracycline), while some states restrict treatment to the traditional silver nitrate solution.

Some parents object to the use of silver nitrate. The swelling conjunctivae and eyelids that result interfere with the infant's ability to open her eyes. It therefore disturbs the family's earliest hours together and the bonding process, which is enhanced by eye-to-eye contact (see pp. 248–251). Antibiotic ointment does not cause as much inflammation and is preferable to silver nitrate in this regard. Application of either antibiotic or silver nitrate can be delayed one or more hours after birth, in order not to interfere with initial parent–infant contact. Parents should inquire about this before birth.

Chlamydia (see pp. 166–167) has replaced the gonococcus as the most common cause of eye infection in newborns in this country. Since silver nitrate is not effective against chlamydia and erythromycin is effective against both chlamydia and gonorrhea, an argument can be made for using erythromycin exclusively in treating the eyes of the newborn. Although tetracycline is also officially recommended, its effects have not yet been as well studied. Again, this should be discussed with the physician before birth.

PKU Test

As mentioned in Chapter 2, the PKU (phenylketonuria) test is done soon after birth on several drops of blood obtained by pricking the baby's heel. It is usually done in the hospital without parental participation, but, since more babies are being discharged early or are born at home, it may be done either in the office or at home after the baby has had several feedings.

After the heel prick is made, the drops of blood are squeezed from the foot until the spaces provided for them on the test card are filled. This is obviously disturbing to the newborn. One resourceful mother in my practice nursed her baby through this uncomfortable procedure and demonstrated that she could calm her infant most of the time. I subsequently recommended this approach, with success, to several other mothers. The Bandaid on the heel can be removed the following day.

This test is done to identify the 1 baby in 10,000 with a biochemical disorder that can lead to mental retardation if left untreated. These babies are unable to process the amino acid (simple protein) *phenylalanine* found in human and cow's milk. As this chemical builds up in the blood, it damages the brain. Once identified, the condition is treated by restricting phenylalanine in the diet.

In a pregnant woman with PKU, the exposure of the fetus to high maternal blood levels of phenylalanine is likely to result in mental retardation and small head and brain size (microcephaly).

Thus, a woman treated for PKU during childhood must resume the low phenylalanine diet before conception and during her pregnancy, to prevent damage to her baby. PKU in either parent increases the likelihood of an offspring with the disorder. So, not only should the baby be tested, but the affected parents need to know about their disorder. Affected adults should alert health professionals in order to take preventive measures before pregnancy.

Testing Newborns for Drug Exposure

Unfortunately in today's society the most common toxic influence to which babies are exposed before birth is illicit drugs taken by a drug-dependent mother, including crack, cocaine, marijuana, and heroin. Accordingly, some hospital nurseries are adopting a policy of testing infants for such exposure so that treatment and preventive measures can be begun. A favored sample source is meconium, the stools formed before birth, which provides a months-long record of in-utero drug exposure.

Signs of Illness

Serious signs of illness in an infant are the following. A doctor or nurse should be contacted immediately.

- A fever above 100.5 degrees (see the following discussion)
- Diarrhea (frequent watery, foul-smelling, loose stools)
- Continuous vomiting at feedings, or vomiting that shoots out several feet from the baby (remember, however, that simple burping may sometimes be "projectile")
- Weak or absent sucking
- Blood in stools or in vomitus
- Labored breathing
- Persistent or unusual crying

Use a *rectal thermometer* to take the baby's temperature. Shake the mercury column down to below 98.6 degrees and grease the bulb end with petroleum jelly taken from the jar on a tissue (to avoid contaminating the jar). Lay the baby face down across your lap and gently insert the thermometer about one inch into the rectum, holding the thermometer between index and middle fingers with palm down to grasp and hold the buttocks together. This allows you to move with the baby if he or she wiggles and to prevent the thermometer from breaking. Keep the thermometer in place for three minutes, then wipe it off with tissue to read it.

As for other worrisome symptoms, parents should trust their own instincts and consult the doctor or nurse if any unusual or sudden change in the baby's appearance or habits persists. See also Appendix E for books on children's health.

Jaundice

During the first week check the baby daily in natural light for jaundice, a yellow color of the skin and the whites of the eyes. Any yellowness darker than "just visible" should be reported to the doctor or midwife. Yellowness as deep as the color of lemon peel or egg yolk and jaundice of any kind during the first twenty-four hours warrant *immediate attention.*

Jaundice is produced by the buildup of a chemical called *bilirubin.* Normally present in humans of all ages, bilirubin is a break-down product of hemoglobin from red blood cells that have died. The bilirubin is carried by the blood to the liver, where it is combined into the bile for elimination through the intestine. The newborn's liver normally takes a few days to reach peak efficiency in processing bilirubin. In addition, a newborn's red blood cells are reducing in number, to accommodate the infant to life outside the uterus, thus liberating more hemoglobin and, hence, bilirubin. For both these reasons, the newborn is apt to develop jaundice. If any other disorder that increases red cell destruction is present—such as maternal antibodies against fetal cells, as in Rh(D), or ABO blood type incompatibility (see p. 59)—the likelihood of jaundice is even greater.

Bilirubin in the blood above a certain level can injure the brain, especially in a premature or sick baby. Hence, jaundice needs to be assessed and treated if excessive. While full-term babies normally develop jaundice, only a small percentage require therapy. Experienced midwives and doctors can estimate the degree of jaundice by simply looking. If the level seems high, an exact measurement of bilirubin can be made on several drops of blood obtained by pricking the heel.

The garden-variety physiologic jaundice in infants makes its appearance on the second or, more likely, on the third day, peaks on day four or five, and is pretty much gone by day seven. There is no evidence that giving extra water will decrease jaundice, and water supplements will interfere with breast-feeding. If jaundice occurs during the first twenty-four hours, contact your doctor right away, for the level is likely to move quickly into the dangerous range.

The mainstay of treatment of jaundice is light (phototherapy). Light activates a chemical in the baby's skin that breaks down bilirubin. The infant is placed naked with her eyes covered under one or two special fluorescent lights for as long as it takes to lower the bilirubin. Nursing can continue while "under the lights." With the help of a doctor or midwife, phototherapy can be given in the home as well as in the hospital.

Borderline levels of jaundice can be treated by exposing the baby to natural sunlight near the window at home. In babies whose severe jaundice is not controllable by phototherapy, bilirubin is removed by withdrawing blood bit by bit and replacing it with donor blood having a normal level of bilirubin. This procedure is known as *exchange transfusion*.

A relatively common form of jaundice is related to breast-feeding, as noted earlier in this chapter (p. 262).

Automobile Safety

As noted in Chapter 3, car safety is a critical issue for riders of all ages, but especially for infants and children, since automobile accidents are a leading cause of death and disability in this age group. Even in the absence of a crash, infants and children are at risk from the swerving and stopping of a car. In many of these situations the child is thrown from the car. Until they are four years old and weigh forty pounds, children require *special safety devices*. (After this age the car's lap and shoulder belts can be used.)

In general, rearward-facing devices are better for infants, and car seats that hook over seat backs are unsafe. Car seats must protect children from both front and rear crashes, cushioning them and keeping them from being thrown free. In addition, the seat must have a head restraint to protect against whiplash and have restraining belts at least 1.5 inches wide to hold the upper parts of the child's body. Any seat constructed of easily bent, bare metal or flimsy strapping, or padded only with thin sponge rubber or sharp or pointed hardware, is unsafe and to be avoided.

In 1982 the U.S. government established guidelines for child and infant car restraints. Many states have passed laws requiring the use of restraints that meet the federal guidelines until children are large enough and old enough to use the belts that come with the car.

Whenever infants are transported in a car, even on their first ride home from the hospital, a specially designed restraint should be used. It should be installed and used according to the manufacturer's instructions. The back seat is safer than the front, and the center of the car is safer than the sides. Everyone else in the car should use seat belts, too (whether or not inflatable airbags are installed). In a crash, unrestrained passengers can literally crush others, as well as hurt themselves. A practice to be especially condemned is holding an infant in one's arms in a moving vehicle. In a crash, the baby will either be released or crushed by the person holding him or her. If you are driving or riding and need to remove the baby from the restraint, pull off the road and stop the car.

By insisting on restraint use in your car right from the start, you will find it much easier to enforce this policy later when your child is old enough to protest. He or she simply will never have known anything different.

7

Complications
of Pregnancy
and Birth

Breech Presentation

Breech (buttocks-first) birth has been feared for centuries because of increased risk to the baby during labor and delivery. Through modern obstetrical techniques, the risks have been greatly reduced. It is now reasonable to expect successful birth whether vaginally or by cesarean section.

About 3 percent of term pregnancies involve breech presentations. The more premature the baby, the greater the likelihood of a breech birth. In fact, it can be said that all babies are breech at least some of the time during the pregnancy. The explanation lies in the ratio of the size of the fetus to the volume of amniotic fluid. Early in pregnancy the fetus turns every which way. As the fetus grows, it occupies more of the intrauterine space, and there is less room for turning. After thirty-six or thirty-seven weeks it is unlikely that the fetus will flip over by itself. Without manipulation, a breech tends to stay a breech.

Prematurity is not the only factor associated with breech presentation. In multiple pregnancies (pp. 338–341) at least one twin is likely to be breech. Breeches are more common with various birth defects. For example, a baby with Down syndrome (pp. 134–

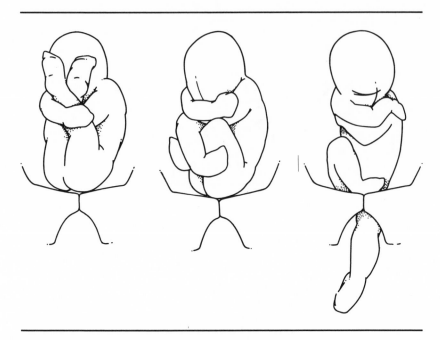

Figure 19. Frank breech   **Figure 20. Complete breech**   **Figure 21. Incomplete breech**

136) is twice as likely as a normal baby to be a breech. Breeches are also more common in hydramnios (p. 311) and in women who have carried many pregnancies. Sometimes more than one factor is operating, for example, when prematurity and a congenital defect are associated. In about 80 percent of breeches, however, there is no known cause.

There are three common types of breech presentations. In a *frank breech* (see Figure 19) the legs are flexed on the abdomen, and the lower legs are straight or near straight at the knee. This position makes it very difficult for these babies to turn over on their own, since the legs in effect splint the body. In this sense, frank breech can be said to maintain breech position and may explain why a majority of breeches at term are of the frank variety.

In a *complete breech* (see Figure 20) the thighs are flexed at the groin, but the legs are bent at the knees. In an *incomplete breech* (see Figure 21) one or both hips are not flexed (that is, they are straight), and one or more of the feet or knees lies below the level of the buttocks of the fetus. This type of breech is also called a "footling" breech because one of the feet is usually lying low.

The most common type of breech is the frank breech, accounting for 38 percent of all breeches weighing less than 2,500 grams (about 5 pounds) and 51.0 to 73.0 percent of those weighing over 2,500 grams. The corresponding figures for complete breeches are 12.0 percent and 11.5 percent, respectively. For incompletes, the figures are 50.0 percent and 20.0 to 24.0 percent.

The frank breech is the only type in which the inlet to the pelvis is filled as well or nearly as well as in a normal head-first presentation during labor. When a foot or leg is adjacent to the buttocks, as in a complete or footling breech, the fit is not nearly as good. Because of this the umbilical cord is much more likely to prolapse (come out) around the buttocks and foot into the vagina (pp. 336–337). The consequences of a prolapsed cord can be serious. At worst, the baby can die due to interruption of his or her blood supply, which results from cord compression. At best, if the prolapse can be controlled temporarily by properly positioning the mother and pushing the baby back up into the uterus, an immediate cesarean section is usually done.

Compression of the umbilical cord by the baby's head as it passes through the birth canal during the end of labor is a risk in vaginal breech deliveries because it may lead to fetal asphyxia and even death. Mild compression may depress the baby at birth and result in the need for resuscitation. There is always the potential for some degree of brain injury, with possible long-term consequences for the baby.

In addition to the threat of cord compression during breech delivery, there is also an increased likelihood of physical damage if the head does not pass easily through the birth canal and force has to be applied. Overall, the risk of death for breech babies delivered vaginally is several times that of vertex (head-first) births. In this statistic the position used by the mother and the experience of the attendant are not taken into account.

There have been major shifts over the past fifty years in the approach to delivery of the breech baby. With improved techniques of surgery and anesthesia by the 1960s and 1970s, the overall results of cesarean section were found to be superior to vaginal delivery in terms of death and injury to breech babies, and cesarean section was widely practiced. Then, in the late 1970s, researchers found that in most cases frank breeches could be allowed a trial of labor, with cesarean section done only if necessary rather than routinely. The outcomes in the cesarean-delivered and vaginally delivered infants were found to be essentially the same in the university hospital settings where the studies were performed. More recently, some obstetricians have approached the nonfrank breech with the point of view of sectioning only if necessary, with similar excellent results.

Aiding somewhat in the selection of breeches that can safely be allowed a trial of labor are X rays or CT (computerized tomography) scan (using much less radiation) to measure the dimensions of the pelvis, X rays (or CT scan) and ultrasound of the fetus to determine the relationship of the head to the body (babies whose heads are extended back are not considered safe candidates for vaginal delivery), a better understanding of the signs of fetal distress (whether through electronic or stethoscope monitoring of the fetal heart rate and pH testing—see pp. 154–155—of the baby believed to be in difficulty), and generally improved obstetrical techniques.

The best results achieved to date demonstrate that in breeches for whom a trial of labor is considered appropriate, about 45 percent can safely deliver vaginally, while 55 percent will need cesarean section, a significant drop over the figures of a decade ago. (See also discussion of breech as a factor in the cesarean section rate, p. 290.)

Another interesting recent development is a growing recognition that the squatting position may offer significant advantages in the vaginal delivery of a breech baby. It is known, for example, that the area of the pelvic outlet increases as much as 28 percent when a woman squats. Efforts are currently under way to test this hypothesis.

Finally, it must be said that the medical malpractice crisis evident since the mid-1980s has strongly influenced obstetricians—even those decreasingly few skilled in vaginal breech deliveries—to section breeches without exception. Even taking into account the risk of cesarean sections (see pp. 287–288), problems in a breech baby delivered vaginally are hard to defend against the claim that a cesarean section could have avoided the problem.

Faced with this legal reality, many physicians have simply abandoned breech vaginal delivery.

Vaginal delivery of a breech presentation is carried out in most hospitals with the services of two physicians:

- The *obstetrician*
- An *assistant obstetrician*, who is especially needed if forceps are used to guide the birth of the head

The birth of the head of a breech is the critical time. In the usual birth, the head, which is the largest part of the baby, leads the way and is born before the rest of the baby. Once the head has cleared, it is unusual for any other part of the baby to get stuck (see p. 337, "Shoulder Dystocia"). But in a breech, the head is the last part to be born. Thus, passage of all but the head is no guarantee that all will be well. Not only can the head get stuck, but at the same time, the cord will be compressed between the head and wall of the birth canal, an invariable characteristic of a breech vaginal delivery. So time is of the essence.

Forceps are often used in delivering the head to protect it and avoid undue traction on the neck. Four obstetrical hands are needed, two to apply the forceps and two to support the rest of the baby's body. With one hand, the obstetrician supports the baby's trunk and arms with a towel and pulls upward. The legs are supported and pulled upward with the other hand. The first obstetrician inserts the forceps into the vagina over the sides of the baby's head. The forceps bend downward at the perineum, and the handles lock below the baby. As the forceps exert traction on the head, the assistant pulls upward on the body until the head clears the perineum. As mentioned before, It appears likely that giving birth in the upright or squatting position may help avert the use of forceps and episiotomy.

In a cesarean section for a breech presentation, the ideal incision, in terms of avoiding cesarian sections in future pregnancies, is a *lower-segment transverse incision* (see pp. 284–291 on cesarean sections). Particularly when the fetus is premature, the lower, non-muscular part of the uterus may be underdeveloped, forcing the obstetrician to make a vertical incision, thereby destining the woman to repeat cesarean sections during subsequent pregnancies.

Because of the many issues surrounding the care of breeches, identifying these babies prior to labor is important, so that adequate plans can be made. At the physical examination of the uterus during one of the routine prenatal visits (pp. 40–49), clues to a breech include feeling the head high in the abdomen and hearing the fetal heart tones *above* rather than below, the mother's umbilicus. Ultrasound examination can then confirm the situation. (Ultrasound examination done for some other reason may also uncover an unsuspected breech.)

A safe way to convert a breech to vertex presentation before the onset of labor by turning the baby has been sought for some time. Two methods have been tried: positioning of the mother and manual rotation. In the *positioning method*, a woman lies on her back on a hard surface with her buttocks elevated on a pillow for ten to twenty minutes three to four times a day after the thirtieth week of pregnancy. She does this for up to four weeks or until turning has occurred, whichever is earlier. While the success rate of this maneuver has not been carefully studied, it appears to be effective in some cases.

In the *rotation method*, an attendant rotates the baby manually. One of the attendant's hands is placed on the mother's abdomen over the baby's head, the other over its buttocks. The hands are moved in opposite directions as the baby is gently stroked around. The maneuver takes a few minutes to perform. *External cephalic version*, as this maneuver is called, should be done by an experienced attendant. Some doctors first use ultrasound to locate the placenta and avoid the maneuver in cases where the placenta is near to or covering the opening to the cervix (see pp. 323–324 on placenta praevia). Some doctors recommend trying this method only in the hospital and, even during labor, using intravenous drugs to relax the uterus and thereby facilitate the maneuver. To avoid injuring the baby, the breech must not have settled into the pelvis.

The fetal heart rate is determined at the beginning and end of the procedure, and some doctors check it midway through as well. A marked increase, decrease, or irregularity of the rate is a sign of fetal stress and is an indication for the immediate return of the baby to his or her original position. The fetus is turned through the shorter of the two possible arcs so that the head takes the shorter route to the pelvis. Following a successful turning, a woman is asked to stay in an upright position for the rest of the day. If necessary, the procedure may be repeated once. Usually, if the baby does not stay in the vertex position after two attempts following the thirty-seventh week, no further efforts at turning are made. The expected success rate is about 70 percent at the thirty-seventh week and does not increase subsequently. Since there is a higher rate of reversion before the thirty-seventh week, thirty-seven weeks is considered the optimal time to do the procedure.

Reported complications of turning a breech manually include the death of the baby (presumably due to twisting and entanglement of the umbilical cord), placental abruption (p. 324), and rupture of the uterus. There are no good statistics on these complications, and they are considered rare. Nevertheless, many obstetricians do not subscribe to the notion of turning a breech and will refuse to perform the procedure. Not all obstetricians are experienced with the procedure, and it is done now less than in the past. If your obstetrician is not comfortable with it and you remain interested, ask for a consultation with a physician who has experience turning breech babies.

Carpal Tunnel Syndrome

Hand pain is quite common in pregnancy. Mainly occurring in the half of the hand that includes the thumb, and especially the middle finger, it is associated with "pins and needles" and numbness. It is caused by pressure on the nerve (the median nerve) that goes to these parts of the hand area as it passes through the wrist (carpal tunnel). This pressure seems to be related to the accumulation of fluid characteristic of pregnancy.

The symptoms vary widely in intensity, most commonly ranging from merely "annoying" and "interfering with sleep," to "intolerable" in a small minority of women. While the pain is focused in the hand, aching can be felt as high up the arm as the shoulder. In more severe cases, some degree of weakness may occur as well. Either one or both hands may be affected.

In most cases, complete improvement occurs after delivery. Symptoms may be relieved through the use of painkillers and by splinting the hand for part of the day or at night. If all else fails, the disorder can be corrected by a fairly simple operation done under local anesthesia.

Cesarean Section

Cesarean section ("C-section," for short) is the surgical procedure used to deliver a baby through an abdominal and uterine incision in cases when vaginal delivery is judged impossible or dangerous. While documented attempts at cesarean section date back to the seventeenth century, consistent success did not occur until well into the twentieth century. By the World War II era, cesarean section proved to offer dramatic benefits in dealing with such life-threatening problems as placenta praevia, placental abruption, eclampsia, and severe disproportion (all discussed in this section). During the 1960s and 1970s doctors increasingly recognized that cesarean section could benefit maternal and infant health even when life itself was not immediately at stake. For example, babies who had previously been delivered by forceps while still high in the birth canal (so-called midforceps delivery) were found to do much better in terms of neurological problems (fewer cases of cerebral palsy, learning problems, etc.) if they were instead delivered by cesarean section. Certain kinds of breeches were also found to do better after cesarean, rather than vaginal, birth.

While it is hard to deny the enormous contribution made by cesarean section, concern is now being expressed by doctors, midwives, and childbirth educators that in the United States too many of these operations are being performed, with the figures now hovering at nearly one-quarter of all births and close to one million deliveries per year in this country (making it the most frequent form of major surgery). A critical reappraisal of the reasons for cesarean delivery now under way has already led to leveling off in the percentage of deliveries handled with surgery.

The childbirth education movement has responded to the increased frequency of cesarean section will help for the women involved and a constructive critique of the problem. Educators have urged that the term *cesarean birth,* rather than *cesarean section,* be used to emphasize that a birth, not merely an operation, is occurring. Fathers are being welcomed to the operating room, and early parent–infant interaction is encouraged despite the surrounding distractions. Discussion of cesarean birth is now included in prenatal classes, and organizations have been formed to meet the needs of women who have undergone or will undergo cesarean sections and of those who contemplate vaginal birth after a cesarean (VBAC). (See Appendix C for these resources.)

A TYPICAL CESAREAN BIRTH

In most hospitals, cesarean section is performed under spinal or epidural anesthesia (see pp. 209–215). As a rule, general anesthesia is reserved for true emergencies, when time does not permit spinals or epidurals, or when these techniques have proved unsuccessful. Prior to surgery the lower abdomen is shaved from just below the navel to the pubic bone. A catheter is inserted in the bladder and left in place until after the operation. The skin is vigorously scrubbed with surgical soap, and sterile drapes or an adherent plastic covering are placed over the abdomen to leave only the lower belly uncovered. The obstetrician and surgical nurse wear sterile garb—gowns, caps, masks, and gloves. All others present, including the husband or partner and birth attendant, wear surgical scrub suits, masks, and caps in the operating room. Anesthesiologists and obstetricians usually reserve the right to ask nonprofessional participants to leave the room during an emergency. Policies on participation by husbands or partners may vary from one hospital to another. Women are advised to clarify this issue ahead of time.

A vertical screen is usually placed above the woman's upper chest so that she cannot see the surgeons. However, she is able to hear them and can carry on a conversation with those around her. Ideally, she should feel no pain, but if she does, she should report it so that measures to stop it can be taken. She may feel some tugging and pressure, especially during the delivery of the baby. Once the amniotic sac is opened, she will hear the noise of the suction machine drawing the amniotic fluid from the uterus into a collecting bottle. Following the removal of the amniotic fluid, the obstetrician reaches into the uterus to take hold of the head, which is then worked through the incision. The assistant presses the top of the uterus to help push the head out. In a breech delivery, of course, the legs are delivered first.

After the head is born, the obstetrician clears the amniotic fluid from the baby's nose and mouth with a bulb syringe. If meconium (the baby's stools) has been passed into the amniotic fluid, this suctioning is more intense and is done with a plastic catheter. As the baby is delivered, the obstetrician will usually ask the anesthesiologist to inject a dose of Pitocin into the mother's intravenous infusion to cause the uterus to contract. It is also common practice, following delivery of the baby, to give the mother a single dose of intravenous antibiotics to prevent uterine infection. To prevent their passage into the baby, antibiotics are given to the mother after the umbilical cord is clamped. The cord is cut and the baby handed to the nurse or pediatrician, who carries the newborn to a nearby warming table. The baby is further suctioned and examined; when clearly doing well on his or her own, the baby is wrapped, capped, and handed to the father.

Meanwhile, the surgeons remove the placenta and sew up the incisions in the uterus and the abdominal wall. From beginning to end the surgery usually takes between thirty and forty-five minutes. After the operation the mother is wheeled to the recovery room. The baby should be able to remain with the parents, even though there may be a brief period during which he or she is taken to the nursery for weighing, measuring, and eye treatment.

During the postoperative period medications are administered to the mother to deal with the pain of the incision. Blood pressure, pulse, urine flow, amount of bleeding, and the tone of the uterus are checked every hour for four hours. Afterward, checks are carried out every four hours for the first day.

By the day after surgery, many women can drink fluids, and the intravenous infusion can be slowed and pulled out after forty-eight hours. The urinary catheter is usually removed after twelve hours. On the second and third days, "gas pains" from ineffective bowel action are common, and a rectal suppository or enema is often helpful. Women can usually begin walking with assistance on the day after surgery. Early walking promotes quick recovery and prevents the formation of blood clots (thrombi) in the veins of the legs (thrombophlebitis). These clots can break off and travel through the bloodstream and heart into the lungs. By the third postdelivery day, the mother can usually bathe safely; on the fourth day her skin sutures or clips can be removed. As soon as she feels well enough, she can begin breast-feeding the baby. On the fifth postdelivery day, the mother and baby can usually go home.

RISKS OF CESAREAN SECTION

Since it is a major operation, cesarean birth is not without risks. Although the overall maternal mortality rate in the United States is extremely low (9.9 deaths per 100,000 births in 1978), cesarean birth carries a two- to four-times greater risk of maternal death than vaginal delivery. Cesarean birth also carries an increased risk for such complications as thrombophlebitis, uterine infection, urinary tract infection, and the complications of anesthesia. It carries all the economic costs of major surgery and, in comparison with vaginal delivery, causes a delay of at least one week before a woman can return to her normal activities.

Cesarean birth, some authorities say, may actually be safer than these figures suggest. The excess mortality may be related more to preexisting conditions in the mother than to the operation itself. The deaths appear in statistics in the group of cesarean-related deaths, wrongly causing it to appear that the operation itself was the cause.

There is growing evidence that cesarean birth can be done with very few maternal deaths, even in sick women. A report during the 1980s of 10,000 consecutive cesarean births at the Boston Hospital for Women, which included some extremely sick women with disorders like eclampsia, diabetes, and heart disease, showed not a single death of a mother.

Improvements in the operation continue to be made. It is now recognized that the traditional position of women who undergo cesarean births (flat on the back) is related to some complications for the baby. The harmful effects of this position are now clear: the heavy uterus presses on the large artery and vein that run along the woman's spine, interfering with both the return of blood to the heart and the outflow of blood from the heart to the body in general, and to the uterus, placenta, and fetus. Various degrees of fetal distress can result. To avoid these problems, doctors now tilt the woman to one side during the operation in order to roll the uterus off the major blood vessels. Other measures to reduce complications were described earlier: use of intravenous antibiotics at the end of the surgery; early walking to prevent phlebitis; and the use of spinal or epidural anesthesia instead of general anesthesia whenever possible.

Risks to the baby have also been reduced. The baby is more likely to have temporary breathing problems (known as *transient tachypnea* of the newborn). These problems are thought to be due to the absence of the squeezing out of fluid from the chest, which occurs normally in a vaginal delivery. Also, there is a risk of prematurity, with its associated problem of respiratory distress, because gestational age is sometimes not judged correctly. However, accurate tests to determine fetal maturity have minimized this problem.

WHEN ARE CESAREANS NECESSARY?

The cesarean birthrate in the United States increased from 5.5 percent of all births in 1970 to 15.2 percent in 1980. The rate was up to 24.7 percent in 1988, and dropped slightly to 23.5 in 1990.

According to a 1980 National Institutes of Health (NIH) report that looked at ways to reduce the rate of cesarean sections, the diagnostic categories that had the largest effect on the increase in the rate between 1970 and 1978 were *repeat cesarean, breech presentation, dystocia,* and *fetal distress.*

Repeat cesarean section has been identified as the category most amenable to correction. In the past, doctors applied the dictum (first pronounced in 1916) "once a section, always a section," because they feared that the scarred uterus would rupture during a subsequent labor. This risk is a real one with the "classical" vertical (up-and-down) uterine incision, which involves the body or middle portion of the uterus rather than its lower segment. The chances of tearing the scar are far less, however, with the transverse (side-to-side) lower uterine incision now in wide use. This incision cuts through part of the uterus that is less muscular and less full of blood vessels. Thus, in a subsequent labor, if a tear should occur, bleeding, which can threaten the lives of both the mother and the fetus, is less likely. Although obstetricians now make every effort to use only this transverse lower uterine incision, it is not always possible to do so.

If a previous vertical incision was made into the body of the uterus or into the lower uterine segment, the currently recommended course is to forego subsequent vaginal birth (the risk of rupture is 1 to 3 percent). In the case of a vertical lower uterine segment scar, there is a good likelihood that the incision actually extended into the upper uterine segment, with increased risk for tearing during subsequent labors. If, in making the lower transverse segment incision, tearing or deliberate cutting resulted in a T- or J-shaped incision (as opposed to a curved-line incision), repeat cesarean section is also recommended.

This discussion of the intricacies of incisions and scars emphasizes the importance of obtaining records on the previous cesarean birth. The doctor who deals with a subsequent pregnancy needs these to plan the course of labor and delivery.

In comparing the safety of VBAC with elective cesarean delivery, it must be pointed out that there have been no randomized control trials in which women are assigned at random to one or the other route of delivery. (Few women would agree to participate in such a study, which is the major barrier to accomplishing it.) A number of studies of women who have had a single cesarean delivery and who subsequently attempted a vaginal birth have demonstrated that about 80 percent are successful. Furthermore, whether women with a previous cesarean birth delivered by elective surgery or vaginally apparently makes no difference in rates of tears of the uterus, and the use of oxytocin (see pp. 202–204) (to stimulate uterine contractions) does not appear to increase the rate of uterine tears in vaginal delivery after cesarean birth. There is no reported difference in outcomes among the babies.

The best estimate for the rate of uterine tears during labor and vaginal delivery among women with a previous cesarean delivery of a single baby is less than 0.25 percent. Such tears should be readily treatable by surgery and are less serious and less common than many other complications of labor and delivery that require surgical correction.

Although limited, the data available on women who have had more than one VBAC strongly support this practice. There appears to be no limit on the number of VBACs a woman can have.

With respect to monitoring the fetus during a VBAC, there is no reported study that compares continuous electronic fetal monitoring (see pp. 146–147) to intermittent listening to the fetal heart. Most obstetricians insist on continuous monitoring even in the absence of such data. Birthing centers are just now beginning to enroll women who have had a previous cesarean birth. These practice issues await clarification.

While the case for VBAC is very strong, obstetricians were slow to support it. The slow-to-change attitude of obstetricians toward VBAC is an example of the conservatism of the medical profession regarding many maternity care practices.

In the case of a *breech birth*, the NIH report recommended that vaginal delivery is an acceptable choice for full-term breech babies under the following circumstances:

- The expected weight of baby is less than eight pounds.
- The woman has a normal pelvis.
- The baby is in a frank breech, that is, with legs extended and head flexed.
- The doctor and his or her assistants are experienced in vaginal breech delivery.

Because of the risks of a vaginal delivery, the woman and her family need to be fully informed and involved in the choices to be made. (For further discussion of breech presentation, see pp. 277–283.)

Dystocia, or *failure to progress in labor*, is another reason for cesarean birth. It was identified by the NIH report as an explanation for much of the increased rate of cesarean birth in the United States. A reduction in the number of cesarean births done for this reason seems possible. For example, in 1988, 7.6 percent of all births in the United States were accomplished by cesarean birth for dystocia, while in a study done at the busy National

Maternity Hospital in Dublin, Ireland, at about the same time only 0.7 percent of all births occurred by cesarean birth for this reason. The difference may be due to varying approaches to the care of women with ineffective uterine contractions. While oxytocin and other nonsurgical measures to stimulate labor were routine (see pp. 199–200) in Ireland, cesarean birth was more quickly resorted to in the United States.

In considering *fetal distress* as reason for cesarean birth, the NIH report recommended further studies to improve the accuracy of the diagnosis of fetal distress, the development of new techniques for making the diagnosis, and improved nonsurgical ways of dealing with this problem. In particular, more widespread use of fetal blood testing was recommended.

Having presented this discussion of cesarean section, I thought it would be useful to look at what you yourself can do to minimize the need for an operation and to maximize your chances of having a vaginal delivery. One of the best summaries on this topic is contained in Table 6, distributed by the organization, C/SEC (see Appendix C), and reproduced without change. While I generally agree with these recommendations, I also refer the reader to the discussions of specific topics—for example, eating and drinking in labor (see pp. 201–202)—found elsewhere in this book.

C/SEC provides mail and telephone counseling on questions concerning cesarean childbirth, cesarean prevention, and VBAC (vaginal birth after cesarean). C/SEC publications can be obtained individually or in quantity for parents, support groups, childbirth educators, and health care professionals.

The topic of cesarean birth is a touchstone for many issues in contemporary obstetrical care. Once you understand this subject, you also understand a great deal about prenatal care and labor and the choices involved.

Death of a Fetus or Baby

While most miscarriages occur during the first trimester, fetal death can occur at any time right up to and during labor itself. Causes include intrauterine growth retardation (see pp. 312–315),

Table 6 How to Prevent an Unnecessary Cesarean

Reasons for Cesareans	Don't's	Do's

Dystocia (difficult labor)
Also called
  CPD (baby's head too big or at the wrong angle to fit)
  Failure to progress
  Prolonged labor
  Arrested labor
  Uterine inertia
	DON'T be impatient. It is all right if it doesn't go fast or if it is different from the way you or the doctor expected.	**DO trust your body to work right.** Unless there are obvious problems, stay home during the early, slower part of labor, usually until contractions are 3–5 minutes apart, at least 45 seconds long, and strong enough to take your whole attention. If you are less than 3–4 centimeters dilated when you get to the hospital, go home again unless contractions are very strong and close together.

	DON'T lie on your back or stay in one position through labor. Lying on your back, even with pillows behind you, will make labor slower and more painful.	**DO** change positions often. Stay upright as much as possible, alternating standing, walking, kneeling, sitting, rocking, being on hands and knees, or on your left side. Go to the bathroom at least once an hour.
	DON'T have an intravenous (I.V.) or electronic fetal heart monitor unless there are definite medical problems.	**DO** agree to an I.V. or electronic monitor only when medically necessary. If they are, ask for an I.V. pole on wheels, and the monitor to be disconnected some of the time so you can walk, perhaps 45 minutes out of each hour.
	DON'T lie down or hold your breath when pushing. If you push lying down or leaning back, you have to push the baby uphill.	**DO** squat, stand, be on hands and knees, kneel, sit on a toilet, or lie on your side to push. When you squat, your pelvis is bigger.

Table 6 *Continued*

Reasons for Cesareans	Don't's	Do's
	(continued) Holding your breath, holding your legs up, or digging in your heels all tense your bottom, making the birth longer and harder.	**DO** push only when you feel your body pushing, just as long and hard as feels right. **DO** keep your mouth and throat loose and open, avoid holding your breath unless you want to. Make as much noise as you want. It will help. **DO** concentrate on opening up and letting go.
	DON'T break the bag of waters artificially. They are an important protection for the baby.	**DO** say no to breaking your waters unless there are special circumstances.
	DON'T use Pitocin (a drug to start or speed up labor), just because labor is slow, the waters have broken, the due date has passed, or for convenience. Some labors are normally slow, and some babies take longer to be ready for birth than others. If the waters break before labor, the risk of immediate infection is very small if you are healthy to begin with, and continue to eat and sleep well.	**DO** let your baby decide his or her own birthday, and let your body decide how labor will go. **DO** wait for labor if the baby is "late" unless tests show he or she may be in trouble. **DO** wait for labor if the waters break, unless there are signs of infection. Stay home, don't take baths, use tampons, or have sex. Eat and sleep normally.
	DON'T stop eating and drinking in labor. Labor is hard work, and both you and your	**DO** eat lightly as you feel like it in labor—soup, toast, yogurt, cereal, applesauce, Jello.

Table 6 *Continued*

Reasons for Cesareans	*Don't's*	*Do's*
	(*continued*) baby need food and fluids. The hospital may keep you from eating and drinking for fear you might vomit if you have general anesthesia. It is very rare to have to go to sleep for the birth, and keeping you from eating and drinking doesn't get rid of the danger anyway.	**DO** drink lots of juices, sweetened herb tea, broth, or other clear liquids. Stay home in early labor so you can eat and drink what you feel like, unless you know you have complications or will be having anesthesia.
	DON'T take drugs for pain in labor if possible. They will not take away all the pain, but may slow labor, and make you so groggy it is harder to cope. **DON'T** have epidural anesthesia in labor (to make you numb from the waist down). It may weaken contractions, slow labor, and make it much harder to push your baby out.	**DO** learn and use other ways to reduce labor pain before using drugs or anesthesia. Most important is to let go all tension. Walk, change positions, have someone massage, stroke, or hold you, take a long bath or shower (even in the hospital), use warm compresses where it hurts, learn and use relaxation and breathing techniques.
	DON'T be afraid and anxious. Fear makes you tense, which slows labor down and makes it hurt more.	**DO** learn as much as you can about birth so you feel more confident. **DO** have someone you know and trust with you at all times to love, support, and encourage you. If possible, go to a trained midwife and plan to give birth in a home-like place such as a birth center or birthing room rather than the regular hospital maternity unit.

Table 6 *Continued*

Reasons for Cesareans	Don't's	Do's
Fetal distress (the baby is not getting enough oxygen)	**DON'T** rely solely on the electronic fetal monitor to check the baby's condition. The tracings are hard to understand and may seem to say the baby is in trouble when he or she is fine. The belts may feel uncomfortable and keep you from moving around as much as you'd like.	**DO** ask that your baby's heart be monitored by someone listening with a stethoscope on the outside of your belly, unless there are definite problems. If the machine says the baby is in trouble, change position, for instance, such as sitting straight up. Ask for another test to confirm distress, such as fetal scalp sampling (a test which involves taking a tiny bit of the baby's blood through your vagina and testing it for oxygen), or fetal acoustic stimulation (making a loud noise outside your belly to try to startle the baby).
	DON'T lie on your back or lean back for long. The weight of your uterus may cut off the baby's oxygen supply.	**DO** stay upright, out of bed, or lie on your side.
	DON'T use Pitocin to start or speed up labor when it can safely be avoided. It can cause contractions to be too strong, long, and close together for the baby to take. It may make labor harder for you, so you are more likely to want pain drugs.	**DO** use Pitocin only when there is a clear medical reason. Be patient, or use other ways to stimulate labor: take a rest, walk, take a long bath or shower to help relax, get rid of anyone or anything which is making you afraid or worried, have sex if your waters have not broken, rub your nipples or have someone else do it.

Table 6 *Continued*

Reasons for Cesareans	Don't's	Do's
	DON'T take drugs for pain in labor if possible. They go directly to the baby and may depress ("down") him/her.	**DO** use all the things listed above to help you cope with the pain of labor before turning to drugs or anesthesia.
	DON'T have epidural or spinal anesthesia in labor. They may make your blood pressure fall, which means less oxygen can get to your baby.	
	DON'T lie down or hold your breath when pushing. It can cut down the blood going to your uterus, so your baby gets less oxygen.	**DO** squat, stand, get on hands and knees, kneel, sit on a toilet, or lie on your side to push. Push only when you feel your body pushing; breath out while pushing as long as you can.
	DON'T hyperventilate (overbreathe). This happens when you breathe fast and deep, and cuts down the oxygen going to your baby.	**DO** relax and let your upper body go. **DO** take slow deep breaths during contractions. If you feel dizzy, tingly, or numb in your fingers, toes, or lips, cup your hands tightly over your mouth and nose and breathe into them for a few seconds.
	DON'T be afraid and anxious. Fear can make less blood go to your uterus so your baby gets less oxygen.	**DO** use all the things listed above to help you feel relaxed and safe.

Table 6 *Continued*

Reasons for Cesareans	Don't's	Do's
Breech presentation (baby coming bottom or feet first)	DON'T agree to rigid rules about doing cesareans for all breech babies.	DO ask what position your baby is in about 8 weeks before the due date. DO learn about and do an exercise to help the baby turn if he or she is breech. DO find a doctor who knows how to do external version (turn the baby from the outside before labor). DO find a doctor who is experienced and confident in delivering some breech babies vaginally.
Premature birth/ Low birth weight Toxemia High blood pressure Placental separation	DON'T diet, or be careless about what you eat. Gain at least 22–28 lbs.	DO learn about the right foods, and eat them every day. DO find out if you qualify for WIC programs.
	DON'T stop using all salt. You need salt to hold extra fluid, so your blood supply will increase.	DO salt your food to taste.
	DON'T take drugs of any kind if possible.	DO avoid all drugs, even those given to you by another doctor unless you check them with the doctor or midwife you are seeing in pregnancy.

Table 6 *Continued*

Reasons for Cesareans	Don't's	Do's
	DON'T drink more than a little alcohol or things with caffeine. Alcohol can cause some birth defects.	**DO** drink only a little beer, wine, hard liquor, coffee, tea, chocolate drinks, colas, other sodas with caffeine—or none at all.
	DON'T smoke. It can cause a miscarriage, premature birth, a baby that is too small, or other problems.	**DO STOP SMOKING.** **DO** ask your doctor or midwife to refer you to someone who can help you stop smoking or drinking.
Having had one or more cesareans before	**DON'T** have a cesarean just because you had one for your last baby. A vaginal birth will be safer for both you and your baby than a planned, scheduled cesarean in most cases. **DON'T** schedule a cesarean even if you know you need one. That way you know the baby is ready. Even a short period of labor will be good for the baby.	**DO** go into labor and plan to deliver vaginally unless there is a new reason for a cesarean in this pregnancy. **DO** use all the information in this book to help you have a safe, normal birth if possible. **DO** wait for labor to begin before a planned cesarean.

Source: Reprinted, with permission of the author, Elizabeth Shearer, "Preventing Unncessary Cesareans, A Guide to Labor Management and Detailed Bibliography," (Framingham, MA C/SEC Inc., 1989).

accidents to the umbilical cord (pp. 336–337), preeclampsia (pp. 327–329), poorly controlled diabetes (pp. 174–175), smoking (pp. 175–176), or placental abruption (p. 324). These deaths may occur before or during labor. High-risk fetuses deserve careful testing before and during labor (see pp. 139–157).

In a 1980 study from the Boston Hospital for Women, involving about 17,000 pregnancies of over thirty-seven weeks, there were sixty-four fetal deaths. Lethal congenital birth defects accounted for fifteen, while thirty-two were normally formed infants who died from asphyxia. The remaining deaths were from other miscellaneous causes. The asphyxiated group is the focus of much attention, because these fetal deaths theoretically could have been prevented using currently available technology. Of this group, twenty-one died before labor, three in labor, and eight following labor. At least in theory, the largest group—that in which the deaths occurred prior to labor—could have been spotted before it was too late, but in practice many of the affected pregnancies showed no obvious signs of trouble. On the basis of findings like these, some obstetricians now argue that all pregnancies should be screened with nonstress or contraction stress tests to identify the approximately 1.6 per 1,000 fetuses in danger of dying before birth, as well as those likely to experience trouble in labor. While the cost of such screening would be great, the result could be fewer fetal deaths or handicaps due to asphyxia. However, given the limitations of our present methods of testing, it is also true that many more unnecessary cesarean sections would also be performed. More accurate tests are the answer. Death can also occur at the instant of birth, if, for example, the shoulders are trapped in the birth canal (p. 337) or the cord is compressed during the birth of the head of a breech baby (pp. 277–283). Apart from occurring prior to birth, deaths can occur at various times after birth as well. The most common cause of such postdelivery deaths is prematurity.

Deaths before birth are called *intrauterine deaths* or *stillborns*. Fetal death after the eighteenth or twentieth week is usually suspected by the woman herself who no longer perceives fetal movement. The absence of growth of the uterus is another clue. Death is confirmed by a failure to detect the fetal heart tone either by fetoscope or by ultrasound; by a decrease, loss, or failure of increase of chorionic gonadotropin; and by lack of fetal growth as determined by ultrasound.

If a fetus has died and labor has not occurred, there are good reasons to bring about delivery promptly. Women commonly experience severe psychological problems in carrying a dead fetus. And, especially after several weeks have passed, absorption of the dissolved fetal tissue into the mother's blood can cause widespread and harmful clotting of her blood.

If a death has occurred in the third trimester, labor can often be induced with oxytocin. In the second trimester, when the uterus is relatively unresponsive to stimulation, several choices exist. A dilation and evacuation, or D and E, may still be effective. Alternatively, uterine contractions can be stimulated by prostaglandins, which can be administered as a vaginal suppository, by injection, or intravenously. Common undesired effects of prostaglandins are nausea, vomiting, and diarrhea, and some women develop fever. Medication can be given to counteract these side effects.

If the fetus cannot be delivered through the induction of labor because of some mechanical problem (such as a placenta praevia or cephalopelvic disproportion), a cesarean section (pp. 284–291) may be necessary.

After the birth of a stillborn child, the risk of future stillbirths, postnatal death, and handicaps in surviving infants is more than doubled. In the case of two stillbirths, the combined risk increases fivefold and affects one-third of subsequent fetuses. The more that can be learned about a stillbirth, or early fetal death, from autopsy study, postmortem x-ray and ultrasound studies, and chromosomal analysis, the more information can be given to the parents to guide them and other parents in future pregnancies.

EMOTIONAL AFTEREFFECTS
OF PREGNANCY LOSS

The reaction of the parents to a stillbirth largely depends on the gestational age of the pregnancy and their own personalities. The closer to the predicted time of birth, the more likely they are to have identified with the fetus as a full-fledged human being.

In recent years investigators have paid great attention to how people cope with loss and death. They have identified some principles that can be helpful to those who mourn. They also can help attendants—physicians, nurses, midwives, labor coaches, and childbirth educators—understand better how they can be most helpful to a grieving couple.

The guiding principles in coping with a death include dealing with the reality of the situation; fully communicating feelings, beliefs, and fantasies; and using others appropriately for support.

Parents are encouraged (but not required) to look at, talk to, and hold the dead baby, even one with deformities and even after autopsy, if not before, as well as to be alone with him or her if they so wish. Photographs may be useful for later recall, to help make the unbelievable real again, as may retrieved locks of hair or pieces of clothing. Naming the child can also help concretize the reality of the baby's having been alive. Crying is healthy and should be fully accepted, not denigrated or suppressed.

The decision to obtain an autopsy and chromosomal studies must be made quickly. Both procedures are desirable to obtain information about the cause of death (and thereby remove fantasies about it) and to provide important information for future pregnancies. The medical examiner should be contacted when a death occurs out of the hospital; he or she may request an autopsy as a matter of course. The parents should expect that the attendants will share the findings of the autopsy with them as soon as they are made available.

The parents should be encouraged to hold a simple funeral, memorial service, burial, or cremation, even if they would not otherwise be motivated to do so on religious or philosophical grounds. The funeral as a rite of passage makes death real and allows the couple to experience the sympathy and support of friends and relatives. Funeral services for infants are generally not expensive.

Bereaved parents should be aware of the physical and psychological elements of normal grieving. These include unusual physical sensations such as headache and chest pain; the welling up of intensely sad feelings, especially during the first few weeks and for up to a year or more after the death; a recurrent bizarre experience of believing that the baby is still alive; and the fear of angry feelings that the parents may direct toward themselves, each other, the attendants, and others. In one typical study, over 50 percent of parents who had lost a baby experienced anger, guilt, irritability, loss of appetite, preoccupation with the death, difficulty in sleeping, and intense sadness.

Parents should talk with each other about their feelings, listening to each other at length. Most will need to discuss the events surrounding the death many, many times before resolving their grief. If one parent is reminded of the dead baby by any association (a toy, an anniversary, the birth of a friend's baby), it should be shared with the other parent as well.

Bereaved parents also need to pay careful attention to the needs of their living children. It does not help to hide sad feelings from children. Being honest about one's own feelings helps children express themselves and deal with their own conflicted feelings. Parents should listen carefully to a child's reactions, reaching for the deeper meaning underlying the words and behavior. Often, young children will see themselves as the cause of the death. Such self-blame in young children is not unlike that of the parents themselves. Parents commonly search their own actions and thoughts for a possible cause of the death, such as initial feelings of ambivalence toward the pregnancy, failure to stop smoking, or a cavalier approach to nutrition or other preventive issues. Parents need to accept the child's feelings fully while supplying the necessary corrective information: "It may feel that the baby died because you didn't want us to have him, but the way you felt had nothing to do with it." By helping a child in this way, the parent can clarify his or her own responses and also strengthen family relationships.

Ideally, the parents should meet with the attendants at the time of the death and several days later. Questions about procedures at the time of birth and their effects—what was or was not done—should be answered fully. Other family members who may want to join the second meeting should be welcomed. A third meeting to review the death and mourning should be planned for three to six months later. The results of the autopsy are shared with the parents when they are received, providing another opportunity for the parents to ask questions.

Support groups for bereaved parents now exist in many communities and can be a great help. Childbirth education organizations, such as the local affiliates of the ICEA, can direct parents to such groups. (See Appendix C, and Appendix E for books that might help.)

In certain hospitals bereavement teams have been established. Members of the team can include a nurse, a neonatologist, a social worker, a pathologist, and a psychiatrist.

Parents are usually advised not to plan another baby until they complete their mourning, which means waiting, on the average, six months to a year after the death before conceiving another child. Women in particular may have an intense desire to have another baby immediately in the belief that their pain and feelings of emptiness will thereby be relieved. It may be preferable not to act on such impulses but to wait and then plan for a new baby who will have an identity of his or her own. However, individual differences in psychology and physical factors such as advancing age of the parents play a large role in these decisions. Parents, while respecting and considering the advice of others, should act on their own well-considered and heartfelt intentions.

Disproportion

Cephalopelvic disproportion (CPD) refers to the inability of a particular fetus to fit through a particular pelvis. When the cervix fails to dilate as expected, and/or the baby does not descend in the birth canal after an adequate trial of labor, sometimes augmented with Pitocin stimulation, this condition is suspected.

As might be expected, labors complicated by CPD are long, hard, and frustrating. The lack of progress is discouraging to the woman, her partner, and all those attending the birth. One particular physical finding associated with CPD is caput, or swelling of the baby's scalp (see p. 244).

Once CPD is diagnosed, the attempt at vaginal delivery is discontinued, and a cesarean section (see pp. 284–291) is carried out.

Ectopic Pregnancy

An ectopic pregnancy is one in which the fertilized egg implants somewhere outside the uterus. The word comes from the Greek *ex*, "out of," and *topos*, "place." While most ectopic pregnancies by far are located in the fallopian tubes, they can occur at other sites as well, including the ovary, the outside of the uterus, or within the abdominal cavity. Ectopic pregnancy is by no means rare. Various studies have shown a frequency ranging from 1 in 64 to 1 in 230 pregnancies. Apparently the rate is increasing. All sexually active women of childbearing age should know the commonly occurring symptoms of this disorder and, if necessary, be ready to act quickly to get help.

The greatest danger of an ectopic pregnancy to a woman is that the growing embryo can erode blood vessels in her fallopian tube and cause internal hemorrhaging. A woman can go into shock and even die from such blood loss, a complication that is fortunately uncommon today. The symptoms and signs of such serious blood loss, which should be kept in mind, include *light-headedness, dizziness, pallor, and sweating along with rapid pulse and falling blood pressure* (seen initially when sitting or standing; later on, when lying down).

A more common symptom of ectopic pregnancy is *lower abdominal pain*. Pain occurs as the embryo distends and erodes through the fallopian tube, especially at the point when it actually breaks through the walls of the tube. Furthermore, the free blood in the abdominal cavity can irritate the diaphragm, producing *pain* in the shoulders when the woman breathes.

Because the growth and development of the ectopic embryo and placenta are eventually halted, hormonal support of the pregnancy is also halted, and growth of the endometrium (inner lining of the uterus) is affected. This endometrium is shed and is recognized as *vaginal bleeding*, another common sign of an ectopic pregnancy. The pattern of this bleeding is usually different from that of a normal period: it is later and lighter, and resembles spotting. However, it is easy to mistake this bleeding for a normal period. As will be discussed, bleeding due to an ectopic pregnancy can also resemble that seen in a miscarriage (pp. 316–322), a condition with which an ectopic pregnancy can easily be confused.

There is usually little difficulty in diagnosis when a major rupture occurs in a woman who knows she is pregnant. Besides vaginal spotting, symptoms include sudden sharp, stabbing, one-sided lower abdominal pain; shock; tenderness in the abdomen, and exquisite tenderness when the cervix is moved; a tender mass on one side of the uterus; and a soft swelling caused by pooled blood felt behind the cervix on rectal examination. A woman with these classical symptoms should be wheeled straight to the operating room.

However, most ectopic pregnancies are more subtle during the early phase of rupture. Over a period of days to weeks symptoms of mild lower abdominal pain, vaginal spotting, and tenderness on pelvic examination develop in a woman who may or may not know that she is pregnant. Any combination of these findings may be present in any degree of intensity. Women and their medical attendants must keep the possibility of an ectopic pregnancy foremost in their minds if a diagnosis is to be made early. It is often difficult to distinguish ectopic pregnancy from appendicitis and other conditions.

Determining whether a woman is indeed pregnant is the first step in establishing whether her symptoms could be related to an ectopic pregnancy. Several tests can help, including a pregnancy test that measures human chorionic gonadotropin (HCG) as early as five to nine days after conception in both intrauterine and ectopic pregnancy. (See pp. 39–40, "Pregnancy Tests.")

Since the level of HCG normally doubles every three days, if this increase fails to occur (taking the shape of a flattened curve), or if there is an actual decline in the level (a falling curve), a pregnancy in trouble is indicated. And one possible reason for trouble is ectopic pregnancy. Thus, serial measurements are often made to determine the normalcy of a pregnancy when signs and symptoms such as spotting and pain raise doubt.

By five to six gestational weeks, ultrasound examination can detect a fetal sac in the uterus. In a pregnant woman its presence argues against an ectopic pregnancy, while its absence argues for it. But ultrasound cannot detect an intrauterine pregnancy younger than five to six weeks, so it is not useful as a diagnostic tool in ectopic pregnancies suspected before this stage. (In very rare cases—1 in 5,000—intrauterine and tubal pregnancies can coexist. Thus, while the presence of a fetal sac in the uterus argues against an ectopic pregnancy, it does not completely exclude it.) Ultrasound is also useful in detecting fluid behind the uterus, which is blood from a leaking ectopic pregnancy.

Direct visualization of a fallopian tube with a laparoscope (passed into the abdomen through the umbilicus) can identify a fallopian tube that is swollen and/or ruptured by an ectopic pregnancy. (The laparoscope is a kind of flexible, pencil-thin telescope through which light beams are transmitted through bendable fiberoptic channels.)

Another diagnostic measure is the identification of blood in the pelvic cavity using aspiration with a needle passed through the vaginal wall just behind the cervix. The finding of such blood is strong evidence for an ectopic pregnancy in a woman who is pregnant.

Even with these advanced diagnostic approaches and our heightened awareness of the problem of ectopic pregnancy, this disorder can still escape detection. Ectopic pregnancies that occur in the part of the fallopian tube contained within the wall of the uterus, so-called *interstitial pregnancies,* are particularly treacherous. About 2.5 percent of ectopic pregnancies in some series studied are of this variety. Because of the site of implantation in interstitial pregnancies, no mass is present in the tube, and the uterus enlarges much as it would in a normal intrauterine pregnancy. Because of the strength of the wall of the uterus in contrast with that of the tube, rupture of the pregnancy is likely to occur somewhat later, between the end of the second and the end of the fourth month. When rupture does occur, the bleeding is likely to be brisk, and it requires urgent attention.

During an operation for a ruptured ectopic pregnancy every effort is made to preserve the tube, although its ability to transport a fertilized ovum successfully will be reduced, and its likelihood of again harboring an ectopic pregnancy is increased. However, in advanced tubal pregnancy it is often impossible for the surgeon to remove the products of conception without also removing the tube itself.

The site in the fallopian tube where the pregnancy occurs determines the surgical procedure performed. Ectopic pregnancies near the open end of the tube grow under its surface, not in the central lumen or core, and can often be removed without cutting through the tube. Those nearer to the uterus, which usually grow within the lumen of the tube, must be cut out; afterward, the surgically severed ends of the tube are reconnected. In an interstitial ectopic pregnancy, the uterus itself may have to be removed (hysterectomy) along with the tube and the products of conception. Depending on the location and size of the ectopic pregnancy and the associated blood clot, surgery is performed under visualization with a laparoscope, with its various mechanical attachments (pincers, etc.), or through a lower abdominal surgical incision. Recovery from the former procedure is usually easier and quicker.

If at laparoscopy the ectopic pregnancy has not ruptured, it may be possible to dissolve it by direct injection of a solution of concentrated glucose, prostaglandin, or methotrexate. There has been some success as well with methotrexate taken by mouth.

Rh(D) negative women should be given RhoGAM at the time of treatment for an ectopic pregnancy, in order to prevent sensitization to the Rh(D) factor and resulting risk to subsequent pregnancies (see pp. 57–59).

While an ectopic pregnancy may have all the symptoms of a miscarriage, it is important to distinguish between the two conditions. Sometimes this is not possible, using currently available tests. Therefore, if a D and C is done because of a suspected incomplete abortion (miscarriage) or purposefully to interrupt a pregnancy, it is important to submit the curettings (scrapings) to a pathologist for examination. The absence of fetal tissue strongly suggests (but does not alone prove) an ectopic pregnancy and should prompt a search for this disorder. Some ectopic pregnancies are discovered in this way.

While the cause (or causes) of ectopic pregnancy is often not certain in an individual case, several factors are known to predispose a woman to this disorder. Each of these factors has to do with changes in the structure and function of the fallopian tubes. Prior infection of the tubes (salpingitis), most commonly from chlamydia (pp. 166–167) or gonorrhea (pp. 169–170), is perhaps the most common. The practice of vaginal douching in women who carry chlamydia is also associated with ectopic pregnancy.

The fallopian tubes can be malformed in their development, with narrowing, blind pockets and misplaced openings. They can be scarred and stunted from prior inflammation within the abdominal cavity (such as caused by a ruptured appendix). Uterine tumors such as fibroids can block the entry of the tube into the uterus and predispose a woman to tubal implantation. Either the failure of a previous operation on the tube to restore its ability to carry fertilized eggs or sterilization procedures (especially those in which the tubes are tied rather than cut as well as tied) can also set the stage for an ectopic pregnancy. Finally, the woman who has had one ectopic pregnancy is at increased risk for another; her subsequent pregnancies have about a 10 percent chance of again being ectopic.

Women at increased risk for ectopic pregnancy should be monitored closely and should get in touch with their doctors when they intend to conceive. Monitoring includes early diagnosis of pregnancy through hormonal testing, serial measurements of the human chorionic gonadotropin (HCG), the hormone made by the placenta which normally increases at a predictable rate in early pregnancy, ultrasound, and increased awareness of the earliest signs of rupture—measures involving both the woman and those caring for her in pregnancy.

The earlier an ectopic pregnancy is recognized (ideally, even before symptoms occur), the better. Surgery done before rupture not only spares the woman a potentially life-threatening condition and much inconvenience, but also offers a better chance of leaving an intact and functioning fallopian tube.

The issue of ectopic pregnancy is closely tied to that of infertility. Infertile women are at increased risk for ectopic pregnancies, and women who have had an ectopic pregnancy are at increased risk for infertility. Even with the best of today's care, only 50 percent of women who have had an ectopic pregnancy can expect to become pregnant. Of these, only 60 percent can expect to deliver a baby (30 percent of the original group), and 10 percent will go on to have a repeat ectopic pregnancy (5 percent of the original group).

Tubal problems that contribute both to infertility and to ectopic pregnancy can sometimes be repaired by microsurgery. When such measures fail or cannot be performed, the defective tubes can be bypassed altogether by using intrauterine fertilizations or embryo transfer. The dramatic successes of "test tube baby" research have so far dealt with these kinds of situations. In this successful technique, the egg is removed just prior to ovulation through use of a laparoscope and fertilized with the partner's sperm in a test tube. The resulting fertilized ovum is then implanted in the uterus, and the pregnancy proceeds normally.

The point needs to be made that although the problem of ectopic pregnancy can be dealt with today much more effectively than in the past, its prevention is a major unresolved issue, which is growing in importance. Furthermore, from the point of view of achieving fertility, present-day treatment is far from ideal. And the loss of an ectopic pregnancy carries all the emotions associated with a pregnancy loss (see pp. 300–303), even though the woman will also feel relieved to have survived a life-threatening situation.

Gallstones

During and after pregnancy there may be an increased incidence of symptoms due to stones in the gallbladder. These symptoms include attacks of crampy upper abdominal pain, more often on the right side and sometimes radiating to the right shoulder, often accompanied by nausea and even vomiting. In addition to the obvious discomfort and inconvenience of such symptoms, there is a danger that a gallstone will actually block the bile duct and interfere with the flow of bile, a more serious problem. There is also some evidence that the gallbladder is less efficient in emptying itself of bile during pregnancy and that this might contribute to the formation of stones.

The standard recommendation is to remove stones (and the gallbladder that contains them) when they cause symptoms and preferably before they obstruct the bile duct, a development that significantly increases the mortality and morbidity associated with surgery. In pregnancy this approach needs to be balanced against the risk to the fetus, especially in the first trimester when miscarriage has been reported to occur with such surgery and general anesthesia. For this reason, surgery is postponed if possible until after delivery or, at least, until the second trimester. How the new technique of laparoscopic gallbladder removal will affect this equation remains to be seen.

Hydatidiform Mole

Hydatidiform mole is a rare tumor of the very early placenta. In the United States it occurs in 1 out of 1,500 pregnancies. In this condition, there is no fetus present, and the uterine cavity is filled with tissue that looks like a cluster of small grapes.

The symptoms and signs of hydatidiform mole are marked nausea, elevated blood pressure, uterine enlargement out of proportion to the duration of the pregnancy, a markedly high level of chorionic gonadotropin (one of the pregnancy hormones), and occasionally, the spontaneous passage of the hydatidiform "grapes." Ultrasound shows a characteristic picture, which includes absence of any evidence of a fetus, and naturally no fetal heart action can be detected.

A hydatidiform mole that penetrates deep into the wall of the uterus is called an *invasive mole,* a form of nonspreading cancer. Another danger of a hydatidiform mole is its potential transformation into a true cancer known as a *choriocarcinoma,* which can spread (metastasize) from the uterus throughout the body. Vaginal bleeding is a common symptom, and as in the case of hydatidiform mole, the chorionic gonadotropin level is very high. (Choriocarcinoma can also arise in the uterus after a pregnancy is terminated either by delivery or abortion.)

Treatment of a hydatidiform mole consists of removal of the abnormal tissue through a dilation and suction curettage of the uterus. In some cases, the mole must be removed through an incision into the uterus reached through the abdomen (hysterotomy) or even by complete removal of the uterus itself (hysterectomy).

Following removal of a mole, it is important to follow the chorionic gonadotropin level until it falls to within normal range. Until it does, the possibility exists that cancerous changes in the mole have occurred and that not all of the abnormal tissue was removed.

If the hormonal levels do not fall, or if they rise—a finding that suggests cancer—the woman can be treated with drugs with an excellent outlook for cure. (Choriocarcinoma that does not arise from a mole is dealt with similarly.)

Hydramnios and Oligohydramnios

Hydramnios means excessive amniotic fluid, and *oligohydramnios*, a relative lack of it. When the size of the abdomen is, respectively, larger or smaller than predicted, these conditions are suspected. The diagnosis is confirmed by ultrasound. More often, too much or too little amniotic fluid is detected by an ultrasound exam done for some other purpose.

Each disorder is a symptom of some abnormality in the pregnancy that must be carefully checked. For example, congenital abnormalities of the fetus that interfere with swallowing or with production of urine can result in hydramnios and oligohydramnios, respectively. However, an explanation is not always found, particularly when the increases or decreases in fluid are small and detected only by ultrasound.

If excessive, hydramnios can, in itself, represent a problem for the woman. If it interferes with breathing, it may need to be treated by withdrawing amniotic fluid through amniocentesis (see pp. 139–141).

Oligohydramnios presents hazards to the fetus such as interference with development of the lungs, which do not then fill normally with air at birth; deformities of the arms and legs (because of severely restricted movement); and twisting or compression of the umbilical cord, which can interfere with the fetus's oxygen and food supply to the point of malnutrition and even death. Injecting salt solution into the amniotic cavity is being studied as a way of buying some time for the fetus in trouble until delivery can be accomplished.

Intrauterine Growth Disturbance

The growth of a fetus becomes of concern if its birth weight is 10 percent less than that predicted for its gestational age. By this definition, the growth of about 7 percent of all fetuses is too slow. Prematurity alone does not mean that the growth of the infant is disturbed, by this definition, since premature infants can be normal or subnormal in weight for their gestational age.

One type of growth disturbance is called *asymmetric intrauterine growth retardation.* While the length and weight of affected fetuses are abnormally low, their heads may or may not be small. Their mothers are more likely than the mothers of infants of normal weight to be ill in pregnancy, with high blood pressure, chronic kidney disease, or advanced diabetes. In some of these pregnancies growth failure appears related to impaired circulation in the uterus and placenta, so that these fetuses are undernourished. In many other cases the cause of the growth impairment is still unknown.

A second type of growth disturbance is known as *symmetric intrauterine growth retardation.* The overall growth of these fetuses, including their heads, is stunted. This is usually due to an illness of the fetus—irrespective of the health of the mother or the placenta. The illness can be genetic or due to an infection or toxin. Among the causes are chromosomal abnormalities (see pp. 132–137), the congenital rubella syndrome (see pp. 172–173), congenital cytomegalovirus infection (see pp. 167–168), the fetal alcohol syndrome (see pp. 176–178), and fetal exposure to cocaine (see p. 179).

A third type of growth disturbance is known as *dysmaturity* or *postmaturity* (see pp. 326–327) because this disorder occurs most commonly in fetuses whose gestations have exceeded forty-two weeks. These babies show signs of having regressed in nutritional status. Their length and head size may be normal, while their weight may be reduced. After birth, they look as though they have lost weight: their skin is loose, dry, and wrinkled; and they have little of the fine, long body hair (lanugo) of the normal newborn. Their nails are long, and their skin may have a yellowish cast, resulting from staining by meconium passed in utero. (Meconium, the feces of the fetus, may be passed into the amniotic fluid when the fetus is subjected to stress.) Growth retardation of these infants seems related to problems in the placenta. For reasons yet unknown, their placentas seem to have "given out" after having reached a certain age and are unable to supply the nutrients and oxygen needed by the fetus.

Growth-disturbed fetuses run more risk for death before, during, and after labor. They are more likely to have difficulties as newborns and require special attention. Some of these difficulties include low blood sugar, low blood calcium, and temperature instability (hence the use of infant warmers).

The long-range outlook for growth-disturbed fetuses depends both on the cause and on the events surrounding birth and the immediate period following birth. For example, a baby with the congenital rubella syndrome is at great risk for permanent physical handicaps, and a postmature infant who has suffered lack of oxygen compounded by meconium in the lungs (which interferes with breathing at birth) is more likely to have resulting neurological handicapping. On the other hand, many babies who are small for gestational age but have a normal head size do perfectly well. Head size seems important in predicting the outlook for these babies. For example, a study from the Queen Charlotte Maternity Hospital in London showed that children who were small for gestational age and had head growth that began to slow before twenty-six weeks of gestation demonstrated significantly lower scores in perceptual performance and motor ability at five years of age when compared to a matched control group of children who were normal for gestational age. Head size was of greater predictive value than weight or length, a logical relationship, given that head size corresponds to brain growth.

During every pregnancy the growth of the fetus should be monitored at each prenatal visit. In fact, the routine measuring of the height of the uterus is intended primarily to determine whether or not fetal growth is occurring. But the size of the uterus provides only indirect evidence, since it depends not only on the growth of the fetus but on the amount of amniotic fluid present, as well as other factors.

At present, ultrasound is the most accurate means of assessing fetal growth (see pp. 151–154). Examination by ultrasound allows measurement of the diameter of the head, the circumference of the abdomen, and other body parts. It makes possible a reasonably accurate prediction of fetal weight based on a combination of measurements of the fetal body. In addition to assessing the maturity of the fetus, ultrasound can also provide helpful information on the maturity and health of the placenta.

A series of ultrasound examinations of infants suspected of growth disturbance can show whether or not growth has occurred. Techniques for assessing fetal growth by ultrasound are undergoing constant improvement. A continuing problem, however, is that of identifying growth interference early enough to remove any treatable cause.

Because of increasing precision in determining fetal growth by ultrasound, many obstetricians advocate its routine use for this purpose (as well as for other reasons). But we do not yet know how often a growth-disturbed baby would be overlooked if ultrasound were used only in pregnancies that can be identified as being at high risk for this disorder. Studies to date do not support such an approach.

Currently there is no effective intrauterine treatment for the fetus whose growth is impaired. Researchers are trying to find ways to increase blood flow to the placenta and to supply the fetus with nutrients by injecting them directly into the amniotic fluid. Research on how the placenta works and what can disturb this is also a high priority.

The preventable causes of growth disturbance are the responsibility of each individual. Pregnant women who smoke should stop, and rubella immunization should be routine before pregnancy. Deficient diets should be corrected. For the high-risk woman, bed rest, especially on the side (to prevent the uterus from pressing on the great blood vessels and impairing blood flow to the placenta), may be useful, but its benefit has not yet been proven.

When growth disturbance is suspected, the status of the fetus's well-being requires monitoring through available tests such as the biophysical profile and umbilical artery pulsation analysis. Consideration is given to early delivery if the fetus seems in danger. Plans should be made for the delivery to take place in a maternity center equipped to care for high-risk newborns.

Late Childbearing

As more women have babies later in life, there has been an understandable concern about what risks to the babies are related to maternal age. Good data—that is, from well-designed studies of representative populations—have been hard to come by until recently. A group of Swedish physicians conducted an excellent study and reported their findings on this question in the August 19th 1992 issue of the *Journal of the American Medical Association*. They found that there are indeed risks associated with late childbearing, apart from the previously recognized problems of a higher rate of miscarriages (spontaneous abortions) and of chromosomal abnormalities (see the discussion that follows). Compared with women aged 20 to 24 years, women aged 30 to 34 had significantly higher chances of late fetal deaths (1.4 times as likely), babies with a very low birth weight (1.2 times) or a moderately low birth weight (1.4 times), and very premature infants (1.2 times) or small-for-gestational-age ones (1.4 times). Among women aged 35 to 39 years the risks were even higher: babies with a very low birth weight (1.9 times) or a moderately low birth weight (1.7 times), very premature babies (1.7 times) or moderately premature ones (1.2 times), and small-for-gestational-age infants (1.7 times). The odds for a problem were highest among women 40 years and older: babies with a very low birth weight (1.8 times) or a moderately low birth weight (2.0 times), very premature babies (1.9 times) or moderately premature ones (1.5 times), and small-for-gestational-age infants (1.4 times). Thus, special care is called for during pregnancy with late-childbearing women.

Older women must also make decisions early in pregnancy about amniocentesis (pp. 139–141) and chorionic villous sampling (pp. 141–142) for identifying a fetus with chromosomal abnormalities. After age thirty-five the risk of a fetus having Down syndrome is greater than the risk of losing a pregnancy as a complication of an amniocentesis done to obtain fetal cells for chromosomal analysis. For this reason, we recommend that all women thirty-five or older consider having an amniocentesis during the second trimester of pregnancy. Waiting until the second trimester for amniocentesis makes sense in that older women have a higher spontaneous rate of miscarriage in the first trimester. By not doing the procedure until after twelve weeks, those who miscarry will thereby spare themselves this testing.

Miscarriage

A remarkably high percentage of pregnancies do not end in the birth of a live baby. While fetal death can occur at any gestational age, most deaths occur early in the first trimester, often even before the pregnancy is recognized. Such deaths are referred to medically as *spontaneous abortions* (or miscarriage), to distinguish them from induced or deliberate abortions.

The statistics on miscarriage are sobering. The chance in a first pregnancy is about 20 percent. After having a miscarriage in her first pregnancy, a woman runs a 28.2 percent risk of one in a second pregnancy. After two miscarriages, her risk rises to 37.9 percent; and after three, to 50 percent. Women who have had one miscarriage in a pregnancy that follows a normal pregnancy run a 16.1 percent risk in subsequent pregnancies. The more live-born children a woman has, the less the risk, and the more miscarriages or stillborn births after live-born births, the greater the risk of future miscarriage.

For any average figure, the percentages tend to be higher the older the woman. For example, a twenty-year-old runs a 15 percent chance of her first pregnancy ending in miscarriage; a twenty-five-year-old, 15 percent; a thirty-five-year-old, 25 percent; and a forty-year-old, 40 percent.

Genetic defects are at the root of most miscarriages. Of first-trimester miscarried fetuses of less than eight weeks' gestation,

70 to 75 percent are estimated to have chromosomal abnormalities. Between eight and twelve weeks, 40 percent of spontaneously aborted fetuses are chromosomally abnormal. In all, about 60 percent of first-trimester miscarriages are estimated to have chromosomal abnormalities. Because in some instances the source of an abnormal chromosome may be one or both parents, chromosomal analysis of the parents may be part of the evaluation of recurrent miscarriage (see pp. 125–139 on genetics).

Another 20 percent of first-trimester miscarriages result from the joining of two recessive lethal genes, one from each partner. (See p. 127.) Each of us carries between six and ten such genes. If partners each carry one or more of the same recessive lethal genes, their mating carries a 25 percent chance for two such genes to combine. Such combinations lead to the death of the fetus. Chromosomal abnormalities and recessive lethal genes taken together account for approximately 80 percent of all first-trimester miscarriages:

Another 10 percent or more first-trimester pregnancy losses appear to be related to immunological factors, which also appear to be among the most common causes of recurrent early pregnancy loss. In one example, there is an association between early spontaneous abortion and the production by the mother, for unknown reasons, of antibodies to her own thyroid gland. Another immunological disorder, incompletely understood and somewhat controversial, involves production by the mother of antibodies directed against phospholipids in her own tissues and those of the placenta and fetus. When the antibodies attach to the phospholipid receptor sites in the tissues, a destructive process, varying in intensity from woman to woman, is initiated. Why a woman's immune system does this is not known. In the mother the results of this immunological attack on her own body include blood clots in veins and destruction of platelets (see pp. 325–326, "Platelet Disorders") circulating in her blood. In the placenta the result is both interference with function and impairment of the nutritional support for the fetus, which can lead to early miscarriage, intrauterine growth retardation (see pp. 312–315), and possibly preeclampsia (see pp. 327–329). In the fetus the antibodies may destroy platelets and heart tissue, impairing heart function. The full-blown condition in the mother is known as the antiphospholipid syndrome. A tip-off to its presence is a (falsely) positive test for syphilis during the first prenatal visit (see pp. 56–57). Many mothers with this condition are also diagnosed as having lupus erythematosis. Some success has been reported in treating the antiphospholipid syndrome with aspirin or cortisonelike hormones, but much more needs to be learned about it.

An example of a hormonal explanation for recurrent miscarriage is *inadequate luteal phase,* in which, following ovulation and the formation of the corpus luteum during the menstrual cycle, insufficient amounts of progesterone are produced (for reasons unknown) to sustain an early pregnancy. Spontaneous abortion results. Hormonal treatment has been successful in this disorder. The study of immunological and hormonal factors in pregnancy loss appears to be a fruitful area for further research.

Infection of the fetus with certain viruses (for example, mumps and rubella) is a known cause of miscarriage, and infection is a major cause of spontaneous abortion in cattle. Thus, it is quite plausible that as yet unidentified infections could also play a role in miscarriage in humans.

Completing the list of causes of spontaneous abortion, including those in the second or third trimester, is a group usually designated as "environmental," meaning the environment of the fetus. Some of these factors are known, while others are as yet merely speculative. Among the known factors are anatomical abnormalities of the uterus and cervix. Instead of forming one chamber, the uterus may consist of two chambers with various degrees of separateness that range from partial to complete. This defect can be corrected surgically with a reasonable chance of success. Another well-known, but fortunately uncommon, problem is *incompetent cervix.* This disorder is characterized by painless dilatation of the cervix in the second trimester or early in the third, followed by rupture of the membranes and the subsequent expulsion of a fetus that is usually too immature to survive. The same course of events tends to be repeated in subsequent pregnancies.

Surgical treatment of incompetent cervix involves sewing the cervix together early in pregnancy, tying it up with a suture like a purse string to close the cervical opening. The operation is done after the first trimester and before cervical dilation of four centimeters is reached. It is said to be 85 percent successful. The sutures are removed at once if uterine contractions begin or if the amniotic membranes rupture. Although some cases of cervical incompetence seem to be due to stretching of the cervix during an earlier dilation and curettage, the cause of this disorder is not well understood.

Despite the fact that much is known about the actual causes of miscarriage, the human mind is rich in supplying imagined causes as well. Intense and unjustified feelings of guilt and self-blame for "causing" an abortion often result. Rare is the woman who does not search for some additional cause—what she did or didn't do, what she felt or didn't feel—even though there is no evidence that individual behavior or feelings play a role in spontaneous abortion.

Probably the greatest "noncause" of miscarriage is sexual intercourse. So often one hears the lament: "If only we had not had intercourse, this would not have happened!" While it is true that intercourse may be the precipitating factor in the *timing* of spontaneous abortion, the pregnancy would have aborted anyway, perhaps several days later, if intercourse had not occurred. *Intercourse cannot be said to cause miscarriage,* which is primarily, as we have seen, a result of genetic abnormalities.

Other common examples of "noncauses" of miscarriage are horseback riding, skiing, and car accidents. A fall, like intercourse, could affect the timing of a miscarriage, but not cause it. Mixed feelings about the pregnancy (what woman does not have them?) can also cause guilt, as can considering an induced abortion to terminate the pregnancy (few feelings are more guilt arousing). Women worry about morning sickness and not having eaten well as a result (presumably, so the fear goes, leading to malnutrition of the fetus), having had a cold or flu, having taken an alcoholic beverage either before or after knowing that one was pregnant, having taken acetaminophen (Tylenol) for a headache, and so forth. While feelings of guilt are understandable and the search for rational causes only human, the facts simply do not support any of the above factors as having anything to do with miscarriage. While drinking, smoking, and medications can affect the *health* of the fetus, they do not cause miscarriage. Women with recurrent miscarriages need to be evaluated for treatable causes.

The onset of a miscarriage is signified by vaginal bleeding. As long as the cervix has not dilated and fetal or placental tissue (sometimes euphemistically referred to as the "products of conception") has not been passed, the term used to describe the bleeding is *threatened abortion*. At this point there is no good way to predict whether the bleeding will stop and the pregnancy proceed normally, or whether an abortion will occur.

Traditionally, women who bleed are sent to bed and told to avoid intercourse and tub baths, to help prevent infection of the uterus should rupture of the membranes occur. As we have seen, it is also true that intercourse or orgasm may precipitate, or at least speed up, a miscarriage that is about to occur. Bed rest has never been convincingly demonstrated to prevent miscarriage, nor is there any reason to believe that it could or would. Given the causes just discussed, it is easy to see why it would not work. Nevertheless, going to bed and "taking it easy" seem to be ingrained responses to vaginal bleeding and are still widely recommended.

In cases of threatened abortion, it is important to review the steps to take if it progresses and tissue is passed before reaching the hospital or a doctor's office. Such tissue should be placed in a sterile (or, at least, clean) receptacle and taken promptly to the hospital for careful study by a pathologist. If the miscarriage occurs in the hospital or doctor's office, the doctor will follow the same procedure. The purpose of this recommendation is to determine whether or not the symptoms were results of a spontaneous intrauterine pregnancy, as opposed to an ectopic pregnancy (pp. 304–309) or a hydatidiform mole (pp. 310–311). If the bleeding stops and all is well, the condition is commonly referred to as the *cyclic bleeding of pregnancy*, a diagnosis that can be made only in retrospect.

If crampy uterine pain occurs in addition to the bleeding, the chances of a miscarriage increase. If there is a gush of amniotic fluid and dilation of the cervix, the miscarriage is inevitable. Once tissue is identified or the intact fetus in its sac is seen, a miscarriage has occurred (or is occurring). Continued bleeding and cramping lead to suspicion that parts of the pregnancy remain in the uterus, and these will have to be removed by dilation and curettage (D and C), described in subsequent paragraphs. Otherwise, cramping and bleeding will continue, with the possibility of significant loss of blood and the increased risk of infection.

Sometimes it is not clear whether or not a miscarriage has occurred, especially when no tissue is identified and no cervical dilation is observed. This uncertainty can occur either when the woman is examined after a complete miscarriage or when nothing has yet emerged. The latter condition is referred to as a *missed abortion;* it is the same as an intrauterine fetal death, which may or may not be associated with bleeding or cramping when the fetus dies.

When there is uncertainty about whether or not a miscarriage has occurred, ultrasound can be helpful; it can detect the presence or absence of the fetus and determine whether it is alive or not. Other signs of a lost pregnancy are the failure of the uterus to continue to grow, the loss of the associated signs of pregnancy (breast enlargement, etc.), and a failure of the predicted increase in chorionic gonadotropin, the hormone commonly measured by the various tests of pregnancy. Instead of rising, the level may flatten out or actually decrease.

The D and C is the technique used to complete an incomplete abortion. When done to remove the contents of the uterus, a D and C is more accurately referred to as a D and E (dilation and evacuation). If done during the first trimester, it may be performed in the doctor's office as well as in a hospital. It involves dilating the cervix to the point that a plastic cannula can be inserted into the uterus. The woman lies on her back, her legs spread and supported by straps or knees stirrups. A pelvic examination is performed to assess the size and position of the uterus. Next a clamp is used to grasp the rim of the cervix to stabilize it. The unanesthetized woman usually experiences this maneuver as a pinch, which eases over the next few minutes. Then the vagina and cervix are cleansed with an antiseptic solution. If the woman chooses to be awake through the procedure, local anesthetic may be injected around the cervix to reduce the pain of stretching. The uterus is next measured by passing a metal or plastic measuring rod (sound) into its cavity and recording the depth of insertion. A series of small metal dilators of increasing diameter are inserted into the cervix to stretch the canal to the desired size. Next the plastic cannula is inserted. It is attached to a suction machine that draws the contents of the uterus out through the tube. The cannula is rotated and moved back and forth to have contact with the entire interior of the uterus. It is then removed and the size of the uterus rechecked with the sound (it should now be smaller); the clamp on the cervix is removed, and the procedure is completed.

If this procedure is done in a hospital, as is usually the case, general anesthesia (p. 215) is commonly used. The woman is asleep and unaware of what is happening, which can be an advantage for some and a disadvantage for others. When done without general anesthesia, a painkiller such as Demerol can be given prior to the procedure to take the edge off the pain, which women describe as similar to that of strong menstrual cramps. While anesthetizing the cervix with local anesthesia lessens the pain associated with cervical dilation, it does not affect the pain caused by intrauterine manipulation. Once the uterus has been entered, the D and E takes about five minutes.

To minimize bleeding after the procedure, many doctors prescribe Ergotrate tablets (see pp. 204–205), which cause the muscles of the uterus to clamp down. Sometimes antibiotics are prescribed as well to prevent infection. Such medications are taken every four to six hours for one or two days. The removed tissue is always sent to a pathologist for examination to make sure that fetal tissue is identifiable, thereby excluding the possibility of an ectopic pregnancy or hydatidiform mole.

Many women like to have their partner or a friend with them during an office D and E. While doctors vary in their receptivity to such requests, I have found that a partner's participation is supportive to the woman as well as the doctor, during the procedure. Couples can use the D and E as an opportunity for the partner to demonstrate his support, as well as learn about the price women sometimes pay for being the members of our species who can conceive and bear children.

All losses of pregnancy, whether through miscarriage or induced abortion, will arouse strong emotions in the woman experiencing them. If she can acknowledge these feelings and give herself time to rest or be with close friends, she will recover more completely.

Placenta Praevia
and Placental Abruption

Placenta Praevia refers to a low-lying placenta that partially or completely covers the inner opening to the cervix or is close to the edge of the cervix. The problem with this location is that bleeding occurs as the cervix stretches before and during labor. Before the onset of labor, painless bleeding that stops of its own accord is the most common sign of placenta praevia. In the typical case, the woman awakens in a pool of blood. Usually the amount of the first bleeding is not sufficient to cause symptoms of blood loss.

When placenta praevia is suspected, the diagnosis is now made primarily by ultrasound, which is highly effective in locating the placenta. When the placenta covers the inside of the cervix entirely or in major part, there is no alternative to a cesarean section. However, the placenta is often next to or near the cervix, in which case vaginal examination by the obstetrician is also needed to determine exactly where it is and whether a vaginal delivery can be tried without too much risk of bleeding. Such an examination is safely done only in the operating room with an intravenous infusion in place and running, and an anesthesiologist standing by so that an immediate cesarean section can be done if bleeding ensues. Such a "double setup" is also used to diagnose placenta praevia when ultrasound is unavailable.

Once placenta praevia is diagnosed, the pregnancy is considered to be high risk, even when the bleeding has completely stopped. The woman should be admitted to the hospital and stay in bed up to the time of delivery. Because of the high risk of hemorrhaging in labor, delivery should be accomplished by cesarean section after the fetus reaches a mature thirty-seven weeks' gestation. If hemorrhage recurs before thirty-seven weeks or fails to stop after the first bleeding, cesarean section is performed immediately as an emergency procedure.

The case of placenta praevia is not known. It affects about one-half of 1 percent of all pregnancies and is more common the more children a woman has had and the older she is. Previous induced abortions may also be a factor. It appears that placenta praevia may be involved in some first-trimester miscarriages. Now that ultrasound is more commonly used during pregnancy, it has been found that in the second trimester a significant percentage of placentas are low lying, even though few of them become placentae praeviae at term. (In fact, there is little justification for repeating ultrasound examinations to follow the course of these early placentae previae, as is common practice.) This observation suggests that the placenta is actually capable of migration during pregnancy. Why some placentas move and others do not is not understood.

Placental abruption refers to a peeling away of the placenta from the uterus with associated bleeding between the separated placenta and the uterus. It is the other major cause of bleeding late in pregnancy. The accumulated blood may be trapped within the uterus, or it may escape between the amniotic membranes, passing through the uterus and cervix into the vagina, where it is recognizable as vaginal bleeding. Other symptoms and signs are (1) spasm (increased muscle tone) of the uterus; (2) pain and tenderness over and in the uterus; (3) signs of shock due to blood loss (sweating, pallor, light-headedness on sitting, clammy skin, and so on); (4) changes in the pattern of the fetal heartbeat or complete loss of the fetal heart tones. Since there are various degrees of abruption, the signs and symptoms also vary. At one extreme the fetus may die and the mother be in profound shock from blood loss; at the other extreme, the mother may show no vaginal bleeding, the fetal heart rate may be normal, and only persistent uterine pain points to the problem. Sometimes partial abruption can be totally without symptoms and be discovered only after the placenta is examined following birth.

Once the diagnosis of placental abruption is made, delivery should be accomplished promptly by cesarean section after the woman's blood volume is brought back to a stable level.

Placental abruption occurs in less that 1 percent of pregnancies, and its cause is not known. It is reported to be more common in women who have high blood pressure during pregnancy (see pp. 327–329 on preeclampsia) and in the second born of twins. The risk for recurrence of placental abruption in a woman who has already experienced this complication is about ten times the normal rate.

Platelet Disorders

Platelets are blood cells (coexisting with red and white cells) that play an important role in blood clotting. A fetus with insufficient platelets is at risk during labor and delivery for bleeding into the skin or elsewhere. Particularly worrisome is bleeding that occurs within the skull. A common cause of low platelets in a fetus is transplacental passage from the mother of antibodies that destroy platelets. Women who are most likely to produce such antibodies have a condition known as *autoimmune thrombocytopenia* (*thrombocytopenia* means "low platelets"). For unknown reasons these women make antibodies that destroy their own platelets. As a result, many will have had bleeding into the skin and possibly other organs. Some will have had their spleens removed as a treatment. They are at increased risk for heavy bleeding from the uterus at the time of birth, whether vaginal or cesarean. For many of these women antibodies to their platelets are the only self-directed antibodies they produce. They are said to have *idiopathic* (cause unknown) *thrombocytopenic purpura* (bruising). Other women who make antibodies to their platelets also produce antibodies to other body tissues. (See, for example, the discussion of the antiphospholipid syndrome on pp. 317–318.) Treatment of these mothers during pregnancy, if indicated, consists of cortisonelike drugs taken by mouth.

The treatment of a fetus when the mother has autoimmune thrombocytopenia is not standardized. It is possible to identify a fetus affected by low platelets before birth by sampling its blood through a needle guided by ultrasound imaging into the umbilical blood vessels. During labor, after the membranes have broken, a sample of blood for a platelet count can be obtained from the baby's scalp (see pp. 154–155). If a fetus has low platelets, a decision must be made about the safest route of delivery (cesarean birth may be safer, but this is not yet clear) and about possible treatment before birth (about which not much is known). Following birth the baby may require additional treatment including transfusion of platelets and exchange transfusion to remove platelet antibodies from his or her blood.

Although not discussed here in any detail, some babies have

low platelets because of destruction by maternal antibodies directed against the baby's, but not the mother's, platelets. The platelet types of mother and baby are different. Just as Rh(D) negative mothers respond with antibodies to Rh(D) positive fetal red blood cells (see pp. 57–59), so mothers can produce antibodies to fetal platelets that are different from theirs.

Postdate Pregnancies

What to do about pregnancies that extend beyond forty gestational weeks (the gestational age applied as an average figure to all pregnancies as the estimated date of delivery), even when the age of the pregnancy is well documented (which is often not the case), is not known at present. We cannot even answer the question of how long a pregnancy should last. Just as women's height varies, what is "term" for one woman might not be so for another. While the vast majority of fetuses older than forty weeks are normal and will survive, a minority are at increased risk of fetal death during labor or after birth. Some of these fetuses have major malformations. Others suffer from progressive malnutrition and asphyxia related to failing placental function. Loss of amniotic fluid (oligohydramnios, see pp. 311–312) also plays a role in their compromise. No studies have been done which prove that delivering all fetuses by a certain gestational age will reduce this fetal loss.

Mainstream obstetrical practice is to induce labor at forty-one gestational weeks if the cervix is favorable for induction (see pp. 202–204, 332 on induction of labor). When conditions for induction are not optimal at forty-one weeks, surveillance of the fetus is done at least once weekly by some combination of non-stress test (see pp. 149–150), contraction stress test (see pp. 150–151), and fetal biophysical profile (see pp. 149–150). Fetuses at certain levels of risk according to the tests are then delivered by induction or cesarean section. Also, induction is carried out at any time when the cervix is ripe. By the end of forty-three gestational weeks (not a common occurrence), current obstetrical practice is to deliver all babies whether or not testing shows them to be at risk according to the test used.

In the best study to date, a randomized control trial of the Canadian Multicenter Post-term Pregnancy Trial Group (published in the June 11th 1992 issue of the *New England Journal of Medicine*), the rates of death and illness among the babies in the early (at forty-one weeks) induction group were the same as in the group of babies whose mothers' labor was allowed to begin on its own, assuming no problems were detected by a monitoring program like the one previously described. One difference in outcomes was that the early induction group required fewer cesarean deliveries than the wait-and-monitor group, 21.2 versus 24.5 percent (both interestingly high figures). There is a *pressing* need for more randomized control studies to answer the question of what is best for the postdate pregnancy.

Preeclampsia and Eclampsia

Preeclampsia-eclampsia, also known as pregnancy-induced hypertension, is a multifaceted disorder of pregnancy. Its cause is still unknown. It is characterized by high blood pressure, the presence of protein in the urine, and/or edema (swelling) after the twenty-fourth week of pregnancy. Relatively common, it affects up to 6 or 7 percent of all pregnancies and can seriously threaten the well-being of both the fetus and the mother. Preeclampsia can also be superimposed on existing hypertension.

Blood pressure and urinary protein levels are routinely checked during prenatal visits (pp. 48–49, 55–56) in order to detect preeclampsia. When blood pressure rises above 140 (systolic) over 85 (diastolic), or if the systolic pressure increases 30 points over the prepregnancy level, or the diastolic pressure increases 15 or more points, preeclampsia is suspected. A urinary protein level of "two plus" or greater, as measured by the dipstick method and/or the excretion of more than 500 milligrams of protein in the urine over a period of twenty-four hours, is considered significant.

The accumulation of fluid (edema) in the skin of a pregnant woman, especially in the hands and face, can be a sign of preeclampsia. While edema, especially in the legs, is normal in pregnancy, rapid, sudden weight gain and development of edema point to the diagnosis of preeclampsia.

Preeclampsia can also cause symptoms such as upper abdominal pain, nausea, and vomiting, without elevated blood pressure, or protein in the urine. This is less common. Laboratory tests of liver function and blood count are then used in the diagnosis.

The possible effects on the fetus of preeclampsia include intrauterine growth disturbance (pp. 312–315), premature labor (sometimes this must be induced) and prematurity (see pp. 329–336), stillbirth (pp. 291–303), low blood platelet counts (see pp. 325–326, on thrombocytopenia) and placental abruption (p. 324). Risks to the mother include convulsions, hemorrhage into the brain with possible permanent neurological deficits, loss of vision (usually temporary), hemorrhage into the liver, kidney failure, and at the extreme, death. Whenever convulsions occur, *eclampsia* is said to exist.

While most of the symptoms of preeclampsia can be controlled, there is no real cure yet for preeclampsia other than ending the pregnancy through the birth of the baby. There is now accumulating evidence from controlled clinical trials that aspirin taken in low doses during the second and third trimesters can reduce the risk of preeclampsia and of the birth of very low birth weight babies. It is possible that aspirin treatment will find its way into routine prenatal care. Calcium supplements may have a similar effect on preventing preeclampsia.

When measures to control preeclampsia fail, the baby is delivered as a last resort, either through induction or by cesarean section. Since convulsions can occur even after delivery, the mother is carefully monitored for the next seventy-two hours. In rare cases, convulsions can occur after delivery without any signs of preeclampsia having occurred prior to labor. In considering early delivery, the gestational age and well-being of the baby, as determined by tests such as biophysical profile (see pp. 149–150), are balanced against the risks to both mother and fetus if the pregnancy continues.

If convulsions have occurred or seem impending, the standard treatment is magnesium sulfate administered intravenously. Headache, confusion, an increase in blood pressure, abdominal pain, nausea, and vomiting can signal impending convulsions.

Despite much research, we do not yet know the cause of preeclampsia. It appears to be related to unexplained constriction of the blood vessels in the uterus, which in turn deprives the placenta and the fetus of much-needed blood. In about 20 percent of women with preeclampsia, the abnormality of the blood vessels of the uterus is related to preexisting kidney disease (with or without high blood pressure), which will persist after delivery, either along with high blood pressure or with the potential for developing it later. In the majority of women with preeclampsia, however, the changes in the kidneys follow the changes in the blood vessels of the uterus. In both types of cases the woman's blood volume decreases and her arteries constrict too much, thus leading to a rise in blood pressure.

Unless there is preexisting kidney disease, preeclampsia is primarily a disease of a woman's first pregnancy. The women most apt to develop preeclampsia are teenagers or women over age thirty-five who are poorly nourished and have blood relatives who have had preeclampsia. Also at increased risk are women with hypertension, renal (kidney) disease preexisting the pregnancy, those with diabetes (see pp. 174–175), and women who use contraceptives that prevent exposure to sperm, such as diaphragms. A woman who has not demonstrated preeclampsia during her first pregnancy is unlikely to develop the disorder in subsequent pregnancies unless the baby has a different father; this finding suggests that the man also contributes something to the disorder. Other predisposing factors are multiple (two or more) fetuses (pp. 338–341), diabetes (pp. 174–175), hydatidiform mole (pp. 310–311), and fetuses whose red blood cells have undergone destruction by maternal antibodies (pp. 57–59 on Rh(D) incompatibility).

Prematurity

PREMATURE LABOR

Premature labor that results in the birth of premature babies is a major problem in maternity care and is still largely unsolved. An estimated 10 to 15 percent of all live births are premature. Depending on the degree of immaturity, premature babies run a higher risk of disability and death, and they face longer and often costlier hospitalizations. Much of our infant mortality rate (high by international standards among industrialized countries) is attributable to premature labor and birth.

Labor is called premature in the following situations:

- The fetus weighs less than 2,500 grams (roughly five pounds)
- The fetus is younger than thirty-seven weeks' gestational age
- The mother is experiencing regular uterine contractions, with the cervix thinning out and widening—the cardinal signs of labor (see p. 188)

The onset of premature labor is signified by menstrual-like cramps; tightening in the stomach; dull low backache; pressure in the lower back, pelvis, abdomen, or thighs; and intestinal cramping. Any of these symptoms should be promptly reported, because the earlier that premature labor is recognized, the greater the chance of arresting the progression to delivery. Childbirth classes are increasingly emphasizing this point.

While we do not yet know the causes of most premature labors, contributing factors include multiple birth (pp. 338–341), abnormalities in the structure of the uterus, hydramnios (p. 311), poor weight gain in an underweight woman (pp. 86–93), bleeding prior to labor (pp. 323–324 on placenta praevia and placental abruption), intrauterine growth disturbance (pp. 312–315), intrauterine fetal death (pp. 291–303), preeclampsia and eclampsia (pp. 327–329), possibly certain infections (pp. 166–174) and lack of prenatal care. Sometimes premature labor is purposely induced, as in the case of a fetus who has become infected because of premature rupture of the membranes (see pp. 332–333).

There are at least two good reasons for stopping premature labor. The first and chief reason is to allow the fetus to mature in the most natural environment (assuming, of course, that this particular environment—uterus, placenta, and so on—is nourishing and supporting the fetus). The second reason, is to buy time during which the mother can be given corticosteroid hormones to induce the lungs of the fetus to mature so that they will function adequately at birth. (See discussion of L/S ratio, pp. 155–156.) Steroid injections are spaced twenty-four hours apart. If birth can be delayed for at least these twenty-four hours, the steroids lead to significantly less respiratory distress in infants born between twenty-eight and thirty-two weeks' gestation. The effect lasts for up to seven days after completion of the treatment. Beyond seven days, the protective action is reduced and retreatment is considered if premature labor still seems likely. (Recently, it was also shown that premature babies given steroids suffer less often from a severe and sometimes fatal inflammation of the intestines known as *necrotizing enterocolitis*.)

While a number of drugs have been used to stop labor, ritodrine, which temporarily inhibits contraction of the muscles of the uterus is, at this writing, the only drug approved by the U.S. Food and Drug Administration for use in the United States. At first it is administered intravenously in small amounts, which are gradually increased to the maximum safe dose. If labor stops, the drug is given intravenously for twelve more hours and then orally in larger doses for twenty-four hours. If the uterus remains quiet, a lower dose is administered for as long as it is needed, then discontinued.

The initial enthusiasm for ritodrine has dropped off significantly as increasingly sophisticated studies have demonstrated that the 24–48 hour delay in birth sometimes achieved with this drug, which, as stated, can buy time for administering corticosteroids for the lungs of the premature fetus, has not been accompanied by an improvement in outcomes for babies. Furthermore, ritodrine has been found to have risks for the mother, sometimes fatal, which make it unacceptable. Many now question the wisdom of the FDA approval in 1981. One class of drugs under study is the prostaglandin inhibitors such as Indomethacin. Magnesium sulfate is another.

Home-based electronic telephone-transmitted monitoring of uterine contractions in high-risk women can detect the early signs of premature labor. However, evidence of effectiveness of this approach is very weak in preventing premature birth. (Another expensive technology introduced before it was fully evaluated!)

If premature labor cannot or should not be arrested, every effort is made to arrange as safe a birth as possible in a medical center appropriately equipped to deal with the problems of premature infants. Whether delivery by cesarean section is safer is not clear.

The value of the common practice of using forceps and episiotomy in the vaginal birth of a premature baby is unproven.

PREMATURE RUPTURE OF THE MEMBRANES

Premature rupture of the membranes is signified by leaking of amniotic fluid from the vagina prior to the onset of labor. Its cause is not well understood. Smoking (pp. 175–176) and infection (see pp. 166–174) may play a role. One risk of breaking the barrier formed by the amniotic membranes between the sterile intrauterine environment and the vagina where many bacteria reside is that bacteria can enter the uterus to infect both the fetus and the mother.

In most full-term infants, labor follows within hours of the "breaking of waters." Seventy percent of women will be in labor in twelve hours and over 90 percent by twenty-four hours with little to no risk to themselves or their babies. Only 2 to 5 percent will not deliver within seventy-two hours. The policy in many obstetrical centers is to induce labor in those women at term with premature rupture of the membranes who have not gone into spontaneous labor by an arbitrary time, usually twenty-four hours. However, several studies show that such inductions lead to increased rates of maternal pelvic infection and cesarean sections.

There is no evidence to support the common practice of inducing labor in premature rupture of the membranes at term. After confirmation of the diagnosis by vaginal speculum examination, further exams should be avoided to prevent infection. Cultures for bacteria are taken for women at high risk for group B streptococcus (see p. 170), and intercourse and tub baths should be avoided. Signs of infection should be reported promptly.

When premature rupture of the membranes occurs in a preterm fetus, one less than thirty-seven weeks' gestational age, an individualized decision must be made about whether it is safer to induce labor or simply to watch and wait. The major risks being weighed are those of infection of fetus and mother versus those of prematurity. Other concerns arise from the adverse effects of reduced amounts of amniotic fluid on the fetus: underdevelopment of the lungs and deformities of the limbs secondary to prolonged restrictions in their movements.

Diagnostic tests that help in evaluating these risks include analysis of the amniotic fluid for evidence of infection and for the L/S ratio (see pp. 155–156) to determine fetal lung maturity, and the fetal biophysical profile (see pp. 149–150). The currently recommended policy is to induce labor when there is evidence of infection or fetal ill health and otherwise to support the continuation of the pregnancy to allow the fetus to mature (see the discussion of premature labor on pp. 329–332). Administration of corticosteroid medication to the mother to prevent respiratory distress syndrome should the baby be born prematurely has been proven effective. (See p. 158).

If a woman falls into the watchful waiting category, she is followed and follows herself for early development of infection. Tests to assay fetal health are also used.

If no signs of infection develop and the leaking of fluid stops, suggesting that the tear has sealed over, women can remain at home and avoid tub baths and intercourse. If the leaking continues, the women remain in the hospital. If at any time signs of infection develop, labor is induced or a cesarean section is performed.

Tocolytic drugs (see p. 331) to stop labor have not proven effective with preterm rupture of the membranes, except to buy a little time, for example, to transfer the mother to a high-risk maternity center.

PREMATURE BABIES

By definition, a premature baby is one born before thirty-seven weeks of pregnancy. Since babies less than twenty-four weeks old rarely survive, *preemies*, as they are commonly called, are those babies born between twenty-four and thirty-seven weeks of gestation. Prematures vary enormously in how well they do and how much special care they require. The majority do very well.

The immediate problems of the sickest and usually smallest

prematures include respiratory distress syndrome (difficulty in gas exchange because of fluid and protein accumulations within the small air sacs and collapse of the sacs themselves); difficulty in feeding due to weakness; increased incidence of jaundice and increased sensitivity to its effects (pp. 273–274); increased susceptibility to infection; congenital defects, including those of the heart; and danger of bleeding within the brain and the resulting development of hydrocephalus (dilatation of the fluid-filled cavities or ventricles in the brain). The care of these frail babies also can cause problems: the blowing out of a lung overinflated by a respirator (pneumothorax), blindness or impaired vision related at least in part to oxygen therapy, scarring of the lungs due to treatment with a respirator, errors in dosages of drugs and fluids, and so forth.

The smaller and more immature the infant, the more long-range problems are encountered: cerebral palsy, mental retardation, learning disorders, and vision, hearing, and speech problems.

There is no question that the best treatment for prematurity is prevention. This is a goal, however, we still have not reached. Short of prevention, improved care for the sickest prematures in special intensive care units has made a major difference in rates of survival and the quality of life for the infants who survive. During the days before neonatal (newborn) intensive care, fewer than 10 percent of babies weighing 1,000 grams (approximately two pounds) or less, and only about 50 percent of those weighing 1,000 to 1,500 grams (or two to three pounds) survived. Since the introduction of neonatal intensive care, reported survival rates have increased greatly. Survival rates of 45 percent or higher have been reported for babies weighing under 1,000 grams; for babies weighing 1,500 grams at birth, reported survival rates have been 70 percent or higher.

Of those infants weighing less than 1,500 grams, between 2.3 to 10.4 percent will later have moderate to severe handicap, as reported in various studies.

One result of modern care is that many infants who would not have survived in the past now live on, but with various degrees of handicap. In the case of the smallest premature babies, parents and doctors face an ethical dilemma: whether to intervene and bring all of medicine's impressive technology to bear—with un-certain results, probable prolonged hospitalization, and the chance of saving a severely handicapped baby—or to "let nature take its course" and let the baby die. While there is no simple answer to this question, some neonatal care specialists who deal with the smallest babies encourage taking the cue from the babies, watching them for a short while to see "if they want to go on or not."

The decision about how far to go in treating a tiny, sick pre-mature is an exceedingly complicated one, which unfortunately must often be made quickly under conditions of great stress. There are risks regardless of what is finally decided. If the baby does not do well, and particularly if he or she grows into a handicapped child, parents must live with the responsibility of having made the decision to intervene. If, on the other hand, life support measures are discontinued, the parents will have to ac-cept responsibility for deciding to let the baby die.

The best advice I can give in these pressured situations is that parents request an estimate from the physicians about the prob-ability of survival and the probability of survival with a handicap. While each set of parents will deal with such probabilities in their own way, they will be in a better position to make decisions along with the physicians if they have full information on possibilities and actual odds. No decision can be a perfect one—it can only be the best decision that could be made under a particular set of uncertain circumstances.

Present treatment of sick prematures includes a watchful nurse, who is of critical importance; intravenous fluid delivered through finely controlled infusion pumps; respirators; monitors for breath-ing, blood pressure, pulse, and oxygen concentration; radiant heat warmers (or incubators); and feeding tubes. Amidst all the re-quired paraphernalia it may be hard to find the tiny baby. The situation is a very stressful one for the parents, and the staffs of neonatal intensive care units usually try to be sensitive to their needs. They encourage parents to touch the baby, provide liberal visiting hours, support mothers in keeping a supply of milk going through the pumping of breasts and freezing of milk for later use, and make themselves available twenty-four hours a day by phone. They make every effort to include parents in making decisions. Nevertheless, the time that a premature must spend in an intensive care unit until he or she is out of danger and begins to progress is usually fraught with anxiety and concern.

If the baby does well and the tube feedings can be discontinued, mothers can start to nurse their infants. Many such mothers make several visits daily for this purpose and bring milk pumped at home to use when they cannot be present to nurse the baby.

After discharge, the prematures who have been the smallest and sickest will need periodic evaluations by a team of specialists such as pediatricians, neonatologists, ophthalmologists, and psychologists to monitor for handicaps and intervene as early as possible to arrest or minimize them. A recent exciting development is the prevention and treatment of respiratory distress syndrome (see p. 333) with inhaled surfactant, the chemical that is missing in the lungs of these babies.

Prolapse of the Umbilical Cord

Prolapse (or falling through) of the umbilical cord into the vagina is a true obstetrical emergency. The cord may be trapped and compressed between the baby and the cervix, cutting off blood flow to the placenta and the fetus. The fetus can be endangered and even die from such a catastrophe.

Prolapse of the cord is more likely when the fetus does not fit snugly into the lower part of the uterus. Circumstances in which this occurs include breech presentation (pp. 277–283), prematurity (pp. 329–336), twins (pp. 338–341), disproportion (pp. 303–304), and situations in which the amniotic membranes rupture (or are ruptured) before the head or other presenting part has occupied the lower portion of the uterus near the entrance to the vagina.

Cord prolapse can be detected by actually feeling the loops of the cord protruding from the cervix into the vagina. The fetal heart rate is usually depressed. In emergency treatment for cord prolapse, the woman assumes a knees-to-chest position with her buttocks up, on her knees with her chest near or on the bed. This position takes advantage of gravity to shift the fetus higher into the uterus away from the cervix.

This may allow room for the cord to drop back into the uterus or, at the very least, take pressure off it. To achieve the same objectives, the attendant can place a hand in the vagina to push the fetus up higher and work the cord back into the uterus.

Depending on the circumstances and the well-being of the fetus once a prolapsed cord is replaced, the woman may continue labor to delivery vaginally. In most situations, however, cesarean sections are performed because of the high likelihood of repeated prolapse.

Shoulder Dystocia

Shoulder dystocia refers to a baby's shoulders getting stuck during delivery. The upper shoulder can be trapped behind the symphysis pubis. The diagnosis is made if the contraction following the birth of the head fails to result in the birth of the rest of the baby. It is a very worrisome development, one which can be fatal in certain rare cases. The size of the baby in relation to the pelvic outlet is the major determining factor. Large babies such as those of diabetic or very overweight mothers are at increased risk. Recent studies suggest that ultrasound may be useful in identifying the baby suspected of being very large so that a cesarean section can be performed and shoulder dystocia avoided entirely.

There are several turning maneuvers that can be performed to dislodge the shoulders and move them off dead center. These are usually done while applying pressure to the top of the uterus and to the uterus above the pubic bone to push the baby down. Having the woman draw her thighs up onto her abdomen may help increase the size of the outlet, as will squatting, which has the added advantage of bringing gravity into play as well, increasing the effectiveness of the woman's own pushing.

The asphyxia associated with prolonged cord compression during shoulder dystocia may lead the infant to begin breaching movements prior to actual birth, with the danger of sucking amniotic fluid and mucus from his or her mouth and upper airways into the lungs. For this reason, standard practice in cases of shoulder dystocia is to suction the baby's mouth as soon as this diagnosis is suspected.

Twins and Other
Multiple Pregnancies

The thought of twins probably crosses the mind of every pregnant woman and her partner—and with good reason, for twins are not uncommon. About 1 out of 250 births, regardless of ethnic background, will involve *identical* or *monozygotic* twins, those who originate from a single fertilized egg that later halves. The frequency of twins involving more than one egg fertilized during a single ovulation, the so-called *fraternal* or *dizygotic* twins, is more variable and depends on a number of factors. In Caucasians, the incidence of fraternal twins is about 1 in 100; in blacks 1 in 79; in Japanese, 1 in 155. Being a twin increases your chances of bearing or fathering twins.

The age of the mother also affects multiple births: the older the mother, the greater her chances. A Swedish study showed that in first pregnancies, multiple births occurred 1.27 percent of the time, compared with 2.67 percent in fourth pregnancies.

A higher rate of twinning is reported in women who conceive within one month of stopping birth control pills, but this does not hold for subsequent months. The drugs and hormones used to promote ovulation in cases of infertility are notorious in producing multiple ovulations and conceptions. Following hormone treatment, multiple pregnancy may occur as often as 20 to 40 percent of the time. One study showed that after administration of the drug clomiphene to induce ovulation, 6.9 percent of the resulting pregnancies were twins; 0.5 percent, triplets; 0.3 percent, quadruplets; and 0.13 percent, quintuplets. Another study of clomiphene effects showed the rate of occurrence of multiple fetuses to be 13 percent.

The figures quoted for twinning have to do with percentages of babies born. Now that ultrasound has been used to study the course of pregnancies, it is clear that the actual frequency of twin conceptions is much higher, with only one of the fetuses generally surviving to birth. In one study, twin fetuses were identified in thirty women in the first trimester, but only fourteen eventually gave birth to two infants. Eleven of the remaining sixteen gave birth to a single baby and an undeveloped one (blighted ovum), while four others had twin blighted ova, and one had a blighted ovum and a miscarriage.

Determining whether twins are monozygotic or dizygotic (identical or fraternal) is more than a matter of mere curiosity. In this era of human organ transplantation, knowing who can donate to whom can be of critical importance. In all but the rarest instances, careful examination of the placenta or placentas helps to make this distinction. For this reason, great care should be exercised in delivering the placentas of twins intact with the membranes attached.

A common feature of the placentas of monozygotic twins is communication between the blood vessels of one placenta and the other, permitting an admixture of blood. A possible result is that one fetus can have too much of the combined blood while the other receives too little. Depending on degree, this imbalance can harm each of the babies in its own way. The baby with decreased blood volume can be runted (see pp. 312–315 on intrauterine growth disturbance), be hypotensive (have low blood pressure), and have an underdeveloped heart, while the twin with the excess blood volume can be larger, but subject to heart failure, abnormal blood clotting, and the increased likelihood for developing jaundice. The survival of both may be threatened at birth. If one baby has died in utero, the dissolving of the tissues of the dead fetus may liberate materials into the joined circulations, which can lead to clotting of the blood of the other twin, often with grave consequences. Also, because of the occurrence of these blood vessel connections in twins, it is very important that the cord of the first born be clamped immediately before the second is delivered. Otherwise, the blood of the second can dangerously drain off through the cord of the first. Although the path to birth of twins is full of stumbling blocks, modern obstetrics is happily able to clear away many of the obstacles, or at least push them aside.

From the very outset, the twin fetuses are at increased risk. In one study, the average gestational age of twins at birth was thirty-five weeks compared to thirty-nine weeks for singletons. With triplets, the average age at birth was thirty-three weeks; with quadruplets, only twenty-nine weeks. The alleged value of bed rest in prolonging a twin pregnancy, long a recommended practice, is unproven. Twins are more than twice as likely as singletons to be affected with major and minor birth defects. Despite these odds, however, let us emphasize that most twins do just fine, especially since our ability to deal with premature infants has undergone such steady improvement.

The mothers of twins are at increased risk for such complications of pregnancy as preeclampsia (pp. 327–329), anemia, hemorrhage at delivery, and hydramnios (p. 311); and such complications of labor as premature labor (pp. 329–332), prolonged labor, nonvertex fetal presentation, and prolapse of the umbilical cord (pp. 336–337). Thus, pregnancies involving twins deserve special handling in all respects.

The mother of twins needs to eat for three people, not just two. Her caloric intake should increase by 300 calories per day, and she should take sixty to eighty milligrams of supplemental iron. Folic acid needs are also increased. This can be met through either diet or supplementation.

The problems surrounding twins do not end once labor has begun. As already discussed, complications of labor in multiple pregnancies are notorious. A decision will have to be made about vaginal versus cesarean delivery. There is general agreement that cesarean section is the preferred route if the presenting part of one or both fetuses is a part other than the head (for example, breech), especially if the first baby to be delivered is either unusually large or small or if the umbilical cord prolapses. A particularly tricky period in vaginal delivery follows the birth of the first twin.

Ideally, twins should be identified prior to labor and delivery so that appropriate plans can be made. More help is needed at such a birth to deal with the unexpected, and more help is needed afterward to care for the babies.

Ultrasound is the most effective way of diagnosing twins early in pregnancy and can demonstrate the separate gestational sacs as early as the sixth to tenth weeks. The increasingly routine use of ultrasound in pregnancies has resulted in a higher percentage of twin pregnancies being identified early.

One dividend of testing for alpha fetoprotein in the second trimester (pp. 64–66) is the identification of twins, for the presence of more than one fetus is one cause of persistent elevated maternal alpha-fetoprotein levels.

In the complicated situation of twins suspected of having neural tube or other serious congenital defects, amniocentesis must be done on both sacs to determine whether one or both of the twins are affected. The same can be said of twins at high risk for chromosomal abnormalities, such as those carried by mothers who are thirty-five or older, or whose parents are known carriers of genetic diseases. Both twins need to be studied by amniocentesis and cell culture.

Twins are suspected, of course, when the size of the uterus is larger than would be expected on the basis of gestational age. This finding warrants an explanation that includes checking for twins with ultrasound. (Other explanations for a large uterus include an error in dating the pregnancy, hydramnios [p. 311], fibroid tumors of the uterus [p. 78], and, late in pregnancy, a large baby.)

Late in the second trimester and throughout the third trimester, it is possible to identify twins by palpation of the uterus and to hear two distinct fetal heartbeats. There are two separate sites on the abdomen where the heart tones can be heard equally well. The rates are unequal, each beating at a different rate, as recorded by two observers listening and counting simultaneously.

Twins complicate the already difficult issue of therapeutic abortion. In conditions where abortion might be performed for an abnormal fetus, as in the case of Down syndrome (pp. 134–136), the presence of a normal twin, along with the chromosomally abnormal one, creates a dilemma, because routine abortion procedures would lead to the loss of both. There are reports of selective termination of the life of an abnormal twin. In this ethically controversial procedure, the heart of the fetus was punctured with a needle guided through the uterus using ultrasound visualization, resulting in its death. The normal twin in the case went on to develop, be born, and survive without difficulties.

Women expecting twins should plan for more help at home in the early months. Not only will they want time to recover from the extra strain on their bodies, but twins take more time to feed, to bathe, and to enjoy. Once the adjustment has been made and the hurdle of a more complicated birth is past, parents may be delighted and proud of producing two babies after only one pregnancy and labor.

Statistics on Home and Birthing Center Births

For the increasing number of women who consider giving birth outside of hospitals—still a minority choice in the United States and not even an option in many communities—it is reassuring that well-organized home or birthing-center services provide safe outcomes comparable to those achieved by women with similar characteristics who give birth in hospitals. In general, other outcomes are far better for women who begin labor in out-of-hospital settings—for example, fewer cesarean sections, fewer episiotomies, less use of anesthesia, and lower costs.

There is, however, a limitation in such comparisons: to date there has been no randomized control study of in- versus out-of-hospital births, which is the most rigorous way to study the effect of the site of birth on outcomes. Such a study would be very difficult to organize. First, women would have to agree to be randomly assigned to one site or the other. Second, the policies and practices in the two sites would have to be the same. However, this study-design limitation of the existing research no more argues for the hospital than it does for the birthing center or home.

As I stated in the Introduction, I conclude, based on my review of the evidence, that the out-of-hospital settings are currently meeting the highest scientific standards of care. Their practices most closely conform to current research findings on many of the issues discussed in this book. As a matter of public policy we should encourage these settings as laboratories for evaluating maternity care practices. Hospital-based services have much to learn from them.

In the following discussion I present three examples of out-of-hospital birth services on which carefully collected data exist. (I prefer the term *community-based maternity service* to *out-of-hospital birth service* because the latter implies that the hospital should be the reference point, the gold standard of care—a reputation I do not believe it deserves.) As you will see, the three services do not report on the same outcomes. Furthermore, the services reported here are state-of-the-art and may not be representative. I recommend that you ask for similar data from any maternity care service or provider you are considering using. (Also, see Introduction, pp. xiv–xv.)

The best natural laboratory for home-birth-outcome research has been the Netherlands, where national health policy, a noninterventive philosophy of birth, and an excellent support system, including maternity aides who stay during labor and the baby's first week, have enabled midwives and general practitioners to continue to attend many births at home. A study that analyzed data compiled by the Central Bureau of Statistics found no significant differences in outcomes between cities with an almost 100 percent rate of hospital births and cities of similar demography with a 50 percent rate.

Following international trends, between 1960 and 1990 the proportion of deliveries in the Netherlands occurring in the home declined from 70 to 35 percent and is holding steady. However, birth at home continues to be very safe. In a 1990 report of almost 9,000 births, the perinatal death rate was .14 percent, and only 3.1 percent of infants were admitted to the hospital in the first week. (Data on mothers transferred are not available.) The cesarean section rate in Holland is less than 5 percent.

Home birth in the Netherlands benefits that nation's entire system of maternity care. Through the repeated experience and highly visible model of successful normal births in the home, as well as through the prominent role of midwives in hospitals as well as at home, a philosophy of nonintervention in maternity care (relative to other countries) is maintained even for hospital births. The incidence of cesarean section in the Netherlands was 2.0 percent in 1969, 3.0 percent in 1975, 5.0 percent in 1980, and 6.0 percent in 1987. In the United States the rate was 5.3 percent in 1969, 10.2 percent in 1975, 15.2 percent in 1978, and 24.0 percent in 1988.

Pooled data from a family group practice in Cambridge, Massachusetts, during the late 1970s and early 1980s and the obstetrical practice of two physicians in Fresno, California, using similar screening procedures (including a requirement of twenty minutes or less driving time to backup hospitals), involved 875 women seeking home birth. This number is too small for a definitive report but large enough to give one an idea of what to expect. Data on transfers and outcomes for this group are presented in Table A-1. The overall picture is encouraging, with no maternal deaths, modest rates of transfer and intervention, and few major complications. Birth weight clustered in the six- to eight-pound range. Most of the infants born at home had Apgar scores (a less objective measure) of eight to ten at one minute (85.2 percent) and at five minutes (97.3 percent).

However, the stillbirth rate of 8.25 per 1,000 labors begun at home is higher than in other studies. Three of the six stillbirths were predelivery fetal deaths discovered in early labor (having occurred after the last prenatal examination from one day to one week earlier) and took place within one four-month period in the California practice. The stillbirth rate declined as more births were added. These three deaths, along with a similar fatality in the Massachusetts sample, had occurred by the time the birth attendant arrived—without delay—at the home and thus presumably before the woman would have chosen to go to the hospital had she planned to deliver there. In one case vasa praevia (a variant of placenta praevia; see pp. 323–324) was identified as a probable cause, while no cause was established in the other three cases.

All four were judged not to have been site related or preventable. The fifth and sixth stillbirths might have been site related. The fifth occurred because of fetal-placental insufficiency (inadequate supply of oxygen to the fetus) after a prolonged pregnancy of 43.5 weeks (see pp. 326–327). Post-term antenatal screening

Table A-1.   Outcomes of Planned Home Births

	Number	Rate per 1,000 Labors Begun at Home
Total number of women seeking home birth	875	
Lost to follow-up (moved, transferred)	69	
Continued prenatal care	806	
Changed to planned hospital before labor	79	
Began labor at home	727	
Transfers during labor	56	
Postpartum transfers	17	
Maternal	10	
Neonatal	7	
Planned and completed without transfer	654	
Home births	671	
Stillbirths (see text)	6[a]	8.25
Before labor	4	5.50
During labor	2	2.75
Live home births	666	
Cesarean sections	22	30.26 (3.0%)
Maternal deaths	0	

[a]One stillbirth occurred in a hosptal.

Source: Family Practice Group, Cambridge, Mass.; and David Dowis, M.D., and Janet Dowis, M.D., Fresno, Calif.

(urine estriol determination and nonstress tests) failed to predict the problem. Although this birth would have occurred in the hospital according to the subsequently revised protocol in this practice, clinical experience and a review of the literature do not support the contention that electronic fetal monitoring would have reliably prevented the stillbirth. Therefore, it cannot be said conclusively to have been site related. The other stillbirth occurred in a first-pregnancy breech birth after extensive counseling in which attendants explained the risks and advised a hospital birth. When the couple announced their intention to deliver at home with or without professional assistance, the attendants agreed to attend the birth. In the presence of two doctors and two nurses, a stillborn infant who failed to respond to resuscitation measures was delivered. Since electronic fetal monitoring or elective cesarean section might have saved this baby, this death may be regarded as site related, as anticipated by the attendants when they strongly recommended hospital delivery. In all, only two of the six stillbirths in the Cambridge-Fresno series may have been site related, which is of concern, nevertheless.

Data on out-of-hospital birth in the United States are available not only for home births but also for freestanding birthing centers such as those pioneered by the Maternity Center Association of New York City. A report prepared for the U.S. Federal Trade Commission concluded that during its first five years of operation (1975–1980), the Association's Childbearing Center had maintained a high standard of safety and offered low-cost, high-quality care while exerting a positive influence on obstetric care in the New York area and the nation as a whole.

Currently there are 140 freestanding birthing centers in the United States, with 50 more under development. Seventy percent are certified by the National Association of Childbearing Centers (see Appendix C), an organization that maintains very high practice standards. The association reported its statistics in the December 28th 1989 issue of the *New England Journal of Medicine;* the data involved 84 centers and 11,814 women admitted in labor and delivery. Overall, the outcomes were excellent and comparable to or better than the best achieved in a hospital setting among similar women. The intrapartum and neonatal mortality rate was (a low) 1.3 per 1,000 births. Sixteen-plus percent of the women were transferred during labor to a hospital, and 2.4 percent were transferred as emergencies. First-time pregnant women were more likely to be transferred than those with second (or more) babies (29.0 versus 7.0 percent). The rate of cesarean sections (all performed in hospitals) was (a low) 4.4 percent (see pp. 284–291 on cesarean birth), and no mothers died. Seventeen percent of the women had episiotomies (see pp. 219–223). Thirty-four percent had no vaginal tears, 45.7 percent had minor tears, and slightly over 2.0 percent had deeper tears. Internal continuous electronic fetal monitoring (see pp. 146–147) was used in 1.1 percent of the labors (the rest were monitored by intermittent listening to the baby's heartbeat), and 95 percent of the women drank liquids or ate while in labor (see pp. 201–202). Forty-three percent of the women took showers, baths, or both. Twenty-four percent of women in their first labor and 6.0 percent of those in their second (or greater) labor received analgesics for pain relief (see pp. 208–209). (Other forms of anesthesia such as epidurals [see pp. 209–215] were not available in the birthing centers.)

The freestanding birthing centers emphasize continuity of care by midwives (some physicians are involved also); providing prenatal education; and treating pregnancy, labor, and delivery as normal, happy experiences. They do not administer oxytocin to augment labor, nor do they use epidural or spinal anesthetics. They place great emphasis on helping women find what works best for them in labor, drawing on each woman's own strengths. They encourage laboring and delivering in a vertical position (see pp. 216–218 on position in labor and delivery). Their excellent outcomes probably reflect the combined effects of all of these policies and practices, which differ from the standard hospital-based approach and offer a revealing comparison. As a model of care, the birthing center that meets the standards of the National Association of Childbearing Centers has much to recommend it, including reaching women in need of services and reducing the costs of care by as much as 30 to 50 percent. More and more hospitals are adopting a birthing-center approach within their own walls or grounds and achieving similar results, with an added advantage of easier access to facilities and personnel for complications.

Advantages of a Plant-Based Diet

A meat-based diet costs us dearly in many ways, which we are only now beginning to appreciate. Damage to the environment from cattle is not only a problem of the developing world. Serious problems in the American West such as soil erosion, desertification (growth of deserts), stream destruction and pollution, endangerment and extinction of animal and plant species (for example, bighorn sheep, mountain lions, freshwater fish, and coyotes) can be directly related to overgrazing by cattle (of which there are an estimated eighty-three million in the Untied States), often on publicly owned lands.

Grazing cattle contribute to global warming in yet another way. As they digest the grasses and hay in their diet, they produce methane gas, which is expelled from their intestines into the atmosphere. Like carbon dioxide, methane is one of the major gases that contribute to the greenhouse effect. Worldwide, emissions of methane from livestock are substantial. Consider that in the state of Iowa alone there are at any time about twenty million pigs being fattened for market.

There are also economic considerations related to the raising of cattle. Grains and grasses (or similar plants) will feed far more people directly than will the meat from cattle fed on the same grain. By directly consuming the grain, more of us can eat for much less money. Furthermore, raising of cattle is an energy-intensive activity that requires a substantial consumption of fossil fuels. One estimate is that *over half* of the oil we import (much from the Middle East) could be saved if we switched to a plant-based diet. (In addition, we would produce significantly less carbon dioxide by avoiding the burning of this fuel.) At a time of growing water shortages we should take note that producing a meat meal from start to finish (raising the grain, watering the cattle, cleaning the slaughterhouse, and so on) requires about *fourteen times* as much water as a plant-based meal.

For all of these reasons—health, environmental effects, and cost—the positive effects of a widespread shift in eating habits away from meat and dairy products will be enormous, especially if coupled with population control (on which time is quickly running out). The world our children will inherit may depend on such changes. Are we ready to take the step of not merely trimming the fat from the hamburger but actually giving it up or at least significantly limiting its inclusion in our diets?

Support and Professional Organizations*

American Academy of Family
  Physicians
8880 Ward Parkway
Kansas City, Missouri 64114

American Academy of Hus-
  band-Coached Childbirth
  (AAHCC)
Box 5224
Sherman Oaks, California
  91413
(Information on the Bradley
Method

American Academy of
  Pediatrics
141 Northwest Point Road
P.O. Box 927
Elk Grove Village, Illinois
  60007

American College of Nurse
  Midwives (ACNM)
1522 K Street, N.W.,
  Suite 1000
Washington, D.C. 20005

American College of Obstetricians and Gynecologists
  (ACOG)
409 12th Street, S.W.
Washington, D.C. 20024

American Foundation for
  Maternal and Child Health
439 East 51st Street
New York, New York 10022
(Clearinghouse for research on
the perinatal period)

*Where aims and resources are not clear from the name of the organization,
a few words of description are given.

American Society for Psycho-prophylaxis in Obstetrics (ASPO/LAMAZE)
1840 Wilson Blvd., No. 204
Arlington, Virginia 22201

Association for Childbirth at Home, International (ACHI)
P.O. Box 430
Glendale, California 91209

Boston Women's Health Book Collective
47 Nichols Avenue
Watertown, Massachusetts 02172
(Publications include *Our Bodies, Ourselves*, the classic of the women's health movement)

Center for Science in the Public Interest
1875 Connecticut Avenue, N.W.
Suite 300
Washington, D.C. 20009
(Nutritional information and advocacy for a safe food supply)

Center for the Study of Multiple Birth
333 East Superior Street, Suite 463-5
Chicago, Illinois 60611

Choice in Dying: the National Council for the Right to Die
200 Varick Street
New York, New York 10014

Compassionate Friends
P.O. Box 1347
Oak Brook, Illinois 60521
(Self-help group for those experiencing the death of a baby)

COPE
(Coping with the Overall Pregnancy/Parenting Experience)
530 Tremont Street
Boston, Massachusetts 02109

C/SEC inc. (CESAREANS/SUPPORT EDUCATION and CONCERN)
22 Forest Road
Framingham, Massachusetts 01701
(Emotional support and information on cesarean births and vaginal birth after cesarean [VBAC])

Environmental Defense Fund
257 Park Avenue, South
New York, New York 10010

Friends of the Earth
218 D Street, S.W.
Washington, D.C. 20003

HOME
(Home-Oriented Maternity Experience)
P.O. Box 450
Germantown, Maryland 20874

International Childbirth Education Association (ICEA)
P.O. Box 20048
Minneapolis, Minnesota 55420

La Leche League International, Inc.
P.O. Box 1209
9616 Minneapolis Avenue
Franklin Park, Illinois 60131
(Information, education, and support for breast-feeding)

The March of Dimes
P.O. Box 2000
White Plains, New York 10602
(Information and research on genetics, genetic counseling, and birth defects)

Maternity Center Association
48 East 92nd Street
New York, New York 10028
(A well-known freestanding birth center with information and advocacy functions)

Midwifes Alliance of North America (MANA)
600 Fifth Street
Mincett, Missouri 65708
(Nurse and lay midwives in the United States and Canada)

Mothers Against Drunk Driving (MADD)
669 Airport Freeway, Suite 310
Hurst, Texas 76053

NAPSAC, International
(National Association of Parents and Professionals for Safe Alternatives in Childbirth)
Route 1
Box 646
Marble Hill, Missouri 63764
(Umbrella group for the alternative birth movement in the United States, provides information and support)

National Association for the Advancement of Leboyer's Birth Without Violence, Inc.
P.O. Box 248455
University of Miami Branch
Coral Gables, Florida 33124

National Association of Childbearing Centers (NACC)
Box 1, Route 1
Perkiomenville, Pennsylvania 18074
(Information and education about freestanding birth centers)

National Women's Health Network
1325 G Street, N.W.
Washington, D.C. 20005

Parents Without Partners, Inc. (PWP)
8807 Colesville Road
Silver Spring, Maryland 20910
(Resource for the single parent)

Physicians for Automotive Safety
P.O. Box 430
Armonk, New York 10504

Physicians Committee for Responsible Medicine
P.O. Box 6322
Washington, D.C. 20015

Physicians for Social Responsibility
19 Garden Street
Cambridge, Massachusetts 02138
(Information and activism on issues of the threat of nuclear weapons and wastes)

Planned Parenthood Federation of America
810 Seventh Avenue
New York, New York 10019

Remove Intoxicated Drivers (RID)
24 Elm Street
Schenectady, New York 12301

The Sierra Club
730 Polk Street
San Francisco, California 94109
(Activism and information on environmental issues)

Sources for Books and Supplies

Birth and Life Bookstore
P.O. Box 70625
Seattle, Washington 98107

Run by Lynn Moen, the store offers books on all aspects of childbirth and child-care, books for children, pamphlets, cassettes, and records. A useful catalogue, *Imprints*, which appears several times a year, offers listings and helpful reviews.

ICEA Bookcenter
P.O. Box 20048
Minneapolis, Minnesota 55420

The source for all ICEA publications and books from all publishers on childbirth. The catalogue, *Bookmarks*, appears twice a year.

Suggested Reading

HISTORY AND CRITIQUE

Arms, Suzanne, *Immaculate Deception: A New Look at Women and Childbirth in America*. Boston: Houghton Mifflin, 1975.

Bursztajn, Harold; Feinbloom, Richard I.; Hamm, Robert M.; and Brodsky, Archie. *Medical Choices, Medical Chances: How Patients, Families and Physicians Can Cope with Uncertainty*. New York: Routledge, 1990.

Rothman, Barbara Katz. *In Labor: Women and Power in the Birthplace*. New York: W. W. Norton, 1982.

Wertz, Richard, and Wertz, Dorothy C. *Lying-In: A History of Childbirth in America*. New York: The Free Press, 1977.

MYTHS AND TALES OF BIRTH

Franz, Marie von. *Creation Myths*. Zurich: Spring Publications, 1972.

Meltzer, David, ed. *Birth. An Anthology of Ancient Texts, Songs, Prayers, and Stories*. San Francisco: North Point Press, 1981.

WOMEN'S HEALTH

Boston Women's Health Book Collective. *Our Bodies, Ourselves: A Book by and for Women.* New York: Simon and Schuster, 1984.

OVERVIEWS OF PREGNANCY AND CHILDBIRTH

Brewer, Gail Sforza, and Presser, Janice. *Right from the Start: Meeting the Challenge of Mothering Your Unborn and Newborn Baby.* Emmaus, Pa.: Rodale Press, 1981.

Kitzinger, Sheila. *The Complete Book of Pregnancy and Childbirth.* New York: Alfred A. Knopf, 1989.

———. *The Experience of Childbirth* (revised edition). New York: Penguin Books, 1978.

MacFarlane, Aidan. *The Psychology of Childbirth.* Cambridge, Mass.: Harvard University Press (The Developing Child Series), 1977.

McLaughlin, Clara, with Frisby, Donald; McLaughlin, Richard; and Williams, Melvin. *The Black Parents' Guide to Healthy Pregnancy, Birth and Child Care.* New York: Harcourt, Brace, Jovanovich, 1976.

Noble, Elizabeth. *Childbirth with Insight.* Boston: Houghton Mifflin, 1983.

Panuthos, Claudia. *Transformation through Birth. A Woman's Guide.* Massachusetts: Bergin and Garvey, Inc., 1984.

Pritchard, Jack A., and MacDonald, Paul C., *et al. Williams Obstetrics.* New York: Appleton-Century-Crofts, 1990.

Queenan, John T., ed. *A New Life: Pregnancy, Birth and Your Child's First Year.* New York: Von Nostrand Reinhold, 1979.

Soman, Shirley Camper. *Preparing for Your New Baby.* New York: Dell/Delta Books, 1982.

Todd, Linda. *Labor and Birth: A Guide for You.* Minneapolis, Minn.: ICEA, 1981. [Simply written and intended for the pregnant teenager]

Wolfe, Maxine Gold, and Goldsmid, Margot. *Practical Pregnancy. All That's Different in Life Because You're Pregnant.* New York: Warner Books, 1980.

CHOICES AND ALTERNATIVES

Balaskas, Janet, and Balaskas, Arthur. *Active Birth*. New York: McGraw-Hill, 1983.

Baldwin, Rahima. *Special Delivery: The Complete Guide to Informed Birth*. Millbrae, Calif.: Les Femmes, 1979.

Bean, Constance A. *Methods of Childbirth* (new revised edition). New York: Doubleday/Dolphin, 1982.

Berezin, Nancy. *The Gentle Birth Book: A Practical Guide to LeBoyer Family-Centered Delivery*. New York: Pocket Books, 1981.

Bing, Elisabeth. *Six Practical Lessons for an Easier Childbirth*. New York: Bantam Books, 1981. [Lamaze method]

Birth: A Journal of Perinatal Care and Education. Blackwell Publications, 3 Cambridge Center, Cambridge, Mass.: Blackwell Publications.

Brackbill, Yvonne; Rice, June; and Young, Diony. *Birthtrap: The Legal Lowdown on High-tech Obstetrics*. St. Louis: C. V. Mosby Co., 1984.

Bradley, Robert A. *Husband-Coached Childbirth* (3rd edition). New York: Harper & Row, 1981.

Brennan, Barbara, and Heilman, Joan Rattner. *The Complete Book of Midwifery*. New York: E. P. Dutton, 1977.

Davis, Elizabeth. *A Guide to Midwifery: Hearts and Hands*. Santa Fe, N.M.: John Muir Publications, 1981 (New York: Bantam Books, 1983).

Dick-Read, Grantly. *Childbirth without Fear: The Principles and Practice of Natural Childbirth* (revised 4th edition). New York: Harper & Row, 1978.

Elkins, Valmai Howe. *The Rights of the Pregnant Parent* (revised). New York: Schocken Books, 1980.

Enkin, Murray W., Keirse, Marc J. N. C., and Chalmers, Iain. *A Guide to Effective Care in Pregnancy and Childbirth*. New York: Oxford University Press, 1990.

Feldman, Silvia. *Choices in Childbirth*. New York: Grosset and Dunlap, 1979.

Gaskin, Ina May, *Spiritual Midwifery* (revised edition). Summerton, Tenn.: The Book Publishing Company, 1978.

Korte, Diana, and Scaer, Roberta. *A Good Birth, a Safe Birth*. New York: Bantam Books, 1984.

Klaus, Marshall H., Kennell, John, and Klaus, Phyllis H., *Moth-*

ering the Mother: How a Doula Can Help You Have a Shorter, Easier, and Healthier Birth. Reading, Mass.: Addison-Wesley/Lawrence, 1993.

Lamaze, Fernand. *Painless Childbirth.* Chicago: Henry Regnery, 1970.

Leboyer, Frederick. *Birth Without Violence.* New York: Alfred A. Knopf, 1975.

Lesko, Wendy, and Lesko, Matthew. *The Maternity Sourcebook.* New York: Warner Books, 1984.

Long, Raven. *Birth Book.* Palo Alto, Calif.: Genesis Press, 1972.

Odent, Michael *Birth Reborn.* New York: Pantheon Books, 1984.

———. *Entering the World: The De-medicalization of Childbirth.* New York: Marion Boyars, 1984.

Parfitt, Rebecca Rowe. *The Birth Primer. A Source Book of Traditional and Alternative Methods in Labor and Delivery.* Philadelphia, Pa.: Running Press, 1977.

SEX DURING PREGNANCY

Bing, Elisabeth, and Coleman, Libby. *Making Love During Pregnancy.* New York: Bantam Books, 1977.

Kitzinger, Sheila. *Woman's Experience of Sex.* New York: Putnam, 1983.

THE SITE OF BIRTH

Kitzinger, Sheila. *Birth at Home.* New York: Penguin Books, 1981.

Sagov, Stanley E.; Feinbloom, Richard I.; Spindel, Peggy; and Brodsky, Archie. *Home Birth: A Practitioner's Guide to Birth Outside the Hospital.* Rockville, Md.: Aspen Systems Corporation, 1984.

Sumner, Philip E., and Phillips, Celeste R. *Shared Childbirth. A Guide to Family Birth Centers.* New York: New American Library/ C. V. Mosby, 1982.

Young, Diony. *Changing Childbirth: Family Birth in the Hospital.* Rochester, N.Y.: Childbirth Graphics, Ltd., 1982.

LIFE BEFORE BIRTH

Annis, Linda Ferrill. *The Child Before Birth*. Ithaca, N.Y.: Cornell University Press, 1978.

Maurer, Daphne, and Maurer, Charles. *The World of the Newborn*. New York: Basic Books, 1988.

Nilsson, Lennart. *A Child is Born*, New Edition. New York: A Merloyd Lawrence Book/Delacorte Press, 1990.

PROTECTING THE UNBORN CHILD

Abrams, Richard S. *Will it Hurt the Baby?* Reading, Mass.: Addison-Wesley, 1990.

Apgar, Virginia, and Beck, Joan. *Is My Baby All Right? A Guide to Birth Defects*. New York: Trident Press, 1972.

Freeman, Roger K., and Pescar, Susan. *Protecting Your Baby During High Risk Pregnancy*. New York: McGraw-Hill, 1983.

Hales, Dianne, and Creasy, Robert K. *New Hope for Problem Pregnancies. Helping Babies Before They're Born*. New York: Berkeley Books, 1984.

Milunsky, Aubrey. *Choices Not Chances: Controlling Your Genetic Heritage*. Boston: Little, Brown, 1989.

Norwood, Christopher. *At Highest Risk: Protecting Children from Environmental Injury*. New York: Penguin Books, 1980.

Smith, David W. *Mothering Your Unborn Child*. Philadelphia, Pa.: W. B. Saunders, 1979.

EXERCISE AND COMFORT

Balaskas, Janet, and Balaskas, Arthur. *New Life. The Book of Exercises for Pregnancy and Childbirth* (revised). London: Sidgwick and Jackson, 1983.

Benson, Herbert. *The Relaxation Response.* New York: William Morrow, 1975.

Jimenez, Sherry Lynn. *The Pregnant Woman's Comfort Guide.* Englewood Cliffs, N.J.: Prentice-Hall, 1983.

Markowitz, Elysa, and Brainen, Howard. *Baby Dance: A Comprehensive Guide to Prenatal and Postpartum Exercise.* Englewood Cliffs, N.J.: Prentice-Hall, 1980.

Noble, Elizabeth. *Essential Exercises for the Childbearing Year* (2nd edition). Boston: Houghton Mifflin, 1982.

Olkin, Sylvia. *Positive Pregnancy Through Yoga.* Englewood Cliffs, N.J.: Prentice-Hall, 1981.

PRENATAL NUTRITION

Brewer, Gail Sforza, and Brewer, Thomas. *The Brewer Medical Diet for Normal and High-Risk Pregnancy.* New York: Simon and Schuster/Fireside Books, 1983.

Brown, Judith E. *Nutrition for Your Pregnancy. The University of Minnesota Guide.* Minneapolis, Minn.: University of Minnesota Press, 1983.

Cronin, Isaac, and Brewer, Gail Sforza. *Eating for Two. The Complete Pregnancy Nutrition Guide and Cookbook for a Healthy Pregnancy.* New York: Bantam Books, 1983.

Klein, Diane, and Badalamenti, Rosalyn T. *Eating for Two. The Complete Nutrition Guide and Cookbook for a Healthy Pregnancy.* New York: Ballantine Books, 1983.

Lappé, Frances Moore. *Diet for a Small Planet* (revised and updated). New York: Ballantine Books, 1982.

BABY CARE

Boston Children's Medical Center. *The New Child Health Encyclopedia*. New York: A Merloyd Lawrence Book/Delacorte Press, 1987.

Brazelton, T. Berry. *Touchpoints: Your Child's Emotional and Behavioral Development*. Reading, Mass.: Addison-Wesley/Lawrence, 1992.

Jones, Sandy. *Crying Baby, Sleepless Nights (How to Overcome Baby's Sleep Problems and Get Some Sleep Yourself)*. New York: Warner Books, 1983.

Jones, Sandy. *To Love a Baby*. Boston: Houghton Mifflin, 1981.

Kelly, Paul, ed. *First-Year Baby Care. An Illustrated Guide for New Parents*. Deephaven, Minn.: Meadowbrook Press, 1983.

Leach, Penelope. *Babyhood* (2nd edition, revised). New York: Alfred A. Knopf, 1983.

———. *Your Baby and Child From Birth to Age Five*. New York: Alfred A. Knopf, 1981.

Rakowitz, Elly, and Rubin, Gloria. *Living with Your New Baby*. New York: Berkley Books, 1980.

Spock, Benjamin, and Rothenberg, Michael. *Dr. Spock's Baby and Child Care*. New York: Dutton, 1985.

Stoppard, Miriam. *Day-by-Day Baby Care*. New York: Villard Books, 1983.

NURSING

Huggins, Kathleen. *The Nursing Mother's Companion*, Revised Edition. Boston: Harvard Common Press, 1990.

Kitzinger, Sheila. *The Experience of Breastfeeding*. New York: Penguin Books, 1980.

La Leche International. *The Womanly Art of Breastfeeding* (3rd edition, revised and enlarged). New York: New American Library, 1981.

Llewellyn-Jones, Derek. *Breast Feeding—How to Succeed. Questions and Answers for Mothers*. London: Faber and Faber, 1983.

Messinger, Maire. *The Breastfeeding Book*. New York: Van Nostrand Reinhold, 1982.

Presser, Janice, and Brewer, Gail Sforza. *Breastfeeding*. New York: Alfred A. Knopf, 1983.

Price, Ann, and Bamford, Nancy. *The Breasfeeding Guide for the Working Woman*. New York: Simon and Schuster/Wallaby, 1983.

Pryor, Karen. *Nursing Your Baby*. New York: Pocket Books, 1973.

Worth, Cecilia. *Breastfeeding Basics*. New York: McGraw-Hill/Sun Words Books, 1983.

THE NEWBORN BABY AND THE FAMILY

Bower, T. G. R. *The Perceptual World of the Child*. Cambridge, Mass.: Harvard University Press (The Developing Child Series), 1977.

Brazelton, T. Berry. *On Becoming a Family: The Growth of Attachment*. New York: Delacorte/Lawrence, 1981.

Brazelton, T. Berry, and Cramer, Bertrand G. *The Earliest Relationship*. Reading, Mass.: Addison-Wesley/Lawrence, 1990.

Galinsky, Ellen. *The Six Stages of Parenthood*. Reading, Mass.: Addison-Wesley/Lawrence, 1987.

Kaye, Kenneth. *The Mental and Social Life of Babies: How Parents Create Persons*. Chicago: University of Chicago Press, 1982.

Klaus, Marshall, and Kennell, John H. *Bonding: The Beginnings of Parent-Infant Attachment*. New York: New American Library/ C. V. Mosby, 1983.

Tronick, Edward, and Adamson, Lauren. *Babies as People. New Findings on Our Social Beginnings*. New York: Macmillan/Collier Books, 1980.

Weiss, Joan Solomon. *Your Second Child. A Guide for Parents*. New York: Simon and Schuster/Summit, 1981.

BOOKS FOR MOTHERS

Brazelton, T. Berry. *Infants and Mothers: Differences in Development* (revised edition). New York: Delacorte/Lawrence, 1983.

Friedland, Ronnie, and Kort, Carol. *The Mother's Book: Shared Experiences*. Boston: Houghton Mifflin, 1981.

Schaffer, Rudolph. *Mothering*. Cambridge, Mass.: Harvard University Press (The Developing Child Series), 1982.

BOOKS FOR FATHERS

Alliance for Perinatal Research. *The Father Book: Pregnancy and Beyond*. Washington, D.C.: Acropolis Books, Ltd., 1981.

Coleman, Arthur, and Coleman, Libby. *Earth Father/Sky Father. The Changing Concept of Fathering*. Englewood Cliffs, N.J.: Prentice-Hall, 1981.

Parke, Ross. *Fathers*. Cambridge, Mass.: Harvard University Press (The Developing Child Series), 1981.

Phillips, Celeste, and Anzalone, Joseph. *Fathering: Participation in Labor and Delivery*. St. Louis, Mo.: C. V. Mosby, 1978.

CESAREAN BIRTH

Cohen, Nancy Wainer, and Estner, Lois J. *Silent Knife: Cesarean Prevention and Vaginal Birth After Cesarean (VBAC)*. South Hadley, Mass.: J. F. Bergin, 1983.

Cox, Kathryn, and Schwartz, Judith. *The Well-Informed Patient's Guide to Cesarean Birth*. New York: Dell Publishing, 1990.

Hausknecht, Richard, and Heilman, Joan Rattner. *Having a Cesarean Baby* (revised edition). New York: E. P. Dutton, 1982.

Meyer, Linda D. *The Caesarean (R)evolution: A Handbook for Parents and Professionals* (revised edition). Edmonds, Wash.: Chas. Franklin Press, 1981.

Norwood, Christopher. *How to Avoid a Cesarean Section*. New York: Simon and Schuster, 1984.

Wilson, Christine Coleman, and Hovey, Wendy Roe. *Cesarean Childbirth: A Handbook for Parents*. New York: New American Library/Signet, 1981.

PREMATURE BABIES

Avery, Mary Ellen, and Litwack, Georgia. *Born Early. The Story of a Premature Baby*. Boston: Little, Brown, 1983.

Manginello, Frank, and Digeronimo, Theresa. *Your Premature Baby*. New York: Wiley 1991.

Pfister, Fred, and Grieseme, B. *The Littlest Baby: A Handbook for Parents of Premature Children.* Englewood Cliffs, N.J.: Prentice-Hall, 1983.

PREGNANCY LOSS

Berezin, Nancy. *After a Loss in Pregnancy.* New York: Simon and Schuster/Fireside, 1982.

Borg, Susan, and Lasker, Judith. *When Pregnancy Fails: Families Coping with Miscarriage, Stillbirth, and Infant Death.* Boston: Beacon Press, 1981.

Friedman, Rochelle, and Gradstein, Bonnie. *Surviving Pregnancy Loss.* Boston: Little, Brown, 1982.

Kubler-Ross, Elisabeth. *On Death and Dying.* New York: Macmillan, 1970.

Peppers, Larry, and Knapp, Ronald. *Motherhood and Mourning: Perinatal Death.* New York: Praeger, 1980.

LATE PARENTHOOD

Brewer, Gail Sforza. *The Pregnancy-After-30 Workbook.* Emmaus, Pa.: Rodale Press, 1978.

Daniels, Pamela, and Weingarten, Kathy. *Sooner or Later: The Timing of Parenthood in Adult Lives.* New York: W. W. Norton, 1982.

Price, Jane. *You're Not Too Old to Have a Baby.* New York: Penguin Books, 1978.

Rubin, Sylvia P. *It's Not Too Late for a Baby: For Women and Men Over 35.* Englewood Cliffs, N.J.: Prentice-Hall, 1980.

ICEA Resolution on Disclosure of Information About Obstetrical Practices*

The International Childbirth Education Association, in keeping with its philosophy and goal, "Freedom of Choice Based on Knowledge of Alternatives," supports disclosure by maternity care providers of information about their obstetrical procedures and practices to pregnant women and the public in the following resolution.

Whereas,

Health care consumers have a right to information that pertains to their bodies and their health and that helps them to make informed choices about where and with whom they give birth,

Pregnant women base their choices of birth practitioner and birth place on many factors, including individual and facility obstetrical management practices,

Education of pregnant women about all aspects of pregnancy, childbirth, and its management helps to improve the outcome of pregnancy,

* Adopted by the ICEA Board of Directors 10 February 1988.

Information provided by practitioners and facilities about their obstetrical procedures and practices can serve as the basis for constructive communication and discussion between the pregnant woman and her practitioner and can encourage her active participation in decisions about her health management,

The increasing use of obstetrical tests, technologies, and procedures frequently does not demonstrate an association with improved birth outcomes for low-risk pregnant women,

The inappropriate and/or excessive use of some obstetrical procedures (e.g., cesarean delivery, episiotomy) unnecessarily exposes childbearing women to serious health risks, can delay the establishment of family bonds, and wastes health care dollars,

The public dissemination of practitioner- and facility-specific rates of obstetrical procedures has the potential to promote self-regulation of health care providers and thereby to help decrease the utilization rates of unnecessary procedures,

Shared information and decision making between health care providers and pregnant women lead to shared responsibilities and risks, thereby diminishing the potential for lawsuits.

Therefore, the International Childbirth Education Association supports the establishment of mechanisms facilitating disclosure by maternity care practitioners and facilities of information about and utilization rates of their obstetrical procedures and practices to women early in pregnancy and to the public as a necessary component of informed choice and education for childbirth.

Index

ABOUT THE AUTHOR

Richard I. Feinbloom, M.D., is a family physician and pediatrician currently in private practice in Cameron Park, California and on the staff of the Marshall Hospital. A native Philadelphian and graduate of the University of Pennsylvania, he has taught at the Harvard Medical School, where he directed the Family Health Care Program, and at the State University of New York Medical School at Stony Brook, where he was responsible for the maternity care teaching program for family practice residents and students.

Dr. Feinbloom was chief of the Child and Family Health Division of the Boston Children's Hospital Medical Center and co-founded the Family Practice Group of Cambridge, Massachusetts. While at the Children's Hospital, he worked with the newly formed health education department and edited and coauthored the first editions of the *Child Health Encyclopedia* and *Pregnancy, Birth, and the Newborn Baby*. He is coauthor of *Medical Choices, Medical Chances: How Doctors, Patients, and Families Can Cope with Uncertainty,* a guide to decision making in medicine for patients and physicians.

Richard Feinbloom has twice been a consultant to the International Childbirth Education Association and is a founding member and past president of the Physicians for Social Responsibility. He is married and the father of three young adults.